El Camino

The Penn State Series in Lived Religious Experience

Judith Van Herik, General Editor

The series publishes books that interpret religions by studying personal experience in its historical, geographical, social, and cultural settings.

Lee Hoinacki, El Camino: *Walking to Santiago de Compostela*

Lee Hoinacki

El Camino
Walking to
Santiago de Compostela

The Pennsylvania State University Press
University Park, Pennsylvania

To my classmates

Library of Congress Cataloging-in-Publication Data

Hoinacki, Lee, 1928–
    El camino : walking to Santiago de Compostela / Lee Hoinacki.
      p.   cm.
    Includes bibliographical references (p.   ) and index.
    ISBN 0-271-01612-4 (cloth : alk. paper)
    1. Spain, Northern—Description and travel. 2. Christian pilgrims
and pilgrimages—Spain—Santiago de Compostela. 3. Hoinacki, Lee,
1928– —Journeys—Spain, Northern. 4. Santiago de Compostela
(Spain) I. Title.
DP285.H65   1996
914.6′1—dc20   95-49302
                                                     CIP

Second printing, 1997

Copyright © 1996 The Pennsylvania State University
All rights reserved
Printed in the United States of America
Published by The Pennsylvania State University Press,
University Park, PA 16802-1003

It is the policy of The Pennsylvania State University Press to use acid-free paper
for the first printing of all clothbound books. Publications on uncoated stock
satisfy the minimum requirements of American National Standard for
Information Sciences—Permanence of Paper for Printed Library Materials,
ANSI Z39.48-1992.

El Camino

"Here, with each step, I am always in place, in some place, going to the next place. . . ."

—from Chapter 2

Foreword by Judith van Herik   vii

First, Thanks   ix

How It All Began   xi

1. St. Jean Pied de Port to Roncesvalles   1

2. Roncesvalles to Zubiri   13

3. Zubiri to Pamplona   21

4. Pamplona to Cizur Menor   29

5. Cizur Menor to Puente la Reina   37

6. Puente la Reina to Estella   45

7. Estella to Los Arcos   53

8. Los Arcos to Logroño   61

9. Logroño to Nájera   69

10. Nájera to Santo Domingo de la Calzada   77

11. Santo Domingo de la Calzada to Belorado   87

12. Belorado to San Juan de Ortega   97

13. San Juan de Ortega to Burgos   105

14. Burgos to Granja de Sambol   113

15. Granja de Sambol to Castrojeriz   121

16. Castrojeriz to Frómista   129

17. Frómista to Carrión de los Condes   137

18. Carrión de los Condes to Sahagún   145

19. Sahagún to Mansilla de las Mulas   153

20. Mansilla de las Mulas to León   161

21. León to Villadangos del Páramo   169

22. Villadangos del Páramo to Astorga   177

23. Astorga to Foncebadón   185

24. Foncebadón to Ponferrada   195

25. Ponferrada to Villafranca del Bierzo   203

26. Villafranca del Bierzo to El Cebreiro   211

27. El Cebreiro to Samos   221

28. Samos to Portomarín   231

29. Portomarín to Palas de Rei   239

30. Palas de Rei to Arzúa   249

31. Arzúa to Monte del Gozo   257

32. Monte del Gozo to Compostela   267

Notes   281

Index   297

Foreword

Judith Van Herik, General Editor

In the fall of 1993 Penn State Press launched a new series in religious studies scholarship. Entitled "Lived Religious Experience," the series publishes books that interpret religions by studying personal experience in its historical, geographical, social, and cultural settings. Nothing disqualifies a book from being considered for this series unless it is centered on concepts rather than people. The series may include biographical or autobiographical works but is not limited to this genre.

Lee Hoinacki's account of his pilgrimage is the first title in the series.

When Edith and Victor Turner wrote the American Council of Learned Societies Lectures, published as *Image and Pilgrimage in Christian Culture* (Columbia, 1978), they correctly noted that pilgrimage was a neglected area of study. Partly because of their work, this is no longer so. Many books and articles exist, in religious studies and in cultural anthropology. But to our knowledge, none does what Lee Hoinacki offers herein.

What religious people—ordinary and "specialists"—consider to be most real, most important, truest, and most beautiful is our interest. This is to be found on every page of *El Camino: Walking to Santiago de Compostela*. Lee Hoinacki's tale of his walk across northern Spain is captivating in many ways. His feet, socks, and each step are felt by the reader: one can sense the stones, rain, and winds encountered on his walk. As another friend has said, no one could have written this book when the road to Santiago was truly still a pilgrim's trail, and now that it is also a tourist route, no one has the history to walk and write as Lee has done.

Hoinacki's account of his peripatetic musings in 1993 encompasses traditional theology, childhood memories, reflections on his parents and children, considerations of the "natural" world and its despoliation by the automobile, and a discovery of the meaning—then, there, and to him—of the Rosary, the Virgin, sacrifice, sonship, and other Christian, Jewish, and Islamic themes. At the same time, the reader meets the motley characters of the camino, past and present, long dead and newly hatched, female and male, on foot and on bicycle.

The reader can discover this for herself. We urge you, however, to attend carefully to Hoinacki's accounts of the wandering cow in the abandoned church on a rainy night and his frustration at being too scrupulous to eat the green asparagus that nobody in Western Europe wants anyway.

El Camino: Walking to Santiago de Campostela is a perfect companion for travel and travail.

First, Thanks

I wish to thank the following persons who carefully read the manuscript, offered fine suggestions, and made pertinent corrections: Judith Van Herik, William A. Christian Jr., Mother Jerome Nagle, O.S.B., and Patricia Mitchell. Philip Winsor's enthusiastic reception of the manuscript made publication possible. Barbara Duden gave me an excellent pocket knife for the Camino, and provided a gracious house where I did much of the writing. Sebastian Trapp loaned me a first-rate backpack, and instructed me on how to treat sore feet. Alfons Garrigós gave me the map I followed, together with sound advice. I enjoyed the privilege of access to Valentina Borremans' library and the hospitality of her home in Mexico. In Santo Domingo de la Calzada, I was warmly received by Father José Ignacio Díaz and his staff, especially Maite Moreno. Carl Mitcham of Penn State University made thoughtful arrangements that my work there be pleasant and fruitful. In State College, I could always count on Peter Bohn for a place to sleep, a good meal, and lively conversation. To Ivan Illich, I am grateful for the idea of walking to Santiago de Compostela. I hope the text itself expresses what I feel toward all the people I met on and along the Camino.

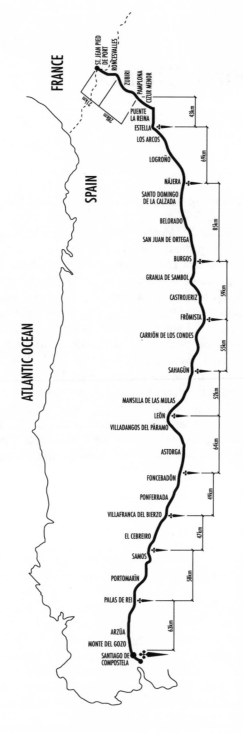

Map of the journey from St. Jean Pied de Port to Santiago de Compostela.

How It All Began

Bremen, Germany
January 20, 1996

In 1962, I first met Spaniards in Mexico and Chile, and was introduced to the haunting and surreal movies of Luis Buñuel. Through these experiences, I came to sense a terrible truth expressed by the eminent and controversial historian, Américo Castro. During three centuries of a destructive error, he says, Spaniards have tried to live, *desviviéndose*. By this he means the attempt to create a national life in the very act of denying the essential components of the historically specific Spanish mode of being—*el ser español*. After these encounters, mysterious and puzzling for a midwestern American, an unquenchable desire formed quietly but firmly deep inside me: I wanted to visit the country in which such paradoxical and powerful passions governed men's hearts. Thirty-one years later, my still strong wish was granted.

I was living in Germany, and a friend suggested that I go to Santiago de Compostela, a place in Galicia, at the *finis terrae* (end of the earth), which became the most visited city in the West during the High Middle Ages. Except for this one fact, I knew nothing further about its history. My friend explained that it was a pilgrimage site, that many believed in the presence of Saint James the Apostle's body there, that pilgrims, walking to and from Compostela, established roads that can still be traced today. I then read a short, popular booklet on the subject . . . and began to wonder. Why did these thousands—or maybe millions, no one knows how many—travel from as far away as Galway on the west coast of Ireland? Long before the age of modern media, maps and transport, men, women, and children found their way over mountains and through forests to the extreme end of the known world. What drew them to a tomb that was, in the beginning, nothing more substantial than a hermit's solitary retreat in the countryside? I concluded that there was but one way to find out: To walk to Compostela myself.

I immediately decided to read nothing more, neither about pilgrimage nor about the famous shrine itself. I felt that the less I knew, the more open I would be to whoever or whatever awaited me along that path, thickly traversed as it had been for a thousand years. From long experience, I have found that I learn by articulating to myself what I have felt and begun to think—by writing out what has happened to and in me. So when I started walking, I carried a school copybook and pen. Each night, before falling asleep, I wrote down what seemed to touch and affect me that day.

After returning to Germany, I typed out my notes and showed them to the friend who had suggested that I go to Compostela. He and other friends then urged me to consider making a book out of these comments. Fortunately, I had access to sources and time to write. I learned something of the *camino,* the way, and increased my knowledge of Spanish history. This involved the attempt to understand the popularity and meaning of the *camino* in the context of three distinct peoples, Catholics, Muslims, and Jews. For more than seven hundred years, the first two fought to rule the Peninsula, while the Jews, a large and important community, struggled peacefully to be faithful to their tradition, from Roman times until their final expulsion in 1492.

The present text is the nearly verbatim account that I made each night—what I experienced on the *camino.* I have interwoven historical information and interpretative remarks insofar as they illuminate and flesh out what I sensed and thought as I walked.

Castro wrote that, "In Santiago [de Compostela], the pendulum swung from devout submission to the advocates of heavenly mercy, to chaotic or even criminal rebellion." He gives examples from the late Middle Ages. Today, I believe, the pendulum swings farther in each direction—throughout the Peninsula, and beyond. This I learned by the time I arrived in Compostela.

1

St. Jean Pied de Port to Roncesvalles

May 4, 1993

E arly morning . . . I get off the train in Bayonne, in southwestern France. Here I must buy a ticket for a local train that goes to St. Jean Pied de Port, a town on the French-Spanish border, where I shall start walking—to cross the Pyrenees on the first day of a pilgrimage to Santiago de Compostela. But suddenly, I shudder . . . with fright. I'm sixty-five! Am I acting like some kid, attempting a rash, foolhardy adventure? Should I have talked to someone who has experience walking over mountains? I haven't seen a doctor for ten or fifteen years, maybe longer . . . I don't even remember. I should at least have gotten a medical examination. This much I surely owed my children. But they didn't suggest it, and they voiced no opposition when I told them that I planned to walk across Spain.

None of my friends tried to dissuade me. On the contrary. Their enthusiasm flowed over into gifts for the journey. One loaned me a good, thick sleeping bag; another, an excellent large backpack that rides on my hips; another, an ingenious Swiss army knife. Finally, and perhaps rather incongruously, the friend who had originally suggested that I might be interested in Santiago de Compostela loaned me an old but sturdy-looking pair of Italian mountain shoes, with the firm and confident exclamation, "Here, put these on—they'll take you all the way to Compostela!" I tried them on and, amazingly, they fit. I had vaguely heard, and strongly believed, that shoes might be the most important item of my equipment. Today, however, I'm worried. Maybe I just imagined that they fit me . . . maybe *this* was an imprudent way to start out . . .

The station is open, but no one is working at the ticket window—it is still too early. The schedule, high on the wall, indicates that there are two trains to St. Jean Pied de Port, but this seems to depend on the season. Looking around the empty and cold room, I spot an electronic information machine, something I had never seen before. Fortunately, my French is just barely good enough to decipher the instructions. One touches the screen at a certain place, depending on what information is wanted. I press. I am presented with a screenful of alternatives and must choose and press again. After I go through about a dozen actions of narrowing down the mass of information that the machine contains, I arrive at the time of my train's departure, and the cost of the ticket. I have just over an hour to wait, and enough French francs to buy the ticket.

Before leaving Germany, I had procured the amounts of French francs and Spanish pesetas that I calculated I would need—all at the official, posted rates, which I knew I could trust. What a tremendous difference from earlier times! In the sermon, "Veneranda dies," found in the *Liber Sancti Jacobi,* the twelfth-century author—probably Aymeric Picaud, a French cleric—details the various ways in which money changers and

Fig. 1. Petrarca-Meister, "Pain," c. 1520. Bayerische Staatsbibliothek, Munich.

others cheated the pilgrims of that era. After listing examples of the different schemes and frauds, he addresses the criminals:

> Oh you cheating innkeepers, dishonest bankers and wicked merchants, turn back to the Lord your God, drop your evil actions, abandon your avarice, rid yourselves of your malevolent deceits! What will you say on the Day of Judgment, when you see all those whom you defrauded accusing you before God? Know that you have despised God in your innumerable crimes. But if you do not repent the numberless frauds carried out against the saints, namely: Santiago, Peter, Giles, Leonard, the very Mother of God, St. Mary of Puy, St. Magdalene, St. Martin of Tours, St. John the Baptist of Angély, St. Michael the Sailer, St. Bartholomew of Benevento, St. Nicholas of Bari [saints whose churches were popular places of pilgrimage then], you will have them as your accusors before the Lord, for you have exploited their pilgrims.

In the very different world of the twentieth century, I walk away from the machine, certain that it has not deceived me. In fact, if I had had to deal with an impatient or distracted employee, I might have had insuperable difficulties understanding the French. Nevertheless, I feel a certain unease. Another machine has appeared; another person has disappeared. A cold, electronic efficiency, yes. But I've lost the possibility of experiencing an elementary human drama: Will this person, whom I approach for help, reach out to me, struggle to help me understand the language, or will the information I need be brusquely and rapidly spit out; do I dare ask for it to be repeated, slowly . . . ? Does this denial of the fleshly feel of my and the other's person contribute to the further destruction of nature?

Stepping out into the street, I feel the sharp, clean quiet of the early morning air—no traffic yet. But across the street, a café is already open. Its exterior, appearing friendly and quaint to me, an American, invites me to walk over. Why not treat myself to a *café au lait?* Since leaving the house in Germany, I've taken nothing except from the supplies in my backpack.

The coffee seems expensive, but I shall not be drinking another here in France. It is also not as good as I've had in Italy. I wonder what the coffee will be like in Spain. Too many comparisons, too many countries visited superficially, too many distracting experiences. What will happen to me on the *camino?* (Literally, "way" or "road." As will be seen, the word has many strong and rich connotations, from a muddy dirt path to the self-designated character of Christ—"I am the Way . . ." [John 14:6].) Will this be a singularly *different* kind of journey? At times, I've felt uncomfortable reading some of the historians. They tend to write as if there is *one ca-*

mino, one pilgrim, *one* experience—the true one, *el verdadero.* They seem to be searching for some kind of authenticity, some kind of unitary truth. But this is to collapse the fears, the dreams, the ambitions, the heterogeneity, of innumerable persons stretched out over twenty centuries into one ideal type. This can't be.

As I come out of the café, I see an old man and woman—that is, they appear older than me—across the street, both with backpacks, and he carries an umbrella. Walking out of my vision, they hold hands. Sewed on the back of their packs is a piece of yellow material, in the shape of a shell—the traditional emblem of a Santiago de Compostela pilgrim. My first sighting of a genuine pilgrim. All the pictures of European pilgrim iconography show nothing compared to the excited *feel* of accosting the real thing, in the early morning light, right before my eyes. I wonder, are they just starting? or returning? But they seem much too feeble to endure the long walk to Compostela.

Soon it's time to get into the two-coach train for the hour-long ride to St. Jean. Amazing—this small town, already in the mountains, is served by a daily train that ends there. I notice that it's electric—as all the trains I've taken were since leaving Germany. Today, I shall begin a thousand-kilometer walk, thanks to atomic power. What should I feel, think, about this? Is it just another of the infinite number of contradictions that the modern world presents me? But I freely put myself into it. I could have walked; the German pilgrims in the Middle Ages did that. But I'm reminded of what happened to two Frenchmen who walked from Paris to Compostela a few years ago. Several times, while still in France, they were picked up or harassed by the police, suspected of being vagrants or criminals. What about those who arrive in a jet? Are they pilgrims? What must one do to walk with the dead? Can I join these ancient wayfarers, making the compromises I've made?

Well, the questioning is over, the train arrives in St. Jean Pied de Port. It's time to find out something mundanely practical: How do I get from the train station to the *camino?* I must hurry, for it's nearly eleven o'clock, and I want to cross the Pyrenees before dark. Excited, I'm almost running out of the train station. But that is eminently foolish . . . I have to cross mountains today . . . something I've never done in my life. I must try to be calm . . . find my way through the town . . . not get lost . . . save my strength . . .

I have a rough map, mostly just lines, indicating the *camino,* with the names of towns and villages through which I will pass, and the distances between them. For each larger town, there is a simplified street map. Looking at this, and asking people I meet, I hurry to get out of St. Jean. There are two routes from here to Roncesvalles, my destination on the other side of the mountains. I want to find the one that is a marked trail; the other runs alongside a road. Shortly after leaving the town, I realize that I am going along the road, not the trail. But how long will it take me to go back into town and find the other way? Will I still get to Roncesvalles today? For there are no towns on the trail, no place to stop for the night.

I decide to continue along the road. This, too, is considered the *camino*, and I am afraid I do not have time to find the trail. I shall be walking over the ancient Roman route.

A bright sun blesses this early spring day. In St. Jean, I was tempted to stop at one of the sidewalk cafés where the waiters were just putting out bright, checkered tablecloths for lunch. But then I remembered the written comment of a Spanish pilgrim, walking with his companions from Madrid in 1928, facing a similar kind of temptation: "Well, that's the Sancho Panza which each of us carries in himself."

Yesterday, back in Germany, as I did my daily walk with the backpack, my left knee pained me. Off and on, it felt that way during the seven days that I practiced, "to get in shape." I thought that since I spend almost all my time seated at a desk, and get no real exercise, I should get out and do some preparation for this enterprise. So, early each morning, I shouldered the pack, filled with some books to give it weight, and walked for two hours along the river near our house. Each day, I felt a little more excitement about the coming adventure. After one week, I could wait no longer. Although I had done nothing more than walk along that level path for those few days, I filled the pack, put on the mountain shoes—which continued to feel quite comfortable—and jumped on the train.

But now I begin to feel some apprehension, in spite of the lovely day. What if those irregular pains in the knee turn out to be something serious? What if I need some kind of medical care—when I do not carry any "health" insurance at all? What if I become a burden to my children through this vain traipsing through an unknown foreign country? What if I never make it to Compostela? Ah, but this kind of maudlin thinking is worse than letting Sancho Panza take control of me. I must try to open myself to what lies before me among those who have preceded me. There were many young men, of course, but the records also list single women, and families with children, some of whom were infants. One account says that a blind man, named Folbert, walked to Compostela—from Germany!

Ahead of me, alongside the road, I see a man, going more slowly than I. Gradually, I overtake him. He, too, is walking to Compostela, from France. If I understand him, he started in Brittany, coming all this way on foot. Here, indeed, I have met my first fellow pilgrim. Since I am walking faster, I move on ahead. I had also made the decision, before starting out, that I would walk alone. I felt that only in this way would I be able to explore the secrets of this *camino,* which, I believed, might be possible if I could accompany those who went before. But, from my reading of pilgrim reports and historical studies, it appears that, up until quite recently, pilgrims had to fear unscrupulous innkeepers and food merchants, and robbers. Robbers fell into two general categories: First, there were those who dressed as pilgrims and preyed on the real pilgrims with various kinds of artful thievery. For example, the malefactors, appearing to be pilgrims, would enter the regular hospice for the night. There, they would drug the tired wayfarers while they slept, and rob them. In the fourteenth century, most of the criminals caught doing this turned out to be English. The other kind operated simply as highwaymen. But as late as 1928, the young men from Madrid, mentioned above, were put under arrest twice by the Guardia Civil—the national police force. The first time they were let go only because they carried a *salvoconducto* signed by one of the top army generals in Madrid. The second time required a call to the governor of Madrid, who happened to be the father of two of them!

Proceeding alone, carefree, with no thought of any danger at all, I walk through the town of Valcarlos. I am in Spain! There are signs indicating a border post, but no one is around to check on foreigners coming into the country. I pass a parked car from which three men emerge. They too appear to be pilgrims, starting out here. Later, walking much faster than I, they greet me and one, a young man who carries a good stout staff, evincing an interest in someone obviously much older, encourages me to find a staff, too. It will be a great help, he assures me. I remember, again, that the pilgrim staff is a regular feature in the iconography of Santiago Peregrino. There is even a special blessing for it. One of the young Madrid pilgrims carefully writes down in his report (*relato*) the street in the city where he bought his, made of ash. He mentions, wistfully, that it disappeared, along with all his belongings, in the sacking of his house by "the Reds" (in the Civil War). He rejoices in the music of its regular tapping the earth as he walks, and believes it to be quite indispensable. Later, when I find a newly fallen tree near the road, I cut myself a staff with my new pocketknife.

I stop once to eat some bread, cheese, and fruit. I also carry water in a plastic bottle, one of three items I had to buy for the journey. Friends told me I should also get a plastic mat to put on the ground under the sleeping bag, and a poncho. Soon, I have to pull this out of my pack and put it on, for it begins to rain. It covers both me and the backpack, so is unwieldy, quite large and difficult to drop over my head. I need several tries to succeed.

After a few hours of climbing the mountain—the ascent is always gradual, never really terribly steep—I start to feel tired, and the pain, too, begins, first in my feet, then in my legs, reaching my back and shoulders until my entire body aches. Curiously, I am able to distinguish two distinct but "complementary" feelings—pain and exhaustion. I can think of nothing to do to relieve the pain. If I could sit down, get the weight of the pack off my body, and rest, I think I should be able to handle the exhaustion. But I cannot sit on the ground—it is too wet, and I could not simply stand up again with the pack—it is too heavy. So I watch for large rocks on which I can sit, resting the bottom of the pack, too, on the rock. The rain runs off them, so they are not so wet.

I have no idea how far I've walked, nor the distance remaining to Roncesvalles. I am beginning to feel that I cannot go on much longer—the pain and the exhaustion are just too much for me. But I find no roof, and I cannot spend the night on the ground with the rain drenching me. I have no tent, since I heard that there are shelters along the *camino*.

Coming around a bend in the road, I see what looks like a cave—a dry place out of the rain. It is a few meters up a steep hill next to the road, a kind of cliff. I try climbing up, and fall down. Too slippery, too sheer. I take off the pack, put it on some stones under a tree, and try again. Even without the pack, I cannot get up the incline. I have no choice . . . I must go on.

It seems now that I have all my attention fixed on the road ahead, looking out for a rock on which I can rest. Now and then, I find a guard rail on this mountain road, and I learn to perch myself and the pack on the narrow metal edge for a few moments.

My thoughts veer wildly over strange memories, distant events, the history of this *camino*. Why am I here? How did I get myself into this? Slowly, my imagining takes shape . . . a single notion appears before me: This is a penitential exercise. I have somehow been led here to do penance for my sins. The pain and exhaustion will be measured out to me in accord with what I need to bring a balance back in my life.

But then I remember reading somewhere that intense pain brings unconsciousness—this has happened to prisoners under torture. If that occurs to me, alone out here in these mountains, the whole exercise will be finished. And maybe me with it!

Mulling over this predicament, a prayer forms in my heart. I pray that the pain not become so great that I faint, that the exhaustion not be so total that I fall down, unable to get up. It does not occur to me to pray for relief; only that I be able to bear what is given to me, that I not lose this marvelous opportunity to bring a balance, a certain justice, into my life. Or, at least, to make some first modest steps in this direction, since I cannot know of what this justice would consist.

In the midst of these tortures, I explore distant realms—I think of all those who preceded me, crossing these mountains . . . and then I am struck with the clear and unquestionable realization: They're still here. And they're interested in me! They are even more eager than I that I reach Roncesvalles tonight . . . They are here to help me, to carry me over the next rise, around the next cliff . . . I have only to ask them. So I turn to them, to them and to the angels. According to one story, angels carried or guided a boat with the body of Saint James the Apostle in it, after he was beheaded in Palestine, to Galicia. There, he eventually became Santiago, and that's the source of everyone's pilgrimage. There would never have been a Compostela (at that time a forest, now a city) without the belief that the body of the Apostle was buried there.

I cannot tell how much time passed between those prayers and the realization that I am no longer going up. The path becomes level, it even seems to descend now and then. I remember, from the map, that when this happens, one is near Roncesvalles.

Later, I look up and see a monument and a small church or chapel— they are dedicated to Roldán, Roland. Here, on August 15, 778, the mythic hero whose legend is told in one of the great epic poems of Western literature, the *Chanson de Roland,* fell, mortally wounded, to die. He was at the head of the rear guard of Charlemagne's army, which was returning to France. The main force had already crossed the mountain when Roland's troops were attacked at Roncesvalles. Almost all were wounded or killed. With his last breath, Roland blew a call on his horn, appealing to his uncle, Charlemagne, for help. A colorful account is found in the *Liber Sancti Jacobi,* where the author says that Santiago had appeared to Charlemagne in dreams, asking him to follow the Milky Way to Galicia, where he would find the Apostle's forgotten and hidden grave. He should make this route secure, free from the Moors who had invaded and overrun Spain in 711, so that pilgrims from France and the north might be able to reach the tomb.

The *Liber Sancti Jacobi,* also called the *Codex Calixtinus,* is one of the most studied documents of the Middle Ages. It is composed of five books relating various stories connected with the Apostle James (Santiago), and pilgrimages to his tomb in Galicia. In accord with a custom of the time, authorship is attributed to a prominent person, in this case, Pope Calixtus II. Book IV, however, in which the story of Roland occurs, is presented as the work of Archbishop Turpin, a contemporary of Charlemagne.

Those who write serious books of history say that Charlemagne came to Spain at the invitation of the Islamic ruler of Catalonia, to help him in his fight with a fellow Islamic ruler in Córdoba. After crossing the Pyrenees, Charlemagne laid siege to the Christian (!) city of Pamplona. From there, he proceeded to attack the Islamic city of Zaragosa. Unable to conquer it, and learning of troubles in his own Frankish kingdom, Charlemagne left Spain. His army was ambushed at Roncesvalles, not by Moors, but by Christians—Navarros and Vascos (people from Navarra and Guipúzcoa—the Basque region)—in retaliation for his attacks on them when he entered Spain. Perhaps Roland never existed.

Here one begins to enter some of the many layers of mystery to be found in the *camino*. In the late seventeenth century, Domenico Laffi, an Italian cleric from Bologna, passed here on his way to Compostela. He describes, in great detail, what he saw in the church in Roncesvalles: the great horn of Roland and two maces, belonging to two warrior companions of Roland, among other objects. Outside, he saw a small chapel that Charlemagne had built, with Roland's tomb inside. On the grounds nearby, he found the huge rock that Roland split with his great sword, "Durandarte" (meaning, "with it one strikes heavy blows"), before he died. He did not want the sword to fall into the hands of any "coward or Sarracen," so he hit this rock with it to destroy it. However, after three strokes, he only succeeded in splitting the rock—the sword remained intact. Before continuing on their pilgrimage to Compostela, Laffi and his unnamed companion, an artist, carved their names—first and last—on Roland's stone tomb itself with a sharp knife.

The empty chapel and small monument that I see appear to be quite recent constructions. The chapel that Laffi describes must have been down in Roncesvalles. Well, the warriors of Charlemagne were not the last French troops to come through here, after wreaking havoc in Spain. And I am too exhausted to think about all this.

I start down the road and soon see a large building in front of me. It turns out to be the pilgrims' *refugio*. This and El Cebreiro—many days ahead of me—are the two oldest places on record offering assistance and shelter to pilgrims. After eight hours of struggling over a mountain pass, I have completed the first day's journey. Learning that one should inscribe himself as an official pilgrim, I set my pack down on a bench and, after lying on the bench myself for some minutes, slowly make my way to the office. I can walk, just barely, but the pain is terrible.

The rain has stopped. The sun is setting. I find the office, where I meet two or three Spanish pilgrims. A friendly priest inscribes us and gives each of us our *credencial*—the document that should be stamped in each place where we stop, and that is then presented at the pilgrim office of the cathedral in Compostela. If we wish to sleep in the *refugios* of the *camino,* we must show this *credencial* to be admitted. The priest also informs us that there will be a special *Misa de Peregrino* (Mass for pilgrims) at eight this evening.

The church is between the office and the shelter, so I think that maybe

I can make it. The priest tells us that we can get a good, inexpensive meal in the village, in the bar, not the restaurant section, of a local establishment. But I don't think I can walk that far. And there is no need, since I still have food in my pack.

I return to the shelter, and find a dormitory with cots. There appear to be about ten persons in the room, but I am too weary to notice or do more than perfunctorily greet them. I lie on the thin mattress, unable to move, until eight. Again, slowly, each step a torture, I make my way to the church. There, I can with difficulty get my body to make the position changes to follow the liturgy. It seems there are a goodly number of people, but I am too tired to distinguish any individual—I only vaguely sense people around me.

In fact, I am unaware of the Mass itself. My mind is working again, not wandering, not troubled, but strangely settled, something like a gentle concentration, something I've never known before. I'm not here looking at myself, as I was out there on the *camino,* in the rain. I simply am myself, aware of myself, as the recipient of a lovely gift—the grace to make this pilgrimage. In fact, I cannot rid myself of the idea that this is the greatest grace I have yet received in my life. But this seems so strange, absurd even, after such a day—eight hours that seemed to drag on and on, filled with the worst kind of doubt, discouragement, suffering, tiredness. Why is this such a special favor? And yet that is the clear, powerful feeling that has taken hold of me, in spite of my present exhausted state—in the midst of the confusing obscurities out there: the finding of Santiago's tomb, Frankish warrior myths, the enigmatic presence of the Moors, the huge numbers of pilgrims over a thousand years, and the paradoxical feelings inside me. Well, I did the right thing in not bringing any books to read. I had decided that solitude on the *camino* should be accompanied by reading nothing when I stopped to rest, in order to open myself to the experience of these people. I see I'll have enough to think about.

At the end of the Mass, several others and I go up to receive a special Pilgrim's blessing. I am too tired to know what is being said. The rite extends back at least to the twelfth century, and takes this form today:

Priest: Oh God, You Who took up your servant Abraham from the city of Ur of the Chaldeans, watching over him in all his wanderings, You Who were the guide of the Hebrew people in the desert, we ask that You deign to take care of these your servants who, for love of your name, make a pilgrimage to Compostela. Be a companion for them along the path, a guide at crossroads, strength in their weariness, defense before dangers, shelter on the way, shade against the heat, light in the darkness, a comforter in their discouragements, and firmness in their intentions, in order that, through your guidance, they might arrive unscathed at the end of their journey and, enriched with graces and virtues, they might return safely to their homes, which now lament their absence, filled with salutary and lasting joy. Through Jesus Christ Your Son, Who lives and reigns with You, in the unity of the Holy Spirit, one God, forever and ever.

May the blessing of Almighty God, Father, Son, and Holy Spirit, descend on you.

All: Amen.

Priest: May the Lord direct your steps with his approval, and be your inseparable companion on the entire *camino.*

All: Amen.

Priest: May the Virgin Mary grant you her maternal protection, defend you in all dangers of soul and body, and may you merit to arrive safely at the end of your pilgrimage under her mantle.

All: Amen.

Priest: May the Archangel Rafael accompany you on the *camino* as he accompanied Tobias, and protect you from every injury and obstacle.

All: Amen.

In former years, there were special blessings for the pilgrims' clothes—they wore a distinctive garb, their sack—in which they carried food, and their staff. Pilgrims were immediately identified by their dress and what they carried.

Back in the *refugio,* I abandon myself to the comfort of a hot shower. An incredible luxury. Feeling much better now, I eat some food from the pack. Since I have a sleeping bag, I want nothing else tonight. I put on my pajamas, crawl in and pull up the zipper. This has surely turned out to be the strangest day of my life.

But then I begin to suffer terrible chills and violent trembling. I have no control over my body; it's as if the shaking has taken possession of me. What to do? Should I call out to the others in the dormitory? Should I pray? What is happening to me? I've never experienced anything like this. Then, after some time—I have no idea how long—my body seems to warm, to become calm . . . I am quiet . . . I sleep.

2

Roncesvalles to Zubiri

May 5, 1993

I awaken . . . and lie here, listening. It's still early, not quite daylight. I try moving my arms and legs a bit in the sleeping bag. No pain. I unzip the bag and get out. Still no pain. I walk to the toilet. I feel fine! Am I the same person I was last night? Am I the same body? I'm actually ready to start walking again, eager, in fact. I dress quickly, and get out a piece of sausage, some cheese, bread, and fruit from the pack. There is a large table in a dining and gathering area, and soon several others join me there. Everyone seems cheerful and ready to set out for another day on the *camino*. I organize the pack, pick up my staff, and say goodbye to Roncesvalles.

I notice that there are a number of buildings here, and the place, I know, is rich in history. In the Middle Ages, there were several large shelters here—called *hospitales* then—which were famous all over Europe for their hospitality. At that time, the pilgrim received both bed and board. There also seem to be some interesting shops. But I am impatient; I want to get out on the *camino;* I have no interest in historic architecture and attractive souvenirs. Everything has probably been rebuilt several times over the centuries. The only place I feel I have a chance of finding what so many have sought is out here, under the same sky that sheltered the earlier wanderers, rooting my feet into the same soil.

I pass through hilly country; not really anything to match the mountains of yesterday, though. There are lovely forests, and everything dripping freshly from yesterday's rain. I notice some black spots on the ground, and I had seen them yesterday, too. When I come to a rock, I sit down and can reach one of them. It's a snail! So, now I must walk more carefully, not to step on them.

After several hours, I begin to feel something new, something never before experienced. I strongly sense, with my whole self, that I am moving from one place to another. Puzzled, I nevertheless clearly realize that I have never tasted anything like this, never known about this. I am not passing *through* space, as one does in a car or airplane. This is a radically different sensation. I feel I am in a place; actually, in an infinite number of places. I am not in an undifferentiated space—what one feels in many modern places that, really, are non-places; they are simply repetitions of concepts—the concept of hospital space, shopping mall space, airport space, highway space, suburb space, and so on. Here, with each step, I am always in place, in some place, going to the next place, one centimeter or half a meter farther on. There is something solid about where I am—at every moment. And all my senses seem to be more open, more aware; they seem to be taking in much more. It's as if I'm plowing through infinitely different perceptions, for with every step I *am* in a different place, and each place has its own unique character. At each step, if I stop and sense where I am, what is around me, I know, I see, that it is different from the previous place. Is this what poets mean when they celebrate the wonders of creation?

Being out here, *in* creation, I sense, too, that the light is always specific to the place and the moment. There is no such thing as undifferentiated light, as more or less light. The character of light changes constantly, with the soil under each step, since light, too, is particular, and contributes strongly to my sense of this place and moment differing from all the others. As the thickness of the air changes with each meter of elevation, so too the quality of the light in each distinct space. Part of my sense of fixing a certain place in my memory derives from the nature of the light illuminating or hiding that scene or spot. In this place, for example, I shall never forget the way the early morning light filtered down through the pine trees, with just a suggestion of mist here and there.

Perhaps this is the way to get at one of the wonders of yesterday that is repeated again today—the sense of something beautiful. Much of the time yesterday, and most of the time today, I can see only a few meters ahead. There are no grand vistas, no distant horizons. There is only this place where I am, whose features I feel, and the prospect of other places just a meter or two ahead. And they are *other places.* There is no destination to which I am rushing. There is only this earth that I touch in so many ways, and the promise of a new earth, a new soil, under, around me, in the next step. Does the experience of newness, the pleasure of novelty, induce me to see beauty? that is, to see . . . creation?

I am also keenly aware that I have no sense of direction. I'm not at all clear about where I am, nor where I'm going. I have heard that one should follow the yellow arrows—painted on trees, rocks, fence posts, an old wall. The good people who work to maintain what is called the *camino francés,* the one mapped out by Aymeric Picaud (following common opinion, I'll assume him to be the author) in the fifth book of the *Liber,* have painted these arrows to guide people like myself who have no idea in which direction to walk. Now and then I find that I've missed one and must backtrack until I find an arrow again, and attempt to follow its direction more carefully. Without these arrows, I would immediately be lost. As I was totally dependent yesterday on the ancient pilgrims to carry me along, today I feel my dependence on the modern ones who have marked the path.

After some hours, I begin to feel the pain and exhaustion of yesterday. But it is not the same. The awful intensity is there, but something new also comes in to influence me, to fill me. There is no mistaking what begins to permeate me, what I feel, along with the discomfort, but it is somehow more real, going more deeply into me . . . a quiet joy. I have the clear sense of seeing the world, as creation, for the first time—at sixty-five! In conventional terms, I am surrounded, both yesterday and today, by an attractive landscape. But that is not what I experience; I do not look at a scene; rather, I move into what I see, I become more and more immersed in a new kind of beauty, the creation as good, that is, a good specifically made to be enjoyed as beauty.

In addition to this wonder of myself stepping into the natural world, I also enter the *camino*—a millennial path stretching out before me for hundreds of kilometers, laboriously trod by humble saints and the most awful sinners—and I am becoming a part of this great multitude, my European ancestors. The very idea seems both real and unreal: Here I am, with my feet firmly on the ground in some unknown but authentic *place* in northern Spain, following the Milky Way to *finis terrae,* the place which Middle Ages folk believed to be, literally, "the end of the earth." Strangely, modern maps still call the place by that name.

It's only the second day, and already I feel that the cost, trouble, and pain are as nothing when I acknowledge that I am being introduced to experiences whose existence I never suspected, which I could never have dreamed of. To imagine . . . I might have died without knowing this.

After nine hours of steady walking, I come to Zubiri, a place that seems to be a small town. I ask for the *refugio,* and am directed to a building behind a fence. It is a classroom in a school, converted by the people of the town into a dormitory, with showers and toilets at one end. There are eighteen double bunks, placed closely together. When I arrive, two young women are just finishing their work of cleaning the place—I see that they missed no spot of dirt. As they leave, they arrange a bouquet of flowers on the large table at the front of the room. They obviously came from someone's garden, and their grace is not diminished by the fact that they modestly stand in a plastic milk carton.

A strange world this *camino.* I arrive at the border, propelled by atomic power, and now meet two lovely smalltown people who freely devote part of their day to clean and make attractive a place for me to sleep. And I assume the townspeople have made this hostel available for us, organizing the maintenance, and paying for the hot water in the shower.

It begins to rain, and several other pilgrims arrive . . . one, a man from Barcelona, perhaps a few years younger than me, an exuberant, cheerful person. Out of his pack, he extracts a box, and carefully opens it to show me an array of homeopathic remedies. Confident of their efficacy, he feels ready for anything. He tells me that there is a bakery nearby that will stamp our *credencial,* but that the woman will not open the place again until tomorrow morning. He has learned, however, that a small store down the street possesses a valid stamp and we can go there to get "certified" tonight.

Reflecting on his medical kit, I wonder if I should have been more solicitous for my own supplies. Before starting out, I had read a list of items that one should carry. These included medicaments for both constipation and diarrhea, sunburn oil, liniment for sore muscles, some antiseptic like iodine, Band-Aids, aspirin, toilet paper, and two pairs of solid walking shoes. I ignored the recommendations, except for the aspirin. The friend who loaned me the backpack suggested that I take a couple of rolls of Leuchtoplast, a kind of adhesive tape, for blisters (none so far). This is the extent of my traveling medicine chest.

Every *camino* guidebook—and there are many available, especially in Spanish—gives a list of suggestions: what to take, what to be careful about, and so on. The very best of these, in my opinion, is included at the end of the first volume in an account written in the mid-eighteenth century by Nicola Albani, who walked from Naples to Compostela. (The second volume describes his return journey to Italy.) I also found this the most exciting and attractive—that is, because of the character of the author—of all the *relatos* I know. Albani, who walked alone, lists some suggestions for anyone wanting to use his book as a guide in making the pilgrimage to Compostela.

First, no one should undertake such a long journey without *un buen compañero,* one who is true in heart and soul, who shares your outlook. If such a one cannot be found, you had better set out alone, for you know the proverb, "better alone than badly accompanied."

Second, never set out in time of plague or war. When Albani walked, both raged in Italy and southern France. His difficulties with the public health authorities, and with Italian, French, German, and Spanish troops are astounding. Once, at Genoa, he had to take off his pilgrim garb and disguise himself as a *paisano,* and accompany those bringing produce into the walled city, since he did not have the necessary health certificates. He had to pass three separate checkpoints; the city was besieged by both plague and war. Another time, while sleeping in the forest, he was awakened by approaching soldiers. Hiding himself under some thick underbrush, he listened in terror as the men, deserters from one of the armies, described how they had robbed and killed a person they met. It seems miraculous that he survived all these encounters.

Third, no one should go who does not enjoy good health and a strong constitution. And you had better be accustomed to accepting what fortune brings, good or bad, because if not, according to Albani, "you'll surely die on the way." (From the experiences he endured, he knows whereof he speaks.)

Fourth, you need strong legs, and you had better not be overly meticulous about what you eat. Rather, be ready to eat whatever you find or whatever you are given. If you're looking for delicacies or cleanliness, you'll never find them, you may die on the way, and you'll certainly fall ill.

Fifth, never walk at night, nor with someone of whose character you have any reason to doubt. In the places where you find shelter, never be the life of the party; the less said about money the better; never take out gold or silver coins in front of others; never mention the route you will take the next day. The false pilgrims who stayed in the shelters and who are described in detail by Picaud in the twelfth-century *Liber,* were around in Albani's eighteenth century. One thief, who made off with Albani's money while he slept, was a truly ingenious rascal. The pilgrims were locked in the room from the outside. Albani had sewn his money inside his trousers, and put these under the mattress on which he slept. When he awoke in the morning, he discovered that his pants, together with one "pilgrim," were missing from the room. Looking up, he noticed a tiny window near the ceiling. But he could not believe that it was large enough for a man to crawl through.

Sixth, those especially who wear (the distinctive) pilgrim dress, and who hope to receive blessings in the holy shrines, must walk with the fear of God; otherwise, it's all a loss. Further, you should be enterprising, astute, clever like a serpent, and intellectually alert so that no one can deceive you, and you should adapt yourself to the customs of the place . . . never speak badly of another nation; and it's a great advantage if you speak any foreign tongue. Also, you cannot be shy about asking for alms—if you're ashamed to beg you'll die of hunger. Lastly, you had better have a strong stomach for the sufferings you'll undergo in God's service.

A literary-religious tour de force, Albani's remarkable book leads the reader into the adventures and thrills, the dangers and deceits, which an eighteenth-century pilgrim found on the *camino*. But again and again, I had the feeling that the worlds described by Albani in the eighteenth, and Laffi in the seventeenth century, were rather similar to those found in Picaud's twelfth-century account. They are certainly closer to Picaud's than to mine.

My world seems totally other. In a few moments, I shall walk a couple of meters to take a hot shower. Is the time distance from Picaud and Albani an indication of my spiritual distance from them? Can I ever hope to step into their world? But what is their world? One of the most common appellations of Picaud's Middle Ages is "Era of Faith," and of Albani's eighteenth century, "Age of Reason." But from examining these pilgrims' respective documents, the reader cannot help but suspect that the religious sensibility of Albani may be more delicate, more far-reaching, than that of Picaud. This judgment, however, may depend on two very different modes of literary expression, and not on the character of the men themselves. Almost every document, when examined closely, seems to raise questions rather than provide answers. The precise point of my interest must be, I think, these people. I must get beyond the written evidence to their hearts, to *them*.

Wondering, I take a shower, relaxing in the relief that the warm water brings to my aching flesh. And then I find a restaurant down the street . . . where I am certain the food will be good . . . I'll not need Albani's strong stomach today . . .

Back in the shelter, other pilgrims arrive. A couple from Pamplona give me a small shell. At one time, those who traveled to the Holy Land were called *palmeros* because they returned with palms; those who made the pilgrimage to Rome were called *romeros,* and those who went to Compostela, *peregrinos;* these returned with a shell. In many pictures, one sees that pilgrims fastened small shells on the wide brim of their hat; the larger ones are attached to their gown or cloak. There is also a tradition that people who had been to Compostela on pilgrimage asked to be buried with their shell. In Scandinavia, 123 of these shells have been excavated in thirty-seven different places. In the city of Lund, in the south of Sweden, 39 have been dug up. This is the largest number found in any single site in Europe. From such evidence, scholars have attempted to estimate the number of pilgrims who traveled from these distant lands to Compostela. And I have, in my pack, a black, wide-brimmed hat to which I sewed some small shells. I picked them up along the Pacific shore when I visited a friend in a remote Indian village in the south of Mexico, and later put them on the hat, thinking I would need to identify myself in this way as I walked. Seeing me with my pack and staff, no one mistakes me, I feel sure, for anything but another foreign *peregrino*. But perhaps I should wear the hat when I go to look for food, having left my pack and staff in the shelter. Then, possibly, I look like a tourist.

A young man comes in the *refugio;* he is from the Canary Islands. He has a very small pack, and tells me that he carries no water. He expects to drink from the natural spring fountains he finds along the way. Chapter 6 of Book V in the *Liber* lists which rivers are safe for drinking and which not. Picaud says that one river, the Salado, not far from Puente la Reina— which I hope to reach in three or four days—is deadly to both man and horse. When Picaud and his party arrived there, they found "two *navarros* seated on the bank, sharpening their knives, which they use to skin the horses of pilgrims, which drink that water and then die." He asks the men if the water is good to drink. They answer yes. Two horses of Picaud's group are led to the river, drink, and "die immediately." The two *navarros* silently and unceremoniously skin them. Picaud writes that the *navarros* lied to him in order to obtain some free horsehide. When I first read this, similar scenes of disreputable characters sharpening knives in an isolated landscape while strangers approach came to me from Hollywood Westerns. In chapter 7, Picaud describes the people and regions of the *camino.* His hatred for the *navarros* reaches such an intensity that he even details their supposed fondness for various unusual sexual customs, including bestiality. It appears to me that the memories of what happened between the Frankish army and the *navarros,* three hundred years before Picaud, were still very much alive on both sides.

I envied the small pack of the young man. I had already decided that my pack is too heavy, and I review each item: Is it really necessary or not? On this point, the conventional lists of advice are absolutely correct: Carry the lightest pack possible. It is usually said that the extreme maximum should be ten kilograms. I hope to find a post office in Pamplona and send superfluous things back to Germany.

Another pilgrim enters the room—a huge young man from Canada, the first English-speaking person I've met. He tells me that among his motives for walking to Compostela is his desire to lose weight. Crossing the Pyrenees from St. Jean Pied de Port, he found the trail that I could not locate. Up there, snow was still on the ground, and he could not make it to Roncesvalles in one day. His father had insisted that he take a small one-man tent. He put himself in this and spent the night on the mountain-side, in the snow. Perhaps I was lucky not to have found that trail.

It's about nine o'clock, time to get in the sleeping bag. During the nine hours of walking today, through forests and over small mountains, I found myself turning often, naturally, to my fellow pilgrims who, I felt, would be taking a great interest in me, would be looking out for me, would carry me through another day. And it happened. In spite of the exhaustion and pain, I am here, I've completed another stage in this journey, supported, during the day, by those who preceded me, comforted, at night, by the friendliness and companionship of those resting with me here. A great peacefulness envelops me. I am walking into a new world, a new place . . . that I did not know existed. But I'm still puzzled. I don't recognize this place; I don't know what it is.

3

Zubiri to Pamplona

May 6, 1993

S trange . . . I awaken, get out of bed, feel pleasantly
refreshed. The change from what I felt the night
before is almost too great to be believed. I would never have imagined
that sleep could restore one so dramatically. True, I go to bed about nine
and get up at six; I fall asleep immediately, and do not wake up until
morning. One piece of advice I read said that you should rest for an entire
day about once a week. If I continue to feel like this each morning, I need
never stop until I reach Compostela. But maybe I'll suddenly collapse one
of these days. Maybe that knee will go from merely being filled with pain
to being altogether useless.

Yet I feel so good, so eager to step out into the morning air. The sun is
shining, but drops of water from yesterday's rain cling to all the vegetation . . . until I pass by. I become thoroughly wet, brushing past the
bushes that line the path. Along here, the *camino* becomes something like
a ditch in many places. A high bank on one side, thick vegetation or an
ancient stone wall on the other, the space for walking varying from two to
four meters wide. In the bottom of the ditch, after the good rain, water
runs. It is a continual challenge to find stones or solid mud on which to
step. All my efforts are directed to one end: not to step in water that will
come over the tops of my shoes. I have a belief that I should keep my feet
dry. Each day I put on two pairs of clean socks, and so far this has

worked very well. Not a sign of a blister. Yet all of the accounts complain of blisters . . . Maybe my time is yet to come.

Down below me on the right, a hundred or more meters away, a highway runs parallel to the *camino.* Now and then, the vegetation is low enough that I can see the traffic. It seems to whiz by effortlessly, covering great distances rapidly, while for me every step is slow and awkward. And I must be sharply awake. Yes, there are differences. A driver and his or her passengers can be almost anesthetized, perhaps some of them are, by their stereo . . . while I move in a heightened state of consciousness, alert to many aspects of my surroundings at every instant. I am moved to ask the question: How can one move across the earth?—not how *does* one, but how *can* one? Does my action approach some primordial, purposeful movement?—not a Weberian ideal type, not a Platonic form, and not a Jungian archetype. Rather, something like an Aristotelian final cause. So that my motion, going from Germany to the French-Spanish border, made sense only because it was something ordered to real movement; it had meaning only in terms of what it would permit: the movement of walking, a true action.

These slow steps then, in some sense the only genuine way to move across the created earth, are a criterion, an ordering principle, allowing me to judge the possibility of all transport of people through space. Thoreau seemed to understand this, as he saw the railroads introduce mass transport.

> True and sincere traveling is no pastime, but it is as serious as the grave, or any other part of the human journey, and it requires a long probation to be broken into it. I do not speak of those that travel setting, the sedentary travelers whose legs hang dangling the while, mere idle symbols of the fact, any more than when we speak of setting hens we mean those that sit standing, but I mean those to whom traveling is life for the legs. The traveler must be born again on the road, and earn a passport from the elements, the principal powers that be for him. He shall experience at last that old threat of his mother fulfilled, that he shall be skinned alive. His sores shall gradually deepen themselves that they may heal inwardly, while he gives no rest to the sole of his foot, and at night weariness must be his pillow, that so he may acquire experience against his rainy days.

Obviously, my experience is much richer than anything I've known in any vehicle, much more real, actual; against it all other motion will either acquire or lose meaning. Here is something open indeed to exploration and reflection. As I struggle to get through the mud, to avoid the deeper water, each step is a distinct and separate act, a new adventure. Each step also seems to be a particular and special grace—the gift of one more half meter toward Compostela. I would never have seen this, never have known, that each step nearer the sacred place is actually a gift. How could it ever have happened that, on my own initiative, I would have learned that the *finis terrae* existed? . . . that I would set out to go there by a true action of moving across the earth, from one place to another place, the places being infinite? The two French pilgrims of a few years ago who were picked up by the police before they left France calculated the number of actual steps they would take in getting to Compostela. They must have had some sense of this kind of movement.

But it seems more and more difficult to find a place to put my feet so that the water does not go over my shoes. I watch for an opening where I might climb up on the bank—higher ground will mean that the water has run off . . . it's all down here where I'm trying my best to avoid it.

Finally, I succeed in getting up the bank; I'm in a forest with some brush—enough to keep me damp as I walk through it. I then come out on a kind of field where the wet grass is so thick and so high that it is almost like walking in water. Perhaps I was better off in the ditch. Or maybe it's better drained along here. I look for a place to descend again.

And now I learn something new. Having grown up in central Illinois, and never having walked in hilly or mountainous country, I never knew that there is a great difference between going up and going down—at least for me. Climbing, I am slowly weighed down by exhaustion. Descending, I am sometimes tortured with pain. But as the hours lengthen, I welcome this variation. On level ground, I am tired and ache—both feelings press in upon me to dissolve me. But if I'm climbing or coming down a hill, I only have to contend with one, getting a good rest from the other. It seems that the pain and weariness are greater today; but, luckily, my tolerance increases accordingly. Before starting, I had thought that I would find the walking easier as I grew more accustomed to it. Well, that opinion is quickly shattered as an illusion.

In spite of these feelings, I still see the beauty—it's always there, all around me, pressing sweetly in upon me. I seem to move only through beauty . . . if I don't look down at the highway! The landscapes are never what is conventionally called "spectacular." But the experience of the succession of places is unmistakable; everything confirms yet again what I see. The particularity of each place seems to add up to an infinitude of *different* places. Moving at this pace, I actually see particularity, I sense a uniqueness that stretches out forever all around me. At times, the effect becomes awesomely dramatic. Once, looking up, I see a mountain—right in front of me!—standing between me and what must be Pamplona on the other side. But then, because of the vegetation and the depth of the ditch, I lose sight of it. My next sensation is that it has disappeared. The *camino* must have wound around it; it must have had a side, an "ending," which I didn't see. But I'm not aware of a directional change in my walk. How wonderful—to be so close to the earth, and yet to be striding over it.

After seven hours of tiring and difficult excitement, I come out on a road. And there ahead of me, just as the map indicated, some kind of institutional structure appears—a convent. Almost wiped out by the day's exertions, I reach out to ring the bell. A nun answers. I ask her if this is the *refugio*. Yes. She shows me where to go—the entrance is around on the side of the building—and says that they ask for a donation of 300 pesetas—less than two dollars and fifty cents.

I walk to the door, noticing that the sun is still shining brightly against this side of the building, and will be there for some hours yet. I go in-side—all is very simple, but extremely neat and clean. I take off my shoes, clean off the mud, and put them out in the sun, hoping they will be dry for tomorrow's march. I then wash everything that has been soaked in sweat or covered with mud. I carry one bar of strong laundry soap, which serves nicely for bathing, shaving, and washing my clothing.

This appears to be the only "problem" on the *camino*: how to get clothes washed and dry. Basically, laundry comes down to two items: my one towel and the many pairs of socks. The other things are not so ur-gent. I have tried rigging up strings across the back of the pack, so that, from the rear, I must look like a walking clothesline. But on days like today, or if it rains, this arrangement doesn't work at all. This afternoon, the sun looks good and strong; I should have dry, clean shoes, and clothes for tomorrow.

After a hot shower—that alone was worth more than 300 pesetas—I go looking for something to eat. I notice that there is a fully equipped kitchen in the *refugio*. That means I can go out and buy food and cook it myself—undoubtedly, the ideal practice, but I am too tired; I just cannot face searching for a food store and shopping.

A couple of blocks down the street I find a place that is reputed to offer a decent *menú del día*. This is the daily special and if one is lucky it can be quite substantial and pleasantly palatable. Today I am especially un-lucky. The price is reasonable, but the food is scanty and terrible.

In three days I have found three very different kinds of shelters, one seemingly run by church personnel (Roncesvalles), one by the town (Zubiri), and one by a religious order (here). The other two places had a box on the wall with a sign, asking for a donation. But there was no suggested amount and everyone was completely free to drop something in, or ignore it.

The history of these places, now called *refugios* or *albergues,* formerly called *hospitales,* is rich and varied. Kings have built them, the most famous of these being the huge one in Compostela, ordered to be built by Ferdinand and Isabella at the beginning of the sixteenth century. *Refugios* have also been constructed and endowed by bishops, religious orders, the military orders, noblemen, and private persons who had the means to carry out this good work. Some have also been built and maintained by *cofradías*—confraternities, organizations of laypersons who may have been pilgrims themselves, and who wish to provide this service for other pilgrims. I have not heard of any ancient foundation that has continued until today, but perhaps I'll learn of one before I get to Compostela. In the Middle Ages, the *hospitales* were highly organized. I see that today, too, there are a few rules: for example, one needs a *credencial* to get in (the religious at the door stamped mine for me when I showed it to her), and the pilgrim is allowed to stay only one night, unless special permission is obtained (for sickness, I assume).

For me, walking, I am always interested to know where I can find the next *refugio,* for this will determine how far I walk the next day. Up to now, my map, which was copied from a popular Spanish guidebook, has been a reliable indicator.

And so, I have been surprised by what I found in Book V of the *Liber.* All the authors state that this is the first travel guide written in Europe, the forerunner of all the thousands of tourist guidebooks written since then. It is indeed an interesting document but, for me at least, a strange kind of guide. Probably written about 1140, it tells much about the *idea* of pilgrimage in the twelfth century and, as I noted above, about the animosity between the French and the people on this side of the Pyrenees, the *navarros* and *vascos.* But there is not a word about a place to stay if one goes to Compostela, starting from the mountains, as I did. The chapter devoted to *hospitales* (chapter 4), speaks of three: one in Jerusalem, one at Mont-Joux (in the Alps, for those going to Rome), and the one called Santa Cristina, in Somport, a town in France before one gets to the mountains at the Spanish border. This chapter, with eleven lines the shortest in the book, is apparently a symbolic statement affirming that there are *hospitales* on the roads to the three great centers of medieval pilgrimage. This is a very different concept than the one I would have about what is helpful in a guidebook. But I may not know how to read it. Perhaps the medieval pilgrim knew, from these three instances, that there were other shelters along the way; literary custom revealed this. And, from other documents, I know that there were *hospitales* along the *camino* when the *Liber* was written.

The longest chapter in the *Liber* (chapter 8, 709 lines), which describes the *santos cuerpos,* the holy relics in the churches that one should visit on the way to Compostela, is almost twice as long as the next longest, that on the city and tomb of Saint James the Apostle (chapter 9, 397 lines). And of the 709 lines describing relics in chapter 8, only 19 refer to relics in Spain. The others are found in France, along the four routes that led to the two places in the Pyrenees where pilgrims crossed into Spain. These two routes then joined at Puente la Reina, now just one or two days ahead of me.

Here one enters a region of the *camino*'s strange world—the place of relics in the medieval religious imagination. It is clear, from the space he devotes to them, and the way he writes about them, that the relics that one could see *and touch* on the *camino* to Compostela, were very important to Aymeric Picaud. The tradition of venerating relics antedates Christianity. And there is some evidence that pilgrimages to shrines of relics were popular in Spain before the Romans arrived here in the third century B.C. People have sought—and seek—to physically touch sources of power, whether this be the power to destroy, to heal, to comfort, or to forgive.

When the Moors invaded Spain in 711, they quickly conquered the land, advancing even beyond the Pyrenees, but were stopped at the famous battle of Poitiers, in 732. Only one part of Spain successfully resisted the invasion, encompassing the mountainous country of Galicia—where, according to tradition, the body of Santiago would be discovered around 830—Asturias, and the region of the *vascos* (these last not subdued by the Romans either). In this area, local leaders tried to establish themselves as monarchs, continuing the tradition of the Visigoths, and to found a kingdom from which they could launch attacks against the Moors. Some Christians, fleeing from the advancing Moors, brought with them to this region, near Oviedo, a *Santo Arco,* a box of relics. This collection was honored and promoted by the early rulers as an integral part of their legitimacy and of the nascent kingdom's very foundation. A magnificent church was built by them in Oviedo to contain the *Santo Arco.* This became a famous place of pilgrimage, though its importance would be overshadowed later by Compostela. Records show that many pilgrims visited Oviedo on their way to or from Compostela.

Some modern authors attempt to establish the proposition that "faith in the thaumaturgical power of relics" was the principal motive for making a pilgrimage in the Middle Ages. When this is said, there is usually the corollary, implicit or explicit, that such faith would be regarded as superstitious by a more enlightened age, such as our own. Today's irrational beliefs, however, are usually lacking any sensible ground or foundation; they point toward abstract, oftentimes arbitrary constructions or fantasies, such as the GNP, insurance systems, technological solutions. The people who walked to Oviedo or Compostela could see and touch the sacred objects that remained from the lives of people who manifestly reached heroic heights of virtue and power. I suspect, though, that the motivations of people then were as mixed and as varied as those of myself and of others I meet on the *camino* today.

Aymeric Picaud's guide reflects the religious geography and mentality of the people for whom it was written. Yes, they needed to know which water was good and which poisonous, but their principal interest was to enter a universe of power and blessing, of wonder and forgiveness, through seeing and touching the remains of these great figures who stand before God as intercessors for fallen creatures still on the *camino*.

A modern reader might find more useful material—for getting to Compostela—in the long and rambling sermon, "Veneranda dies," attributed (today, one would say, "falsely") to Pope Calixtus II, and found in Book I of the *Liber*. Here, Picaud provides detailed descriptions of all the many kinds of fraud perpetrated by money changers, merchants, innkeepers, and other *pícaros* who lay in wait for the innocent and unsuspecting pilgrim.

After an insufficient and rather contemptible lunch, I return to the *refugio* to rest. I think I've covered about twenty kilometers today, perhaps the same as the first two days. Well, I hope I can increase this in the days to come. If not, I'm going to be a long time on the *camino*. From their *relato,* I learn that two young Spaniards in 1937, during the Civil War, averaged forty-two kilometers a day! In July! One of them, a priest, appeared to wear a pilgrim gown much like a cassock.

In the shelter, there is a larger room with comfortable chairs. And, on a table, the guest book. I have seen these in the other two shelters, also. Each person is free to write some comment, and sign it if he or she wishes. I check to see the last date in 1992 when a pilgrim passed through here: December 29th. The first person to sign the book in 1993 was here on January 1st! I'm aghast. What must it be like to walk the *camino* at that time of the year? At the higher elevations there is snow, and I've heard that it can be deep. Many of the arrows are painted on rocks. How would one see them to find his way? It appears that someone is out here every day of the year, maintaining the living presence of a thousand-year-old tradition. I'm quite overwhelmed by the idea. I decided to walk in May because I heard that in the months of June, July, and August the *camino* would probably be filled with thousands of people because this is a Holy

Year and the government has launched a huge international promotional campaign—for tourists. But I would have been afraid to come earlier because of the cold and snow.

So far this year, 137 persons have signed the book. But not all pilgrims stop at this or any specific *refugio*. And perhaps not all who stop sign the book. I guess the only way to get a complete record is to count the names of those who check in at Roncesvalles and then present their *credencial* at Compostela. But this would not include all who make the pilgrimage, for some start at other towns along the way. A friend of mine started at León when he walked to Compostela a few years ago.

I leaf through the book, reading some of the remarks. What a rich mine this is. What an interesting project this would be—to study these records. Some people evidently have given much thought to what they write. One person was especially acute: *"Me duele todo el cuerpo, pero 'no hay dolor'"*—"My whole body aches, but 'there is no pain.'" It is sometimes a subtle delight to read Spanish—people are able to express sentiments and ideas with a kind of grace and incisiveness that cannot be caught in a translation. English seems inadequate to get the fine nuances. One must be able to read it in Spanish. And this has been one of the genuine daily pleasures of the *camino* for me—to greet and speak with people in their own language.

I brought along my Latin Breviary that, for the past few years, I have been saying each day. But I have been too tired to open it. That must not be a suitable prayer for the *camino*—at least not for this pilgrim. Strange. When I was packing in Germany, I noticed my father's Rosary lying in the desk drawer. Not thinking, or perhaps moved by sentiment, I picked it up and dropped it in the backpack. I know that he said it regularly. And it was the custom, at the time he died, to wind the Rosary around the body's hands in the casket. This was the traditional way to present the corpse for family and friends who came to the wake. When they closed the casket, the funeral director removed the Rosary and gave it to me, the eldest child. And it has been in my desk, untouched, ever since. Tomorrow, I must look in the pack and get it out. Perhaps I will learn that this prayer is connected with the *camino,* it fits the rhythm of walking.

Alone in the dormitory, I get ready for bed. As I crawl into the sleeping bag, three young Canadians, one of whom I met in Zubiri, come into the shelter. They bring food with them and start cooking in the kitchen. I am too tired to do more than weakly greet them. As I lie still, the trembling chills start again . . . they go on and on . . . it seems they will never stop . . . finally, I must have fallen asleep.

4

Pamplona to
Cizur Menor

May 7, 1993

I get up early, find that I am marvelously renewed—a new man!—eager to be out on the *camino* as soon as possible. The usual breakfast of bread, cheese, and fruit, while I dream of a cup of coffee . . . I've had none since the *café au lait* in Bayonne. After yesterday's late afternoon sun treatment, the shoes look to be in fine condition. I make up the backpack and set out for Pamplona, about five kilometers away. This will be my first big city on the *camino*.

I guess it would be interesting to explore the city, but I've decided to confine myself, as much as I can, to the open space of the *camino* itself. I'm afraid of distractions. And this will be a place full of them. I suppose that it's a modern city of over a hundred thousand persons by now; tradition says it was founded by and named for Pompey, Caesar's rival. Between the French, the Moors, and the native *navarros,* it has been fought over many times. In the sixteenth century, Philip II again fortified it, making it the most impregnable city in northern Spain.

But when I think of Pamplona, I am reminded of Ignatius of Loyola. Born a *vasco* in 1491, Ignatius served first as a page, then as knight in the houses of relatives and connections. Participating in various military and diplomatic adventures, he found himself in 1521 in Pamplona, helping to defend the city against a French army. On May 20th, a cannonball fractured his right leg badly, and damaged the left one. When able to be moved, he was taken to the family castle of Loyola. There, he decided to submit to the painful surgery involved to break his leg again and reset it, for the first setting had been done badly.

I suppose the story of Ignatius is well known, being one of the great dramatic tales of European history, but perhaps by recalling some of its features I can better understand the *camino* and bring some new light to the darkness of our century. Completely immobilized, the thirty-year-old knight could only indulge in reminiscence. Tiring of this, he asked for something to read. The only books available in this Christian castle of warriors were a Life of Christ and a book containing the lives of some saints.

These stories strongly affected the worldly young man. When able to move on his own, Ignatius took his sword and traveled to the famous place of pilgrimage in Catalonia, Montserrat. There he hung the weapon up beside the image of the Virgin, and went to a nearby cave in Manresa, to explore the worlds of prayer and penance.

While living in the cave, he began writing one of the powerfully influential books of the West, the *Spiritual Exercises*. He includes a prayer that he said, and that he left for others. Once, when I showed it to a Spanish friend, he read it and paused for a minute or two, then remarked, "Why, that's the prayer my mother said every day of her life!" He had no inkling of its origin; in fact, no knowledge of Ignatius. The prayer:

> *Alma de Cristo, santifícame,*
> *Cuerpo de Cristo, sálvame,*
> *Sangre de Cristo, embriágame,*
> *Agua del costado de Cristo, lávame,*
> *Pasión de Cristo, confórtame,*
> *Oh buen Jesús ¡óyeme!*
> *Dentro de tus heridas, escóndeme,*
> *No permitas que me separe de tí.*
> *Del enemigo maligno, defiéndeme,*
> *En la hora de la muerte, llámame,*
> *Y haz que vaya hacia tí,*
> *Para que con tus santos*
> *Te alabe por los siglos de los siglos.*
> *Amen.*

> Soul of Christ, sanctify me,
> Body of Christ, save me,
> Blood of Christ, inebriate me,

Water from the side of Christ, wash me,
Passion of Christ, comfort me,
Oh good Jesus, hear me!
Within your wounds, hide me,
Do not let me be separated from you.
From the malignant Enemy, defend me,
At the hour of death, call me,
And grant that I go to you,
With your saints to praise you,
For all eternity.
Amen.

In 1523, Ignatius made another pilgrimage, this time to the Holy Land. On his return to Spain, he turned himself into a student, sitting down with much younger men for about twelve years, to get an education. He made his lengthy pilgrimages safely but, while studying in Spain, was arrested and imprisoned twice by the Inquisition. In each trial, he was able to establish his innocence—of heresy—and was set free.

The geography of faith through which Ignatius traveled is very different from the one mapped out by Picaud. Ignatius did not journey to the place of Spain's most famous relic, rather, to the mountain of the country's most mysterious presence, Montserrat, where there are no bones, only the ancient, blackened (from pilgrims' candles) image of the Virgin and Child. In his next pilgrimage, he goes to Jerusalem, the place of the empty tomb. Ignatius began with a look into an icon; later, he searched the darkness beyond all icons. Many pilgrims to Compostela emphasize the relic, its real presence. One, however, believing that that tomb, too, is empty, rejoices, saying that it is for the pilgrim himself to fill the tomb . . . This is the secret joy of the place.

As soon as I arrive in Pamplona, I consult my rough street map. I want to get through the city by the most direct route possible, with two stops, the post office and a shoe repair shop.

I find the post office easily, needing to detour only two blocks. There I buy a pasteboard box, fill it with all the unnecessary weight from my backpack, ship it back to Germany, and get a supply of stamps for post-cards. Continuing to cross the city, I see a shoe repairman and ask him if he can put some new innersoles in my shoes. The old ones have moved around and curled up . . . not very comfortable. He glues in some good-looking thick ones, and I am on my way again.

I feel as if I have new feet. And my attention seems to be absorbed by this; I don't notice the city, I don't pick up any of its flavor or color. Well, the *camino* is to be found in the traditional mud and forest, field and mountain, which have not changed much over the centuries, but not in urban developments.

At about noon, I arrive in Cizur Menor, which seems to be a kind of suburb a few kilometers beyond Pamplona. I could walk farther; it's still quite early in the day, but I've heard there is a good *refugio* here and decide to look for it. I've come only about ten kilometers, but perhaps the rest will be good for me. I'll try for a greater distance tomorrow.

With a couple of questions, I quickly find the location of the *refugio.* There is a high wall and a solid gate. I ring the bell. A woman answers, welcomes me, and leads me through a pleasant garden, past a well-designed old house, and to an attractive, low building set back in the garden. This is all owned and operated by a private family. The woman says that she charges 500 pesetas—about three dollars and eighty cents. The building is light, airy, the clean bunks are not pushed closely together. There is a kitchen and, of course, shower and toilet. I am surprised to see that the room is divided by a curtain. I understand that the bunks on one side are for women, on the other, for men. This is the first shelter with that convenience. The modest behavior of the pilgrims in the previous shelters had prevented me from thinking that such might be useful. Since I undress completely to get into pajamas each night, I just turn my back on the part of the room where women happen to be. Well, this place seems almost too agreeable and comfortable. But it is nice to be able to rest in such a tastefully arranged setting.

Another pilgrim arrives. It is the Frenchman I met my first day on the *camino.* He is limping badly. The woman, Doña Maribel Roncal, asks him about his feet, speaking fluent French. She tells him to take off his shoes while she prepares a treatment. Then she makes a mixture of warm water, vinegar, and salt, and tells him to soak his feet in this. She stamps our *credenciales,* and explains that these can be stamped at various places in a town: the police station, the office of a parish church, the city hall, many places of business, or the *refugio.* Each of these places will have a rubber stamp with the particular logo of that establishment or institution. The *credencial* has outlined spots so that one can get these stamped in sequential order. I've already noticed that each stamp is an interesting and different design.

Then the Señora gives each of us a list of the *refugios* between here and Compostela. She explains that there are others, but these are the ones that meet her personal criteria of what a *refugio* should be. She is quite proud of her place—and rightly so, I would judge—and thinks that all the *refugios* should be equally well furnished. Well, maybe . . . Privately, I think that perhaps her facility is a bit sumptuous, but I must admit that I am thoroughly enjoying the agreeable atmosphere and the physical comfort of her lodging. She goes on to recount various anecdotes about the *camino.* In the Middle Ages, there were at least two *hospitales* for pilgrims in Cizur Menor. Some ruins of the church adjoining one still exist on a hill, but most of the stone from the shelter itself has disappeared—probably carried off to be used for other buildings. Good stone does not decay or rot.

It is evident that the *camino* and its pilgrims are important to her; such interest and enthusiasm are refreshing to see. I discover that her English is also quite good. Knowing three languages, she can probably speak to nearly all the pilgrims who come through.

Today, I need only wash my socks. That chore soon finished, I find a comfortable spot in the sun and leaf through a magazine that was on the table, something called *Peregrino,* which seems to be dedicated exclusively to the *camino.* After a few moments, however, I am interrupted by three young men who approach and introduce themselves. They come from a local TV station and want to interview a pilgrim for a program they are producing. Since I am the only pilgrim present who speaks Spanish, the leader of the group requests an interview. I ask him to explain a bit more of what he wants to do. He says that he thinks most of the programming on television is not very good. He would like to change that. He has great hopes for this medium. He wants to produce serious things, shows that will make people think, that will introduce new or important ideas. Today, he wants to speak with a pilgrim. He suspects that the fascination of the *camino* is much more than tourism and historical sentimentalism. Indeed, as experience it might have some depth to it. He would like to capture this for his TV audience.

Somewhat apologetically, he acknowledges that he himself is not a practicing Catholic, but he feels that there must be some validity to the "spiritual" character of the *peregrino.* He doesn't mention the word "superstition," perhaps not to offend me—he doesn't yet know my sentiments or thoughts—but I can sense that the word is there, hanging in the air between us: Is it possible that belief in Santiago is something more than a medieval superstition, seized today by the government and tourist agencies for their own purposes? He asks if his companions may set up the equipment for an interview.

I ask them to wait a moment. I am still uncertain what to answer; I express certain reservations. I tell him that I have not owned a TV set for many years. I never watch television, except for maybe an hour each year when, altogether, it takes me that long to extricate myself from situations where I find a set turned on in front of me. Long ago, thinking about television, I came to make a distinction between the images and the medium, between the content and the form or manner in which that content is projected on me or at me. Early on, I decided that the issue was *not* the content, but the form. Questions concerning dumb situation comedies, movies of classical drama, foolish games, or pornography were quite unimportant. I was interested in how this mode of presenting images, *any* images, would affect my ability to see myself as a person, my sense of self as a moral creature. What kind of person would I turn out to be if I let myself be exposed to electronic images coming at me in this way? I am suspicious, since each time I have let television invade my private interior space, I have been left feeling uncomfortable, sometimes disturbed.

Further, when TV sets first appeared, I guessed that the infant industry would soon attract quite talented people to work for it. Inevitably, this would lead to greater and greater manipulation of my sensibilities. I can stop reading a book at any word, to think about it, to argue with the author, to reach up and check what he says with a reference book and so on. Nothing like this is possible with television. Or maybe I never learned how to watch it. When television was invented, I was already too old to learn how to take in its pictures. But that greatly bothers me: *receiving* pictures. It seems to be radically different from what I experience out on the *camino.* There, I continually walk *into* the picture, I *create* the picture, I *am* the picture.

Looking at the young man, I suggest that I can illustrate the argument, perhaps, by what is happening here between the two of us. As I've talked with you, I've seen your face, your eyes. I've listened to your request. In some modest way, I've come to know you somewhat, to trust you. I feel I could say something about my motives for being here in the middle of Spain, walking through mud and rain, sun and wind, sore and tired every day, and I'll be doing this for at least three more weeks. This is not the kind of activity advertised in the American media for people my age, who are supposed to be retired, relaxing on a golf course.

Because I can look into your face I am not afraid to say that, some months ago, I found myself in a small chapel in Spain, what is called a chapel of the Blessed Sacrament. The altar was filled with flowers and lighted candles and, in the center, something called a monstrance—with the Host in it. Now this is not so common today in Catholic churches. Devotional practices change over the years. But people kept entering that chapel, people oblivious to me, sitting there, and to others whom they did not know. All their attention and concentration were centered on the Real Presence in which they believed.

Remaining there some hours, I wondered about those people in the chapel, and about the others who walk to Santiago de Compostela—the multifarious multitude that has been wending its way there for over a thousand years. Again and again, I asked myself: Why did they leave their familiar homes? Why did they journey so far? What drew them to that unknown place, the *finis terrae?*

I finally came to form the beginning of an answer: If you wish to find out, go.

You see, I said to my interviewer, I'm interested in what is immediate, tangible, what I can touch. Television was designed to remove you from the immediate and, by that stratagem, may make it progressively more difficult that you ever see, touch, smell, taste, or hear again. This, I suspect, is what television ultimately does to people.

He answered that he was impressed with an idea of Umberto Eco: television was communication at a distance.

Yes, I agreed, perhaps it is. But I am not interested in communication. Communication is something that takes place between machines, not between people. Communication works through bits, zero-one. I want to hear your accent, the traces of the place from which you come. I want to see the smile on your face when you hear my accent. I do not want to speak to anyone into whose eyes I cannot look. How could I say these things into a dead microphone? How could I speak to a void? How could I turn myself into a communicating machine?

Let us assume there is a large TV audience for your program, I propose. How could I speak *virtuously* to a huge crowd of undifferentiated and unseen eyes and ears? Yes, it's possible that I have motives that go beyond the emptiness and degradation of tourism. But if that is true, how could I prostitute them so shamefully? How could I participate in such monstrous exhibitionism? What would be the moral character of my motives to parade myself before an abstract audience?

And to be more candid, I don't really know yet why I am here. If I am especially blessed, perhaps I'll find out when I reach Compostela. We could meet there for a cup of coffee and discuss what happened to me on the *camino.* Who knows? I may have a tale to tell by then.

I apologize to the television producer for wasting his time, and for seeking such a high ground from which to pontificate. His two companions had long ago disappeared. He smiles, graciously accepts the apology, and definitely appears at ease, with no trace of resentment; we exchange good-byes, shaking hands. I may have been a pleasant afternoon diversion for him. He is probably inwardly amused at the obscurantist and retrograde rantings of the old codger.

I wonder if this young man rested his gaze on the trees and flowers here in this garden. Did he recognize the reality of *this* place? Did he realize that the space we occupied was special? That we filled a unique space through our sensory contact, creating a place here? Now it's lost because he is gone. But it was real then and we could make it real again.

The world of communications, however . . . is there anything real in that? And, ultimately, is there any truth that does not grow out of immediate sense experience? Or that must somehow touch that experience? Is the world of information and communication one gigantic deception, one outrageous scam? Are many of today's *pícaros* to be found there, working the crowd? But now the crowd is not a few unwary pilgrims to be fleeced, but millions of modern sophisticates to be amused.

It's late afternoon; I should think of eating. Maribel Roncal said that a woman sells things to eat in a house down the street. There is no regular store here in this village or suburb, but we can buy supplies from this woman and cook our dinner here in the shelter. The Frenchman and I decide to look for her house.

I have come to learn that in some places here in Spain a house and even a place of business might be just a door in what looks like a wall or another building running along the street. There is often a number beside the door and, if a place of business, sometimes a hard-to-see sign. Of course, especially in the larger towns and cities, there are also modern signs and supermarkets. But we are unable to find the door of the woman, and decide to try what seems to be the only restaurant in town. The meal is excellent, but sets me to thinking. There must be attitudes, together with habits of mind, heart, and body, which lead either toward or away from the *camino*. I believe, for example, that if I felt the need to read the newspaper each day, I could not seek to meet all those who found their way on the *camino*—their own *camino* (way) on *the camino*. Since I have learned that regional dishes are especially delightful to my sensibilities, I suspect that they might act, like the newspaper, as a debilitating distraction. Hence, I try to find the most common fare, only what I need to sustain me in my walk to the next *refugio*. But I've still much to learn: How to eat simply and well in Spain? One of the difficulties is that each place is so different—but that is its beauty and charm, too. On one street, you find the bakery; on another, the sausage shop; on another, the meat market; on yet another, the greengrocer, and so on. And the streets, for a stranger, are a confused jumble. I've seen supermarkets, too, but I have not yet entered one.

I learn that the French pilgrim is a retired physician. I think he says that he has been in general practice in a small town or village. But my French is not good enough to get very far into the subtleties of *his* motivation! We are both also interested in our sleeping bags at this time. I think we share a certain enthusiasm for the quiet and wonder-filled solitude of the *camino*. Sleep is important now to enter this space again in the morning.

5

Cizur Menor to Puente la Reina

May 8, 1993

The sun is not yet up when I go out . . . cool enough that I need to put on a sweatshirt before starting. But then, moving well, I feel too warm . . . time to take it off and tie it on top of the pack. Today, I start climbing what seems to be a mountain, La Sierra del Perdón. My body feels good, making the effort. I must be getting stronger. When I reach the top, a fierce wind is blowing. Although the sun is shining, I need the sweatshirt again. Then, when I reach a much lower altitude, it's too warm for so much clothing. With relatively few steps, I move from one climate to another, and they are so different that they require different amounts of clothing. The earth is infinitely variable, just within a few kilometers. If I took the time, I would come to know something of this infinity in all the variation of wild, growing plants throughout the range of different degrees of hot and cold, of more or less rarefied air. But none of this can be known, except for the one who has his or her feet firmly on this soil.

During all this time, the scenery changes constantly, with every step. Underfoot, I feel a different combination of pebbles and rocks each time my foot hits the ground. Not only do I never step in the same place twice, but I never feel the same kind of surface twice. The variations of hardness, softness, and sharpness are never the same. If I look up, the cloud formations are always new. If I gaze around me, the scene is ever unique. Walking, moving rapidly through the different places, I can nevertheless get some sense of creation, of its infinite variety. It really *is* infinite! I clearly sense this. Today, again, I see that the reality that surrounds me is evident, *as creation.* There is no possibility of doubt—its ever changing beauty reveals its character. It is also quite clear where men have touched or affected the creation, and whether they've done this well or badly.

Looking carefully, and walking through places changed by men's work and destruction, at times lightly, at times, heavily, one can make judgments. After the time of these days spent out here treading this soil, I begin to feel an almost connatural capacity to judge: Here, they have acted well, with reverence and respect, there, badly, with contempt and carelessness. I pass many wheat fields, little pasture land, see almost no livestock, and houses are rare. From the size of the fields, I see that large farm machinery is needed to work them. This kind of farming—industrial agriculture—calls for big machines and few people—a depopulated countryside . . . that I now walk through . . . large-scale monoculture. In the United States, some people who have looked closely at and thought carefully about this phenomenon have concluded that it means the destruction of the land, as it has already impoverished or wiped out small rural communities. I wonder what the Spaniards think about it, about what they are doing to their land and villages . . . to themselves.

From the judgments I find myself making, I think I begin to see differently. The *camino* has changed the way in which I see. Leonardo da Vinci believed that one could not see the organs of a dissected body unless they were first drawn. Otherwise, one did not know *how* to see what was before one's eyes. I suspect that this is true of all literate people, and of all things that they "see." The more deeply one is in the world of literacy, the more one will need drawings, by word or picture, of what is there to see. It is only the illiterate person who sees directly, who sees with all his senses, who sees without any mediation or heuristic interpretation. Perhaps this is a kind of exemplary seeing, the primordial act of seeing. Being out here, not having read anything about the *camino* before starting, and reading almost nothing since I left St. Jean Pied de Port, my sensibility has had all the words and pictures cleared away. My senses can now work at their optimum, somewhat as an animal's. I am passing a threshold. The *camino* takes me to life *in* creation.

This year is a Holy Year for the *camino,* since the feast of Santiago, July 25th, falls on a Sunday. Such is the special privilege granted by the pope in the fourteenth century. In such a year, those visiting Compostela and fulfilling the requirements—such as making certain acts of devotion— receive spiritual blessings. This year, the government has developed a multifaceted program to celebrate the occasion. There have been many discussions on how to "improve" the *camino*, and violent disagreements about some of the proposals—for example, to construct a several meter-wide asphalt pavement covering the entire route of the *camino*. One project that seems to have been implemented along here is to plant trees beside the *camino* where there are none already growing. Each young tree is enclosed in a translucent corrugated plastic tube about two meters high, supported by a heavy stick or pole the same height. This seems somewhat bizarre when tourism literature—but perhaps from a different government agency—glories in the ecological character of the *camino*, its celebration of nature. I've noticed many droppings along here from sheep or goats, so it would be necessary to protect young trees from these hungry beasts. But is plastic the only solution?

Today, I take out my father's Rosary, and start saying it as I walk. The fields of grain provide a perfect enclosure, the proper space, in which to pray. These fields may destroy farming in Spain, but their undulating gracefulness supports the soaring of my spirit. How can one understand such an experience? Is this what it means to be confused today? I know that these industrial agriculturists, if they continue much longer, can only destroy: They produce ever new kinds of desertification. And yet I can calmly pray in the midst of their depredations. Has our age also invented new forms of the grotesque? What used to be considered a type of compromise is now the grotesque. But it takes a new kind of vision to see this, a peculiar insight, a purification of the senses.

By the time I arrive at my destination, I have completed ten of the fifteen Mysteries, the five Joyful (the Annunciation, the Visitation, the Nativity, the Presentation, the Finding in the Temple), and the five Sorrowful (the Agony in the Garden, the Judgment before Pilate, the Scourging, the Carrying of the Cross, the Crucifixion). In four or five hours, I've recited the Hail Mary at least a hundred times, the Our Father ten times. I used to say five mysteries—fifty Hail Marys—in about fifteen minutes. Today, I needed a couple of hours. Maybe I'm learning to pray. After this experience, all my thoughts and feelings lead me to one conclusion: This is the ideal exercise for the *camino*, this is exactly what I must do each day as I walk. How miraculous that I understood this so early in my journey, on the fifth day. I still have most of the days ahead of me. And so, I learn yet again: There are no accidents, no coincidences in creation; there are only gifts, whether of pain or of insight, the vision of place or the experience of prayer.

After what has happened to me today, I am ashamed to admit that I cannot recall how many years it has been since I prayed the Rosary. I'm deeply embarrassed to find how much I've fallen into modern superstitions, abandoning ancient truths. And I hope I'm humbled enough to acknowledge the unusually rich character of this gratuitous grace: What I lived through today was a totally *new* experience, having little apparent connection with my past actions of reciting these prayers. As I walked, I fell into a certain rhythmic pattern automatically, naturally, without any forethought or reflection. I said the prayers, the Hail Marys, Our Fathers, and the doxology aloud, speaking the words, one by one, on each breath—one breath, one word.

Somehow I realized that I had hours ahead of me, there was no need to rush; it made no sense to speak the words as in an ordinary earthly conversation. The Other has no need of the words anyway; they are only for me, according to the rhythm of my life at this moment. And that seemed to be the pace of my breathing: Each breath fitted one word; each word rested through one breath. So the prayer became a part of my body in a new way; it came to belong to me, as I was during those moments, those hours; it became *my* prayer in a sense I had never heretofore experienced nor, indeed, imagined.

Each of the words, then, came alive, and savored of a sensible sweetness. Each seemed to fit *that* moment, *that* motion of my body. And each felt new, perhaps as earlier, when each step I took felt new to the bottom of my feet. I was never tempted to hurry the words, to finish, to get to the end. The words themselves seemed to fix my attention. Distractions simply disappeared, vanished into the serene clarity of the bright sky. *That* was certainly something new for me. As, on the first day, the earlier pilgrims carried me along, so today, these prayers . . . a new way of walking over the earth, of learning to be in my place on earth.

I had never before seen—or dreamed of—a prayer fitting so well into a place, a time, a person, and all the surrounding circumstances—the congruences were wondrous, unforgettable. So this is what vocal prayer can be! I recall reading, many years ago, books on prayer. Some modern authors—and maybe not so modern, too—make a distinction between what they call vocal prayer and, another kind, mental prayer. With the former, one speaks words, with the latter, simple, direct thoughts, leading to a "resting in." All these authors agree on one point: The latter is superior to the former. Those who are beginners in something called "the spiritual life" are stuck in vocal prayer; more advanced persons soar in mental prayer. Any person seriously interested in prayer should get busy with the necessary exercises to graduate from vocal to mental prayer as quickly as possible. Today I wondered how many of these pious and sincere authors had ever experienced lowly "vocal" prayer . . .

I could not help but reflect on the extent and centrality of walking in the Joyful Mysteries. For example, Mary walks through the mountains to visit her cousin, Elizabeth (the Visitation); Joseph and Mary walk to Bethlehem to be inscribed in the census (the Nativity). These are the humble and hidden events that introduce one to the Incarnation—to God become Man and Woman. Perhaps the very act of walking is important to come to the Incarnation, to find the Incarnation. I feel pretty certain that I need sense experience, the fleshly experience of my body, to come *to believe* in my body. This seems amply established by reflection on my sensory response to the *camino*. The *camino* has made me truly feel my body. Perhaps I need this perception leading to this faith to carry me to belief in the Incarnation. I cannot find my way to believe that God became flesh until I experience belief in my own flesh. Struggling to conquer the obstacles of the *camino*—whether from outside or from my own inner weaknesses—I come to feel my flesh in every step. Every step, then, may be a privileged move toward the Lord.

Perhaps this too is what the thousands who preceded me learned when they walked. Then this may be why they were here—that is, from my perspective, looking back. And this may be what they are trying to tell me. Perhaps it takes this much pain and fatigue for one to come to believe in his body. As I now see that there is a certain character to prayer that I never before knew, so there may be a certain way of believing in my body that I never knew. And, of course, there is much in the mystery of the Incarnation that I did not know, and much that I shall never—in this vale of tears—come to know, but I have learned something. This apparently simple prayer, the Rosary, associated, for example, in the drawings of the great artist Goya, with old (disreputable) women, joined to this mundane act of walking across Spain, a pilgrimage, may be uniquely powerful to carry me to God in the only place where he can be found/touched—in the Incarnation. Yet another surprise of the *camino*.

While saying the Rosary, I also passed through three small villages. I had expected to buy food in such places to put in my pack for breakfast and supper. In the first village I asked if there were a place to buy food. No. Nor in the second, but I learned there that a small truck comes to the village at a fixed hour each morning with fresh bread and other provisions. I did not have the luck to hit that village at the proper time, however! It was obvious that people in these villages had cars and many of them probably drive to larger nearby towns for jobs. Perhaps they also shop at the supermarkets in those places, too. Yesterday, I walked through a very small farm village. It was clear from the sights and smells that most of the houses and their adjacent buildings were occupied by working farmers, not by people with jobs in town or city. But there was no place to buy bread, so those people, too, must depend on a daily delivery truck. Vehicles change peoples' lives here, too.

I am puzzled at one place to find a yellow arrow, painted on a rock, pointing to a plowed field. Since the rock only weighs a kilogram or two, maybe it got changed around. But it appears that the *camino* should be going forward. I try to sight a straight line to a point on the other side of the large field and start walking. When I get to the other side, I again find an arrow! Several times today I have been directed by the arrows to walk through a wheat field. It appears that there is a fight between the farmers, wanting to cover all available space with their crops, thereby covering the ancient trail, and the people interested in preserving the *camino,* as closely as possible, according to Picaud's twelfth-century directions. It must be much more of a struggle to establish the *camino* in the larger cities and growing suburbs. But most of today's walk is through colorful, open country where, as on the other days, I pass by many early wild-flowers. There are striking new blooms today: red poppies. What a bright and cheerful companion to find along the way. And I feel good about being able to walk much faster today, with less pain. The *camino* is toughening me up.

After about five and a half hours' walk, I arrive at another famous place on the *camino,* Puente la Reina. Here, the early pilgrims had to cross the Río Arga, across which a bridge was constructed, specifically for them by a queen, hence the name of the bridge and town. It is not clear which of two possible queens is responsible (La Mayor, wife of Sancho III, or their daughter, Estefanía), but the bridge was probably built in the eleventh century. There were also several *hospitales* here.

I soon come to the *refugio,* maintained by the Padres Reparadores, a religious congregation of men who operate a large minor seminary here. A friendly brother in the office stamps my *credencial* and directs me to the *refugio,* an older building converted into a comfortable shelter. There are several showers and toilets, and the bunks, to my astonishment, are three high. Since no one else has yet arrived, I can choose a bottom one in a quiet corner. The water is wonderfully hot, and there is a well-designed washboard sink for doing clothes. But I can find no good place to hang them to dry. Since the large room is empty, I stretch my clothes-line—which I always carry with me—from one bunk to another in front of an open window.

After taking a shower, I think about looking for food. There is no kitchen, so I decide to eat in a place that the brother who welcomed me told me about. They offer a good *menú del día,* he said.

I'm still not prepared for Spanish towns. What appears to me as the irregularity of the street patterns always confuses me. It's all very *sim-pático* if one is just wandering around like a tourist, enjoying the maze of architecture and color, people and odd shops. But to look for a specific place to which I have the directions continues to be a major challenge. Walking all round what appears to be the center of the town, I finally find a restaurant, but not the one the brother had mentioned. This one charges 1,250 pesetas for the *menú*—just over nine dollars and fifty cents! I have set myself a kind of goal: to spend about one thousand pesetas a day on both food and lodging. With this meal alone, I'll exceed my limit. Well, perhaps I should look at out-of-pocket expenses from some other perspective; for example, activity over passivity as an ideal. I should go out and search for the individual items of food, rather than sit down at a restaurant table and have them brought to me, all prepared. I can also thereby better choose the necessary, rather than the exotic or "interesting."

I go in and am surprised to find that I am the only diner. I suspect that it is still early for Spaniards to eat their main meal. The young woman who comes to wait on me, by the manner of her friendliness, not by anything she explicitly says, indicates that she knows I am a *peregrino*. And before I have ordered anything, she brings me a small plate of delicious ripe olives. I order the "daily special," which generally means bread, wine, two dishes (*dos platos*) and dessert. Soon, the first dish comes—a thick soup of cooked brown beans, flavored with garlic and herbs. She proudly tells me that these are from a local farm. With a side dish of hot green chile peppers, they are really delicious—just the kind of food to satisfy my taste.

The second dish is a small piece of steak and French-fried potatoes, which, as I have heard, is a popular way of serving potatoes in Spain. For dessert, there is rice pudding (*arroz con leche*), a popular dish. There is also bread—good, hard-crusted rolls, and a small pitcher of house wine (excellent)—enough for about two glasses. I eat everything she brings me, except that there is too much bread. I had prepared for this, and put what is left in the bread basket into a plastic bag I carry in my pocket. Given what I have to pay, I leave nothing behind except the tip. I must add, though, that the quantity and quality—of both the good food and gracious service—were certainly worth what I paid. This is clearly not the world described by Aymeric Picaud.

Returning to the *refugio*, I discover that one of the Canadians has arrived, the huge one. He invites me out for a cup of coffee, and we go to a nearby hotel coffee shop. I eagerly order a *café con leche*—my first coffee since leaving France almost a week ago. It seems years ago. What a glorious, sensual luxury. How did I manage to walk all these days without indulging such pleasure?

I find some fruit and cheese at a small supermarket, and bread at a bakery, so I'm prepared for tomorrow's breakfast—and for this evening, if

I am hungry. Fresh bread is baked every day at these bakeries, but there is often only one kind: a long loaf of white bread with a good, solid crust. I miss the variety of dark breads available in Germany. Bakeries in the larger towns will sometimes have whole wheat loaves, which I buy if they are available. But they seem to bake only a few of these each day for, if I arrive later in the day, I am often told that they are sold out. There is always enough of the standard white bread, however. The Spanish student pilgrims of 1928 note that the bread changed from region to region as they walked, and all of it was good. Today, it appears that industrial standardization controls most of the bread-making in Spain.

The shelter is quiet . . . there are very few people here tonight. I wonder what it would be like with the dormitory full of pilgrims, stacked three high. Each night I find myself in a very different place; no one *refugio* is like another. It's something like the villages—as if each has been constructed independently, idiosyncratically, no one consulting with the people at the next *refugio* or in the neighboring village. It's very much the opposite of the chain-store effect, which seems to be the pattern of so much modern space. And although each village or town is different, I have eventually managed to find my way around, and to sleep quite well every night.

The creation of space today, as in the new hotel down the street, is often so self-consciously novel that I respond with immediate boredom rather than with any intensified awareness. In the villages, however, I am sometimes seduced by the visual and poetic force of the artless lines and patterns. Then, when I settle down in a *refugio,* I feel that I've arrived in a real place, I'm immersed in an extra dimension of dignity that delights. This may be something like the great chain of being; here, it's a great connected circle of unique places, attached to one another like the beads on a Rosary. The challenge, then, is not to break the connection; one's life should go from one genuinely differentiated place to another. For example, if I were to abandon the pattern one night and seek an elegant tourist hotel, I would break the chain, I would fall out of place, I would be lost. And I would be unable to move the next day, for I would have no place from which to start.

6

Puente la Reina
to Estella

May 9, 1993

M y first Sunday on the *camino*. Last night, without thinking about it, I checked on the hours of Mass today. Here, at the Minor Seminary, there is a High Mass at eleven this morning. With lots of young, trained voices, that should be a grand celebration, a prayer I would thoroughly enjoy. But then the day would be half over before I could start walking again, and I want to reach the next *refugio* in Estella today, a goodly distance from here. What should I do? In some of the literature, there is solemn talk about the necessity of "religious exercises" on the *camino*. I believe there are special prayers and suggested routines. But I've never considered looking into any of these formulas. Perhaps I'm much amiss, too careless or cavalier. On the other hand, there may be something more complicated lurking below my options this morning. From the finding of Santiago's body until today, there has existed a certain tension between individual initiative and institutional order or rules.

According to the old legend, Pelayo the hermit saw heavenly signs near his retreat in the forest, early in the ninth century. But it was Teodomiro, the nearby bishop, who authenticated the newly discovered tomb as belonging to Saint James the Apostle. From the very beginning of the Christian Revelation, hermits have been persons who follow the invitation of the Lord, the promptings of grace, independently of the regularized order of the community. In a certain sense, one can see them as a protest against the institutionalization of the Gospel's call (*vocatio,* from which "vocation" comes). The drama between Pelayo and Teodomiro continues today. At times, institutional support greatly helped pilgrims, as when civil and ecclesiastical authorities promulgated legislation protecting pilgrims or established *hospitales* along the *camino.* At other times, I feel, the work of these same authorities destroyed the possibility of a pilgrimage and grossly distorted the man of the Gospel, Santiago Peregrino. Most of the created legends, campaigns, and promotions "from above" cluster around the figure of Santiago Matamoros, the Moor-killer. Santiago Peregrino, however, is largely the creation of innumerable individual pilgrims who began walking from all over "Europe" to Compostela immediately after the discovery of the tomb, and continue today from all over the world.

These pilgrims from beyond the Pyrenees made Compostela a Carolingian (French)—then "European"—center of pilgrimage, before the cult spread throughout the Peninsula. Specifically Spanish devotion was only local. And there is no mention of Santiago as protector against the Moors—the Matamoros—until the eleventh and twelfth centuries. Then *this* figure became more popular in Spain, as the Reconquista slowly and fitfully advanced. The figure of Santiago Matamoros does not appear in central European iconography until the fifteenth century, perhaps in response to the Turkish threat in that part of Christendom.

One of the most gifted and remarkable of the Spanish pilgrims, Raimundo Lulio (Raymond Lull), arrived in 1263. After experiencing a vision of Christ on the cross, Lulio, a *catalán* (from the province of Catalonia) poet, distributed his goods and made a pilgrimage to Compostela. There, he composed a prayer:

> I ask for and seek to find an ART by which Christian truth can be shown to unbelievers, in order that good men might spring up to assimilate and expound it, that Pope, Emperor, kings and princes promote the study of Arabic and Hebrew, facilitate missionary expeditions and organize a crusade of universal scope. All of this being oriented toward concord between Christian and Saracens, including their respective clergy, because at bottom they are very close to one another.

Lulio learned Arabic and visited popes, kings, and princes, trying to convince them to establish schools for the study of Arabic and Hebrew. He also traveled to Africa as a missionary. In a later vision (1272), he thought he saw the principles of the ART he sought. These principles centered around the divine attributes and the elementary structure of nature, to which adherents of the three faiths could agree. He wrote in Arabic, *catalán,* and Latin, being a pioneer in the use of the vernacular for theological work. There is a tradition among Spanish Franciscans that relates that Lulio was a lay member of the Third Order of Saint Francis. The Franciscans honor him as the Doctor Illuminatus. From his life, work, and the prayer, one can see that his was a singularly open spirit, reaching out to the Other, in an age when the hands of Christians often wielded swords. Reflecting on this history, I decide to set out early. Today, I'll neglect the institutional directive, and attempt to reflect on the principles of Lulio's ART, while keeping my eyes along the way open for a church where my arrival will coincide with the hour of Mass.

Leaving the city, I am surprised by seeing the restaurant that the brother told me about yesterday. Well, too late now. If I ever come back, I can try their *menú.* After some time, I cross the Río Salado, near the place where Aymeric Picaud claims his two horses died from drinking the water. The river's name, Salado, means "salty"—the same name Picaud gives—a condition that has not changed since the twelfth century. Other authors have disputed Picaud's claim; they think the water could not have killed the horses. It's salty, and does not taste good; but it's not poisonous.

A family of gypsies passes on the road in front of me. The man—a small, wiry, scowling, tough-looking fellow—walks rapidly, holding a rope fastened to the halter of his scrawny horse. The small covered wagon seems to carry a woman and child. A hungry-looking dog runs behind them, tied to the back of the wagon. They appear to be extremely poor; the figures evoke only sadness—another scene to remind me of Goya's power to portray what he saw. There is such pathos in so many of his drawings. But I am reminded of something else, too: the amusing encounter between the three Spanish students in 1928 and a larger group of gypsies along the *camino.* The boys called them a "tribe of gypsies," and believed that they were staring at them (the students) with the idea of forcibly making them members of "their clan"! But then the gypsies let them pass, while a young woman from the group cried out, "Jesus, what tall handsome fellows!" (a rather weak translation of, "¡Jesú, y qué talluito son lo mozo!"). The leader of the gypsies noticed that two of the boys, from their similar appearance, were brothers, and added, "What a good team they would make!" (meaning also, a team of work animals). The boys could only come up with "Thanks," and hurry on nervously. From the slight note of fear and apprehension in the tone of the telling, one can see that these upper-class youngsters were not accustomed to dealing with the familiar and earthy banter of gypsies. I only wish that the unfortunate-appearing family I met were so jolly and carefree.

The ground here is covered in many places with red poppies, too. I'm just in time to get all the first flowers of Spring. According to Chaucer, this is the time when a man's heart turns to thoughts of pilgrimage. But I don't expect to meet anyone so richly caparisoned as some of his pilgrims.

For the first time, I notice many vineyards on each side of the *camino*. But it's still too early to see anything on the bare vines. And since I know nothing about grapes, I have no idea whether they look good or bad, well or ill cared for. Since the best-looking fields show no signs of weeds, or any growth other than the vines, I suspect there must be a heavy use of herbicides. But the ground is also cultivated between the vines, so they might use cultivation to control weeds. I wish I knew more about it, more about the *land* of these people.

After about six hours of walking, I am getting close to Estella, but have not passed any church where there was a Sunday Mass. Several times, I think I am in Estella but, when I ask, discover that it's just another small village; I still have a few more kilometers to go. I begin to feel especially tired, but it's a kind of depression, a new kind of exhaustion . . . perhaps because now, in these final kilometers, I have to walk along a highway, and the Sunday traffic is heavy and decidedly unpleasant. Nothing here to lift my spirits.

While still in the more open country, I finish all fifteen Mysteries of the Rosary. But I am distracted a few times when I have to ask people for directions. And then the question arises: When I meet someone, should I put the Rosary in my pocket, hiding it, or leave it dangling in my hand? Strange . . . in Germany, I see Muslim men unself-consciously fingering their prayer beads in public. Why do I feel a certain embarrassment, and raise such a question? I decide to make a kind of compromise. When I'm actually saying the Rosary, I carry it. When I meet someone, I might pull up some of the beads into my hand, so that I am not so ostentatiously waving the whole string at them. Beyond that, I'll not worry about the observers. They can think what they wish.

Tired, I arrive in the town itself, and wander around for a time—once making an actual circle around some blocks—unable to figure out where I am going. Finally, I find a police station, get my *credencial* stamped, and also receive what seem to be clear directions to the *refugio*. By this time, I feel nearly dead from exhaustion.

In 1090, a king, Sancho Ramírez, founded the town of Estella with a group of French immigrants, repopulating territory won back from the Moors, thereby moving the *camino* route about three kilometers. People found the site to be a most picturesque place and, helped by the pilgrim traffic, it thrived greatly. The *Liber* notes that pilgrims in the twelfth century would find good bread, excellent wine, a great quantity of meat and fish there, and that the town was full *de toda felicidad*—a grand place to stop! The records show that there were soon many *hospitales* and *hospederías*—guest houses. Each parish established its own *hospital,* and these were usually operated by a *cofradía.*

According to an episcopal letter published in 1988 by the Spanish bishops through whose dioceses the *camino* passes, Estella is the seat of the oldest Confraternity (*cofradía*) of Santiago pilgrims in the country. The first record of such an organization (though it was not here in Estella) appears in 1120. One of the most famous was that of Paris, which continued in existence for four hundred years. These organizations were usually made up of persons who had made the pilgrimage to Compostela. When they returned to their respective cities, they would form an association, hold annual meetings, work to promote the pilgrimage, sometimes build *hospitales* for poor pilgrims, and arrange for the burial of their members. The Confraternity in Paris held a banquet for members in 1388, with 809 persons attending. They consumed five oxen, eighteen pigs, and three thousand eggs. Their annual banquet in 1578 became so rowdy that the police were called in.

Confraternities were also active in the Low Countries, Germany, and England. In Spain, the organizations worked to provide shelters, improve roads, and build and maintain bridges along the *camino.* Today, confraternities remain active in several countries of Europe.

I finally reach the *refugio,* or so I believe. It is in an apartment building, dirty-gray in color, constructed perhaps twenty years ago, and appearing ready for the wrecking ball. Other apartment buildings nearby seem to be empty and abandoned. The door is locked and no one is around. Hard to imagine a more dreary neighborhood—I've come a long way from the joyful beauty of Señora Roncal's lovingly cared-for hospice.

The town preserves its memory with some amazing stories. Around the year 1270, the bishop of Patras, a city in western Greece, decided to walk to Compostela. Wanting to leave a gift fit to match the dignity of the famous shrine, he took with him a shoulder bone from the body of Saint Andrew the Apostle, who had suffered martyrdom in Patras and was buried there. The bishop arrived in Estella on foot, with no attendants, since he wanted to travel like the poorest pilgrim. There he became ill and, without telling anyone who he was, sought shelter in the *hospital,* along with the other penniless pilgrims. His condition rapidly worsened and he died almost immediately, with the precious relic under his clothing, in a special box fastened to his chest.

They buried him in the cloister of the church of San Pedro. That night the sacristan was shocked to see a mysterious light hovering over the new grave; it appeared that small stars had descended to the place, signaling some presence. Doubtful about the sacristan's tale, the clergy nevertheless stationed themselves near the cemetery to watch during the next night. The prodigy was repeated—a clear sign that they had to dig up the body. Excited and trembling, they started to remove the clothing from the corpse, and were astounded to see a small wooden box attached to the chest. Carefully opening it, they found the relic of Saint Andrew, an enameled copper head of a staff (originally from Limoges), two cruets, and some silk gloves. An enclosed document authenticated the relics. Later, Andrew was declared the patron saint of Estella.

At four o'clock, a man comes to open the door. He apologizes for the shelter, explaining that this is a temporary arrangement. The city is preparing a permanent *refugio*, which is not yet ready. He hopes I will understand the situation. This place comprises two or three rooms filled with bunks, and a bath. The water is hot, the roof doesn't leak—it's now raining outside—and I have a bunk on which to sleep. I need nothing else.

At the end of the twelfth century, someone composed a poem in Latin, praising the *refugio* in Roncesvalles. There are forty-two verses of four lines each. I see that one verse applies nicely to this shelter in Estella:

> *Porta patet omnibus, infirmis et sanis,*
> *Non solum catholicis, verum et paganis,*
> *Judaeis, hereticis, ociosis, vanis,*
> *Et, ut dicam breviter, bonis et profanis.*

> The door is open to all, sick or well,
> Not only Catholics, but pagans also,
> To Jews, heretics, idlers, the vain,
> And, as I shall briefly note, the good and the worldly, too.

The only test for entry is that you appear to be on the *camino;* no questions are asked.

Other pilgrims drift in. The big Canadian arrives, and explains to me that he will take a bus tomorrow to a city nearer Compostela, perhaps to León. He wants very much to walk into Compostela, but he has to report to a new job as a cook in Greece, and he does not have time to walk the entire distance.

Since there are no kitchen facilities here, my companion and I go out to look for something to eat. In the "center" (there might be several) of town, we meet a young couple whom we had seen once or twice before on the *camino*. They have taken a room in a hotel, and are returning to Germany tomorrow. The walking has been hard on them, they are on vacation, and they think it prudent to return home, leaving themselves enough time to "recover from Spain" before they have to report back to work. I am reminded of a scene in the *relato* of the young men who walked from Madrid to Compostela in 1928. The older brother writes that at the door of the house, their mother "gave us a kiss, one long enough to keep us during all the nights of our absence from home." Their father, smiling but in a grave tone, spoke: "If you wish, you still have the opportunity to remain here at home; but if you set out, do not come back to this house without having reached Santiago." Reflecting on these differences—of what? of character? of culture? of times?—I am rather distracted, and follow my companions to a popular and crowded bar where we enjoy a simple supper.

It's still raining, so we hurry back to the gray and glum apartment-house *refugio*. I shall start out again early tomorrow morning, and thus will have no opportunity to explore this town, so rich in legends. One relates how Sancha (also called Leofás), the daughter of the king of Navarra, García Ramírez, was married to Count Gastón de Bearn. After the count died in 1170, apparently leaving no heir, it was soon discovered that Leofás was pregnant and the Bearn family rejoiced in the hope that a son would be born to the dead count. But within a short time, Leofás suffered a miscarriage. Suspicions were aroused and she was accused as the voluntary author of a crime and condemned to suffer trial by water. With her hands and feet tied, she was thrown from a bridge into the river Ega, which runs through the town. More than three thousand persons were present to watch the sad spectacle.

Leofás called out to the Virgin of Rocamador as the witness to her innocence. When she hit the river, her body gently floated over the surface of the water and came to rest on a nearby sandbar. Seeing the impossible in bright daylight with their own eyes, the crowd lifted Leofás to their shoulders and carried her in triumph to her nearby castle. She then donated an elaborate tapestry to the abbot of the Santuario de Nuestra Señora de Rocamador, situated just outside Estella. The stories, the marvels, go on and on. And I wonder . . . have I actually touched the soil of these people? Is there some contact, however tenuous, between them and me, between their faith and mine? Can I rid myself enough of distractions to walk into their world?

7

Estella to Los Arcos

May 10, 1993

I t's still quite dark; I feel fine, however, and it's time to get started. But what is the noise I hear? I look out the window . . . it's raining. What do I do now? I've walked through some hours of rain, but I've never had to start the day in a storm. And it looks pretty desolate out there; the sky is heavily overcast—maybe an all-day downpour. I think of the young Germans in their warm and comfortable hotel room, of the Canadian who will board the bus this morning.

After my usual breakfast of fruit, bread, and cheese, I pack the gear, shoulder the pack, throw the poncho up and over all, tie the hood tightly around my face, keep one arm inside the poncho and grab my staff with the other. And down the street I head, rhythmically tapping the empty sidewalk with the staff, breaking the town's dark silence. No one else is out so early, except for one pilgrim who leaves right after me.

Going through the town, I notice a small supermarket that is already open. Because of the rain and darkness, and the fact that the market is not very well marked, I'm afraid that my companion, some meters behind me, will not see it. I know he is looking for a place to buy some food. I turn to shout to him. As I do so, I put my foot on what I think is a step into the store. It is not; it is an incline for wheelchairs or the dolly transporting goods into the market. My foot slips on the wet concrete, I am thrown off balance, weighted down with the pack. In spite of the staff, I fall directly on my bad knee. It smacks the concrete. Pain shoots up and runs all through me. I think I shall faint right there on the sidewalk. It's awful. The knee has been troubling me almost every day, all day, but I had just about reached the point of not noticing it. One scene alone appears before my eyes: This is the end of my pilgrimage; I'll be on that bus, too.

I attempt to rise. Slowly, I find myself erect; I take a step, another, yet another. The pain is terrible, but I am able to keep moving, ever so hesitantly. I do not stop. Then, after a time—I cannot tell how long it is—the pain starts to subside, and it keeps going down and down until, amazingly, it disappears altogether. Again, something unbelievable. I feel like laughing and crying, shouting and dancing, singing with the rain, blessing all creatures.

The rain continues, but it is not a hard rain. Perhaps one could call it a friendly spring rain. No harm or discomfort intended. Soon, I'm in the open country again; now I feel I'm really on the *camino*. Not so far out of Estella, I notice a collection of large buildings, the Monasterio de Nuestra Señora la Real de Irache. This is one of the oldest monastic foundations in Navarra, some records claiming that it dates back to the time of the Visigoths. During one period, it also housed a university. But from a large sign, I see that the place is now abandoned, and is being renovated by the government—the number of pesetas being spent is noted in prominent figures. Another action preserving the cultural heritage of the country. What a huge place it is. How could it ever be filled with monks? The turns of history: In the last century, the Spanish government threw out the monks and nuns; now it tries to recover the empty architectural treasure of their buildings. I am again reminded of Goya's drawings—showing nuns and monks or friars being forced to remove their holy habits and walk out into the world in lay clothes. The power of his imaginative pen portrays passions no words could describe.

A large building on the right is the warehouse of a winery, the Bodegas Irache. There is a sign and an elaborate ironwork gate. I open it and step over to the wall of the building. A double fountain is built into the wall, with one spigot for water and the other for wine, the winery's Fuente del Vino. Above the fountain, in a recessed alcove, stands an ancient stone statue of Santiago Peregrino. A sign invites all pilgrims to help themselves to a glass of this excellent wine, so that they might make it to Compostela with *vitalidad y fuerza*—vitality and strength. If you want more than one glass, you are asked to come around to the front of the building where there is a retail outlet. There you can buy all you wish. A glass is here, too, sitting on the fountain. I rinse it out with water, and fill it with wine.

Yes, it *is* good wine. I hesitate. I would like more, but I don't want to buy and carry a whole bottle; I don't need any extra weight. What to do? I fill the glass half full. This cannot be too serious an abuse of the vintners' generosity. What a nice thing to do for pilgrims. And how good it tasted—in the rain!

Today, the *camino* passes through vineyards and wheat fields on the muddy paths used by farmers and livestock. The mud makes walking slow and difficult, but I much prefer this to walking along a highway, where I would be splashed by racing cars and trucks. People seem to drive at breakneck speeds here in Spain (as in Germany). Is this a special European phenomenon? Trying to catch up and pass someone else? The Americans, maybe?

Many of the fields are large, and houses, again, few. This seems to stretch out the distances farther. I have the sensation of covering more ground rapidly when there are frequent breaks and changes in the landscape. But the rain, too, may contribute to the sense of moving very slowly today, making the time longer to reach the desired destination.

A pleasant sense of movement through distinct places occurs when I come upon and pass through two or three villages. I see no sign of activity at all in these places, though everything is neatly cared for. I wonder if they are bedroom villages, with most of the inhabitants off at some job in the city.

Yesterday, I passed many fields with long rows of regularly spaced hills in them. There seemed to be nothing in the fields but bare earth—nothing yet growing in the hills—yet there were people working in them. They were all so far from the *camino*, however, that I could not tell what the people were doing nor figure out what might be growing there. Now I pass close to one of these fields and see stray green asparagus shoots popping out of the ground. Asparagus! My favorite vegetable. So this is how Europeans grow white asparagus, keeping it covered so the sun does not turn it green. How much more work to grow this, rather than the green. I've always felt that the white is greatly inferior, both in taste and texture. I've never understood why people eat it.

What a temptation. No one is around. Those green shoots that have escaped from the carefully constructed hills are what the Spaniards probably don't want. They might even feed them to the chickens (or throw them away!), considering them a waste. Oh, how I would like to walk over and break off a few. But I dare not do it. The dirt looks like extremely sticky clay. I would leave a real mess walking to the stalks, and give a bad name to pilgrims—for who else would be out here, walking through the mud, into the fields? And the bottoms of my pants are already covered with mud. I don't need more. I decide to make the sacrifice. The further irony is that I probably cannot find any green asparagus in the market. I can't steal *or* buy it.

After six hours of plodding through the rain, with no stop except for the glass and a half of wine and, later, for drinks of water, I arrive in Los Arcos, feeling—just grand!—almost no signs at all of pain *or* exhaustion. I'm quite ready to keep going for a few more hours. The surprises continue; what a wonderful day. And the Rosary took me deeper *into* the *camino* today.

It takes several inquiries before I can find someone who knows where the *refugio* is located—in a two-story apartment that used to be housing for schoolteachers. Then I have to find the woman who has the key. Finally, I get inside and take off the poncho. I had felt as if the rain was soaking right through it. But that must have been condensed moisture or sweat. The pack is dry. Wonderful. That's the important item. I take off the wet and muddy clothes and put on dry ones. And then I notice a sudden silence from outside. I look out the window. The rain has stopped! A bit of sun comes out.

I am alone in the shelter. Since I am the first pilgrim to arrive, I look around to pick a good bed in a quiet corner. On the second floor, I find a small room with two bunks. Perhaps there will not be so many people tonight and I'll have a really quiet spot. There is another small room with two bunks, and a large room downstairs with a correspondingly greater number of bunks. The place is not very clean, but everything essential is here. I locate a confused arrangement of pipes and valves—the water system. But I can't figure out how it works, so I decide to forget about a shower today. The rain has cooled the day considerably and I can easily forgo so much bathing.

The center of the village is a few hundred meters away. I must go there to get the *credencial* stamped and look for food. But it starts to rain again, hard . . . a pouring cloudburst. If this continues, I'll skip the food today and try to get both that and the stamp tomorrow morning. Since I have only one full change of clothes, I cannot get these wet before the others dry out. I wash out my socks and carefully hang up everything to dry. My staff serves conveniently for holding up the poncho.

Later, the rain stops again. I decide to chance going into the village. Taking my *credencial,* I start out. Once there, I learn that a person in the huge church—large enough for a major city—can stamp my document. I go in search of this person, who turns out to be an elderly woman who, to use uncharitable English, appears to be a battle-ax. I explain what I would like to get from her: a stamp on my *credencial.* She listens impassively, looks at me dubiously, and gruffly tells me to follow her. Slowly, she trudges up the long nave of the darkened vaultlike space, continues past the Blessed Sacrament with the familiarity of accustomed presence—that is, with no pause or sign whatever—and proceeds through a door at the side of the sanctuary. There she turns on the light and I see one of these almost cavernous sacristies—something I've seen before in old Spanish churches. I can never quite believe that such a large room, with so much carving and decoration, is only for the priest to put on his vestments for Mass and the other liturgical services.

The old woman has a kind of table/desk in one corner of the room. I follow her there and hand her my document as she sits down on her chair. She opens a drawer, opens the *credencial,* inks her stamp, and accurately presses it down on the next empty square. She then initials it and writes the date. From long practice, she knows exactly what to do. I thank her. She grunts, "Por nada"—don't mention it.

I start to leave, and notice that she, too, rises. I wait for her to precede me out the door. But she heads for the other wall. There, I see an enormous fuse and switch box. She starts throwing switches. What should I do? I peer out the sacristy door . . . various parts of the distant, empty darkness are suddenly flooded with light. I step into the sanctuary. My God!—a spectacular and confusing mixture of polychromed statues, stone sculpture, painted altarpieces with their gold backgrounds, soaring columns, tall windows, which are dark now because of the darkness outside. I catch my breath; I feel I've been hit with too many artifacts, too richly fashioned, too quickly. Is it beautiful? . . . insane? . . . just hugely impressive? I don't know enough about art and architecture to react in any sensible way, to think some coherent thought. The town seems hardly more than a village. How interpret such an extravagance? I wonder, is this the expression of an ancient faith?

This is the Iglesia de Santa María, which travel books describe as *magnífica, monumental.* It's truly monumental, but I'm doubtful about its magnificence. One can get some notion of the town's historical importance from this monster temple. But for me, understanding the nature of this importance is much more distant and obscure than the church's physical origins.

I think perhaps I made a good decision at the start—to ignore all the art, all the historic Romanesque architecture for which the *camino* is so famous—and on which there exists a huge bibliography—to attempt to see the *camino* only very narrowly. It seems to me that the truth of the *camino,* that which is more enduring, more revelatory is, above all, "out there"—today, out in the rain. Or so I believe. The architecture is too ambiguous, too confusing. I can't take it in, can't work it into what I know; it's too complex, too strange; it belongs to some world for which I have no key. I have no clear idea how to think about it.

Quickly, I step back into the sacristy, thank the generous woman who has turned on all these lights just for my pleasure and enjoyment, and say a few incoherent words about how impressed I am. And then I flee. I want to get outside, into whatever weather is out there . . .

Walking down the street, dazed from my exposure to that wild outpouring of centuries-old Spanish religious sensibility, I run into another pilgrim—the French physician! Both of us happily surprised, he invites me for a cup of coffee. Since this has become my supreme sense pleasure—I have decided that no coffee I have ever drunk compares with the Spanish tincture served in every bar—no matter how small or how elaborate—I joyfully accompany him in search of the town's bar.

It is now late afternoon, the stores are open again after the traditionally long midday siesta, and we go in search of food for today and tomorrow morning. I decide to buy things in a market and eat a cold supper in the *refugio*. After finding a small supermarket-like place—whose owner tells me that he has a brother in California—we get directions to a bakery. We follow them exactly, but when we arrive at what I think is the correct door, we find it closed and locked. I look around, and see a local citizen up the street. I ask him about my problem, since it is already six o'clock. He explains that I must pound loudly on the door. We return and try that. A window opens on the second floor, a friendly face looks out questioningly. I say that we would like to buy bread. She nods and soon comes down to open the shop for us. I suppose that most of the bread-buying occurs in the early morning. And I have noticed that the bakeries are the first places of business to open each day.

The Frenchman wants to buy some stamps, but we have seen no post office. And I feel certain that it would not be open at this hour. I have the impression that the local postal service keeps rather limited hours, and these are confined to the morning. But we pass a shop that seems to sell many different things, all under the heading of, perhaps, dry goods. I ask if it is possible to buy stamps anyplace in the village. I am told that they are sold right there. Then, on a shelf, I notice large, unwrapped plain brown laundry soap. A sign says, *tradicional y pura.* I ask the woman if I can use this to wash myself. Some people do, she answers. Well, when my German laundry soap runs out, I'll try the Spanish variety. I had decided that I should get the soap that is most exactly designed for the most important washing task on the *camino*. That, I figure, is the socks; I hope the same soap then serves the less important areas. So far, that decision has worked out well. Amazingly, my feet still give me no trouble.

It's been an ordinary astonishing day. My usual pattern has served me well: up about 6 A.M., shave sometimes, dress, eat a bit of breakfast, arrange the pack, and get out on the *camino*. Sometimes, if I have it, I eat some fruit while walking, but make no stop during the day except for water now and then. As the fellow from the Canary Islands believed, each village has a *fuente,* a public fountain or spigot where one can drink excellent spring water. I only carry a small amount in my plastic water bottle for an emergency situation; water is heavy. For my destination, I pick a place that has a *refugio* and that I think I can reach that day, about twenty or thirty kilometers away; and they seem to be spaced at about that distance.

Arriving there, washing socks and other clothes as necessary is the very first thing to do, so that they have the longest possible time to dry or start drying before I leave the next morning. If the socks washed the day before were not dry this morning when I start out, I put them in a plastic bag in the pack. They come out now to go on the line to finish drying. Then I usually take a shower and go out to look for food. This action of searching for food in the markets seems to fit the spirit of the *camino* better than being waited on in a restaurant. I have found that if the shelter has no kitchen, I can eat the food cold. If the place where I stop is in a large village or town, I always look for a bar where I can get the special sensual treat for the day, a *café con leche.* After writing my notes, it's time for bed. So far, I've neglected all sightseeing except when, as today, it is unavoidable.

Wittgenstein writes that "nothing is more wrong-headed than calling meaning a mental activity!" I wonder if this statement helps to explain what occurred today in the church. Nothing could happen between all that color and plastic expression, and me. I have not grown up in that world; there is no centuries-old tradition of common familiarity; that is, *this* physical display was not *my* physical history. Contrary to Descartes, I am not a thinking ego; rather, I am a creature who walks and lives in the communal/social accumulation of my tradition. Meaning is not an occult state inside my consciousness. Rather, it is the physical and social interaction between my historical self and the world around me. I can enter the world of the *camino* precisely because I walk into it. I could not enter that world of the church, except tenuously, superficially, vicariously, by reading books about it. Now, for example, the three students' story of the gypsies they met has meaning for me because of the gypsies I met. The beads of the Rosary suddenly have meaning for me because I really say them in community; that is, I breathe and speak every word along with the pilgrims who preceded me, along with those who share a faith with me. I walk directly into their world.

I've left my prosaic day-to-day world far behind. Every morning, I go farther into a strange world of surprises, walking into a new place on a soil never before touched by me, meeting people whose existence I had only imagined. My obedience to awareness, my openness to what comes in through all my senses at every moment, moves me toward the *mysterium* that lies at the end of this journey. How fantastic the rewards of attention.

By some enigmatic instinct, I was led to make the decision to visit no "monuments" before I ever set out. Today's experience dramatically shows that I chose a remarkably fruitful path—similar to what happened to me in deciding to walk alone. If I understand something of Wittgenstein, the only meaning—*sense*—possible for me on the *camino* is through a socially physical experience—wonderfully and abundantly given me as I slog through the mud with my dead companions . . . I "unconsciously" selected the only community of persons who can lead me into the world of the *camino,* which, when I started, was a very foreign world.

8

Los Arcos to Logroño

May 11, 1993

Several times today, realizing that I have not seen a yellow arrow for some time, I stop. What to do? Am I lost? Should I go back and look for the last arrow I passed? But I have a feeling I'm going in the right direction. And I've come to make up my mind that I will not do any unnecessary going back, no side trips . . . no movement that does not take me toward Compostela. The walking is too difficult to extend it any farther than needed.

Each time, except for one, I eventually come to an arrow again. Somehow, my sense of direction—or my guardian angel—saves me. A feeling of simple joy . . . a great sigh of happy relief when the arrow appears again. Another experience I could not have foreseen and that cannot be imagined. One must be here, on an unknown trail, weighed down with the pack, tired, or aware that there is still a great distance to go today, to feel what it is like to find out that one doesn't have to retrace one's steps—for who knows how far?—trying to find the way back to the *camino*.

When I think I should have seen another arrow, and I do not, an inner tension starts to build up, increasing with each step. Am I walking farther out of my way with this step? Will I have to return? And then, finally, each time, the arrows appear again—all the tension flows out—dumped by the side of the path. I can continue with a light heart. And so it seems with everything on the *camino:* The experience is so complex and matter-of-fact at the same time, so carefree and also full of anxiety, that there seems no adequate way to describe it, no possible way to convey the excitement of it—one must come out here and plunge into it. But I do make one wrong turn, or somehow lose the trail once. Happily, I increasingly sense that I have made a mistake before going on too far, go back, and find my way again.

Today, I taste a previously unsuspected sweetness in the words of the Rosary. This becomes especially powerful while saying the "Salve Regina" at the end of each five decades; that is, after five Joyful, Sorrowful, or Glorious Mysteries. This is the ancient prayer to the Virgin, which centuries of monks and nuns have recited or sung together as their last common exercise before retiring to bed—at the end of the canonical hour of Compline. People who visit monasteries often find that this hymn, sometimes sung in the dark while the religious make a procession, carrying small lighted candles, is the most impressive and moving liturgical exercise that they witness there. The words they hear:

> *Salve, Regina, mater misericordiae:*
> *vita, dulcedo et spes nostra, salve.*
> *Ad te clamamus exsules filii Hevae,*
> *Ad te suspiramos gementes et flentes,*
> *in hac lacrimarum valle.*
> *Eja ergo advocata nostra,*
> *illos tuos misericordes oculos ad nos converte;*
> *et Jesum benedictum fructum ventris tui*
> *nobis post hoc exsilium ostende.*
> *O clemens, O pia, O dulcis Virgo Maria.*

> Hail, Holy Queen, Mother of Mercy,
> Hail, our life, our sweetness and our hope.
> To thee do we cry, poor banished children of Eve,
> To thee do we send up our sighs,
> Mourning and weeping in this valley of tears.
> Turn then, most gracious advocate,
> Thine eyes of mercy toward us,
> And after this our exile, show unto us
> The blessed fruit of thy womb, Jesus.
> Oh clement, oh loving, oh sweet virgin Mary.

Why am I able to recall it so easily? But first, how did this prayer get into my memory? I push back through the years of my life, past more than fifty of them, and stop at a small parochial grammar school in Lincoln, Illinois—Saint Mary's. But I suspect the prayer was soon forgotten, for I exuberantly embraced the more worldly atmosphere of the town's public high school. After graduation, such prayer, invoking the Virgin, seemed rather inappropriate to the toughness affected by enlisted men in the United States Marine Corps. But while in college, I read Thomas Merton's *The Seven Storey Mountain*—a thoroughly unsettling experience for a young man seeking a way, a calling, rather than a career. Beginning with questions while he was in college, Merton became a Trappist monk.

I borrowed my brother's car and drove to Our Lady of New Melloray, a Trappist monastery in northern Iowa. There, each night, the monks closed their day by singing the "Salve"—following the ancient Gregorian notation. The visit was inconclusive. After two days, I returned to my college classes, but something—or someone—made a mark on me.

Today, dwelling long on the words, repeating the prayer several times, savoring the exquisite flavor, I am suddenly shocked to realize what the intensity of the experience actually means: This person was unknown to me. The Virgin was a stranger to me. Only now, at my age, do I begin to sense her presence! I might as well have been a modern infidel all these years. How empty and poor was my pantheon.

For a long time I mull over these thoughts, the *feel* of their import. It seems that what I have just learned, how I have just been changed, is of great personal importance. I have been put in a different place; I have been invited to become a different person. From this moment on, I can be a new person since, living in this awareness, in her presence, I will think, feel, act in ways foreign to my earlier existence. Therefore, I cannot but view this grace as the most significant event of the *camino* up to now, its most magnificent gift. But any reason or argument, attempting to "prove" this, would be stupidly superfluous. The familiar presence, together with its intellectual consistency, intuitively grasped—because felt—is all-convincing. It seems then, from this day on, the principal task of each day's walk is to cultivate this awareness with loving attentiveness. For she can introduce me to all the others, to all those whose presence I sense but whose names I do not know and whose faces I do not see. But *she,* in some sense, is known to me. I first made her acquaintance as a child. At that time, she was a familiar figure in my life. But I grew up; I affected a queer sophistication. I wandered in strange company, in a world that I now recognize as barren and desolate. Now I sense that I can step into another world, that I can become the intimate of the companions of my childhood.

Perhaps through the Virgin I shall come to know the most shadowy and mysterious figure of the *camino,* Santiago. The New Testament records very little about this apostle—and that is the only source of information available. His earliest iconographic portrayal—holding a sword—points to the manner of his death, being killed with a sword on orders from Herod. "It was about this time that King Herod arrested some who belonged to the church, intending to persecute them. He had James, the brother of John, put to death with the sword" (Acts 12:1–2 [New International]). Thus end the few words of the New Testament referring to his life. For most of the saints, the image people have of them is constructed out of the events of their lives. Hagiographers have been no less zealous than other biographers who trace all possible leads to learn more about their famous subjects.

Knowledge of saints, as of every historical subject, is a complex mixture resulting from a meeting of facts and a storyteller. Santiago is unique in that he has been molded—in a sense, created—by his miraculous appearances. Beginning with angels and a lighted sky in the early ninth century (indicating the lost place of his burial in Galicia), and continuing with his knightly presence on a white horse, leading the charge at the battle of Clavijo in 852, Santiago was projected into the history of Spain, shaped according to the needs and ambitions, the piety and devotion, of his profiteers and suppliants. Some believe that he is the only saint to be completely identified with his devotees; this is his only existence. But how might we understand this? One cannot depend on the historical sources in a crude, conventional sense. The thousands of pilgrims, out here on the *camino* during these many centuries, through their faith and hope, transformed the bare facts into a rich fabric of transcendental certainty. Detailed questions about the material exactness of every particular can distract one from the composite of finely textured truth, revealed by the *camino*.

In the seventeenth century, there arose in Spain a highly spirited and bitter controversy about the physical existence of Saint James's body in Compostela. The dispute also involved the proposal to make Saint Teresa of Avila the patroness of Spain, sharing this honor with Santiago. The polemical positions on the various aspects of these matters reached such levels of violence that the pope had to intervene, using his authority to impose a kind of peace. But all the arguments over physical truth can lead one to miss the point of Santiago's epiphany in Galicia. The basic issue here is the intensity of people's belief, together with the specific consequences in their lives. This I have learned by being here. But I must remember that one figure stands at the source of the *camino:* Santiago. I must continue to search for him, avoiding the temptation to construct him according to my fantasies.

Santiago first appeared in the Peninsula at the very moment when the people of Asturias, a small and beleaguered enclave surrounded by a militant Islam, began their war for existence as a Christian kingdom. Later, the peculiar character of this people's faith was revealed in two radically different images: Santiago Peregrino and Santiago Matamoros. For me, one is as mysterious as the other. How to imagine the desperate and fearful dreams of such a people? A people for whom heavenly interventions were neither infrequent nor surprising? A people for whom the world rested in God's hands? And what can I think of a saint who walks to his own grave from all over Christendom? Thus did the artists portray him, thus had the people created him.

My *camino* prayer begins to take form. Like almost everything else out here, I had foreseen nothing. Now I want to let my senses, *all* my senses, seek out the numinous. I see that civilization in the peculiarly sophisticated form in which I was molded had transformed them, "refined" them out of existence. The struggle with plodding along each day has restored them, has brought me back to my senses. My desire for the darkness of faith is newly alight. I feel deeply chagrined when I think that, up to now, I have lived with a terribly routinary belief—if it was belief—in the Virgin. Now, perhaps, I can begin to participate with a genuine liveliness in the tradition bequeathed me by my parents.

I pass a small cemetery, surrounded by a high wall. I've noticed that the Spanish tradition of caring for cemeteries is much more casual than that of either the Americans or the Germans. But I would probably never find in those two countries, written over the entrance, what I read here: "Yo que fuí lo que tú eres. Tú serás lo que yo soy" ("I who was what you are. You will be what I am"). Another sentiment that seems to jump out so much more strikingly in Spanish than in English.

I'm getting close to Logroño, a city much fought over—by *navarros* and *castellanos* (people from Navarre and Castille)—since it lay between the two kingdoms. In 1076, Alfonso VI brought this region, La Rioja, under his control in Castille. And he probably built a bridge across the Río Ebro at Logroño, for military purposes and to facilitate the journey of pilgrims, since he was also a great organizer and promoter of the *camino.* It was said that during his reign, "Any woman with her purse full of gold doubloons could travel on it [the *camino*] day or night without fear of trouble." I suspect a bit of hyperbole here.

At this time, al-Andalus, Islamic Spain, was probably the most advanced country in Europe. Its agriculture, science, medicine, architecture, philosophy, and poetry attracted scholars to Toledo and Córdoba from other European countries. When their writings were translated into Latin, the philosophic work of Avicenna and Averroes was seriously studied in European universities. By the tenth century, diplomatic missions from France, Germany, and Constantinople were established in Córdoba. It can be argued that, during the Middle Ages, nearly all expressions of what is commonly called culture—embracing, for example, areas such as science, philosophy, and medicine—that traveled north beyond the Pyrenees, originated in Islamic al-Andalus, not in Christian Spain. Today, one hears inflated claims about the *camino* being a cultural bridge during this period. I suspect that such assertions are seriously lacking in historical truth, and distort the actual character of the *camino.*

Within a few years, two events signaled a radical change in the prospects of al-Andalus as an independent nation. In 1002, the charismatic leader Almanzor, died. Feared by Christians throughout the Peninsula for his sudden and devastating *razzias,* he climaxed his warrior career by attacking and razing Compostela in 997. One legend relates that when he arrived at the tomb of James the Apostle, he found that all the townspeople had fled, with the exception of one old man, calmly and silently lost in his prayers. Almanzor withdrew, without touching the man or the tomb.

In 1031, the Caliphate in Córdoba collapsed. This signified the end of any central authority in al-Andalus. The nation soon broke up into more than twenty small states, continually at war with one another. A strong sense of tribalism—and there were many among the Islamic warriors— tended to dictate loyalties. No single leader ever arose again to unite these warring territories.

In 1085, Alfonso VI captured Toledo. At this time, the Christian princes, if they had not been so occupied fighting one another, could easily have conquered al-Andalus. But that was not to happen until 1492, under the leadership of Ferdinand and Isabella. In 1094, the great and, later, mythic hero El Cid, captured Valencia from the Moors. But he, too, spent part of his life fighting other Christians. Christian princes and troops, with the help of Islamic forces, fought other Christians, while Muslim princes and troops, with the help of Christians, fought other Muslims. When I get to the Río Ebro, I'll be walking across land deeply stained by the blood of these mixed armies fighting one another, a kind of behavior that, in historical time, extends from the Visigoths—late antiquity—until yesterday. All this, too, is part of the enigma of the *camino.*

After seven or eight hours walking, I reach the bridge. A newspaper that I noticed in the bar yesterday predicted possible showers (*tormenta*) today, but I was only barely touched by a few drops in these last kilometers. Happily, I find that the *refugio* is a very short distance beyond the bridge, but is not yet open. There is a police station across the street and the officers let me come in and sit down, since more rain threatens.

There is a story that Saint Francis of Assisi, on his way to Compostela, stopped here in Logroño and cured the son of a man named Medrano.

Out of gratitude, Medrano offered the friars his house and land for a monastery. When Francis returned from Compostela, the work of constructing the monastery was well advanced, thus the origin of the church and monastery of San Francisco.

The people who operate the shelter soon arrive and open the door. It is a very old, handsome building, sitting right on a corner of two streets. Going in the door, I see that it has been completely renovated inside. There is an impressive plaque on the wall, noting the building's recent inauguration as a project of the region's civil authorities. I go up the stone stairs to a desk on the second floor. The two young ladies who opened up are there to receive me. They stamp my *credencial* and ask for a donation of 300 pesetas. Several other pilgrims have arrived, and one of the young women takes us on a tour to introduce us to the facilities. There is a large and well-equipped kitchen with all new equipment, including an automatic washing machine. Out behind the building, I see a very attractive and spacious paved patio that, I notice, also features a good washboard sink for washing clothes by hand. The dormitory is filled with new bunks, packed rather tightly together.

Setting my pack down on a bunk, I take my dirty clothes to the washboard for the first task. There I meet several women from Holland who are walking to Compostela. One is washing her shoes with water—which seems an unwise thing to do. She explains that she has some waterproofing compound that she applies after they dry.

I have only my heavy Italian mountain boots, and need something to put on my feet when I arrive at a shelter. Most of these places have ceramic tile floors—rather cold on the feet. And I need to let both my feet and the shoes rest apart from one another after I get to the *refugio*. One of the attendants at the desk tells me where she thinks I can find some kind of lightweight sandal. She also tells me that there is a restaurant a few blocks from the refugio that serves an excellent *menú* at a specially reduced price for pilgrims. I feel too tired to shop for food; it's a large city and I would have to do some hunting—perhaps a lot more walking—so I decide on the restaurant. My good resolution to care for myself rather than be waited on will have to be set aside today. It also appears that the kitchen will soon be crowded with groups cooking their supper. I suspect that I will see more people here tonight than in any other *refugio* where I've stayed. I have already heard, in several places, that this *refugio*, newly opened, is reputed to be one of the best on the *camino*. Open only a few weeks, it's already famous among the pilgrims.

The young woman also tells me that there is a doctor available who will freely treat any pilgrim who has health problems. It's evident that the people of Logroño have exerted themselves greatly and thoughtfully to provide an attractive resting place for pilgrims. From the size of the building, and the work done on the interior, I see that they spent a large sum of money already. And now they must finance the maintenance, since the pittance each of us pays is surely not enough to cover expenses.

Surprisingly, I meet the French physician again. We walk at a different pace; although we sometimes start at about the same time—for example, this morning in Los Arcos—I arrive at the destination before him. He decides to accompany me to the restaurant and we find that the meal is, indeed, very good and quite reasonable. But I can locate no sandals, and am not willing to comb the city, searching. When we return to the shelter, we see a number of bicycles parked inside the door in the wide front hall. They all seem to be mountain bikes, for me a new kind of bicycle, one on which I have never ridden. People making the pilgrimage on bikes are allowed to stay in the shelters if there are enough beds. Those walking or riding a horse, though, have priority. When I slip into my sleeping bag the lights are still on, and the voices of numerous pilgrims create a confusing but audible sound in the large dormitory.

9

Logroño to Nájera

May 12, 1993

Last night, sometime after falling asleep, I was awakened by the sharp, piercing voice of a woman. She
seemed to be at some distance from me in the dormitory, but she had a
voice that would penetrate thick walls. On and on she rattled, relating the
day's adventures on her bicycle to fellow bike riders. Lying there, rapidly
passing from a feeling of annoyance to a passion of anger, I asked myself,
What should I do about this? There is a large room at the end of the
building where people can gather to talk. This room is the dormitory—for
sleeping. And it's late. How can she and the other bike riders be so inconsiderate? I see that the Frenchman and other walkers are also in their
sleeping bags. Arguing with myself, turning over a few times in the sleeping bag, I finally returned to sleep. But I'm resolved not to remain quiet
the next time this happens. A polite but strong complaint would surely be
in order. The old and modest *refugio* in Los Arcos, although depressingly
dreary in appearance, offered complete quiet for sleeping. For all its
physical beauty, this new and clean dormitory is useless unless the people here respect its essential character: a place to sleep!

After my worst night yet in a shelter, I start out for Nájera at about
seven-thirty. I have to walk a few kilometers on a highway. The *camino*
attempts to follow the route mapped out by Aymeric Picaud in the twelfth
century, but today that is not always a picturesque mountain trail, or a
path winding through magnificent forests. Sometimes the pilgrim has to

share his space with trucks and cars. The road is asphalt, two-lane, with a "shoulder" only about one meter wide on each side. At the edge of the asphalt, the ground drops steeply into a deep ditch. So, I cannot get off the asphalt. When two cars meet, or when one passes another, I am closer than one meter to the speeding vehicle. When large trucks pass me—and there are many—I have trouble keeping my balance . . . a situation strongly conducive to angry and bitter thoughts.

Walking on asphalt is radically different from walking on soil. On the highway, every step is the same; my foot strikes the unyielding hardness of the pavement, never feeling anything different in that step; here, there is no particularity, no place—I sense only a dull and uninteresting sameness. It takes a special act of concentration to imagine that I am in one place, that I have come from another and move toward yet another. I am in a modern space. My steps are reduced to a monotonous trudging along; I feel resentful, hoping at every moment to see a yellow arrow that will send me off on an exciting path of stones, mud, gravel, dirt, anything but asphalt. Off the road, there are always surprises—a small stream with a log for crossing, a turn into a new field of wildflowers, a grove of unusual trees foreign to me and always, at intervals, a village, different from the last one passed and from the next one to be reached. The soil in its infinite possibilities, imprints a new, different pattern on the bottom of my foot with each step. A meditation on this variety can carry me through many kilometers, while I lose sense of the time.

The vehicles, roaring past, produce most of their awful sound by the violent parting and disruption of the countryside air. I am hit more by air shock than by noise. The very quietness of their motors and other moving parts testifies to the sophisticated engineering that has raped the earth so wantonly as to set them shooting through their space. I am saddened and depressed by the thought: So many human talents and earthly goods brought together cunningly to manufacture a monster that, often imported into Spain from some faraway place, can only transport people or freight, burning up in an instant the rich fossil remains that needed thousands or millions of years—and much more than time—to reach their perfection. Where is the proportion? Where the balance? If what I learned on the first day about sin, justice, and pain is true, at what cost and in what form can this centuries-old, world-spanning disorder be righted? Who would be the prophet to denounce such waste? Who would be the people to hear her? Who the strong woman, the courageous man, to act on the hearing, to turn back the forces of thoughtless destruction?

This is what it means to live in an economy: to be forced to get into these vehicles, thus despoiling the earth; to live off what these vehicles carry, thus impoverishing the soil. Is there some way to think about this? Is there a way toward a restoration of limits? of propriety? of order?

I pass several cemeteries today, each surrounded by an ancient wall with a wrought-iron gate in the middle of one side. Over one such gate I read:

> De esta comedia VIVIR,
> es el prólogo NACER,
> la narrativa DOLER,
> y el epílogo MORIR.

> In this drama . . . To Live,
> the prologue . . . To Be Born,
> the narrative . . . To Suffer Pain,
> the epilogue . . . To Die.

There does not seem to be much care of the graves; the grass is not cut, weeds proliferate. I started to think they were abandoned, until I noticed one or two fresh graves in each one. Since I once worked caring for the abandoned cemeteries in my county, and was quite proud of the condition in which I kept them (although often I was the only person to see them), I now take a kind of nostalgic interest in all old cemeteries.

I come to a long, high wall, surrounding some kind of industrial complex. The path runs right along beside it. Looking up, I see that someone has painted a poem, one stanza following the other, on the wall. Each rhymed stanza asks a question and suggests an answer: Why do you go to Compostela? To celebrate nature? To enjoy the freedom of the open air? To fulfill a vow? To seek a special grace? To perform some penance? and so on, for about ten questions. The final stanza states: No, not for any of these reasons; only the "One Up There" knows what pulls you to Compostela.

I have seen similar thoughts and expressions in the guest books in the *refugios*. I guess this is a kind of popular literature inspired by the *camino*. I wish I had more leisure to enjoy it. But concentration on the walking itself leads me into more wondrous places than I can ever hope to absorb; perhaps it will indeed work to make me into a different person . . .

The Rosary again carries me into hitherto unknown realms. Today, the Glorious Mysteries—the Resurrection, the Ascension, the Coming of the Holy Spirit, the Assumption of the Virgin, the Coronation of the Virgin as Queen of Heaven—especially caught and held my attention. And it felt as if the Spirit, too, had been previously unknown to me, a stranger. I recalled the words of the Lord, promising to send his Spirit:

> . . . I will ask the Father, and he will give you another Counselor to be with you forever—the Spirit of truth. The world cannot accept him, because it neither sees him nor knows him. (John 14:16–17)

> . . . the Counselor, the Holy Spirit, whom the Father will send in my name, will teach you all things . . . (John 14:26)

> . . . when the Spirit of truth comes, he will guide you into all truth. (John 16:13)

And after hearing a detailed explanation, concerning his coming death, the Apostles still ask themselves—afraid to question Jesus directly—what's he talking about? "We don't understand what he is saying" (John 16:18).

It now appears to me that I, too, have not understood. How many times have I heard these words over the years? And today I hear them as if for the first time. How good it is to take the time to ponder these words. And I have the time, hours and hours. I'm beginning to understand how I relate to the *camino*, how I—my feet, my heart, all of me—enter into the *camino*. But how do I enter these words? Thinking long about this, I found a suggestion in Wittgenstein, a man who, supposedly, was neither Jew nor Christian.

> Christianity is not based on a historical truth; rather, it offers us a historical narrative and says: now believe! But not, believe this narrative with the belief appropriate to a historical narrative, rather: believe, through thick and thin, which you can do only as the result of a life. Here you have a narrative, don't take the same attitude to it as you take to other historical narratives! Make a quite different place in your life for it.—There is nothing paradoxical about that!

That seems clear to me. As the *camino* is a question of my whole self at this moment, so faith in his word is a question of my whole life through time. And the experience of the *camino* may lead me to the life of faith.

When I started out this morning, I was rather apprehensive, worried. According to the map, I had to walk thirty kilometers to arrive at Nájera, perhaps farther than I have walked in one day. But it's been a fine day for walking, partly sunny and partly overcast. I feel only a bit tired as I approach the town, the historical capital of La Rioja, when the rulers of Navarre held their court here. These people, in the tenth and eleventh centuries—before Alfonso VI of Castille succeeded in adding the town to his kingdom in 1079—were enthusiastic supporters of the *camino*. For example, they constructed and endowed *hospitales* for poor pilgrims. There is a tradition that San Juan de Ortega, whose tomb I should reach in two or three days, built a bridge here in the first half of the twelfth century.

The town appears quite small—the center of a kingdom? Without much trouble, I soon reach the *refugio,* which is located in a huge complex of buildings built up against the face of a mountain on one side of the town. This is the Monasterio de Santa María la Real, founded by the king of Navarre, Don García, in 1052. A sign on the door says that it opens at four. Everything in the town is closed up for lunch and siesta. Given the fact that there *is* an economy here in Spain, I find this its most gracious custom. It seems to be observed faithfully in all the small towns and villages, but I am not sure about the cities. It's nice to see that buying and selling do not dominate the entire day.

But, lucky for me, bars remain open at this time and the town is large enough to have one—or several. Sometimes they also serve food or have a restaurant attached. But now I'm only looking for a *café con leche.* In fewer than five minutes, I'm successful. I set my pack and staff against the wall, take a seat at the bar, and order. The perfect refreshing pause after seven hours of walking. The place is agreeably quiet—just the right tone after coming in off the *camino.* Only one other customer at the other end of the bar. And the television is turned off! That's unusual. All Spanish bars that I have seen always provide two services: high on one wall a large color television set inviting everyone to numbness and, on the bar, the day's local newspaper. So, I am particularly lucky today and can sit in silence while I catch up on making notes. Of course, there are other amenities also: I can order one coffee and sit here for hours. I will never be given the impression that I should order another, or leave.

When it's time for the shelter to open, I shoulder my pack and walk over. I am met at the door by a Franciscan, and he tells me that six friars live here. I see that the monastic part of the complex could probably house hundreds. I also notice that this is the entrance for tourists, who are charged a small entry fee. Well, I'll look into that later. One door off the entrance hallway opens into the dormitory for pilgrims—a large room with bunks. There is only one small window in the meter-thick wall, and I climb up to open it to let in some air. I have found that Spaniards generally leave the windows in a place like this closed, thereby allowing the room's cold and dampness to increase.

In the bathroom I find sinks with hot water, but no shower. So I bathe in the sink, wiping myself dry with paper towels. Some days ago, I abandoned the attempt to get a towel dry for a daily shower, and bought a roll of paper towels. I need only six to dry myself, and the roll weighs very little in the backpack.

I walk the short distance to some stores and find an extremely light pair of slippers. Now, that need is met! There is no kitchen in the shelter, but I can make a good meal from a can of sardines, or a slice of ham, together with bread, cheese, frozen vegetables (one can often buy them in bulk, just the amount wanted) and fruit. In a bakery early this morning, I took my place in line behind several women waiting their turn. The first one in the line turned to me and told me to come to the front of the line, ahead of all. As I've noted before, people know who I am: a foreign pilgrim on his way to Compostela; they unfailingly demonstrate a solicitous and friendly courtesy. I cannot imagine a warmer reception in a foreign country. When I open my mouth to speak, they see that I know their language, and their faces light up in expressive pleasure. Furthermore, today I was fortunate in another small matter—early enough to get whole wheat bread.

I return to the shelter with my new slippers and supper. Putting on the former, I walk into the corridor to catch a glimpse of whatever it is that attracts the tourists—of whom there are a few. Just beyond this hall, I enter a traditional cloister walk surrounding a garden. The delicate stonework between the pillars is so wondrous as to deny the fact that it is stone. At one end of the walk, I enter a kind of small hall or chapel. In the back there are about a dozen large tombs with a life-size figure on the top of each. The *navarro* royalty are buried there. I wonder, are there stoneworkers in Spain today who could do such things. And, if so, are there enough for every small town like this? But if there were, would there be any work for them to do? Could this or any society afford such beauty today?

At the back of a small chapel, which seems to be carved into the mountain, I am startled by the unusual eyes of a Virgin. Slowly approaching the polychromed statue, I see that the eyes are bright and luminous, haunting and reaching out; they exude peace and quietness; they are both expressionless and the mask of a powerful passion. I am caught as in a trance before such a strange revelation. Is this what draws tourists to this place? I learn that Don García, the founder of the monastery, was out hunting one day. His falcon flew into a cave in pursuit of a pigeon. The king entered the cave, searching for his falcon. Inside, he discovered a statue of the Virgin illumined with a lamp, with a "terrace" of white lilies at her feet. The story fits the statue perfectly. Such an unusual and striking piece of work demands an origin similarly out of the ordinary. I can only stand in silent wonder . . .

I continue to be mystified by these churches and monasteries. They are generally large, if not huge. Many, of course, have disappeared. Some still exist in ruins. Others are empty, abandoned. Here, I find a handful of religious left in this place. At the entrance of each settlement—village, town, or city—there is a sign indicating the significant ecclesiastical structures there, together with dates. I don't remember seeing any signs indicating secular buildings. Is the architectural history of Spain composed only of religious structures? The signs must be for the tourists, since the people of the place would either know these facts or not be interested; and it is something they take for granted. Is that the principal purpose of these places now? . . . quaint or impressive relics to entertain and edify the tourist? . . . histories in stone to satisfy the appetites of moderns, addicted to consumption but increasingly bored by the available choices?

The structures all make me wonder, ask questions. But I don't feel that these are the good questions for me. So far, the architecture seems marginal, quite incidental, to my quest. But if I stumble directly into it, as today, I'll take a quick look. A tourist guide told me that there is a magnificent set of choir stalls up in the church. I learn that the friars do not use them. Perhaps so few would feel lost among so many empty places. If monks or friars were there chanting, I would certainly want to be present, but another empty artistic treasure only confuses me. And I suspect that they could be a distraction, like reading books each day, or walking with a companion. The place that awaits me out there in the fields and on the mountains will never be found if I am distracted.

Ideally, perhaps, it might be preferable to have a tent and sleep alone in the fields each night. But the tradition of the *hospitales/albergues* is so rich that I want to taste it. And exchanging a few words with a friendly fellow pilgrim is surely a good and pleasant thing to do. A few minutes ago a man from Holland appeared, a bit younger than me. This is the second time on the *camino* for him. The first time he started from Holland and it took him three and a half months to reach Compostela. That's really reaching back to the practice of his ancestors in the Middle Ages.

I enjoy my cold supper, and slip into the sleeping bag to ward off the dampness of the darkened room. Only two or three others here—it will be a quiet night.

10

Nájera to Santo Domingo de la Calzada

May 13, 1993

A fter several hours, it starts to rain . . . at times, not so hard, at other times, a downpour. I keep thinking that this poncho is no good because I feel damp under it. But each time I arrive at the shelter, the backpack is dry—so I can put on dry clothes. And the rain does not interfere with walking at all.

The mud is not so sticky today. Most of the path is large gravel scattered on clay. Sharp, distinct points of pressure come through the soles of the shoe with every step, so walking provides me with a new kind of pain. But this also makes my steps more real; I am in continual contact with a genuine soil; an artificial surface has not removed me from the earth. Asphalt is not so difficult to take because it is hard, but because it is unnaturally uniform. Walking on it, I have the sensation that I am bluntly removed from a living soil and confined to a deadening monotony that can lead nowhere.

Occasionally, I come upon homemade signs, designed to encourage the tired pilgrim. Today, three were placed along the *camino:*

Ánimo, que ya queda menos

Take heart, you don't have so far to go.

And, farther on:

> *Pronto llegarás a Santo Domingo*
>
> Soon you will arrive in Santo Domingo.

To confirm one's faith, the sign painter put up:

> *Peregrino, vas por buen camino*
>
> Pilgrim, you are on a good path.

Then, I saw something new today while saying the Rosary. Hours of breathed words, lingering images of mysteries and slow, meditative reflection revealed something I had long ago forgotten, abandoned: regular morning and night prayers, the kind one says kneeling beside the bed. The thought strongly impressed itself on me: *This* is the way to begin and end the day. I remembered that I was taught this practice as a young child by my parents. What happened during all those years since then? Once, as an adult, after the death of my mother, I was visiting my father. I happened to notice that he knelt beside his bed for his prayers before retiring. I suspect he did the same in the morning. He had been taught this as a child and had clung to the practice for eighty-odd years. What an example of fidelity! How much I still have to learn—from him. Today I learned that he is here, too, along with all the others who accompany me to Compostela, each one removing yet another veil. I hope he tells me something about the Holy Spirit. I'm eager to learn more about the Spirit's presence.

After about five hours, I see the edge of Santo Domingo de la Calzada. I feel pretty good and have probably covered twenty kilometers. I think there were only about two hours of rain—nothing to notice. The town appears to have a festive atmosphere—colored paper decorations hanging in all the central streets of the "old town," where the *refugio* is located. And then I remember a photo that caught my eye as I walked past a newspaper stand—maybe yesterday—and that showed that Santo Domingo was celebrating its *fiesta patronal*, the day honoring the man for whom the town is named. Santo Domingo de la Calzada is noted for its weeklong festivity. That must be going on now, from the crowds of people—dressed in Sunday-best—and musicians I meet in the streets.

Santo Domingo is probably the saint most popularly and intimately associated with the *camino*. Born in the eleventh century in Viloria, not so far from here, Domingo began life as a shepherd. As a young man, he tried to become a monk, but two monasteries refused to accept him. He then began to live as a hermit, establishing his hermitage in a forest—a place now occupied by the town named for him.

The route to Compostela passed near the hermitage where Domingo lived, and he noticed the hardships and difficulties of the pilgrims. The very forest was a good hiding place for criminals who preyed on them; rivers in the area were difficult to cross. Eventually, he dedicated himself to helping pilgrims: clearing a wide path through the forest, building and maintaining bridges, turning his hermitage into a *hospital* where he personally cared for them.

Alfonso VI, passing through (1076) and seeing the good work accomplished by Domingo, and himself being interested in the *camino,* granted Domingo land to carry on his various activities. Domingo died on May 12, 1109, and is buried in the town's principal church. He is credited with constructing and maintaining the *camino* between Nájera and Redicilla, a town beyond Santo Domingo de la Calzada.

The people gaily direct me to the *refugio,* located in the "center" of town in an old, beautifully restored building, with a long parklike plaza in front of it, the openness of which contrasts nicely with all the narrow streets leading up to it. In the *refugio,* I find an office that is the place where the magazine *Peregrino* is edited. I go up the stairs to the dormitory, find there are two large ones, with bathrooms, kitchen, and dining room between. I wash my socks and enjoy the warmth of a hot shower. I wonder . . . if I traveled with a tent, how could I ever get a hot shower? Am I ready to forgo that? If I don't get wet and cold from rain, my clothes are soaked in sweat when I arrive at a shelter. And I must wash socks almost daily to have enough dry and clean ones. Today, I hang them out on a line that extends over the roof of a neighboring building. Fortunately, I had thought of this before I started, and brought along a supply of large safety pins. With these, I always fasten the washed clothes to the line so that the wind does not blow them off—perhaps to a place, as I see today, where I cannot recover them.

After the shower, I feel like doing something and, noticing the well-equipped kitchen, decide to try to cook a hot meal. Late in the afternoon, when shops open again, I go out to look for a market. Walking down the street, I see that everything is still tightly closed. That seems odd, until I notice a small sign on a door: Closed for the fiesta. I learn that today is the final day of celebration, and all business stopped at noon! Everyone is getting ready for tonight's evening party.

Returning to the shelter, and looking around the kitchen, I find two bananas that a pilgrim says he is leaving there because he doesn't want them. There are many cartons of milk and a lot of eggs in the refrigerator—obviously not the property of any single person. And I find a can of powdered chocolate.

While I am hard-boiling some eggs, a man comes up and offers me a dried codfish that he finds too much to eat. From my pack, I get a piece of bread. So, I enjoy my meal, certainly enough to sustain me until the next day. And I still have a small piece of *chorizo* (a highly seasoned sausage) and bread in the pack. That will do for breakfast. Later, I can surely find a place to buy some fruit.

There are about a dozen liters of milk in the kitchen, all in paper cartons, none refrigerated . . . my first experience with milk that requires no refrigeration until after you open it. Not eager to find out what it tastes like, I mix it with a lot of powdered chocolate. On the cartons I read that the milk comes from the Spanish Red Cross and is not for sale. It must be surplus milk. But this is the first time I have seen it in a shelter kitchen. That might be a useful project—collect surplus food and stock the shelters with it—making a substantial saving for the pilgrims. Here, too, there is no charge, just a box on the wall, asking for a donation. I have decided to put in 300 pesetas each time, the amount I have heard asked most often in those shelters that have a set charge.

An attractive, young-looking woman comes into the room. It turns out she is an American from Monterey, California. Curious, I ask her age. Twenty-three. (I had thought she looked about sixteen.) And you are walking alone? Yes. Have you had any problems? Well, I arrived late in Estella, and couldn't find the shelter. Since I don't know Spanish (and walking alone!), I had difficulties asking directions. Finally, I found a bar open and went in. There a man seemed to understand my predicament and asked me to come with him. After walking several blocks, we came to a large building. He rang the bell. A nun came to the door! She invited me in and they gave me a hot supper and a bed for the night. So I suppose I must say that I've had no problems.

Later, she asked me a couple of questions that surprised me. She wondered if it would be permissible for her to attend Mass in a church. Sure, I answered. Why not? Well, I'm not a Catholic, she replied, and I don't want to do something that is not proper.

She also asked my opinion about another question that troubled her: Are the people of Spain offended to see this American walking through their country? Such a thought had never occurred to me. I thought that people would be delighted to see someone who had come so far to walk in their country. But then I remembered a story I had heard. In a certain town, some pilgrims assist at Mass during their pilgrimage to Compostela. The celebrant of the Mass makes no mention of them in his announcements, and says nothing about the *camino* in the sermon. After this, during the Prayer of the Faithful—when people are free to offer their own petitions—one of the pilgrims asks for the success of their pilgrimage. At the end of these petitions, the priest adds another: "For those who do not enjoy vacations and can in no way take off during the summer." The pilgrim who relates the incident had the distinct impression that the priest was alluding to the pilgrims as a privileged group who had the money and time to indulge in a walk across Spain.

The question of the young woman makes me think that there is a fine sensitivity in her concern and a subtle truth in the priest's implication. Those of us out here are, in many ways, highly favored persons—whether I think of my good health, the time and money at my disposal, or the very idea itself of walking the *camino,* a place undoubtedly sanctified by many over the centuries.

Trying to bring some coherence out of these confused thoughts, I walk the hundred or so meters to the church. As I arrive in the small plaza in front, I see a striking building on the other side, and learn that this is a *Parador Nacional,* a hotel operated by the government. These are located all over Spain, in places where the administration in Madrid feels that a first-class hotel should be located—for tourism?—but where the economic uncertainty of the investment prevents the private sector from taking the risk of establishing such a venture. Some are located in ancient, renovated buildings, like this one, and some in completely new constructions.

I walk over to the *Parador*—a solid, graceful structure, restored with conspicuous taste and refinement. I step in to look around, and immediately feel that I'm somewhat out of place, in a rather luxurious hotel. Beyond the lobby, there is a spacious lounge, and I dare to go that far, in spite of my dress and appearance. Taking a good look, but being careful not to touch anything, I walk back out, stopping at the registration desk to ask if they have any brochure or such about the hotel. The correctly polite young lady directs me to a nearby table. She does not appear to feel that I am a potential guest.

I learn that this magnificent palace-like building is presented as the historical continuation of the work begun by Santo Domingo, who established a shelter for pilgrims here. If this is the site of his *hospital,* then it is also the site of his hermitage in the forest. The soil of this place has certainly been transformed over the centuries!

A few steps away from the *Parador* and I am in the church. Immediately, I am struck by the high iron grillwork surrounding the stone of the saint's tomb. Today, everything is decorated with flowers. On the front of the tomb, there is a life-size standing statue of Domingo. Something catches my attention, but at first I cannot identify what it is. I continue looking at the statue, in all details manifesting the traditional signs of a pilgrim, as one sees in European art, over and over: a staff, a shell, a gourd (for water or wine), a sack or satchel (for food), the pilgrim cloak and a Rosary . . . but, of course, the Rosary! I had not thought of it before, but all the pictures and statues seem to show it. This *is* the prayer of the *camino*. Strange how I "fell" into it. I did not carefully choose this, as I had chosen which clothes to take along. I was given this—by my father. He does join the innumerable pilgrims to lead me into the *camino*'s secrets. The Rosary is no more decorative in these representations than the staff or gourd. As I need to drink each day to continue walking, so I need to say the Rosary—if I wish to enter the sacred space of the *camino*.

Turning the other way I see, built into the wall, a kind of gilded cage that holds two live chickens. I had been waiting to see this, wondering if it were true. These two white chickens, a cock and a hen, are here to commemorate the most famous miracle of the *camino,* one known all over Europe, the evidence of which is found in paintings—now mostly in museums, and stories—now collected in scholarly editions. With such a popular legend, there are various versions, and there is a huge literature on the subject. I'll refer to the one described in the *relato* of Domenico Laffi, an Italian pilgrim who came through here in 1670.

Laffi says that when he entered the church, dressed in his pilgrim gown, the chickens, noting his clothing, began to "sing with joy"—which they did whenever they saw a pilgrim enter. He asked the sacristan for a couple of their feathers, which he planned to take home out of devotion (*por devoción*). It is recorded by others that these feathers have miraculous powers. Laffi says that the chickens only eat what the pilgrims throw into their cage. This must be bread that was obtained through someone's charity (toward the pilgrim), *not* purchased, for the chickens will not eat bought bread—and they can tell the difference. Another pilgrim records the belief that if you throw bread in the cage and the chickens eat it, you know that you will arrive in Compostela. If they turn it down, you know you will die before you reach the holy city.

As Laffi and his companion leave the town, they pass a small chapel that has a plaque on the inside, on which is inscribed a story of the chickens. In 1090, Greeks from Thessalonica, a man and his wife with their son, were on their way to Compostela. When they arrived at this town, they stayed at an inn for two days to rest. The daughter of the innkeeper fell madly in love with the son, a young man. At night, she silently went into his room, awakened him, and revealed her passion for him. But the young man was greatly embarrassed by this wanton display of affection, reprimanded her, and resolutely refused her advances. Seeing that she could in no way seduce him, her desire turned into a violent hatred, and she burned with an infernal fury, seeking now to avenge herself on him.

Leaving the room, she took one of her father's silver cups and returning later, again quietly, hid the cup in the bottom of the young man's pilgrim satchel. As soon as the family had departed for Compostela, the girl began to make a fuss about a missing cup, saying that she was certain those pilgrims must have stolen it. Thinking she might be right, her father took some town officials with him and went after the pilgrims. Catching up with them, the officers searched their belongings and found the cup. They took the son back to town, found him guilty of theft and immediately hanged him—on the spot where the chapel with the plaque was now located.

The disconsolate parents continued to Compostela. They prayed to God and Santiago, imploring them for the good of their souls and that of their only son. Returning, they were undecided whether to take a different route when they reached Astorga. The father wanted to go by another road to avoid passing the place of their son's death. But the mother wanted to return by that town, and he acceded to her wish.

When the couple neared the location of the hanging, their son cried out to them: "Dear father and mother, that's enough weeping; through the grace of God, of the Blessed Virgin and of Santiago, I am alive; they hold me up here in the air. Mother, go to the judge and tell him I am innocent, I am alive, and I want to be returned to you." Obediently, his mother hurries to the house of the judge. As she enters the door, he is just sitting down to dinner. She excitedly tells him that her son is alive and innocent. The judge laughs cruelly and turns to her: "Oh, how you've let yourself be deceived, woman! Your son is no more alive than these two roasted chickens you see on my plate."

"Oh, what a surprise! Oh, what power of the great God!" Laffi interjects. The two chickens, a cock and a hen, flew off the plate and began to crow! The judge, seeing the miracle, immediately jumped up and gathered some priests and citizens to accompany him to the scaffold. Seeing the hanged man happy and well, they returned him to his parents.

Returning to town, the judge placed the chickens in an iron cage in the church. Laffi adds that they live for seven years. Before dying, the hen lays two eggs. From these, two chicks hatch out, male and female, the same color as the parents—white. The innkeeper and his daughter were punished. Some accounts say they were hanged.

The English writer Robert Southey tells the story in a long poem he published in 1829. In a lilting, imaginative verse, he gives his version of the young woman's fate:

> The Innkeeper's wicked daughter
> Confess'd what she had done,
> So they put her in a Convent,
> And she was made a Nun.

The scene, showing the hanged boy being held up by Santiago, with his two parents standing beside the scaffold, was painted over and over in Europe; the story was written and staged as a drama many times. The latest version, it seems, was recently published by Henri Ghéon, *La Farce du pendu dépendu* (1920). Only in the fifteenth century was the miracle of the chickens definitely placed in Santo Domingo de la Calzada. In earlier centuries, it took place in other cities.

It is easy to develop a rational argument "explaining" the popularity of the story over the years. As more people set out from all parts of Europe for Compostela, the number of dishonest innkeepers and such folk seemed to increase proportionately. The power of Santiago, the justice of God, are vivid and sure in the tale. The characters, their actions, and their fates perfectly fitted the historical hopes and experiences of many people of the time.

Some speak of an age when the faith of people was more naïve, more "simple." Even so shrewd an observer of his own people and country as the great Miguel de Unamuno, writes "of those centuries of a more ingenuous, more simple Christian faith . . ." when people believed that the body of Santiago was buried in Galicia.

A more subtle and sensitive eye is needed to read the reports from that distant time. The people of Asturias faced a fearful foe in the eighth century, the Moors. In the early ninth century, they discovered a great relic in their midst, the bones of the apostle, James the Greater. From these actions and events they succeeded in superseding the limits of merely living; they liberated themselves from "the prison of time"; they created a myth that was truly *historiable*—it is still alive today. In a real sense, these people created the mystery of the *camino*. The condescension implicit in judging earlier people to be more childlike certainly leads to distortions and misunderstandings. For example, one of the miracles attributed to Santiago in the *Liber* shows him saving a man from drowning after the man fell off his ship while sitting on the edge of the rail to take a shit. What could be more *natural* than falling off the ship in those circumstances? The important aspect of the miracle, I suspect, is not a supposedly immature scatological image, but the fact that the man, a pilgrim, was returning from the Holy Land. He had *not* gone to Compostela, and yet Santiago did not hold this against him. Credence in such magnanimity strains our sense of simple.

One can begin to glimpse more of these stories' meaning through reflection on a comment of Wittgenstein. He says that "in religion every level of devoutness must have its appropriate form of expression which has no sense at a lower level." A truth that has meaning "at a higher level, is null and void for someone who is still at the lower level; he can only understand wrongly." I suspect that walking the *camino* at ground level, attempting to touch the places where so many have trod, may lead one to the truth of these stories. One cannot remain at the rarefied level of academics—it is too low.

Returning to the *refugio,* I find the streets filling up with joyful people. But I have no idea how to participate in their celebration, and I need my sleep for an early start tomorrow morning. When I get upstairs, a couple of Spanish pilgrims convince me that I must go with them to get the special traditional food of the feast, cooked mushrooms.

When we step out into the street, we see a huge pot of mushrooms cooking, right on the plaza in front of the building. We go to the other end to get in line. After about an hour's wait, I receive one large mushroom on a small piece of bread, and a small paper cup of wine! Both taste good, but I would not have gone out if I had known they would cost an hour's standing in line. Returning back upstairs, I get into the sleeping bag, hearing music and singing in the distance. But it is too far away to disturb my sleep.

11

Santo Domingo de la Calzada to Belorado

May 14, 1993

I have some difficulty finding my way out of town. Whenever I spend the night in a town shelter, I try to orient myself well the evening before since I will probably see no one on the streets early in the morning, and the streets are almost always confusing. I need more time in each place to learn my way around. But I eventually get to the end of houses and pass the huge Franciscan church and monastery, now seemingly empty and locked up, and the place where Laffi found the chapel. I am on the way to Belorado!

After some hours I realize that this very special and, yes, privileged place of the *camino*, created by all those who preceded me, reveals yet another aspect of its truth; I see another light in its darkness. And this insight follows the curious pattern of all the earlier ones. Every time something like this comes to me, it seems to be more important, in the sense of being more significant, more meaningful *to me* at this moment of my life, than the earlier perceptions. As I progress further into the specific space of the *camino,* I find it ever richer in its intelligible resonances; I learn more about the truth of my life.

At various times, the walking has appeared to be a journey into faith or, rather, in search of faith. Over and over I have come to recognize that, to speak the truth, I could not heretofore call myself a man of faith.

Along with this recurring realization, came another: this is precisely the reason I am here—to become a man of faith; that is why I have been led to this place. The *camino* will take me to the place I must reach before I die, will make me the person I must be when I die, a man of faith. All the voiced declarations over the years, all the "correct" actions, now appear rather empty, devoid of any life. They were all pretense. Now, finally, in the short time remaining to me, I approach the place where I shall receive the gift of faith. This I have always known intellectually, which, I see, is *not* to know. I am not a soul using this body, not a mind putting up with this flesh, not a spiritual ego looking down or through the senses. If I understand Wittgenstein, he puts it nicely: Knowledge does not come from a disembodied mind, knowledge is a kind of social product, it results from the "forms of life," and these are established by the meaning people arrive at in their everyday collective action. This action is earthy, fleshy, historical—exactly the kind of action that I experience here in the community of the *camino*.

The gift of faith, toward which I move, is indeed a gift, a *gratia gratis data,* a grace I can in no way merit or, even less, deserve. It is given out of the pure generosity of the giver. My parents gave me all the forms and the example of lives lived in faith. They and the earlier pilgrims gave me the Rosary. This prayer gives me the Mysteries of the Lord. In them, I find his teaching and his person. All I need is there; all I seek is there. But I am coming to the place where I can grasp these gifts because I came step by step, hour by hour, always with my feet on the ground. The pain removes all empty fantasy or sentimentalism. The breathed words preclude all illusionary intellectuality. Again, I am reminded of one of the first realizations—a very necessary insight—for getting on the *camino:* the decision to walk alone and to read no books.

I entered many places in my life. I have traveled to many different countries. But now I learn about a very distinct kind of step, a real step, a step that takes me to a unique place. So, I have only one more step to take before I die: to become a man of faith. When I take that, I will take the last step, which is also the first step, because faith is the beginning. Theologically, this is where one starts. So, as I end my life, I begin it. As I approach the end of the *camino,* I arrive at its and my source, faith.

Lots of rain today. I approach Belorado, which seems to be a large town. I've walked four or five hours, covering only about twenty kilometers, but I feel too tired to go on farther, and my list says there is a *refugio* here. The rain has stopped, and someone directs me to a building down the street. This seems to be the parish office, and a man—the parish priest?—welcomes me and gives me the key to the *refugio,* explaining how to find it. Walking a few blocks farther, and making some turns down various streets, I arrive at a small church—not the larger parish church that I passed—in a quiet neighborhood. Next door is a kind of church hall. I open the door and am startled to see that the place was once used as a theater. Now, a lower ceiling has been put in, this creating also a second floor. The bunks are up there. Here, where the theater seats were there is a large table and chairs. Up on the stage, they have installed a sink and stove. At one end of the stage, there is a toilet and shower—with hot water.

I set down my pack and head for the market. I've just barely time to buy provisions before the stores close. Today I will certainly cook! I get a slice of ham, frozen potatoes and peas, bread—whole wheat—fresh strawberries and yogurt—a feast. Back in the shelter, I do my laundry and hang everything out in the warm sun that now brightens my day. Shoes and all my clothes will dry today. After a shower, I feel *very* good. I heat the ham and vegetables and enjoy a scrumptious dinner. What an unusual place the people of the parish have prepared for us, different from all the other shelters, a charmingly unique place to stop. Stepping across the threshold of these buildings is like taking another step out on a country trail—it's a new, unpredictable experience every time. In Santo Domingo de la Calzada, the *cofradía* beautifully carries on the tradition of their patron saint. Here, the people have come up with their own expression of *camino* hospitality, an unusually funky restoration of an old building.

I find the rubber stamp in a box by the door. One takes care of his *credencial* himself. There is a sign on the door: "Will the last person who leaves in the morning please lock the door and drop the key back in the mail slot hole in the door?" I take a chair out and sit in the sun to get warm, and greet three Spanish pilgrims who arrive. One is the man with the homeopathic remedies from Barcelona. Here and there, magnificent cumulus clouds move across the sky, an endless story of the atmosphere's beauty.

This would be the perfect afternoon to sit at a sidewalk café for my coffee. But I have not yet seen any such place along the *camino.* Perhaps they are only in the larger cities, and in those places I moved through too quickly to look for a sidewalk café. I get up and walk the few blocks to "downtown" and find a bar where I can indulge the pleasures of taste. I have noticed that some of the pilgrims eat chocolate bars, and the ones I see in the stores look most tempting. But I think I better stop with the coffee . . . maybe that is already too much catering to sense pleasure, a dulling of my perceptions.

In the bar, I find as always, many older men, very few younger ones— just about what I've found among the walkers on the *camino.* The men in the bars seem to be much more intent on playing cards and other games than drinking. The tables have special green removable felt covers. The bars are often well crowded—but not always, as I found in Nájera—and, from their behavior and speech, the men appear to greatly enjoy their friends' company. The atmosphere is one of quiet, warm, and spontaneous pleasure. I too enjoy stopping in these places, even though I am a complete outsider. Infrequently, women come in, usually in twos, and only long enough for a drink or a cup of coffee. They seem to be young, employed women, "professionals" maybe, dressed as if they have come from the office, not from the kitchen, and apparently are more independent and liberated. But I have been in too few bars and at too random times to form any decent generalizations. I wonder, though: Where are the wives of all these men? Where do they meet their friends? Do they have some "club" where they gather? I saw a few sitting in the sun on park benches, but they were only a handful. Enough . . . I'm not a pop sociologist. Better to get back to the sunshine in front of the *refugio*. I need to let the bright Spanish sun soak deep inside me after all that rain this morning.

From the little bit of walking in the town, I've noticed many signs that advertise leather goods for sale, and it seems that there are some small shops or factories where these things are made. This may be a center for such work. I am reminded of something I read about the economics of New Spain. By 1535, cattle and sheep raising had become the principal occupation of wealthier Spaniards. But, unless one's ranch was near a large city, beef production was comparatively unprofitable. The chief value of the beasts lay in their hides, and in tallow that was used for candles and waterproofing ships. The meat of slaughtered beef cattle was often left to rot in the field. In the meantime, the impact of cattle hooves and overgrazing resulted in the land erosion that continues today. The Aztecs didn't need the cattle any more than the Spaniards needed the gold.

On the corner where I turn to go to the shelter, I notice a *zapatería*, which I have always thought meant a shoe repair shop, like the one I visited in Pamplona. But after I turn the corner, something stops me. I return to take another look at the small and not very clean store window of this quite modest and almost hidden store front. There are what appear to be new shoes in the window, and a small sign in one corner reads: "Shoes made to order." From the outside, the place is so tiny and unassuming that I have difficulty imagining what that sign means. Why not go in and find out?

I open the door and step in. More new shoes are displayed on racks. But no shoe boxes. Men's shoes, women's shoes, different styles of shoes.

In the back of the shop, two men are working. I walk up to the counter and one man, the younger, nearly my age perhaps, comes up to wait on me. I'm not certain what I want to say. "Do you make shoes here?" I ask incredulously. "Yes," he answers, quite straightforwardly. "Excuse me," I ask, "but is there a young person learning this work to continue it after you die?"

Just at that moment, a well-dressed, middle-aged woman opens the door and comes in. The man looks at me, at the woman, and asks me if I can wait a minute; he wants to talk with me. He attends his customer, evidently a well-known person who has come to fetch some shoes she left to be repaired. She pays her bill and leaves immediately. The man returns to talk.

The older man in the back of the shop, quietly working at a machine, is his father, from whom he learned the craft of making shoes. He tells me that he has three small electrically powered machines that he installed some years ago to enable him to make a pair of shoes in less time, thereby being able to compete in price with a factory-made product. He shows me how the machines work. It appears to be the kind of operation—using such machines—where the craftsman is still a craftsman, really in control, using the small machine as an extension of his arm and hand. Something similar to a hammer or a knife. But this likeness or difference would have to be studied more carefully.

In answer to my original question he answers that no, no one has learned his craft. He appears to be the last one in town who knows how to make shoes.

I ask whether he has children. Yes, two. And where are they? "Oh, they have gone to the university." I sense I'm entering a delicate area and try to ask, as gently as possible, with no trace—I hope—of accusation, whether he encouraged them to follow in the footsteps of their grandfather and himself. Well . . . no. I can detect a certain confusion and ambiguity in his response. I'm pretty certain that he has been fed the conventional wisdom of the day: The university is a good thing. For his children to go there, the first ones in their family to reach university studies, he should also be grateful. So reads the modern script.

But it is clear that he has no knowledge, no experience, of what goes on there, and even less sense of what awaits them when they graduate. He has no real understanding of the world of employment—he has never been employed. He has never known what it is to work according to a set of apparently rational bureaucratic rules, but always interpreted idiosyncratically in conformity with the personal politics and ambitions of the current supervisors or leaders. He is not bothered by the problems of the labor market or arguments about the labor theory of value because his tradition of work and living is rooted in the soil of a real community. But he, along with everyone in Spain, has been exposed to the illusion that what passes for higher education today is an unquestioned good.

I suspect that he does not reflect on the truth that the skills into which he was born are part of a way of life, are an integral and necessary part of an ancient tradition that contributes to making possible a *human* community; that his place in this community is highly honorable and respected because of the quality of his work and the necessity of his product for the community. He is not able to articulate the difference between this world and that of employment in a bureaucratically organized institution, where you are just one more competitor in a frantic race after the abstract and ever receding goal of progress.

He does not see that he can stand proudly before the modern world of industrial and technological employment where almost no one really makes anything at all, where the uniqueness of individuals and communities is destroyed, and softly say: I am a master, a master craftsman; look at my dress, my hands. I can take the skins of animals and make something beautiful and necessary for my neighbors and those who visit our town. Each pair of shoes I make is truly distinctive, because I made it and there will never be another like it, and because it is made for this person here in front of me, whose foot I have touched, the exact shape of which I know. And even if a machine could be designed to take all the measurements of a person's foot, it would still not be able to look at that person in the face, would never know the place of that person in the community—something only learned through generations of intimate contact—and thus be able to arrive at the proper style of shoe *for that person.*

Further, I am the master of my small shop, the master of my time, of every aspect of my work, of all my skills . . . of my life.

How will his children, no matter how high they rise, no matter how successful they become, characterize their work and their place in a community? Will they ever reach a place like his? Will they ever be able to stand with such dignity? Or is it too late to ask such questions? Or are the questions themselves meaningless?

He picks up various shoes, pointing out their special characteristics, talking of his work in making them. He handles them with obvious care and affection. And they are truly beautiful—the amazing work of one man's hands. How I wish I needed a pair of shoes. How I wish I had time to have a pair made for me. Perhaps he would have some sandals already made that would fit me. I look down at the cheap plastic chemically and machine-made ones on my feet. I am embarrassed that he should see such trash in his shop.

He mentions the deteriorating state of the economy—of the country and of this town. You can walk out and see young men standing around all day with nothing to do. There are not enough jobs. There were rumors that the government was going to establish a school here where young people could learn shoemaking; that a factory would be built to employ them, but nothing has happened. The government should certainly do *something*.

Some believe that the economic problems of Spain should be traced to 1492. In that year the Jews, who had no prejudice against economic activity, and who were important in all economic sectors of the country, were expelled. This action of Ferdinand and Isabella helped seal the fate of the empire of Castille before it was born. By this time, there was a kind of craze in Castille for the title of *hidalgo* (the son of *someone*). For a Spanish gentleman so graced, the military was regarded as the highest profession, followed by that of clergyman and lawyer. The principal activity of lawyers seems to have been to hang around the court, seeking preferment. Economic initiative was simply not honored. The superb craft skill that I see here today has, I suspect, never been adequately acknowledged and respected, in Spain or elsewhere.

This man does not see that the issue is both more complex and quite other than government intervention; one must look to the concepts, beliefs, and customary actions of the society: What is work? What is honorable work? How does work build (or destroy) this specific community? I wonder . . . yes, the government could establish a trade school. Yes, it could also start a factory. And yes, all the young people of the town could be employed. But that would be a very different world from the one of these two men in their shop, a place that dignifies its workers and enriches the community.

I see that his father, he, and his children are caught up in a confusing transition. And I fear it will soon be over. In his bones, he knows that he does good work, that the way he works gives him a good life, that the product of his work graces the people of his town. But all this is ending. Centuries of solid tradition, sustaining the beauty of these lives in this community, will be smashed, destroyed forever, when his children simply walk away. No government, I fear, can remedy that. A new world has beckoned to his children. They are probably succumbing to its temptations. They do not see that the best they can hope for is to become the adjunct of some machine, made of hardware or software. The more sophisticated the machine, the more they will be absorbed into it, commanded and shaped by it. They will in all probability never rise above being employees—not of a firm or business, but of a worldwide complex of machines, markets, financial transactions, and avaricious gamesmen.

My eyes wander over the shop. It is not the standardized, antiseptic display of modern stores. I touch, run my fingers over, the different kinds of leather—I had not realized there are so many. I pick up some of the shoes to look at them more closely—what precious objects they appear! I face this modest artist, this master craftsman and, looking into one another's eyes, we shake hands. I want to linger, but I must go on, I must let him return to his tools; our lives—touching so briefly—must part. I thank him, turn, and uncertainly leave the shop. What could I say to him? Could I speak of the beauty of his initiative and independence? of the wonder of a community where such lives are still found? of the richness of a country where such traditions still flourish? But none of this is true. The government may come some day and confirm what has already happened. The picture I draw is out of date, finished. And the government projects—to create employment, a viable industry, a growing economy—will definitively destroy the world which every day becomes more and more a memory, or perhaps only a dream. But how I wish I could somehow have found the words to say: How much I respect you! How much I would like to honor you! How much your country should seek not to lose you!

Every day, from the distant Tuesday back there in St. Jean Pied de Port, I have walked through creation. I have seen the beauty of the world where people tend to leave it alone, and the places where they work to transform it, sometimes well, sometimes badly. And I have tried to remain "out there," coming inside only to sleep and eat. I have tried to avoid the museums, churches, and monasteries. I think that maybe this exercise, this discipline, somehow cleared my vision so that when I passed that very plain and nondescript shop, my eye picked up something and I stopped. Stepping inside, I was shown a noble and honorable way of living. When have I ever seen such before, so clearly, so simply? Now, having seen something of its substance and form, I understand how fragile it is, how rare. Are there worlds where such traditions still live? Is it possible to revive such lives, such communities? Tonight, at night prayers, I must be especially mindful to acknowledge my thanks for this day. At many times in my life I have felt great sadness, but never, I believe, anything like this. The destruction seems to advance so inevitably, so benignly. The attractive images catch people's attention, the illusions take hold, the old people die, the young just move away. No one seems to possess the perspicacity to see what is happening. No one receives the inspiration to cry out. No one has the courage to rebel. The possibilities of human, earthly goodness and beauty vanish.

In a moment, I am back at the shelter. The Spanish pilgrims, too, have brought their chairs out into the sun. I start to speak about the shoemaker. Although all passed the shop, no one noticed it, no one marked it as being there. One man says that yes, he remembers that there were shoemakers in his town when he was a child. But they disappeared long ago. Now there remains only the repairman—a person of uncertain but rather lowly social standing.

But something else has caught their interest. They direct my gaze to the top of the church tower. What is that, I wonder? A haphazard collection of sticks and leaves stuck precariously up there—but it stays. It's a stork's nest, they explain. The first one I've ever seen. I can just see the mother, but the small ones are hidden inside the nest. Occasionally townspeople, some with cameras, come to observe the birds, attempting to get a glimpse of the young ones. I had never thought about storks before. I guess I never really believed that they exist—except on invitations to baby showers and in stories of the origin of the babies themselves. I wonder how that connection ever started. There must be other stories about this creature, too. That seems such a strange way to build a nest. Such a bird must have interesting histories connected with it.

I'm somewhat tired when I get into the sleeping bag, but I am much more overcome by sadness. In addition, though, I hope I am grateful for having found that shop, for having met that man—a fleeting perception of goodness and beauty, an insight into the possibilities of work and community. I feel greatly enhanced, truly blessed, by the experience. I am not the same person I was when I left Santo Domingo de la Calzada this morning. Again, the *camino* took me to a new and strange place—Belorado. Shall I ever forget it, will I ever see it again? Or has it already ceased to exist? But are there no young men or women in Spain eager to apprentice themselves to ennobling work, to the creation of a strong community? What kind of country will this be when all the artists have died out, those whose inspiration, lifelong dedication, skills, and daily work truly make possible their communities? I suppose there are those who wonder if Spain can give birth to another Velázquez, Goya, Buñuel, or Picasso. But I ask whether the artistic expressions of a community life—a domestic art—needing an unbroken tradition, may not be more important to the life of a people.

12

Belorado to San Juan de Ortega

May 15, 1994

C old and cloudy today, but no rain yet. Hills and forests—perhaps one could call some of them mountains. Coming down one path, I notice some ruins nearby. The sign says that this is what remains of the monastery of San Félix, which flourished between the fifth and seventh century. That's right in the middle of the Visigothic period, after the Romans left and before the Moors arrived. This might be the earliest human structure I've seen in my life. Men, so long ago, shaped these stones, and placed them, one on top of the other, to create their habitation, their place of work and prayer. How many monasteries, convents, and churches have been constructed here in Spain! Occasionally, I hear of a church being built today, but no monasteries or convents. And all the ones I have seen on the *camino* are either like this one, in ruins, empty, or with a token presence of men or women. But I only know what I have seen in a small part of the *camino*. In other places, the picture may be very different. I wonder, is there a monastic life in Spain today? Did large numbers of men enter monasteries again after the Civil War, as happened in the United States, after World War II? So much I would like to know about Spain!

For a long time, I walk through a forest. Slowly, in the silence, I feel myself accepted, taken in, by the trees; I move among them as one among other living creatures. What does this place signify, say? Does it stand for the universe itself? Is it really untouched by symbol-manipulating humans? For the world simply is; in itself, it contains no signs. If I can sense purely enough, this world will enter me directly. In the Renaissance, cloth surpassed wood in the symbolic position of *materia prima,* among the substances worked by man. Then, in the Industrial Revolution, metal became the fundament. And today? How far I am from these trees! The place that sheltered heroic outlaws like Robin Hood; the place to which philosophers like Thoreau retreated; the place that is both sacred and profane, a realm of darkness and of illumination.

The forest path then seems to lead up what is unquestionably a mountain. At the top, with a remote forest service road running nearby, I come to a rather plain stone monument, not very large or imposing. I look closely and find that it was erected in honor of *los caídos*—1936 . . . those killed in the terrible Civil War (1936–39). The inscription reads: "Sus muertos no eran inútiles—su fusilamiento era inútil"—"Their deaths were not useless—their killing was useless." It looks as if the monument is forgotten and more or less inaccessible—except for people on the *camino.* It is clear that no one other than forest workers uses the nearby road. About fifty meters below me, a new highway crosses the mountain. It seems pretty obvious what happened. The new road, engineered according to rational criteria of efficiency, has left far behind, has lost, this witness to another age, to a different way of viewing Spain and the world.

This is the first direct reminder I have seen of that war, a conflict full of darkness and mystery for a foreigner. But I strongly suspect one thing to be clear: Today, the inscription would have to be read in reverse to reflect the truth. Their deaths were useless . . . the people and events shaping the public life of Spain today have made the causes for which both sides fought historically obsolete. Or, in the concept of Américo Castro, they are not *historiable,* that is, enduring through time, such as the work of Cervantes. But the killing *was* necessary . . . the hatreds and passions that then governed men had to be acted out, had to result in brother killing brother. The atrocities committed on both sides were horrendous; men were fighting with the ferocity of a *religious* war. One sees in the Caprichos of Goya, the agonies of Unamuno, the sadness of Ortega y Gasset, and the movies of Buñuel the terrible personal records of Spain continually fighting an intimate and violent battle against its past. Although each army believed that it fought for ideals totally opposed to those of the other, at bottom they were both inspired by one and the same ideology, that of purifying the nation of those who believed in the wrong gods.

Throughout Spanish history, from the time of Saint Isidore (570–636)— the first proponent of a Spanish state, and the author of a treatise de-

Fig. 2. Martin Schongauer, "Saint James as the Moorkiller," c. 1472. Graphische Sammlung Albertina, Vienna.

signed to help Catholic clergy make an intellectual argument with Jews—those who did not adhere to the "official" faith have been persecuted, killed, and expelled. Laws regulating the behavior of groups identified as distinct from Christians (found in the *Titol de los Hereges, É de los Judíos, É de las Sectas* [Concerning heretics, Jews, and sects]) can be traced back at least to the time of the Visigothic king, Recaredo (586–601). The origins of this kind of stance in the Christian West seem to be found in the Edict of Milan (313) in which the Emperor Constantine recognized the Christian religion as the official one of the Empire. For the first time in the history of what became Europe, civic rights became dependent on one's adhesion to certain articles of faith. Each country has interpreted and applied this policy differently. In places where the policy was enforced, Jews and heretics were the first groups to suffer. Interestingly, one of the very few places in Europe where Jews have been safe since antiquity is Rome. In Spain, after the Islamic conquest (711), the policy was extended from Jews and heretics to include Muslims (infidels). But from year to year and place to place it was applied (or not applied) *quite* differently.

The only pattern or consistency that I can discern, from Visigothic times until today, is that religious leaders generally take the lead in advocating a policy of intolerance and hatred toward those who have the wrong faith. For example, in 1085, when Alfonso VI captured Toledo, he let the Moors keep and use their mosque. After he had left the city, however, the archbishop took it away from them and turned it into a Christian church. Alfonso X (1252–84) tried to protect the Jews, but pulpit oratory inflamed the Christians against them. In 1391, the virulent sermons of Fernán Martínez provoked fanatical attacks on the Jews of Seville, and these spread throughout the country. Only the Jews of Portugal and Islamic Granada were spared. Some cite 1391 as the end of Spanish Jewry, since great numbers chose baptism rather than die. In 1411, Saint Vincent Ferrer, the most popular preacher in Spain at the time, believing that the Jews still represented some kind of threat, again roused the Christians against them.

When Granada fell on January 2, 1492, Hernando de Talavera, Isabella's confessor and a saintly *converso* (convert from Judaism), was named archbishop. In eight years, his gentle approach, respectful of the person of the Moors, made no converts. Cardinal Ximénez de Cisneros, one of the strongest characters of the time, was appointed to replace him. The Cardinal repudiated the conditions of the peace treaty and attempted to force conversions. A bloody war followed.

Recently, the Bishops' letter of 1988 says that Santiago had protected the Catholics of Spain, especially in the "Reconquista." This is the name, with powerful "mystical"-religious connotations, given to the action begun in the Battle of Covadonga (718) and ending in the capture of Granada (1492)—the series of campaigns and sieges that finally returned the entire Peninsula to Catholic rule. The secular expression of the people's devotion has been mandated, the Bishops say, in the Voto de Santiago, a tradition uninterrupted until today—which is not quite true, since the Cortes abolished the Voto in the nineteenth century; Franco reinstated it in this century. The Voto, a tribute whose exact content changed over the years, was paid by the secular authorities of some provinces or all of Spain (this, too, varied with the time and place) to the church in Compostela, out of gratitude to Santiago for his divine intervention in the Battle of Clavijo (844). There Ramiro I, with the help of Santiago seated on a white horse, defeated the Moors, thereby reversing the infamous tribute of *las cien doncellas.* Delivering a hundred virgins every year to the Moorish ruler had been imposed after an earlier Christian defeat. Historians today believe that Pedro Marcio, writing in 1150, is responsible for these stories, and that the battle and tribute never existed. There was a battle, however, at Simancas in 939, where the Christians under Ramiro II defeated the Moors. Controversies over the issue of the Voto constitute one of the longest and most discussed disputes in Spanish history.

The image of Santiago on a white horse, leading the charge against the Moors, fixes the figure of Santiago Matamoros (the "Moor-killer"), and becomes the symbol of the Reconquista. He is later seen in various battles during the Reconquista, and continues this intervention in the New World, killing Indians there. In Europe, there are two Santiagos, Peregrino and Matamoros, but in the Americas only the Moor-killer is known.

Some believe that without Santiago, Spain would never have come to realize its destiny, that Santiago is the origin of the Christianization and greatness of Spain. Early in the Reconquista, a battle cry was heard: "¡Santiago y cierra España!"—"Santiago and Spain for the Spaniards!" One of the powerful images connected with this campaign is the *Cruz de Santiago*—the Cross of Santiago. As a flag or banner, the background is white with a red cross, pictured in the shape of a sword, which it is meant to symbolize. During the forty years of Franco's rule, the government made an intensive use of Santiago to legitimize the ideology of the state. And in many ways, the Reconquista, finally ending perhaps with the Civil War of 1936–39, was a religious crusade.

Pope Alexander II had preached a crusade against the Moors in the Peninsula in 1065. In 1096, Urban II announced the first European crusade against Islam in the Holy Land. There were at least thirty-five—mostly French—expeditions of crusaders who came to Spain to assist the Christians there. This volatile and dangerous mixture of religious faith and political ambition reached a kind of climax after the Reconquista when all Jews and Moors in Spain were given a choice: conversion or emigration. The Inquisition then continued its work of guarding the orthodoxy of the faith of all inhabitants of the land. This included a campaign enforcing a *limpieza de sangre* in the people (a cleansing of their blood). But the mad fury of the recent Civil War indicates that the task was not accomplished in those distant centuries.

The three student pilgrims of 1928, on reaching Compostela, pray to Santiago for *La Patria,* that he make it powerful and Christian. In 1937, the priest and the young *requeté* (Carlist militiaman) pray for the salvation of Spain, praising the men of the army, who fight until Spain is "purified and cleansed"—which means killing the wrong kinds of Spaniards. When the Republic fell in 1939, thousands again went into exile—not Jews and Moors, but Christians whose ideology was not pure enough to save them from death or long imprisonment. By this time, the initiative for ensuring that only correct beliefs would be respected in Spain had passed to the secular authority. Here on the mountain top, these people erected a monument. But their children do not see it, probably would not understand it, or have any interest in it.

One might doubt whether Santiago actually appeared in Coimbra (1064)—another important battle of the Reconquista—valiantly fighting on his white horse, but there is no question of the belief of those who fought subsequent battles, certain that Santiago was on their side, that they could not lose. This attitude was so highly developed by the end of the Reconquista that a historian like Américo Castro can say that Santiago's influence was crucial in determining the specifically Spanish character (*el modo peculiar de ser*) that came to include a belief in the sword of Santiago, joined to an economy of conquest and booty. One can argue that this mentality, especially prevalent in Castille, is one of the factors contributing to the fact that Spain did not develop economically as other European nations. The idea of a Reconquista may have been more powerful after 1492 than before. The mental, emotional, and spiritual hold of this notion over the hopes and ambitions of Catholic Spaniards seems to be much more universal and deeply ingrained *after* the formal Reconquista ended in the fifteenth century. One sees that the Reconquista, as shaper of people's moral universe, was a distinctly modern phenomenon before modernity, in the sense of transforming the personal invitation of the Gospel into an inflammatory and aggressive institutional imposition. For example, rather than offering the good news of the Gospel to the judgment of each person's heart in the New World—as Saint Paul had done on the Areopagus—a Spanish religiosity was inflicted on the Indians as on an undifferentiated mass.

Albelda, a chronicler writing in 880, notes that the Saracens occupied the Peninsula, but that the Christians battled them day and night until they were expelled. Castro believes that the Catholics developed the concept of a holy war in response to the Islamic challenge, thereby creating a certain (peculiar) notion of "Christian," a people professing a warlike faith. Further, they needed some cry to oppose the war whoop of the Moors, "¡Mahoma!" In the classic *Poema del Cid* (1140), one reads:

> *los Moros llaman: ¡Mafómat!*
> *e los Cristianos: ¡Santí Yagüe!*
>
> the Moors shout: Muhammad!
> and the Christians: Saint James!

This then developed into the nation's slogan, "¡Santiago y cierra España!" expressing a powerful exclusivist vision of national character and the possibility of a collective soul. The faith of people in this form of a holy war was real, the battles were real, men died. But where is this faith today? And what relation is there between my search for faith, these earlier generations of faithful, and the absence of faith in Spain today—as in the young man in Cizur Menor? Of one thing, at least, I am certain: the faith of these earlier centuries was not simple.

Somewhat tired and cold—but not wet, no rain today—I arrive at San Juan de Ortega, named for a follower of Santo Domingo de la Calzada, who also spent his life working on the *camino*, and helping pilgrims. There are many extant documents relating to his life, so the details are known. Born about 1080, as a young man Juan was ordained a priest. Then he went to work with Santo Domingo. When the latter died, Juan made a pilgrimage to the Holy Land (1109). On his way back, his ship was wrecked. Miraculously saved through the intercession of Saint Nicolás de Bari, he promised to build a church in the saint's name. This, in origin, is the present church, its location selected because of the region's dangers for pilgrims. Thieves who robbed them took refuge in this forest. Juan also established a community of Canons Regular, attached to the church; they assisted pilgrims who stopped here. According to tradition, Juan built or repaired bridges in Logroño, Nájera, Santo Domingo de la Calzada, and other places. His will, witnessed and signed by nineteen persons, is still preserved. After his death on June 2, 1183, the name of the church and village was changed to honor him. Laffi records that in the seventeenth century he himself got lost in the forests near here, and survived on mushrooms until he could find the monastery and church. Without the yellow arrows I, too, would have been lost. Although the present forest is one planted, probably by the government, it's still very much a forest.

Today, there is a huge, empty monastery (part of which is used as a *refugio*), a church—being restored—and, from what I can see, only a few houses. The saint's monumental tomb is in the church. A large tourist bus is parked nearby. The passengers soon come out of a bar, board their bus, and leave. I meet several Spanish pilgrims who walk the *camino* on weekends only, and a German couple who are walking halfway this year and the remainder next year. Sitting on a bench in the sun, I eat my lunch from the backpack. I have heard that there is no place to buy food here. There is also a story, however, that the parish priest serves all pilgrims a famous garlic soup. But I wonder where the parish is; the few houses seem to be lost in the forest-covered mountains and some scattered fields.

Several other pilgrims arrive and we enter the bar, at the end of what seem to be the buildings of the old monastery. Just off the bar there is a parlorlike room with a fire in its fireplace. Some of us take our coffee in there and let the comfortable warmth penetrate our bodies. What a nice way to end the day's walk.

Soon, a man arrives and opens the adjoining building. There he receives us, stamps our *credencial,* and admits us to the monastery/*refugio.* I don't see any monastic cells; the bunks for pilgrims are in two large rooms. I try to open a window, since the coldness and dampness inside are worse than outside. A certain bone-chilling uniformity permeates these stone buildings on cold, wet days. There are several hot showers and many sinks in the bathrooms—one for men and one for women—but a sign says that one may not wash clothes. That strikes me as a strange rule, and I've never before seen it.

By evening, about twenty people have chosen bunks in the two dormitories. I notice that one pilgrim is taking a nap with a small battery-powered radio turned on, softly, at his ear. Someone comes in and announces that the soup is ready, and we all file downstairs to a large, extremely plain dining room. Each one is given a bowl of soup and a piece of bread. Delicious! How good it tastes! I could eat three or four more bowls and at least half a loaf of bread. I slowly look around to see if there will be seconds. No luck; it's all gone. My companion at the table is from Holland. He and his wife are on a two-person bicycle. They must be taking the highway, for they never could have gotten over that mountain path today.

Back upstairs in my sleeping bag, I try to sort out the experience of that monument. I see now that not only have people "created" Santiago, they have made two of them. Are they completely separate? or somehow joined? Some authors think that Santiago, the *jinete celestial* (the celestial warrior), was only created around the twelfth century, when the documents describing his appearances at Clavijo, Coimbra, and to Charlemagne (in the *Liber Sancti Jacobi*) were, apparently, first written. But pilgrims were going to Compostela two hundred years before these writings. Later, especially in the fifteenth century, the idea of making a pilgrimage to Compostela was conflated with the idea of going on a crusade—under certain conditions, one could obtain the same spiritual benefits.

What seems clear is that many of these people, in imagining Santiago according to their needs and fantasies, *used* him. In Aristotle's categories of friendship, theirs tended to be utilitarian, not very disinterested. But this is not to pass moral judgment. Rather, I want to make the attempt to get at the truth of Santiago today, the truth for me. By studying the past, I hope to find the Santiago who fits my world, not because I make him fit, but because I see how *I* make myself fit *his* truth. I can only do that if I face the truth of the past, not to judge it with my criteria, but to learn from it.

13

San Juan de Ortega to Burgos

May 16, 1993

A cool but sunny Sunday, comfortable for walking. No problem getting an early morning start, since there is no complicated maze of village streets—only the clear yellow arrows and pleasant rural surprises. About ten kilometers from Burgos, I reach the top of a mountain and, in the far distance, see the city before me. But the way down from that mountain turns out to be a winding path and road through several small villages, and never provides another open view of the city. The continual variety of fields and houses, however, holds my attention until I reach the outskirts of Burgos.

As I walk down the street, heading for the center of town, I pass a number of phone booths. Each has one side covered by a large poster, the *peregrino* mascot for this Holy Year. There seem to be six versions of the one figure, supposedly representing a pilgrim walking. Done with simple lines and bright, primary colors, the pictures are designed to catch your eye. They appear to be inspired solely by the famous drawings of Mickey Mouse with, perhaps, a postmodern touch. This official poster of the Holy Year seems a singularly gauche effort—at least to my sensibilities.

I have heard that the existence or status of a shelter in Burgos is doubtful and unknown. So, when I arrive at the cathedral, I decide to start asking there. This church, Santa María la Mayor, is regarded as one of the great examples of Spanish Gothic architecture, and the number of shops in the immediate area selling post cards and souvenirs testifies to intense tourist interest. I enter, find a priest walking along a kind of corridor, and ask him about the *refugio*. He is uncertain; he thinks maybe a new one is being built; the old one was in the major seminary; they might know more about it. He adds that this seminary is only several blocks away.

I have no trouble finding the place, an enormous gray building sitting on a hill. It's probably no more than twenty or thirty years old, but it will only become more dull and undistinguished with age; very much like those apartment houses in Estella. How could Spaniards design and put up such ugly buildings? I thought the Church had some kind of reputation as a patron of the arts. The only highlight marking this structure is its size—and that was badly calculated. I can see that almost all the windows (one for every student's room, I guess) are tightly closed up with those shutters that slide down out of the wall. Obviously, very few seminarians are living here.

I enter the huge lobby and find a doorman in a room at one side. I ask if there is a *refugio* here. He hesitates, then speaks, but his manner is quite uncertain and somewhat apologetic. He agrees, though, to show me the facility. We walk down a hall on this, the ground floor, and he opens a door that reveals a large, gymnasium-like room, dark and apparently empty. The man then leads me farther along the hall to a bathroom, where I find a toilet and two sinks, but no shower. I thank him and he returns to his post.

First, I must do laundry, since I could do none yesterday, and there is a good sun today. The sinks are suitable for this, and the lack of hot water is no hindrance. Returning to the gymnasium—it could only have been that—I am able to pry open one of the shutters; the others are all rusted shut. They haven't been opened in a *long* time. Looking out, I see a large courtyard, with two wings of this enormous building, on my right and my left. All observable windows have their shutters tightly closed; the rooms are most probably not being used. Putting a chair under the high window, I am able to reach the sill and climb up. I take the chair with me to get down on the outside. There, I tie my clothesline between a metal pole in the yard and the window shutter. With the washed clothes hung up in the bright afternoon sun, the task is completed.

Now that I've let some light in the room, I look around and discover a stack of foam mattresses in one corner, and a few more chairs. The mattress covers are quite greasy and dirty, but that will not interfere with my sleeping bag. I can easily understand why the man acted as he did—he was probably deeply embarrassed by what he had to offer this foreigner.

Heading out to look for food, I stop to thank the doorman and tell him that all is really fine—which is the truth—the seminary offers all the essentials. I ask him about stamping my *credencial,* and he tells me that the rector has the stamp. He is out, but is expected back later in the day. I ask him about places to buy food, and he recommends a nearby bar where, he says, I can eat quite cheaply. Markets here seem to be closed on Sunday.

The bar is only two or three blocks away, and a kind of plate lunch is good and very reasonable. While waiting for my order, I notice that the day's newspaper has a story on Compostela, so I read this while I eat. The director of UNESCO was at the University of Compostela to receive an honorary doctorate. In his acceptance speech, he says that the *camino* may be declared a *patrimonio de la Humanidad*—whatever that means. On October 27, 1987, the *camino* was already declared the *primer itine-rario cultural europeo—un patrimonio histórico, literario, musical y artís-tico* —the first European cultural itinerary—a historic, literary, musical, and artistic patrimony. The story seems to imply that some high-level trading was taking place in Compostela. But the director was not yet at liberty to say that the deal had been closed. He goes on to claim that the *camino* is related to the *conservación de la naturaleza* (conservation of nature). But he doesn't elaborate on the statement. The writer of the story adds that the French government has asked that its portion of the *camino* be included in any such declaration, for this, too, is *un sitio cul-tural y natural transnacional* (a cultural and natural transnational site).

I was saddened by what appeared to be an invasion of the *camino* by these latter-day Philistines—modern carpetbaggers. How many of them have crossed its mountains? How many of them have sought to learn its secrets, not in elegant social salons, but out there in its rich solitude? How many of them have arrived at a *refugio* wet, cold, wracked by pain and exhaustion, yet buoyantly happy to be there, to have accompanied the pilgrims of old for a few more kilometers, to have walked into the darkness of the *camino,* through the *naturaleza,* yes, but reaching be-yond? It appears that the academic and political opportunities of the *camino* are increasing. Perhaps next I'll read that the *camino* is now nec-essary for the ecological salvation of Europe. After all, it worked so well in the past for the religious, social, and political salvation of Spain. I was reminded of the official mascot, the updated Mickey Mouse pilgrim seen all over Spain this year—the trivialization of the hopes of so many, of those who sought Santiago, and of those who sought to rob innocent pilgrims.

I have heard a good story, from the fifteenth century, of how a pilgrim, reversing the more common drama, tricked a tavernkeeper here in Burgos. Coming into the room, the pilgrim said to the woman behind the bar, "Miss, could you put one measure of wine in the cup, and I'll take it to my companion who is just outside the door, watching his horse? And by the way, could you keep an eye on my staff?"—leaving his pilgrim stick there against the bar as a kind of pledge. Going out the door with the tavern's silver cup, he was never seen again! Paradoxically, the story is placed in Burgos, the city of the *camino* best known for its generous treatment of pilgrims.

I walk the block or two to the cathedral, and am able to assist at Mass there. Today's Rosary, out on the *camino,* was a quiet seeking, a further venture into belief, a further grasping of the Mysteries.

It's a warm, sunny afternoon. I pass an ancient stone arch and find a promenade that appears to run a great distance through the center of town. I should, perhaps, walk it, but that looks like too much further exercise. It is filled with trees, bushes sculptured into various shapes, flowers, grass, and wide walks. The people of Burgos must be proud of such beauty running through their city. I find a sidewalk café imme-diately—the one I have been dreaming about! The coffee costs 200 pesetas, while the substantial lunch cost only 500 pesetas. Well, I must expect to pay for a stylish coffee shop in such a prime location. A steady crowd of well-dressed citizens strolls by, all out to enjoy the warm spring day.

Two young men at a neighboring table greet me, and we begin to talk. One of them is a recently ordained priest, the member of a new congrega-tion, which has only about six or seven persons so far. Somehow the conversation gets off into a discussion of modern technology, about which the young man is most enthusiastic, while I am skeptical and criti-cal. I cannot help musing . . . Ignatius started with only a handful of men. Are this man and his group in that same heroic tradition?

They leave, and my thoughts turn to Burgos, which, from here, looks like a most attractive urban space. The city was founded around 884 and, historically, was reputed to be the principal city of the *camino.* There are a number of secondary reasons for this reputation (for example, two sep-arate roads from France met here, the one I am taking and the one that comes down from Bayonne), but the really important one is its tradition of hospitality toward pilgrims. Early in the growth of the *camino,* kings of Castille—with their court here at that time—started building and endow-ing *hospitales* for pilgrims. For centuries the most famous of these—and one known all over Europe—was the Hospital del Rey, founded in 1195 by Alfonso VIII. It was thought to be the best place for pilgrims to stop be-cause of its organization, its income, the royal prestige attached to it, and its services—material and spiritual—for pilgrims. In the sixteenth century, there were confessor-chaplains there who could speak the languages of all European pilgrims. Records attest to the quantity and quality of food and wine given to the travelers. It continued to function until the nineteenth century, and the buildings—now much changed—still stand today, housing a law school.

Other kings, individuals, and religious orders also established *hospitales*. In the fifteenth century, a German pilgrim, Hermann Künig von Vach, in his guidebook for Germans, noted that he had counted thirty-two places to stay. But not all these would have been large. Nevertheless, the city had only about ten thousand inhabitants then. Many documents refer to it as the city of hospitality, par excellence—which helps me to understand the chagrin of the unfortunate doorman when he led me to that dark and deserted gymnasium.

Some authors believe that the greatest attraction in Burgos, drawing pilgrims here, is a crucifix with corpus, El Santo Cristo, in a chapel attached to the church and monastery of the Augustinians. One tradition holds that it was made by Nicodemus of the New Testament. Sometime in the late Middle Ages, a merchant found the crucifix in a box floating in the sea, and gave it to this monastery as a gift. A French pilgrim who stopped to see the cross in the seventeenth century, Mme. d'Aulnoy, wrote that more than a hundred lamps lighted the chapel where the image was kept, some made of silver, others of gold. She also counted sixty silver candlesticks, higher than a tall man and so heavy that two or three workers would be needed to move them. The chapel was also filled with offerings and ex-votos. A life-size figure of the Crucified was on an altar, behind three curtains whose borders were covered with pearls and precious stones. To Mme. d'Aulnoy, the corpus gave the appearance of real flesh. The friars had assured her that it sweat blood every Friday. Laffi also stopped here in the seventeenth century, and registered the powerful impact of the crucifix on him: "[T]his holy image would move even the stones to compassion, if they were capable of such feeling."

In the eighteenth century, a French pilgrim, much more skeptical, also visited the chapel. He calls the friars Dominicans, an obvious mistake, since all the other documents clearly state that this was the Augustinian foundation in the city. Otherwise, his account is similar to that of his more pious fellow countrywoman, Mme. d'Aulnoy, some twenty-five years earlier. He records that the Spanish believe the image responsible for many miracles but, to this pilgrim, the greatest miracle is the wealth of this monastery. Revealing his feelings about the place, he states that the friars are huge, indeed fat, and very ignorant, for they hardly know a word of Latin.

Also in the eighteenth century, another French pilgrim, Guillermo Manier, after looking at El Santo Cristo, records what the friars told him: that the body sweats blood, that they must trim the beard once a week and occasionally cut the nails on fingers and toes. He mentions that this is also required with another famous crucifix in Galicia.

I suppose that many modern persons, reading these reports, would be inclined to accept the debunking Frenchman's as the most appropriate, the most sensible. And postmodern folk might be intrigued by the possibilities: the contrast between a bloody corpse and the curtain of pearls and jewels; between the behavior of Nicodemus, who came to the Lord at night, the dimly lit chapel, and the words of Christ, "I am the light of the world" (John 8:12). But I wonder if a truly *sensible* path to people's devoted pilgrimage to this place, to this image and its stories, is not *their* sense of a truth to be felt here, the truth of the Incarnation. If they believed that God really took on flesh, that their contact with this reality is, ultimately, their only *camino* (way) to God and to their happiness, that is, their salvation. And, being honestly aware of their weaknesses, natural laziness, and disinclination to seek the difficult, what could be more fitting than that an all-loving God, taking pity on them, would make possible this perhaps unusual but certainly sensible evidence of his love for them? The accounts that I have seen are testimonies to *faith,* not visions of "supernatural" spectacles.

The two French pilgrims cited above say that they *heard* about the sweating of blood, the necessity of trimming a beard; they do not claim to have *seen* these things—they took them on faith, perhaps naively. When Queen Isabella visits the chapel, she expresses a wish to have one of the nails holding a hand to the cross—she wants to carry off a pious relic. (Several places in Europe claimed to have the actual nails that held Christ to the cross.) Since she is the queen, it is not possible to deny her request. But when the nail is pulled out, she thinks she sees the arm fall naturally, as if it belonged to a person, not a statue, and faints. El Gran Capitán Gonzalo Fernández de Córdoba, helping her recover, then steps back, overcome with fear, and blurts out, "We don't want to tempt God." They ask that the nail be replaced in the image's hand. Various reports have recorded the awe that people felt in the presence of this crucifix. It may be emblematic of the *camino* itself. A holy object arrives mysteriously by sea . . . someone testifies to its authenticity . . . various persons, or groups, organize the visit of pilgrims . . . some pious fraud may be promoted, enriching certain unscrupulous persons . . . and yet, beyond any improbability of the legend, apart from any willful deception by enterprising entrepreneurs, there lies a truth, a truth accessible only by faith. The pure mystery of faith, like the simplicity of God, can only be approached through multiplicity, complexity, and perhaps when men and women are involved, through the shadows of duplicity, too.

Late in the afternoon, I return to the seminary and learn that the rector is visiting his mother and will not return until tomorrow morning. From my experiences here in Burgos, I think that I had better figure out some way to get the *credencial* stamped tonight, and not hope to find this man in the morning. Fortunately, the cathedral is only three or four blocks away, so I head back there again.

I learn that the sacristan, who has access to the stamp, is assisting some visiting prelate who is saying Mass for a special group. I have only to sit down and wait. I suppose that there is no real need to be so solicitous about getting the stamp in *every* place, but now I look on it as a kind of game or puzzle—to fill in all the squares, and I have decided that I will continue to get the document stamped only in those places where I sleep, so that I will have an exact record for myself. The rubber stamps, each a unique design—and each obtained differently—make up an interesting story in themselves, at least for me.

When I return to the *refugio,* I check on the time the door will be open in the morning—so I can get out—and retrieve my dry laundry. In the toilet, I notice that the doorman has placed about half a dozen rolls of toilet paper. He is probably acting to the limits of his powers to make us comfortable. I wish there were some way I could tell him how grateful I am to have this much shelter, for it is all I need tonight. The excellent lunch and leisurely coffee nicely took care of all my physical and aesthetic needs while I'm in the city.

There is a large sign outside the door to our dormitory, *warning* all pilgrims to stay on this floor alone, since all the floors above are occupied. I wonder with what? I have seen only three or four young men around here today, and only a few windows have the shutters open, indicating that someone is using those rooms. Inside the gymnasium, I greet the three or four other pilgrims who have arrived and arranged a place on the floor to sleep. We few seem lost in the vast space of the room.

Before I left Germany, I imagined that I would often be sleeping on the floor, not having any clear idea what the *camino* is like. But this is the first night that has happened—in *the* city of hospitality, par excellence!

As I get into my sleeping bag, I hear singing; I listen . . . men's voices. They're singing a hymn, and then there is a chant, probably some Psalms. What is this and where does it come from? Finally, I can hear enough to identify the sound as that of a group of men singing night prayers. And it comes from immediately overhead. The seminarians must have their chapel above this gymnasium. I can just barely hear them—the strong, gentle voices of prayer, the final joyful yet sad celebration of the day—a community raising its voice to God. What a magnificent scene it must be! . . . but it comes to me from a great distance, only through the thick ceiling of protective insulation. No one invited us . . . strange people. Are these the future priests of Spain?

14

Burgos to
Granja de Sambol

May 17, 1993

I have no trouble getting out of Burgos, and am soon in the open country again, surrounded by the enormous circle of the horizon. I move, and my world moves with me, a constant and caring companion. The day begins cool and clear, but then clouds slowly advance to cover the sky. My eyes go from ground to sky and back, continually. But the effect on me varies greatly. I can control, somewhat, where my foot strikes the earth—for example, avoiding a sharp-looking rock—but I can do nothing about the sky. And yet I seem to look in both directions with the same sense of interest—as if what I see will then influence my behavior. But so far, the sky is only a continually changing panorama, an always interesting canopy under which I move.

For some kilometers, I walk across what seems to be a *mesa*—a flat surface, high, maybe the top of a mountain. Up here I feel that I am in another world, as if walking across the top of a different planet. The horizon is not the same as when I am "down on the ground." I wonder . . . is there some "explanation" for this? . . . Odd, almost all the land on which I step is new to me; I have never walked through a mountainous country; and the most unusual experience of physical space turns out to be the most familiar because experienced once before, many years ago.

I was in Bolivia in the 1960s, visiting a friend, and he drove me from La

Paz to Cochabamba in his jeep. This meant traveling a long distance across the barren Altiplano before dropping down to the rich farmland around Cochabamba. I could see nothing in that forbidding and somber landscape that looked familiar or friendly to me. I doubted that the strangely dressed beings who stared at us with dark, inscrutable eyes as we passed were anyone I could sit down with and share a joke or discuss literature. And yet, my friend and I, both U.S. priests living and working in Latin America, believed that we could avoid the arrogance of a socio-religious hubris and bring these people *both* the Gospel and socioeco-nomic "development." Was this naïveté? stupidity? vanity?—no doubt, some incomprehensible combination. Shortly after, I walked away from the question; I married and took up academic life.

The flatness ends, and I start down what appears to be a long and gradual descent. At that moment, I see five or six large birds, slowly cir-cling high in the sky, just in front of me. I have only to raise my eyes slightly to see them. Continuing my descent, I look up—they're still there, seeming to float in large circles. Then, suddenly, I remember. I've seen such birds before. They're buzzards! I'm sure of it. Are they waiting for me? I laugh . . . "You're too early in the day." I still feel quite fresh, still in great shape after a good night's sleep. Unless they know something I don't . . .

Now I can see another horizon, one that somehow appears more real or more natural, more of *this* world. The horizon of the *mesa,* seen from up there, appeared rather otherworldly. Sometimes, looking up at a far hori-zon, the distance seems endless; it doesn't seem possible that there could be a destination out there, unseen. It's as if I can see as far as there is to see, and there is nothing there, except for an ever-changing landscape, differently colored fields, rises, sometimes amounting to mountains and, often, villages—on the right, on the left, ahead. If I look back, a similar scene greets me. It does not seem possible that, some hours earlier, there was a place back there—today, a large place—from which I started. Only a few minutes after I left Burgos, I could see no traces of it; it had been swallowed up.

This view of the world from the feet is truly unique. The pace at which I move, the time I have to see, the attention of my body to the space in which it breathes—all lead me to believe that this way of experiencing the world has an elementary quality to it; it is somehow basic to any experience—of the world and of all I might find there. Being out here is, quite literally, a preparation for experience.

As I look out at a really distant horizon, I find it hard to believe that somewhere out there I will reach a destination. I can see so far—and there is no village in front of me yet—that I will surely never traverse that space. When I see a village on the right or the left, at maybe five or ten kilometers, I am tempted to set out for it. I know it's there; I know I can walk that far. And it looks interesting. I imagine that the *camino* really goes through it. And I see nothing ahead, in the direction the arrows point.

Each day, however, I have reached my destination. Sometimes, as I reach the top of a hill, I suddenly see it there, just below me when, five minutes earlier, I had despaired of reaching any *refugio* that day. So here, too, I live in a kind of faith, a belief that the destination will be within my physical limits. Perhaps this experience of limits is very good, especially today, when so many seem not to regard the reality of limits as important. Perhaps this terrible vanity is related to people's lack of experience of limits. There are so many ways to prop up a tired body, to excite crippled senses, to explore unreal worlds, to relieve the ever-recurring ennui. Each day, the place from which I start has a pleasant solidity; the space through which I walk is directly sensed in all its continual variety; the place at which I arrive is within the limits of a man's strength. And although it's only twenty or thirty kilometers from where I started, it's a genuinely *new* place; I've come to some *place.*

This sensation is always reinforced by the fact that each *refugio* has been so different, as has been each village or town; and so, also, with the country through which the *camino* passes. I have seen no "typical" Spanish place.

I suspect that I have never before experienced this kind of space; my sensibilities have been dulled by spending so much time in modern, often undifferentiated space. Modern space is man-made, created with a view always to be familiar, but with some slight variation oriented toward something called "progress." This year's shopping malls, automobiles, planned towns are always recognizable, but they appear more up-to-date somehow than last year's. In the more modern sectors of the cities of the world—at least in all those I have visited—I always find similar spaces, but their similarity is derived from the fact that they copy the same functional space of other cities. Here on the *camino,* the differences—from moment to moment—are never threatening, always interesting and sometimes exciting. Except for the highways and some city streets, spaces seem to have grown into their shape rather than to have been planned. Everything then seems to be itself, not something else, not a copy; there is no confusion through uniformity.

The daily experience of never knowing what kind of space I will go through that day—whether I'll be soaked by rain or burned by sun; climb new mountains or wind around strange kinds of cultivated fields; meet one person, many, or no one—is something I have never known. I would have thought that this would induce some fear or anxiety. Rather, I find that I am eager to stride out into the unknown anew each morning. What *is* happening to me? Perhaps I am learning something about the rich possibilities of adventure within definite limits.

Shortly after noon, I reach Hornillos del Camino, a village about twenty kilometers from Burgos. My map indicates a *refugio* here. The houses and buildings are clustered along the *camino* itself, here becoming La Calle Real, the single street of the village. Where the houses end, I find the shelter, the town *fuente* nearby, with good, spring water; and a small church. It appears that the entire church building has been beautifully restored, but it is locked and I can only see the outside. I walk across the street to the *refugio*—a very small, one-room building with no windows. There is an opening to enter, but no door to close. The floor is hidden beneath a generous coating of dried mud. In one corner, there is enough dirty straw on which to sleep. And that's it. This is certainly the most minimal shelter I've seen so far, and it would probably provide protection from rain. But it's early in the day, and one of the pilgrims in Burgos said that his map, newer than mine, showed a new *refugio* being constructed at a *fuente* about five or six kilometers beyond the town. It may be that the people of the village are building that one to replace this one, and it might possibly be finished. I haven't met anyone in the village whom I could ask, but decide nevertheless to continue walking. Yesterday's paper predicted rain, and the sky is darkly overcast, but I feel fine, ready to step over more ground today.

As I get into the country again, I shiver, struck by a cold, piercing wind. I don't have any extra clothing except for an old sweatshirt, a tissue-thin windbreaker, and the poncho. I thought it would be much warmer in Spain by this time of the year, but no matter. By keeping the sweatshirt dry and walking briskly, I've been comfortable enough. And the hills are not too steep today; I can maintain a good pace.

A few minutes after losing sight of the village, the rain starts. Today, it's a more serious matter—a real deluge with a fierce wind driving it directly into my face. Happily, I was able to get the poncho over me before it started, and decide to keep going forward. After all, it's only five or six kilometers. Surely I can make that . . . and the buzzards disappeared some hours ago. I can't believe that they had any symbolic importance or power.

It was right along here, in the seventeenth century, that Laffi came upon, or was hit by, a swarm of locusts. They formed such a cloud that they completely darkened the sky, and were a considerable annoyance. I have heard and seen different kinds of locusts, but never in such numbers

that they darken the sky. What must they do to the land? Well, I'll probably not find out on this journey.

I meet no one along the road and, after what seems a very long time,
see a small sign: "Refugio—100 m.," with an arrow pointing to the left.
Soon I reach a crossroad or path and take it to the left. I see nothing, but
then the visibility is rather poor and I can't see very far anyway. After
climbing a gentle rise, I see some ruins on the right—only the stone
remains of what were walls. I seem to remember ruins in this area
marked on my map. But no *refugio* in sight. Continuing a few meters
farther, I see what looks like a building on the left. Getting closer, I can
discern a stone structure, with a large window on this side. When I'm
quite near, I see someone standing in the window. It must be the *refugio!*

Passing the building, I turn into a short drive, then find a kind of roofed
porch and a metal door on that side. As I get to the door, it opens and I
am invited inside. With cheers, four Spanish pilgrims, close to my age,
welcome me in out of the rain. I see that they have come in to eat their
lunch. Two of them look familiar from some other *refugio* back along the
camino. They have just finished eating, and offer me the leftovers: almost
a full tin of paté, a couple of sardines, a piece of cheese, and two oranges.
They tell me there is a good spring outside.

They are getting ready to push on to the next town, and strongly urge
me to accompany them. A news report has reached them from someplace: A very bad storm is moving in from the Atlantic. Staying out here
alone in the middle of the country is, in their opinion, an imprudent thing
to do. I'm not so young, they smilingly remind me. I'm wet, it will probably get colder, and I may come down with pneumonia. How could I reach
help? And how can I get dry and warm right now?

I see the buzzards before my eyes, slowly circling, patiently waiting . . .
but this place has already impressed me with a certain charm; it possesses a real attractiveness, and I suddenly feel very tired; I've had
enough of that driving rain for today. Buzzards or no buzzards, storm or
no storm, I decide to stay and take my chances. After all, it's not raining
in here . . . and who knows what tomorrow will bring?

I thank them for their solicitude, and tell them I'm resolved to stay here
for the night. I've got a good sleeping bag, it's dry, I'll be warm enough.
And the clothes will dry out during the night. I still have some bread, one
of the oranges, and a bit of cheese to eat in the morning. I'm certain that
I'll get along fine.

While this discussion was going on, two of them went outside where
they found some dry straw and wood. With this, they start a fire for me.
After this act of kindness, they shoulder their packs, wish me luck, and

set off into the rain. One of them, I notice, has canvas puttees or leggings over his trousers. What an excellent protection from the rain . . . for that is precisely where I'm always soaked: my lower pant legs.

I look around my shelter for the night—a simple stone building, two rooms, only recently completed. This room appears square, about four or five meters across, opening to another rectangular room, somewhat larger. A built-in stone bench runs around three of the walls in this room, and there is a raised stone platform, about one meter in diameter, in the center. On this, the two men built the fire. The smoke rises straight up to an opening in the center of a stone, conical roof. I open the door a crack to create more of a draft so that the smoke goes out the hole. Nothing inside here except walls of stone and mortar, some large windows, and the door. The design is extremely austere, all the proportions and materials excellent. With the wind whistling outside, I feel comfortably immersed in a quietly dignified architectural space.

I put my wet shoes and socks near the fire and prepare to enjoy a peaceful evening in silence and solitude. If no one else appears, this will be my first night all alone in a *refugio,* and a very new one, too. There is nothing to indicate anyone has stayed here before; maybe I'm the first guest. What good fortune to have found such an unostentatious yet graceful room in the midst of the storm—with a fire to dry and warm me. No such comfort was available in the more conventional shelters.

When the rain slackens, I step outside to look around. There is a small grove of trees behind the building, an iron park bench, a picnic table and an outdoor fireplace. Next to this I see a large covered box for wood. This is where the men found the straw and dry logs. So, the people who built this place immediately left it provisioned with the one thing I need. Curious, because no wood is used in the construction itself. I pick up a couple of pieces, not completely dry. I can place them next to the fire to get them ready to burn. Down near the trees, a fountain has been made to direct and collect the spring water. Bits of fallen, dried mortar on the ground indicate, too, that the basic structure is only recently finished. On a sunny day, the entire setting would be most pleasing, but today it's dark, wet, and gloomy. Back inside to the warm fire.

The image of dancing flames. How good it feels, how fascinating it appears. One can sit and watch the ever moving shapes and ever changing light for hours. But, before today, I've never actually done it. Some years ago, when I saw our young son sit silently before an open fire in our house for long periods of time, I used to wonder about his behavior. Was he just wasting time? We had abandoned my tenured university position and were attempting to live a life of subsistence. Building a house, growing our own food, moving away from conventional economic illusions and practices, sometimes inclined me to look askance at "unproductive" activities. I believed that we were recovering more venerable modes of living. Some of the ancients thought that there are four basic elements: earth, air, water, and fire. The tradition, at least in the West, is so old and well established that there must be some important truth in it, a truth that my nine-year-old son intuitively knew, and that I can suspect from the way in which the flames hold and charm me tonight. Only now do I begin to experience what my son could have introduced me to years ago by his unspoken example.

Tonight, perhaps, I'm completing a new stage in my introduction to the experience of the elements. On the *camino,* I've come to an intimate awareness of the earth, the air, and water. The soil powerfully presses itself into me with every step; the air fills my lungs with fresh life in every breath; the pure, sparkling water of the springs continually revives my spirit. Now I've come to know anew Brother Fire, now I have the hours to let the mesmerizing shapes and colors of the flames satisfy my innate craving for variety. Strange . . . the crazy, destructive ways in which so many seek to quiet this longing, with continually new things, persons, sights. One has only to sit alone, in silence, with perhaps a fierce wind, storming outside, resting one's eyes on the bright and vibrant flames.

Once when a number of us had gathered at a friend's house for a discussion, the talk ran into the evening. As the room darkened, my friend went around lighting candles. No lights were ever switched on and I felt, at the time, that the candlelight gave a special tone and character to our conversation. Something very different occurred there that evening than would have happened with electric lights, no matter how well designed or engineered they might be to create a certain effect.

As I learned when crossing the Pacific, one cannot rush; one must take time. Then, I was on a troop ship that took thirty days to sail from San Diego to northern China, with stops in Hawaii, Guam, the Philippines, and Shanghai. There was nothing to do on the ship during these days except read books—and watch the sea. I found myself standing at the rail, at all hours, in all kinds of weather, gazing at the sea. I never tired of that restful yet alert looking. In fact, the ship reached its final port all too quickly. The elements do not reveal their secrets to quick glances, to distracted busy-people.

Now, on the *camino,* I feel that I move each day into a new experience of earth and air. The earth enters through my feet but reaches into every possible nerve in my body by causing tiredness and pain. I am coming to know the *power* of this contact. And I feel that I have an unmediated experience of the air. It seems that the air and I are alone out there on the *camino;* I am always aware of its coldness or warmth, dryness, or wetness. And although I know it is true what Gandhi says, namely, that whatever it is that the air can bring to you, you will receive it much better if your body is uncovered, yet this isn't the climate for *that* exact experience!

I sometimes think that I am out here on the *camino* because of meeting Gandhi in India. Invited there to participate in a conference on economics in the light of Gandhi's life and writings, I lived with some elderly followers of the Mahatma in Wardha, where the great man had established an ashram. For a month, I sat on a mat with these men and some younger women, while they chanted their prayers each day. For a week, while we were at the ashram, I sat in Gandhi's hut—still preserved as he left it— early each morning for a couple of hours in silence. Hearing the strange voices of that hut I realized that I indeed needed to listen, but to the more familiar voices of *my* tradition. The powerful *foreign* quality of what I heard there moved me to understand that I needed to put myself in that kind of silence, but among my own ancestors, among those out of whose loins I have come.

All these people, it is now clear to me, were, above all, people of faith. Beginning with my parents, and going back to the apparently unknown ghosts who walk with me today, I can only feel gratitude, not that I am not a Hindu, but that I, too, like Gandhi, belong to a faith tradition. I, too, derive my strength and direction and (I hope) my character, from this tradition. It is here, on this *camino,* that I have come to meet, to face, all these people and, thus, to learn from them.

I treasure my solitude, but I wish I could share the warmth and glow of the fire with someone else. It seems that I'm selfishly consuming a lot of wood. But I think that I'm now dry enough not to need more tonight. I can leave some for the next pilgrim caught here on a cold, wet night. The shoes feel almost dry, and the embers will finish that job before morning. I can now trust the sleeping bag to keep me warm. Outside, the wind howls, the rain spatters in gusts against the windows. Maybe some kind of storm has indeed arrived from the Atlantic.

I am certainly in a very different place than I was twenty-four hours ago! There, sitting alongside all the flowers, warmed by the sun, watching the Sunday strollers, thoroughly enjoying my coffee—here, enveloped in the darkness, somewhere on an unseen and unknown hillside, with the elements furiously raging outside, surrounded and protected by the sober simplicity of stone. Another wonderfully unique day that I shall never forget.

15

Granja de Sambol to Castrojeriz

May 18, 1993

Since there are no lights in the shelter, I climbed into my sleeping bag early last night. This morning, I awoke in the dark, feeling marvelously rested, as usual. For the first time, I had unrolled the thin plastic pad and put it down between the rock shelf and the sleeping bag. That seemed to be just enough mattress to provide a comfortable bed. Each night I roll up the sweatshirt for a pillow. But that might be a good item to carry along—a small foam pillow.

With my flashlight, I can see to eat breakfast and gather my things together. As soon as there is enough light to see rocks in the path—to avoid the sharp ones and to spot the ones with a painted arrow—I start out. It is still raining, but the wind has moved on to other fields or mountains.

I pass through several small villages. In one, an old lady tells me, "We'll get more rain this afternoon" (at that moment, the rain had just stopped). In another village, a farmer also predicts more rain later today. They want to prepare me for what is coming.

Making my way down and around a turn on a large hill—or small mountain—I suddenly come upon a village, lower down, about a kilometer farther ahead, in front of me. The path leads directly to and then around the village dump, incongruously located on a lovely level place overlooking the houses and buildings below. It looks to me like the perfect site to build one's home. Instead, it is a dumping ground dominated by large, worn-out, or damaged things like old stoves, farm machinery, and various kinds of building materials. Stopping a moment to see what people throw away, I am shocked to see five or six wooden farm carts, all apparently in usable condition, but now abandoned here in the company of broken plastic shelves and bathroom fixtures. These two-wheeled carts, with thin iron rims on the outside of the wheels, made to be pulled by one animal—an ox, donkey, or horse—are familiar to me. I have seen them before—exactly the same, handsome design—on various farms along the *camino*. Since I have seen them in widely separated places— and they most probably did not come from some central factory—many different people must have come to see that the engineering was excellent. Craftsmen in local shops would then make them.

But I have never seen one in use; all were parked near a farmer's buildings. And this is the first time I see them definitively consigned to the trash heap. From this and other small things I've picked up, I have the impression that Spanish farmers quite suddenly jumped from oxcart and horsepower farming to tractors and industrial agriculture. In Belorado, I had the good fortune to meet the shoemaker, a craftsman from an earlier world; here, I am stunned to see a discarded example of the superb work of that world. The craftsmen who made these sturdy carts are probably all dead—and their world along with them. All one can hope for now is that their splendid workmanship be recognized by some enterprising entrepreneur who retrieves their handwork from the village dump to grace the patio of his restaurant. But how could these farmers so casually and indiscriminately cast such artistry among the ugliness of modern plastic and rusting metal trash? I wonder what they felt when they pulled the carts up here for the last time. Does any thought disturb their memory when they pass them today? Have they missed having these workers and neighbors in their community? Have they asked what was lost with these carts?

A pilgrim who walked the *camino* in 1987, during the time of the wheat harvest, writes enthusiastically about the modernity of all the machines he sees. Everything looks so efficient, so progressive. He imagines that there is a series of mechanics stationed at strategic points in the countryside so that the machines can be serviced—for they must not be allowed to sit idle. All his focus is on the machines and their requirements. He does not seem to see the rural communities; he does not ask how the machines have affected them.

For about two or three kilometers, I am on a one-lane asphalt road. I pass one of the new signs that I have seen before on highways: "Camino de Santiago." Each time I come to one, I cry out—loudly—"No! No! The *camino* is not for you people in cars"—shaking my pilgrim staff wildly at the sign. No one can hear me out here, but I feel that I must shout my protest. I assume that most drivers are going to some other destination, not to Compostela. But these signs tell them that they are on the *camino!* They are not. The *camino* is accessible only to those whose feet are on the ground. If you want to be on the *camino,* you must get out of your car, get your shoes muddy, get soaked with sweat, be cold and wet from the rain. You must arrive at the *refugio* tired; then you will experience the joys of the *camino.*

As he came along here in the seventeenth century, Laffi found that the earth was covered with those "accursed locusts." Next to the *camino,* he and his friend found a poor French pilgrim lying on the ground, covered with insects, dying.

> It appeared that God had guided us there to help the poor soul, for hardly had he finished making his confession when he died. Those voracious small beasts had already begun to feast on him.

Plagues and death come in very different forms today. Where Laffi physically sensed a scourge, I must only surmise from some impressive but strange ruins, the most prominent feature of which is a large arch through which the road and *camino* pass. This is what remains of a hospital and monastery of the Antonine Hospitallers. Founded in 1095 by a French nobleman, Gaston de Dauphiné, in Vienne, the order soon spread all over Europe. At some date between 1070 and 1095, Geilen (or Jocelin) had brought the relics of Saint Antony of Egypt to Vienne from Constantinople. Saint Antony (250–356), famous all over Europe because of a biography written by Athanasius in 357, is honored as one of the founders of monasticism, especially that form emphasizing eremitism. It was believed that Saint Antony had special power to cure ergotism, which was called "Saint Antony's fire." The Hospitallers were established to care for persons suffering from this disorder. In Spain, they erected over thirty hospitals. As I walk under the graceful arch, I pray that their spirit, which must remain here among these noble ruins, fill my heart with compassion for those who suffer from especially disfiguring diseases.

Because I started so early, and I've covered no more than about ten kilometers, I approach Castrojeriz at ten o'clock in the morning. The ruins of a castle are on a hill overlooking the town. This was an important fortification originally built in the ninth century. The Muslims stormed and conquered it in 882. After taking the place, they immediately left. A year later, the Christians were back, and strengthened the castle's defenses. The Moors seem to have initiated this kind of warfare, called a *razzia*. It was a sudden raid on a fortified place or town with the sole object of obtaining booty, which might include persons taken for ransom or as slaves.

The first invasion of Spain by the Moors in 711 was supposed to be a quick incursion, with an immediate return to North Africa. Apparently, the leaders were initially most interested in finding a way to keep the newly converted Berbers, whom they saw as tending toward undisciplined fanaticism, content and controlled. The motives for the *razzias* were not territorial conquest and religious aggrandizement. But the "pickings" were so plentiful and easy that first one Arab leader, Tarif, and then his superior, Musa, turned their Berber warriors into an occupying army. There is a story that Tarif—for whom Gibralter is named—after landing with his second expedition, burned his ships so that his North African tribesmen would be forced to follow him up the Peninsula. The story reminds one of the action of Cortés, doing the same thing at Vera Cruz, almost exactly seven hundred years later. When, after some years, Tarif and Musa returned to Damascus, the Berbers' caliph received them coldly, and they lived out their lives forgotten and in disgrace—the two men who began the establishment of a state that, within three hundred years, would be recognized as one of the most advanced in Europe.

In 1131, Alfonso VII conquered the castle of Castrojeriz, held at that time by the *aragoneses* (Aragonese). A contemporary document says that he took the castle, "sacándolo del yugo aragonés, como Cristo redimió del infierno a los pecadores"—rescuing it from the yoke of Aragon, as Christ saved sinners from hell. And so the castle passed from one "Christian" kingdom to another.

I have heard that there is a good *refugio* here in Castrojeriz, and decide that I will stop. I haven't had a shower for several days and those bad weather reports might mean something. In 1495, the monk, Hermann Künig, in his guide for German pilgrims, noted four *hospitales* here, and seven were still operating at the beginning of the nineteenth century. I start asking for directions as soon as I enter the town, for the streets appear more confusing than usual. Several times I stop people to get more information, and then find the shelter in an old building that has been converted into a kind of hostel. Fortunately for me, it is open. As I enter, the sun comes out brightly.

On the first floor, I find a hallway with windows on one side and cell-like rooms on the other; upstairs, a large dormitory. And there *is* hot water. In the back, I see a patio with clotheslines. I open and hang out the sleeping bag, since it smells of smoke. Quickly doing my laundry, I hurry to get it, too, out in the warm sun. The wet shoes will also get dry today.

In the far distance, I can see some dark and menacing clouds, so I'll have to watch. I can't allow the sleeping bag to get wet. Perhaps it's raining in those villages where the people predicted rain, but here the sun is warm and bright. Since the air is rather cool, I'm especially grateful for the sun. I think maybe my only "enemy" is the frequent rain. But I've gotten along with this enemy rather well. I've always managed to get dried out, and have never felt any ill effects from having been wet.

There is a sign asking pilgrims to help clean the place. But recent occupants seem to have ignored that. Since I'm here early, I set to work sweeping and scrubbing. Then, after a shower, I go in search of food. There are a small stove and utensils in the kitchen, so I can cook a hot dinner. After asking directions several times, I locate a produce store, but it has only fresh lettuce. I then discover a kind of supermarket that is just getting started and has only toothpaste, toilet paper, and such. In another place, some blocks away, I find only fresh cauliflower—and I can't possibly eat a whole one myself. I pass the meat market twice, even after getting directions, so small is its sign in a window of what appeared to me to be someone's dwelling. But in all this walking, I pass two places selling fresh fish. Since I don't feel competent to prepare fish, I pass up those opportunities. In the bakery, I buy whole wheat bread, and at a cheaper price than I have heretofore paid. Finally, I acquire enough items to prepare dinner. In my wanderings around town, I pass two very stylish restaurants but, happily, now have no need for them.

These towns have certainly not been arranged for the convenience of occasional visitors like myself. But the monuments are always marked, and I never fail to see a posh restaurant if, as here, there is one. The people who live here know exactly where everything is, as well as any idiosyncrasies of specific shopowners. They and the town have grown up together. If I'm willing to ask a few questions and do some walking, I can soon find out all I need to know—because of the never-failing courtesy of all the people I meet. The more confusing the city, the more friendly conversation I enjoy with the people. What a loss it would be if there were a neatly marked "business section" with signs pointing to it!

After I've cooked and eaten my dinner, I put on my warmest clothes— T-shirt, long-sleeved shirt, sweatshirt, light windbreaker, and black felt pilgrim hat—and head out again to look for a coffee shop. The sun is still shining and, wearing all my clothes, I'm nicely comfortable. I find the coffee down across from the store that had only fresh lettuce. As usual, it's very good. But I wonder . . . scruples again . . . is this too much self-indulgence? After all, I'm on a pilgrimage. And coffee may not be altogether fitting for such a project. Or, to stick with a more basic product, I could buy a liter of that nonrefrigerated milk and some instant coffee.

That way I could drink one large cup in the evening and one in the morning—since I can't carry milk with me. But that would only work when I found the combination of a market with milk and a shelter with a stove. Well, I'll think about it . . . perhaps I am being overly scrupulous.

In the towns, I have noticed offices or small buildings with a large "I" on them. And if I enter the town on a highway, a sign indicates that the place has that office—for information on the "Año Jacobeo" . . . the Holy Year is usually called by its secular name, which sounds rather strange in English: "The James Year." Castrojeriz, although a very small town, has one of these offices, so I stop in to see what they contain or offer. The most prominent object is a large video machine. One presses buttons, according to the kind of information wanted. This appears on the screen, in color, with sound.

A young woman is also here to answer questions. She has many posters, books, and pamphlets on various aspects of the government's promotional campaign. It's all presumably related to Santiago de Compostela and the *camino*. For each month of the year, there is a separate pamphlet listing all the special nationwide events for that period, the "Programación Cultural del Camino de Santiago." These include art shows, concerts, theater productions, lectures, and roundtable discussions. The music, art, and theater for the month I examined had nothing to do with Santiago. From their titles, the lectures were confined to safe cultural aspects of the *camino*, not designed to raise questions that might offend someone. As I've come to believe, however, the presence of Santiago in the history of Spain and in the hearts of those who seek to walk his *camino* is filled with questions demanding serious exploration.

The overall national program is under the direction of the Ministerio de Cultura. At times, I see references to the tourism office also. All the graphics I've seen are of the highest quality. And many different things have been printed. Friends in Germany have sent me stories from the travel sections of their newspapers, informing people of the Camino de Santiago and its special events this year. But I wonder about one of these. A detailed story appeared in *Die Zeit,* one of the principal papers of the country, in which it says that a pilgrim who walks to Compostela can, on arrival, show his *credencial* duly stamped, and thereby claim the ancient privilege of pilgrims: three days free in the *parador.* But the only *parador* in Compostela that I've heard about is the Reyes Católicos, a building put up by Ferdinand and Isabella as a *hospital* for pilgrims, now turned into a four- or five-star hotel. As I found with the *parador* in Santo Domingo de la Calzada, I don't have the clothes for such places. On the other hand, I fantasize about the meals they would offer me there.

I can't really figure out what all the promotion means. Is it anything more than a gimmick to increase tourism? Everything seems designed to have the broadest possible appeal, and I have seen nothing at all on the aspect of the *camino* that fascinates and draws me: the questions connected with faith—the character of my belief as a person moving through real space, reaching various places. So I don't see any of the government's efforts helping or even touching me. And I'm happy to see that the money has not been spent on the *camino*—at least, from what I can see—except for those young trees. If they helped to pay for painting the yellow arrows, I'm certainly grateful for that. And, as I've noted, these *refugios* need some money for establishment and maintenance. Although small, the new one in Granja de Sambol cost a lot of money to build. And it looks as if the hot water system here in Castrojeriz is new. Since no tourist office has interfered with the distances I have to walk between shelters, I can make no complaint about how the government chooses to spend its tax money.

In the late afternoon, a serious man comes with his record book and ink pad to check on the *refugio* and to stamp *credenciales.* He, like others I have met, seems to be a volunteer who offers his time to help with the operation of a *refugio.* There must be many people like this in Spain whom I shall never know—those who contribute time and money that I might enjoy a dry bed, hot water, and a gas stove.

Today, the Rosary again brought me to questions of faith. Each of the fifteen Mysteries, from the Joyful through the Sorrowful to the Glorious, reveals something about the Incarnation, which is the beginning, center, and end of my faith. But the question arises: To believe in the Incarnation, is it necessary to live an incarnate life? Must I live a sensual, fleshly life in order to believe? And, given the character of modern, urban life, how understand the question? One can make the argument that many today have little or no experience of a *sensual* life, a way of living that flows from the various senses' contact with their natural objects. Because of all the technical, mediating "enhancers," designed to improve on the eye, ear, nose, tongue, and skin, one can seriously argue that the senses are farther and farther removed from their ancient objects, the person then becoming more and more isolated in a technically produced solipsistic shell, desperately seeking some kind of escape through fixes like mood drugs and flights into virtual reality.

The farther I walk on the *camino,* the more sensitive my senses seem to become. They are getting true exercise, confronted directly at every moment by their real objects. And this experience of the flesh seems to me vastly different from what I have known through the machines of "health" clubs, or under the regimen of regular exercise in jogging and various forms of calisthenics. Teaching at a university, I looked forward to the twice-weekly meetings with a friend to play handball. But when we moved to the subsistence farm, the daily demands of labor—at times heavy, at times long—introduced me to a new, more complex, more satisfying experience of my body. From those years of good work, I know that my body fits historically older modes of movement better than fashionable or "scientific" exercises. The disembedding that Karl Polanyi studied and that I tried to reverse on my land has produced deleterious effects in areas other than economics.

On the *camino,* my flesh is certainly more immediate to me, perhaps more real. From the first day, I have had trouble with my left leg. The knee pained me terribly; once I developed a blister on the left foot; at times, there were unbearable pains in the heel; another day, an aching shinbone made me cry out in distress. But the right leg is always fine. No matter how awful the daily trudging out on the *camino,* I recover every night; each morning both legs feel ready to set out again. My left side, then, must be the *good* side, the one that teaches me I am flesh and blood, the one that may reveal to me the Mysteries of the Rosary, of my faith.

I've read somewhere that pain is a sign, a sign that one is alive. And pain is certainly universal. Everyone, at some time, in some form, knows pain. Perhaps it is a reminder of the reality of my flesh, of the *delicacy* of my flesh; I need to treat my flesh *well.*

This means to free it from the debilitating and dulling, corroding and corrupting, of the technical Sirens; Greek myth comes in modern garb. Thus the pain I often feel on the *camino* is a good, not a good to be sought, not a good to be enjoyed but, today, a necessary good that opens me to my flesh, to a sound belief in the goodness of the flesh—a belief that can only be reached through a direct, unmediated experience of myself.

Many of us have seen a crèche at Christmas and a crucifix during Holy Week. I now ask myself: What do I see? a plastic Jesus, or a fleshly Jesus? Some of the people who looked at that crucifix in Burgos claimed that it looked *like* flesh. Was theirs the vision I can hope to attain? Will my senses, through their purification and exercise on the *camino,* reach this kind of sensitivity?

16

Castrojeriz to Frómista

May 19, 1994

L ate yesterday, a few more pilgrims arrived at the *refugio,* including the two young Canadians still walking this part of the *camino.* But most of the late arrivals were on bicycles. Whenever there are walkers and bikers in a shelter, I've noticed a consistent division: Most of the people on foot are nearly my age. These two Canadians are the unusual exception. Most on bicycle—almost all of whom are Spaniards—are very much younger. I have met only one or two young Spanish men who are walking. This might have something to do with school vacations. The younger people may arrive only next month. But those on bicycles—and I have the impression that they are as numerous as the walkers—*are* young people, however, a bit older than students. I wonder if this indicates some historical break, like ox to tractor? The older people are still on their feet; the younger ones, on their machines. The older generation still enjoys the independence, the freedom, of its feet. I wonder . . . has the younger generation, now dependent on more and more technological props and distractions, lost the use of its feet?

All the bikers seem to have the latest equipment in bikes, clothes, and outdoor gear—all high-tech. Expensively caparisoned, they contrast sharply with the older people who, like me, seem to be wearing their "everyday" or work clothing. I can't help thinking that the young men, from the way they look and move, remind me of the stereotype, the yuppie. But I've never yet talked to them, except for the Dutchman in San Juan de Ortega, and he appeared to be quite different from the Spanish riders.

It is still cold this morning, so I put on all my clothes again, and venture out under an overcast sky. Since I and all my equipment are dry and in good shape, I have no worry about what the weather brings. The predicted storm must have been another weatherman's fancy. Or it took another route, missing my path.

I walk past some fields of grain and then see, directly in front of me, a mountain—but like none I have ever imagined or seen. It seems to rise straight up out of the ground before my eyes, like a solid wall. And it runs in a straight line, perpendicular to my path, from horizon to horizon. It appears to admit no pass; it must be climbed. Well, I'm much stronger than I was when I started. But I can't imagine how I could get up it; from this distance—about three or four kilometers—it appears that I would need an impossibly tall ladder.

The path continues, heading right for the mountain. When I reach the rocky bottom, I see that there is a trail that weaves back and forth, along the face of the mountain, sometimes quite steep, taking one up toward the top. Getting a firm grip on my staff, I start the ascent. And I have no trouble. I *am* stronger.

At the top, I find myself on a flat *mesa,* another of those otherworldly-feeling places. Almost immediately, I come to a small stone monument, a witness to the *camino,* perhaps to celebrate a successful climb. The *mesa* is not so very wide, and I am soon on the other side, descending from this height, getting back to earth and fields. But after what seems a short time, I face another mountain, higher than the first, but not going straight up. At the top there is a spring with fresh water, and a lot of recent construction. The area around the spring is paved with stone, new picnic tables are placed nearby, and a grove of young trees graces the whole site. Several gravel roads lead up to this place from the country in front of me. People may come up here from different villages for a picnic. Today, there is no sign of any human presence—only a vast emptiness reaching out to a distant horizon.

Walking now through hilly country, I feel a few drops of rain. When it looks as if it will continue, I stop and get out the poncho. Since it is designed to cover both me and the large backpack, I must look quite the misshapen monster when I walk under it. But this time, I can't get it to drop over both me and the pack. After each attempt, I have to take it back off over my head completely, try to fold it so that it falls easily, then toss it in the air over my head. But I can't get it to fall back far enough to come down covering the pack; it always catches on the top of it. Then I see the problem: the rolled-up plastic mat is tied across the top of the pack. It extends out so far on each side of me that the poncho will just barely come down over it. I need to tie this to the pack *vertically*—then there would be much more extra space, not such a tight fit for the poncho.

But the rain is falling harder, I'm getting very wet, there is no shelter in sight, and no time to take off the pack and rearrange the plastic mat. Beginning to feel more and more desperate, near panic, I try yet again, making all the motions slowly and carefully—and it finally falls all the way down in back. I can reach down between my legs, catch the back side and fasten it to the front with a flap—at about knee level. This prevents the wind from blowing the whole thing up over my head. I'm rather wet under the poncho, but I don't think enough rain fell on me to penetrate the pack.

The wind, which made the dropping of the poncho an acutely frustrating exercise, becomes more violent, pelting my face with hard rain. Then the mud turns into real mud, the kind that tenaciously sticks to my shoes, accumulating an ever increasing dead weight at the bottom of my legs. Every few steps, I stop to knock off some of the excess baggage with my staff . . . I've never been able to understand how armies could move through stuff like this . . . But, for me, it feels like another variation of my sense of what can occur between the soil and me. In a new way, the dirt forcefully asserts its reality, its "rights"—it's not something to be paved over and forgotten. And it compels me to make a very necessary and useful effort: The exercise of mind and muscle successfully holds the cold at bay—the exertion reaches all of me; I'm warm from skin to bone.

Approaching a village that must be near my planned destination, I see a large, new sign welcoming pilgrims. Its style and prominence, boasting the village's offer of a *refugio* to tired pilgrims, definitely tempt one to stop. This is the first such advertisement I've seen. Unable to resist this display of disinterested generosity, I decide to stop for a short respite from the rain. I wonder what hospitality stands behind such a sign.

Following the yellow arrows, I come upon no improvement under my feet—village mud clings to my shoes as stubbornly as country mud. The houses that I pass appear to be as modest and unadorned as the rudimentary village "street." My curiosity about these people's offer increases. Then, after a short walk, the houses disappear, and I'm in open country again, still facing a fierce wind. Stopping and looking around, I am puzzled until I can only conclude that the arrows directed me *around* the village, not through it. I've missed the *refugio*. Well, the place is small; it cannot take long to find the shelter. I turn toward a street that seems to lead *into* the village. Almost immediately, at about ten meters, three large and extremely vicious-looking mongrels confront me, barking and growling, daring me to take another step toward them.

This is not my first encounter with dogs; I have met many on the *camino*. Usually, however, they are fastened up with a stout chain or behind a heavy fence. They always bark, and act as if attacking me is their only desire. At those meetings, I grasp my staff with special firmness, and contemplate the ways in which I will swing it if the curs break loose. Since I have absolutely no experience hitting dogs with a stick, my plans are vague and incoherent. A pilgrim of 1987 was so impressed by the number and ferocity of the dogs that threatened and frightened him that he kept a count of them, and several times comments on their savagery. He calculated that about four hundred of these beasts leaped and snarled at him on the *camino*. At the end of his *relato,* he concludes that one must change the old adage: A dog is a man's best friend, to: A dog may be his owner's best friend. These dogs facing me are not chained, and they look extremely serious and determined. In an instant, I decide that I can dry out in Frómista. I turn and resume my struggle with the wind and mud.

As I had guessed, only a few kilometers lay between me and my goal for the day. Six or seven hours of determined walking, much of it a plodding tug-of-war between my feet and the mud, bring me to the edge of town. Almost at that exact moment, the rain ceases to fall and the sun pops out—brilliantly, gloriously! But it's still cool enough that I don't work up a good sweat. After a few questions, I learn that a woman in the center of town has a key for the *refugio*. When I get to her house, she graciously gives me the key, explains where the shelter is located and stamps my *credencial.*

The *refugio* is only about two blocks away, a pleasant building with bunks and hot water, but no kitchen. I wash out my socks, put them and the wet shoes in the sun, and go in search of food. I see a bakery directly across the street, buy my bread, and the man there directs me to a food market, another block or two away. I get a fresh slice of ham, frozen vegetables, bananas, luscious-looking strawberries, and yogurt. Thinking that I would enjoy offering some wine to other pilgrims who, I feel certain, will arrive later, I look over the wine stock. The store is small and has only about a half dozen bottles, all rather expensive. At the cash register, I ask the young woman if there is any wine that is *más corriente*—more common; that is, not so special. She answers yes, and points to some I had not seen. This wine is in one-liter paper cartons, like milk—something novel for me. I pick one up, feeling a bit dubious about the packaging, and ask her, "How is it?" She passively shrugs her shoulders and laconically answers, "Corriente," as if to say, "What did you expect?"

In front of the *refugio,* there is a plaza about twenty meters square, with a border planted in grass and a variety of small trees. Four or five park benches are placed around the edge on the tiles. Happily, one is in the sun: the ideal place to rest and eat my lunch. What a pity that no one is here to enjoy this setting with me—about a block from the main street, only occasionally does a car pass. No one walks by; I'll have to take up all the attractiveness and warmth into myself—for all those who are not here. I suppose the townspeople are at home, eating their lunch.

Two little girls and a younger boy come by to play. They have a long elastic loop, fasten it to a bench at one end, and put the other end around one child's body. Then the girl who is free jumps in and out of the loop, performing a great variety of maneuvers—more than I could have imagined possible. Finally, she holds the loop and the other girl has her chance to perform. The first one is much superior, and I see that this game, requiring nothing except a kind of long rubber band, could keep two children busy for hours, developing their skills in all the possible variations of jumping. And I could watch for hours! Their ingenuity and grace completely absorb my attention. But I can't figure out the place of the younger boy. He never asks to play; he only watches. Does he not know how? Is this only a girl's game? Or is it today the game only of these two girls? I could ask them, but they might be frightened by a stranger speaking to them. After maybe an hour, an adult from across the street calls them home. This seems an amazingly apt game for young bodies, much more elaborate and challenging than the "jump the rope" I know, but needing no more equipment. It would only work, though, with a partner.

I notice several palm trees. That means that the winters here are not severe. What would it be like to walk the *camino* in winter? If I had the proper clothing, it might be an even more exciting adventure than walking in the spring. Although the air would be colder, there might actually be more sun. The high mountain passes would present some difficulties; I've seen photographs where everything is covered with snow. But this is truly fantasy. I'm not yet halfway to Compostela, and I dream of repeating the entire *camino!*

The town glories in an outstanding example of Romanesque architecture, the church of San Martín. This building is all that remains of a monastery founded in 1066 by Doña Mayor, the condesa de Castilla and widow of the king, Sancho III el Mayor. This foundation, an example of a pattern prevailing at the time, is not easy to interpret or understand. Over and over, one sees that the secular rulers took the initiative for ecclesiastical and monastic reform, which, of course, indicates that they were not secular authorities as one understands that today. The monastery of Frómista was also part of the royal effort to repopulate the region after it had been recovered from the Moors and secured in the tenth century.

Sitting here, not far from this church, I think I see a curious and significant historical progression. The original *place* of the Lord was Palestine. This was the physical niche chosen by the Word to dwell on earth, to walk among a colonized, subject people. This locale thus became the Holy Land, the place where one could touch whatever remains He left behind after the Ascension. Pious people traveled there; Christian pilgrimage began there.

Preachers from the Christian community journeyed far from that place to tell all people the Good News. This message of hope was not to be confined to any ethnic group or exclusivist sect. Very soon, the leaders also attempted to establish a new and singular center, Rome. Rome came to be a place of authority over the individual communities scattered around the Mediterranean world. The tombs of the principal apostles, Peter and Paul, were there. Through many events and complex processes, people believed that this was a special place from which the Word's continuing presence on earth emanated. Hence, pilgrims soon accepted the city as a place of power, and it became the object of ritual journeys, pilgrimages. But this center suffered many vicissitudes, an important one being the final break with the Eastern churches in 1054, a cleavage continuing until today. This situation brings into relief several questions: What is the character of a community's center after such a break? Can a community then conceive of its center differently? Since this community began with an Incarnation, what are the physical sources of such questions about a center?

These questions were answered, not by a group of dissidents or new leaders, but by people at the far western extreme of the Mediterranean, two centuries before the break between East and West. On a narrow ribbon of mountainous territory between Islamic al-Andalus and the Atlantic Ocean, the ordinary people of the faith community created a new center in Compostela through the action of pilgrimage. Believing to have found the body of Saint James the Greater in Galicia, countless people from all over Europe walked to the edge of the continent, to the site of yet another epiphany, actively participating in its reality. A new dimension in the historical expression of faith was revealed. People from all social sectors, in unprecedented numbers, braved every kind of hardship and obstacle on the *camino,* bearing silent witness to the substance of their faith by their feet. For the West, they created a new center, a new place, thereby pointing the way to a new vision.

Today, from my experience on the *camino,* I think I discern the outline of this vision. As I've noted many times since I left St. Jean Pied de Port, the ecclesiastical architecture is in ruins or empty; the *religious* structure of the *camino* no longer exists. Like the monastery here in Frómista, it has disappeared. Yet people still walk the *camino.* This fact throws a revelatory light on the historical understanding of sacred places. From this perspective, one sees anew that the significant presence in Palestine is an *empty* tomb; the glory of Rome may not lie in the splendor of ecclesiastical monuments, but in the fact that a privileged people, the Jews, were not persecuted there; the reality of Santiago's tomb may consist principally and essentially in the faith of those who walk there. This nothingness, this weakness, and this darkness allow no place for religion. A new vision of the pilgrim's place is revealed, the place for which he or she longs. In the early Middle Ages, the issue was phrased in this way: *nudum Christum nudus sequere*—to follow the nude Christ nude. Now one can see better the meaning of this truth.

The *camino* is not a path leading to Santiago, but a way to reach Christ—if one can learn how to walk on it. The solitude and silence to be enjoyed in walking alone can lead one, I suspect, to find the meaning of *nudus* today. This is the powerful, liberating truth of the *camino:* It is an initiatory exercise, teaching one some elementary truths about stripping oneself bare. The further one progresses in this way, the further one will walk into the mystery of faith, into nothingness, weakness, and darkness. I can thereby free my faith from religion.

Two or three other pilgrims arrive to break my reverie, among them the man with the homeopathic remedies. He does not drink wine, but the others share my offer. I know nothing about wines, since it was not regularly served in my home when I was growing up. But I have tasted wine that seemed to be of inferior or poor quality; I could tell the difference between this and better wine. *All* the wine that I've drunk in Spain has tasted very good to me. Are wines just better here?

My eyes continually turn to the tower of a church down the street. On the top of the tower, storks have put together a nest. This one seems especially large, particularly haphazard in its construction, and clearly precarious in its attachment to the tower—not a secure place to raise young storks, I would think. But now and then, one of the fledglings raises its head above the edge of the nest and stretches its small wings, so I know the nest has been there for some time already—at least a month for the eggs to hatch out—weathering all kinds of storms and winds. One adult stork flies down or out of the nest, the other remaining behind with the young. They have built the nest and incubated the eggs together, and now cooperate in feeding and caring for the young. Seeing my first real storks back in Belorado, I now find that I can't take my eyes off them. I must be affected by some pre-knowledge, interest, or attraction mysteriously handed down to me, a reflection of the popularity of this bird in European legend.

After seeing them and experiencing this powerful fascination, I have learned something about them. For some people, they are a holy bird, for all, a bringer of good luck. The story that they deliver children is widespread. In some places, citizens have built platforms on their roofs, hoping that storks would nest there, bringing good luck to the house. People have put an old wagon wheel on their chimneys or roofs for the same purpose.

There is one European legend that the position in which a young girl sees her first stork in the spring determines what kind of person she will be that year. If the stork is flying when she sees it, she will be industrious; if clattering (a sound it makes with its bill), she will drop and break a lot of dishes; if standing motionless, she will be lazy. In northern Germany—and similarly in ancient Greece—a stork can be a distant relative, a human. Of course, anyone who would dare to rob a nest of its young, or kill a stork, is inevitably doomed to bad luck.

I never dreamed I would see storks on church steeples in Spain, while walking on the *camino*. What a wonder, what a pleasure. But I'm worried. This church has one of those electronic chiming devices that sounds every quarter hour. These storks *seem* to accept this—they're nesting up there. But who knows? Were they unable to find a silent tower? I hope some are left. I've heard that storks are greatly reduced in numbers because their places of nesting and gathering food are disappearing. How much interference, like these artificial chimes, how much junk can they put up with? Will they, like the shoemaker and horsecart, also die out?

17

Frómista to Carrión de los Condes

May 20, 1993

A s usual, I am the first one out of the house and on the road. I always awake early with a kind of expectation and excitement, as if this day will bring some grand surprise. I'm in a hurry—to be out *there,* to be in *that* space. The *camino* irresistibly pulls me. Starting down the silent street, I raise my staff in salute, bidding farewell to the storks: May their young grow to maturity and find good nesting places, and may they all bring me good luck on the *camino.* Now, in the spring, they could be the patron bird of the *camino.*

For a few kilometers, the trail follows a highway, and I see another of the large new signs, "Camino de Santiago." At the bottom, they read, "Itinerario Cultural Europeo." I have read somewhere that one can think of the *camino* as the first *European* journey, and that this means that the *camino* possesses a *cultural* reality. What can that possibly mean? Someone with the literary grace and talent of Unamuno can write that the "Camino of Santiago is called the Milky Way [*vía láctea*], its clouds of stars guiding the pilgrims to their heart's desire, as the star led the Three Magi." Further, anyone wanting to know Spain well, and wishing "to breathe what remains of her ancient traditional life, cannot fail to make a pious artistic journey [*romería*] to Santiago." Compostela attracted "devout pilgrims from the center of Europe who brought to the heart of Galicia legends, reports, stories and songs, and their pilgrimage was one of the vehicles of European culture then."

But what is this "culture"? What do Unamuno and so many others mean by this term? Is it anything more than a vague connotation, a kind of gloss on the inevitable stories and songs that travelers would carry, the commerce such movement would encourage, the architectural expressions such piety would inspire? I have read some of the stories and songs, I have seen some of the stone monuments. I have been puzzled by them; I have wondered what they mean. Gonzalo Torrente Ballester, another literary light of Spain, believes that the cultural aspects associated with the *camino* are all inspired by its religious sensibility, its religiosity. For him, the principal expressions of what he terms religious faith are to be found, first, in Romanesque and, second, in Gothic art and architecture. Torrente Ballester points out that both Romanesque and Gothic came from northern Europe; they crossed the Pyrenees into Spain. But, as I've begun to question: Can religion and faith be joined so easily? Rather, might there not be a great distance between them? There may be a progression here, beginning with physical expressions appealing to tourists; then, patterns of belief and behavior that hold a people together; then religious manifestations of belief—generally, it seems, superstitions; finally, outside any possible continuum that would include the aforementioned, faith: a loving leap into darkness, absolute trust in the other, death of self.

Some of the comments I hear today suggest that a European *community* is about to be born, and that an impetus toward this can be traced to the *camino;* that some kind of transnational cultural experience is reaching its apogee in a common economic market. This line of thought seems to champion a belief that European tourists coming to Spain have the opportunity to celebrate their common heritage; that, somehow, this began with Santiago. I doubt it. The truth of Santiago lies in a very different realm. To begin, the *camino* exercised a powerful attraction, drawing to Spain both sinners and saints. From the twelfth century on, records attest to the fact that the route was filled with false pilgrims, deviant clerics, sellers of everything, lazy beggars, jugglers, vagabonds, con artists, deserters, vagrants, adventurers, women of questionable morals, fugitives, penitents, and those under civil or canonical sentence (to make a pilgrimage). The very scurrility of these male and female rogues, when viewed together with the heroic virtue of other wayfarers on the *camino,* points to a kind of truth beyond the categories of social or historical phenomena. The *camino* does not point to political or economic togetherness or to the amusement of tourists, but in a very different direction, to the numinous.

Today, I pass a village, Villalcázar de Sirga, whose church, dedicated to the Virgin, reached the height of its fame in the thirteenth century. Pilgrims on their way to and from Compostela stopped there to offer their prayers to the Virgin, and this complex of a physical place, belief in powers from the *más allá* (what is beyond this world) and presenting oneself *there* with the openness of one's heart inspired stories, reports, legends, and songs. The best-known collection is attributed to Alfonso X (1252–84), El Sabio (the Wise One), king of León and Castille. His *Cántigas de Santa María* contains more than verses that relate 360 narratives or stories. The poems celebrate the merciful power of the Virgin, whose famous stone image, La Virgen Blanca, permitted actual contact with people who stopped there; they could touch the statue. Many people would only learn about this place of power as I did: They came across it on their way to Compostela. But there are only a few references to Santiago in all the stories, and these are most curious and instructive.

In one song, the tale is told of a pilgrim making his way to Compostela. The devil, disguising himself in the form of Santiago, appears to him, and tricks him into castrating himself and committing suicide because he had fallen into the sin of fornication before starting the pilgrimage. But the Virgin intervenes and saves him, restoring him to life.

Another song celebrates the miracle of the young man unjustly hanged. Here, the event takes place in Toulouse, not in Santo Domingo de la Calzada, and the family is from Germany, not Greece. The boy is saved by the Virgin, not by Santiago.

A crippled German merchant is the protagonist of another. He and his friends make a pilgrimage to Compostela, hoping for a cure. But the journey is unsuccessful. On their way back to Germany, the crippled merchant becomes blind and his companions leave him near Villalcázar de Sirga. After praying fervently to the Virgin, he is completely restored to health.

The story of the young man who castrates himself also appears in the *Liber Sancti Jacobi,* there attributed to Saint Anselm, archbishop of Canterbury. His name is Gerald, he is from Lyon, and he works with leather and furs, supporting his widowed mother. Single, he nevertheless lives a chaste life. But, on the very evening before he is scheduled to set out for Compostela, he is finally overcome by "the pleasure of the flesh," and fornicates with a young woman. The record does not say, but one can imagine a "going away" party where the powerful mixture of youthful spirits, sentimental longing, and awareness of risk—some pilgrims never returned to their native land—moved him to seek this intimacy in the attractive carnality of the known before facing the fears and dangers of the unknown.

After Gerald's self-castration and self-inflicted death, the devil, accompanied by a disorderly throng of demons, came to carry him off to the place of torment. Curiously, they traveled by way of Rome. Near the city, Santiago met them and rescued Gerald, claiming that he is "my pilgrim." They proceeded to Rome and, in a grassy place near the church of Saint Peter, found a heavenly court of saints, presided over by the Virgin. Santiago, acting as a defense lawyer, presented the case of his pilgrim. The Virgin, recognizing that Gerald is a true pilgrim of "my Lord and Son and of Santiago," ordered that he be returned to life.

The meaning of the *Cántigas* version of this tale seems to be rather clear: You don't have to go to Compostela to be cured and forgiven; the Virgin of Villalcázar de Sirga is not only powerful, but understanding and compassionate. Alfonso, in his *Cántigas de Santa María,* has taken stories current and known in his time, and changed their focus enough to show where his interests lay: in his own kingdom, not in faraway Galicia. There was much competition between places of pilgrimage in the Middle Ages. There were other competitors with Santiago, also; for example, the Virgin of Montserrat in Catalonia, where Ignatius went on pilgrimage. In the long poem of Alfonso, one can see a clear expression of this conflict, this fight for prestige, this struggle to attract the allegiance of the faithful.

I think that Torrente Ballester is correct in that one must start with the faith of those who created the *camino.* To set out on an "artistic journey" to Compostela with Unamuno, however, may be more like a walk into obfuscation. The current government campaign, cloaked with cultural rhetoric but aimed at tourism, appears doomed to leave one with, perhaps, the memory of a few pleasant days in sunny Spain, but nothing more.

I am reminded of that passage in Luke, "When the Son of Man comes, will he find faith on the earth?" (18:8).

Just before noon, I arrive at Carrión de los Condes, on the Carrión River. Early in the Middle Ages, the town was named Santa María de Carrión. Because of the fame of its local rulers, who had the rank of count (*conde*), the name of the town was changed to Carrión de los Condes. One of the counts, Gómez Díaz, and his wife, Teresa, founded the monastery of Saint John the Baptist in the eleventh century. Their son, Fernando, traveled to Córdoba, to help the Muslim ruler there in his wars with other Muslim mini-states. When offered gold and silver in payment for his military services, the knight said that he would prefer to have the body of San Zoilo, a man who was martyred during a Roman persecution centuries earlier. The body of Zoilo had been venerated in a tiny church dedicated to San Félix when the young Christian knight noticed it while he was in Córdoba. Receiving Zoilo's body, Fernando sent it to the monastery founded by his parents, and the monastery's name was then changed. The monastery of San Zoilo became famous for the miracles worked there. According to her epitaph, the Countess Teresa was known for her generosity, building "a church, a bridge and the best possible shelter for pilgrims," and for the fact that "she took little for herself, while distributing much to the poor."

This history illustrates in an especially acute and pure form how faith worked in the lives of some persons connected with the *camino* in the eleventh century. Teresa, born to privilege, acted in a way consistent with a person of faith in her town, a place through which pilgrims passed on their way to Compostela. She provided for their material and spiritual welfare. Further, she helped nurture a son who followed the accustomed path of his social origins, that of a medieval knight or warrior, but in a unique way. Obedient to the faith of his parents, he knew the character of power in that world. Given the opportunity, Fernando chose this power over wealth. He knew that, ultimately, power comes from the *más allá*, from another world, but one can be helped to reach that world by touching the remains of those who have already departed for that place beyond.

I walk by a huge Clarissa convent on my way to the *refugio*. An empty monument, a sign advertises it now as a museum. But I will not go in. I suspect that the time for seeking a living contact with the faith of those who walked before me, some of whom may have lived in this convent, through touching their remains, is past. One must find the forms of faith proper to *this* age. And these, in relation to the *camino*, may be found out there in the high places, out there in the lonely and empty fields, out there in solitude, far from these magnificent but dead stones of medieval architecture. Here the very stones—is this "culture"?—collaborate with the government to turn one into a tourist. Perhaps this is why I have instinctively ignored these ancient hymns in stone. They can no longer sing; they have no voice at all. One hears the voices of angels and forgotten, nameless pilgrims only out there in the forests and mountains.

Coming to the shelter, I pray that it is open. I have arrived here in very good time, but I do not think I can possibly walk another kilometer. The pain now runs all through my weak left leg. And today, the right foot and leg were pierced with pain. For the first time since I started, I really fear that I cannot make it; I will not get to Compostela. I'm just too old and weak to walk so far. But now I need to set this backpack down and rest.

A friendly woman answers the door at what seems to be the house or office connected to a church. She says that, yes, I may enter the *refugio*, which is next door, and opens it for me. Happily, there is no rule prescribing something like a 4 P.M. opening.

After dropping the pack and lying down for a few minutes, I get up and go in search of the post office. It seems that these offices are open only in the morning, which might mean up to 1 P.M. Before leaving Germany, I gave family and friends the name of this town, and told them the date I expected to be here. Since I have heard from no one since leaving Germany, I am now excited by the prospect of mail. I really have been cut off from everyone I know, and they had no idea where I was—except out there on some trail in Spain. I picked this town since it is about halfway to Compostela and I suspected that it was large enough to have a post office, but not so big as to present difficulties finding the building.

As I approach the part of town where I have heard it is, I ask a woman for further directions. She starts to tell me, hesitates, apparently thinks better of it, and then, looking at the streets around us, mentions that the way is rather complicated; she will take me herself. I walk along with her, making several turns among the usual confusion of narrow streets, and we arrive in about five minutes. Thanking her, I enter the building, expectant, anxious. I explain to the man behind the counter that I am a *peregrino,* and ask if there is any mail for me. He looks in his pigeonholes, and returns with several envelopes—from both family and friends! I feel like a child pampered by the good fairies. With my treasure, I return to the shelter.

There is a good laundry sink for scrubbing clothes behind the shelter, together with a large garden and clothesline. After this chore and a hot shower, I'm feeling more optimistic about starting again tomorrow morning. But now it's time to look for food.

There is no kitchen in the *refugio,* and the woman who let me in strongly suggested that I try the restaurant across the street. They serve a very good *menú del día,* she says, for only 700 pesetas. When I enter the first of two dining rooms there, I wonder if I am in the right place. I explain to the neatly uniformed waiter that the woman connected with the *refugio* recommended this restaurant, or so I believe. Could this be the place? Yes, but there is a problem, he says. They are expecting a lot of people who have reservations. He hesitates . . . then asks me to follow him. Taking me to a side table, he brings the menu. There is some choice in the items offered on the *menú.*

All the table covers and napkins are white—cloth. I've never yet been in such a classy restaurant. When I first saw the dress of the waiters—all men, too—and the tables, I was confused . . . I had again lost my way . . . this time, crossing the street!

Two pilgrims walk in, the man with the homeopathic remedies and his friend. I wave them over, and we all enjoy a truly excellent meal, one of the best I've had in Spain. While we are eating, a large group of people about our age, who seem to be on some kind of tour, come in to eat. I am happy to see that there are enough tables for everyone—the waiter who let us sit here need not be embarrassed.

Back in the *refugio,* I take out my notebook and look for the pen. But I can't find it. I look all over the bunk, go through all the compartments of the backpack, but no pen. I have made a rule for myself that whenever I take anything out of the pack, it goes only on the bed, and in no other place. I do this so that I will not lose anything. Unpacking and packing up every day, and in a different place, is a risky activity for me. I am very apt to set things down in some place or other, and then forget them. So far, my rule has protected me from myself; I've not lost anything—until now.

I sit down on the bed and try to think what I could have done with that pen. Then I notice one of my dinner companions at the table in the middle of the room, writing—and it looks as if he is using my pen! I think I recognize it, for I brought a German pen, easily distinguished, with me. But how could he have *my* pen? If I had laid it on the bed, he would not just pick it up without asking me. But I don't remember ever putting the pen on the bed. What to do? I am embarrassed to ask him. How could I put the question? Well, but I have to. That looks more and more like my pen. There must be some kind of mystery here. Finally, working up my courage, I tentatively ask about the pen, saying that I have lost one just like it.

He breaks into friendly laughter. He found the pen just this morning! On the *camino,* he and his friend looked for a place to sit down and rest. While sitting there, his friend saw a pen lying on the ground and picked it up. It seemed to be in good condition, so he gave it to his companion, since he, too, makes notes each day.

I remember when I reached that spot earlier in the morning, I had decided to stop there because I wanted to rest in the sun; it was still quite cool in the shade. For some distance, I had not been able to find anything like a bench along the road—which is always a big help with the heavy backpack. About ten meters from the road I noticed a large log lying on the ground and thought it would make a good resting place. I took off my shoes to give my feet some fresh air, but I have no recollection at all of opening the pack, and I always keep the pen in one of its compartments. How could it have fallen out there? And why did these two men pick that exact spot? And see the pen? And now I see him with it? A whole series of strange questions.

David (who is on the way to becoming a friend) tells me that this is not at all unusual for the *camino.* Things like this happen all the time; it's the nature of the *camino.* For example, he has a favorite hat that fell from his pack one day. A pilgrim coming along later saw a hat in a field and, on impulse, picked it up. When he later arrived at the next *refugio* with the hat, David recognized it and explained that he had lost it.

A cheerful, friendly priest comes in to talk and stamp our documents. He appears to be the pastor of the church that maintains this shelter, and invites us all to Mass in the adjoining church at 8:30 this evening. Since I can probably get back very shortly after my usual retiring hour of 9 P.M., I decide to go. His invitation has a certain warmth, a strong human appeal. It makes me think, yes, I would definitely like to respond to such an invitation.

When I arrive in the church, the priest is leading the Rosary; and then comes the Litany of the Saints and a few other prayers. After my rich experiences of such prayers out on the *camino,* I have the queer feeling that they are somehow out of place here.

By the time Mass starts, there is a good crowd—which seems unusual to me, for it is just an ordinary Thursday evening. The large majority are women. I have no experience of church life in Spain, but from more than thirty years' experience in Latin America, I know that women generally outnumber men in the churches, sometimes greatly so. The other day, in a bar, I had asked myself, Where do the women gather? Could this be part of the answer? Do they also meet their friends here? Or, is there something else? Maybe something more? I recall the Gospel accounts, the stories of women there. The Synoptics mention only women as accompanying Christ to Calvary. They have a special place at the empty tomb after the Resurrection. And there are many meetings between Jesus and individual women in the Gospels whose intimacy is not matched—I think—by similar meetings with men. Is something happening here in this Spanish church tonight that, to understand it, I would have to begin, not with reading sociology, but with meditation on Scripture?

18

Carrión de los Condes to Sahagún

May 21, 1993

I t's not yet really daylight when I set out this morning. Going out the door, I am surprised to meet one of the Canadians who had arrived last night. I ask him where he has been, since I saw him leaving the dormitory with his backpack just before dozing off. He said he found another room upstairs with bunks, and went there, since it was impossible to sleep in the room where the rest of us were housed. He spoke bitterly of the behavior of some who arrived late. Although I put up with this noise, I did not sleep well. A number of bicyclists came in during the evening, making the small dormitory crowded. With their loud talking until far into the night, they also made the place distinctly hostile to sleep. These young men fell exactly into the pattern that I have come to see: They are always inconsiderate, uncivil, noisy. But I never note such traits among these who are walking. Why this great difference? It is something much more than age . . .

After I have been on the *camino* for a few hours, I realize that I have crossed the halfway mark. A rough calculation of the distances marked on my crude map indicates that this must be true. If so, it seems the most important landmark I've reached—for I strongly feel, for the first time, that I can make it to Compostela. The deep doubt and discouragement of yesterday were produced by bad angels—the strength of what I felt clearly indicated *their* desperation; this would be their last chance to mount a serious attack on my resolution to make this pilgrimage. My body has successfully crossed a major threshold; my legs take on a new lightness, my step a new spring. The day is sunny, warmer than usual . . . I'm wearing only a T-shirt today.

Lots of amazing variation in the surface of the *camino*. At times, I'm stepping on a kind of cobblestone, small stones embedded in the hard dirt, which individually penetrate right through the thick soles and inner-soles to the bottoms of my feet and up my legs. Seeing these stones, I find it hard to believe that they can impress their individual character so forcefully on my feet. In some places, there is soft grass. When there is a combination or mixture, I find my feet seeking the grassy side of the trail, or the spot free of stones, for each step. At times, I'm striding on hard clay, a no-nonsense surface that I've learned to prefer dry rather than wet. I suffer a stretch of asphalt, too, but not so much that I can complain.

These new experiences of touching the earth, of actually feeling a soil under my feet, are continually fascinating. There is a tradition that ultimate knowledge is found in touching. The Virgin's quick response, "I know not man," is understood to mean, initially: "No man has touched me." When something sharp or delicate moves my heart, I say, "I was touched." Aquinas notes that all the senses are founded on the sense of touch; it is the most basic one. Further, among all possible sense pleasures, the greatest and most powerful are those experienced through touch, today called the pleasures of sex. The virtue bringing right reason to bear on these delights, ordering them to their proper end, he calls chastity. The extreme or radical form of chastity, virginity, is not more excellent, as a virtue, because the virgin is more chaste than the married person, but because virginity is embraced and practiced in order to free one for contemplation, that is, one becomes unfettered, released for reflection on the things of God, on divine truth. I wonder whether the *camino* so acts on my sense of touch, through my intense absorption *in* touch, that my spirit rises toward those things that are above in some way paradoxically analogous to what the virgin hopes to achieve. That is, the virgin prays to be blessed with divine light through sacrificing the ultimate physical delights. I find my mind continually absorbed in the truths of faith in spite of (because of?) frequent and sometimes continual sensible pain; I'm surprised to find that it's never a distraction.

On the *camino,* I walk into a new, very different world of touch. Not having a regular map, not knowing the route, but being continually in intimate contact with the *camino,* I come to know it only through feeling or touching it. In one of the shelters, another pilgrim proudly showed me his guidebook—the latest, most up-to-date and complete one available, he told me. I leafed through a few pages. They contained detailed written text, photographs, and perspective drawings of what the walker could expect to see at "interesting" places along the way. I was reminded of a remark written by Richard Burton as he made his way up the Nile from Alexandria to Cairo on the first stage of his *hadj* (pilgrimage) to Mecca. He complained that the scenes passed by the boat are of no interest at all—he had seen them all before, in sketches of the pyramids! This was 1853, before the widespread use of photographs. How could one come to be on the *camino,* know the *camino,* without the joy of surprise?

There is much to see—if you have not already viewed it in a picture. My touching the *camino* with all my senses turns my body into a sensorium. With this kind of touching, I come to know the space in which I walk, I come to a felt experiencing of it, I reach a vital familiarity with it— which means that I know how it differs from all the other infinite places behind and in front of me. Seeing the horizon at all times, I come to know what it is to live *with* a horizon—an experience lost to most modern people.

In these days, I realize more fully that, years ago, I must have started acquiring a strong sense of limits. Living on that subsistence farm, acting every day only within a fixed, never changing horizon, I formed a habit, a certain disposition of my soul, the horizon having taken on a normative character. Without being completely aware of what was happening to me, I saw that one could live well, virtuously, today, only if one habitually lived within limits. The pain I felt when I sped over the horizon, traveling from northern Germany to the French-Spanish border on the electric train, was not a new experience for me. After leaving the farm, I have often suffered this affliction. The daily constraints of the farm's horizon habituated me to a certain mode of being. On the *camino,* I need never think of restricting myself; I can act with total abandon. This is the first place, since the farm, that I can freely move without pain, for I do not exceed any limits. Where else in the world could I enjoy such wantonness? With the horizon always "out there," seemingly so distant, I know it is near; I am within its comforting embrace. Before the day is over, I know I will touch it.

I suspect it is because I am continually in touch with the *camino* that I am on such familiar terms with the dead, that I feel them so near me. It is only through the richly sensible and lowly experience of tramping on this soil that I can hope to move familiarly among those who have walked before me, some of whose bodies lie beneath my feet. In some direct and unambiguous way, I share their experience; I can hope to enter their world. Walking alone, I am not distracted; I can be aware of their presence. The greater my solitude, the more I sense being accompanied by them.

I pass through several small villages. In one, I come upon a bar and decide to enjoy my coffee early in the day—a good way to take a short break and to vary my routine. It occurs to me that in some of my habits, I appear to be attempting to take all the surprise out of each day. In another village, I walk by a small market store and stop to buy some food to be carried in the pack. I've learned to be cautious about food—at times it's hard or even impossible to find in the place where I've stopped. Also, I may not make it to Sahagún today.

On my right, I see a range of mountains with their peaks covered with snow. These must be the Picos de Europa, between me and the Atlantic. I've heard that they are very popular for hiking and climbing, but I don't think I will get any closer to them than I am now. My pleasure in them can be only visual, since the *camino* does not pass through, but runs parallel, to them.

Shortly after delighting in this majestic sight, I approach Sahagún. And so I am about to accomplish what must be my first "miracle" on the *camino:* After nine hours, I've completed about forty kilometers—for me, a record distance—and I feel fine. I have no sense of pain in any part of my body. And yesterday I seriously doubted that I could continue. The good angels are definitely in control today. How clear and unambiguous is my experience of them.

Some say that the medieval history of Sahagún is the history of its monastery. The site was first blessed by the burial of a number of persons martyred at the time of Diocletian (284–305). After the Islamic invasion of the Peninsula, the place was attacked by a *razzia,* once in 883, and again by Almanzor at the very end of the tenth century. One of the stories of Charlemagne attributed to the bishop, Turpin, and contained in the *Liber Sancti Jacobi,* says that he founded the town's monastery to celebrate his victory over the Moors. Aymeric Picaud, the probable author, again attempts to associate France with the *camino.* Picaud describes the imaginary battle minutely, but this is the last place along the route of the *camino* where he relates a detailed story. For him, it appears that nothing worth recounting is seen or remembered between Sahagún and Compostela.

Writing in the first half of the twelfth century, Picaud tells of actions that would have taken place at the end of the eighth. Later Spaniards would see a shape and purpose in this combination of religious piety and heroic warfare, naming it La Reconquista, the recovery of the Peninsula from the Moors. They placed its origins in a warrior, Don Pelayo, who grew to mythic proportions after his successful defense of Covadonga, in

Asturias, in 718. This action of Pelayo is described by a church historian, García Villoslada, as

> a marvelous spectacle, a people surrounded by an enemy a thousand times superior who, nevertheless, resist with tenacity and force never before witnessed, always inspired by the religious ideal which enabled them to see their fight as a crusade and holy war in defense of the Christian religion. This ideal of a crusade is that which has made Spain [what it is].

Various authors have attempted to explain the sources of this specific form of religious zeal. For example, Américo Castro believes that it comes from the Jews and Moors. From the example of the Jews, the Christians learned to develop an unbending intransigence based on religious principles. From the Moors, they learned the necessity of fighting a *religious* war. The Reconquista took on the form of a sacred, indivisible action, inflamed by exclusivist sentiments. One can perhaps understand something of this through a careful use of the concept of ideology. As I've come to see, one here meets a peculiarly vicious perversion of faith. The Jews showed that it was possible to remain loyal to one's faith without having recourse to a "holy" war. True, at times of intense persecution, some Jews apostatized. But the Jews of Spain, as a people, did not develop an ideology for a sociomilitary program presumably based on their faith. In this sense, to be a good Jew was to live by a pure faith at a time when, to be a good Christian, one was exhorted to embrace a divinely authorized campaign of bloody conquest.

The historian Vicente Cantarino believes that the Reconquista, together with subsequent modes of belief and action that followed from it and that permeated many areas of Spanish life, took on a specifically aggressive and ascetic monkish sense because of the influence of Cluny, not because of Castro's theory of the *tres castas*—the three "castes" (Christian, Jewish, and Muslim) interacting on one another, the result being a certain Spanish character. Cluny is the name of a Benedictine monastery in Burgundy, and of a monastic reform movement that began there and spread throughout Europe. Alfonso VI (1072–1109) met San Hugo, one of the Cluny leaders, in Burgos and asked him to send some monks to the monastery in Sahagún to reform it according to the ideals and practices of Cluny. In 1079, two monks, Roberto and Marcelino, came for this purpose. Eventually, the Sahagún monastery became the principal Cluny foundation in Spain, with more than fifty other monasteries and priories under its jurisdiction.

Various secular rulers throughout Spain invited Cluny monks to reform monasteries in their respective territories. Castro believes that this was done because they thought that the Cluny monks would help them develop and exploit the *camino*. Other authors violently reject this interpretation. But Sánchez Albornoz believes that the French monks made the *camino* a Cluniac *camino*. Raymond Oursel says that, apart from studying all the documents and biographies of the Cluny movement, one has only to see the physical location of Cluny monasteries in relation to the route of the *camino* to see that such a claim is ridiculous. One does not have to go far into Spanish historiography to find oneself in a minefield.

I have the impression that the Spanish rulers sent regular gifts of money to Cluny—Alfonso VI being the most generous—and worked to introduce the Cluny reforms because of their religiosity, the peculiar form their faith took. They wanted to save their souls. These men and women were no better, no worse, than others who have the power to command. They often sought to satisfy their passions and ambitions to the limit of the possibilities presented. But, somewhere in their awareness of "what is," one sees a reaching toward faith. As Wittgenstein clearly understood:

> Christianity is not a doctrine, not, I mean, a theory about what has happened and will happen to the human soul, but a description of something that actually takes place in human life. For "consciousness of sin" is a real event and so are despair and salvation through faith. Those who speak of such things . . . are simply describing what has happened to them, whatever gloss anyone may want to put on it.

These rulers, in their gifts and actions, demanded and received a quid pro quo. For their money and gifts of land, the rulers received the monks' prayers for the salvation of their souls. They judged that a "reform monk" would be a more holy monk, and a monastery of such monks would have much greater intercessory power before God.

The difficulty with this kind of religiosity is that it raises a serious question: How will those who cannot afford to pay for prayers be saved? The flippant answer is obvious: through their virtue. Then one has only to contend with a double standard.

Sahagún was also famous for its *hospitales*. In the time of Alfonso VI, the monastery built a special hospice that contained seventy beds and was well known among pilgrims for its hospitality. In the fifteenth century, Künig reports that he found four *hospitales* for pilgrims in the town. I have heard that there is still one here, but it takes some questioning before I find it. It seems to be a kind of two-story apartment converted to a small *refugio*. There appears to be some confusion on the existence of a kitchen. I see one, but the man in charge says that it is not available. Later, I learn that if one pays him a bribe, he will allow you to use the stove. No matter. I can eat my food cold in the small dining room.

This town is also the birthplace of the famous Franciscan, Fray Bernardino de Sahagún (1499–1590), often referred to simply as Sahagún. In the sixteenth century, Fray Bernardino worked heroically to learn and record the practices, knowledge, and wisdom of the Aztecs in Mexico before all was forgotten and lost—or destroyed by zealous clerics and inquisitors. His great work, the *Historia general de las cosas de Nueva España,* describes the civilization of the Aztecs. The twelve books are written in parallel columns, Spanish and Nahuatl. When the Inquisition learned what he was doing, it looked upon the work as a dangerous activity and confiscated the books. The books were not burned, however. Rather, they were locked up in a special archive and forgotten for three hundred years. Now that this treasure has been found and studied, some acknowledge Sahagún as the father of modern anthropology.

A few blocks from the shelter, I find some postcards and stamps. I see from a postcard that there is a large statue of Sahagún here, together with many other monuments and historic buildings. But I decide to skip them in favor of resting and reflecting on what happened to me today on the *camino.*

The Rosary took me to places where I sensed something powerful in its impact but clouded in its outline. Words are difficult to find . . . What I can relate appears to me more like a pale, diminished reflection, more false than true, in the sense of being inadequate, not of being contrary. All the Mysteries of the Rosary reveal the love of the Father. If this human way of speaking contains some truth, then one must say that the Father loves the Son above all, as God and as Father. The Son says that He has come to do the Father's will. Theologically, this is the most accurate statement one can make about the Son's actions among the people of Palestine. The Father's will is that the Son submit to the betrayals, hatred, and cruelty He would find among men. The Father demands this because, mysteriously, such pain and suffering are necessary to redeem men and women. If I walk into these Mysteries of faith, I enter a world of love that terrifies. I cannot help thinking of my own children, what I have demanded of them, what I would demand of them. But dare I place these two worlds so close together? Dare I think of them as having anything to do with one another?

Somehow, out there on the *camino* today, I was taken to the place where I had to look at the love of my children anew, where I saw that love is not what I imagined it to be, that one might be asked to suffer greatly in the persons one loves, through *their* suffering. Such a frightening situation does not drive one to ask: Why does this innocent person suffer? but, rather, to meditate on this Mystery of the Rosary and humbly hope for enlightenment. If I become empty enough, I shall understand all I need to know, all I need to love . . .

19

Sahagún to Mansilla de las Mulas

May 22, 1993

T he small shelter in Sahagún filled up last night and, this morning, when I attempted to enter the dining room to eat my breakfast, I found a pilgrim sleeping on the table. The porch on the front of the building provided a fine place to eat and make up my pack for the day's march.

Leaving Sahagún, I find a completely new *camino*, radically different from the one I have known up to now. In 1991, the Consejería de Agricultura de la Junta de Castilla y León decided to improve the *camino* from Calzada del Coto (a few kilometers past Sahagún) to Mansilla de las Mulas, thirty-two kilometers farther along. The *camino* becomes a raised and graded path about three meters wide, running in a straight line to the horizon. It is absolutely smooth, with a covering coat of sand—the perfect bike path! An abstractly conceptualized and machine-made construction, it is punctuated at every eight or ten meters by a newly planted tree, each exactly the same height. Occasionally, at set intervals, there are benches along the path and, less frequently, picnic tables placed in groves of trees, some older, some newly planted. The benches, tables, and a cast masonry sign outside each village are all new, made of some kind of concrete designed to imitate stone. Everything is deadeningly monotonous, chillingly artificial. I'm overcome by an angry and heavy sadness: All the work and money, perhaps the sacrifices, of generous people who attempted to do something good for the *camino,* comes down to this—an antiseptic ribbon rolled across the landscape, an image out of a bad surrealist painting. Dejection envelops and chokes my spirit. This is the way modern technology infects people's imaginations and desires. The uniform bleakness of the path, the cheap slickness of the benches, are simply appalling.

I see that this section of the *camino* has been turned into a technological project, perhaps even reaching the perfection of a *milieu technique,* a concept of Jacques Ellul. This is a milieu essentially formed by the demands and requirements of *la technique:* Everything is conceptualized and then carried out according to technical criteria alone. For example, an abstract concept of orderly efficiency requires that the path be precisely three meters wide, level or with grades determined by mathematical calculation, and of exactly the same material. No human, that is, idiosyncratic, touch is allowed to mar the regularity. No natural grace can be permitted to shine forth. The kinds of trees, their uniform size and distance from each other, must all conform absolutely to "rational" criteria.

Rational here means a kind of marriage—or, in today's jargon, interface—between a Cartesian thinking ego and some physical project. Rational is far removed from the earthy reality of persons, which is manifestly evident in the reaction of a person—myself—to this kind of planned and designed setting: I am quickly bored; for the first time, I find the *camino* depressing, uninteresting. I feel that I have been closed up in a stifling space, an engineered capsule, a sheer, weightless suit protecting me from stumbling over sharp rocks, getting stuck in mud or lost on confusing livestock paths. Today, there are no surprises; I cannot lose my way; there is no need for crudely painted yellow arrows. The *camino* has been deformed and reduced to an industrial road, an extension of smooth freeways with their efficient consumption of distance.

This new *camino* runs through or past many fields of grain, some taller than me and quite unfamiliar. I have to remind myself that this is the evidence of a new year; these crops are the pledge of the earth's fruitfulness. If I look up, I think I can see the same sky I have seen all along. But is this true?

It starts to rain. This is a familiar experience, is it not? Well, yes. It's something like the rain falling on the asphalt highway. But here the surface is not so hard; it is gently graded so that the rain runs off on each side. It has been made to conform to a mechanical criterion, supposedly to help me. It certainly benefits the engineer who planned all this; and the people who made and sold the machines to construct it; and the employed workers who operated the machines. I can move right along at a rapid pace; I never have to watch my footing, attempting to avoid puddles that would run over the tops of my shoes, or rocks on which I might twist my ankle. But am I still walking? Or does this sanitized highway remove me from the earth, swallowing me up into its ersatz space? I can't lose my way, but I've certainly lost the *camino,* the one I've begun to know and embrace with a mixture of awe and delight.

Ellul believes that the technological project is so cunningly perfected and so comprehensively extended that it disorients and blinds those imprisoned in it—namely, most if not all persons caught in the modern sectors of the contemporary world. This encapsulation is concealed and softened by distractions—all the various drugs, games, spectacles, "cultural" activities, gadgets, and toys produced by the technological project itself, that is, all designed to work (read: "amuse," for most; be "interesting," for those with pretensions to intellectual sophistication)—in the setting created by the project. Noting that people increasingly live in a world of artificial images cleverly designed to attract and hold them in the *milieu technique,* Ellul claims that they lose the ability to distinguish between image and reality. That is, they come to think that the artificial bubble *is* reality. Today, out here on this manufactured path—a rather porous cage—I am tempted to believe that I am still walking, that I am still on the *camino.* But precisely because my experience of the real *camino* has been so clear and strong over so many days, I know I am being deceived today.

Must one consciously undertake a similarly arduous cleansing of one's senses to recognize the alluring tentacles of the technological project? Or is something more required? Is a years-long discipline necessary? ascetical practices leading to a new mode of seeing, some sort of radical conversion? These questions occur to me because some people who report that they were on the *camino* describe the space through which I now swiftly move as a "magnificent initiative," "a comfortable and functional road," a "beautiful path of compacted earth." All that is here . . . but I also see something very different . . . or have the fresh air, the sun and rain, the fatigue clouded my judgment so that I am deluded?

What I see seems to be the result of a powerful, clarifying experience. This would never have occurred without two conditions being met: living in a certain tradition, and being able to reflect. But I may not have understood the conditions well. I have thought that, being in the tradition of my parents and so many earlier pilgrims, I should seek the origins of this tradition in faith. Only through faith would I truly be a part of the tradition. But that may have been too quick, too superficial. Perhaps I should have been more influenced by the example and teaching of another great Spaniard of the sixteenth century, Saint John of the Cross. If I understand how this mystic lived and what he taught, I should go out on the *camino* after having worked to divest myself of everything, to empty myself of all tired and routinized thoughts, of conventional feelings, of "normal" passions and desires. In this understanding, I could enter my tradition only through a thorough discarding of all clinging possessions. In this way alone could one effectively cure all the infections of the technological virus. To enter the Western tradition of faith, one would have to be truly free of the pretensions of the Cartesian ego, the idea that the disembodied rationality expressed by this ego has anything to do with being a person, let alone a person of faith. Through stripping myself of "everything," perhaps I can break free from technological imprisonment, free to plod through the mud of the *camino,* free to find a path to faith.

Ellul believes that because people in the modern sectors today are caught in the *milieu technique,* they cannot reflect. He thinks that this is the specific cultural and intellectual tragedy of the modern world: confined to this world, people cannot establish the necessary distance from both themselves and the world, cannot find the requisite quiet and clarity, for genuine reflection. The character of this activity, as it has been practiced in the West, received its definitive expression in the so-called Delphic maxim, "Know thyself." Its first historical source is Xenophon (c. 434–c. 355 B.C.). Christian thinkers emphasized the exercise of this maxim, especially in the twelfth century. Ellul is obviously concerned since, according to this tradition of more than two thousand years a human life, as understood by Greek and, later, Christian thought, is impossible without reflection leading to self-knowledge.

What I have found on the *camino* is that, to the extent that I was immersed in the *camino,* I simply lived in reflection, that kind of reflection that may be expressed best through the notion of recollection—a recalling of the gifts and graces, the errors and self-seeking, the true history of myself as a creature. This has been my day-to-day aware life in this blessed and graced place. In a sense, I have done nothing else but reflect—while walking, while genuinely moving through space. My experience must be a confirmation of his thesis: On the *camino,* I have not been entrapped by the *milieu technique.* I have discovered a realm where I am free from the embrace and blinding miasma of technological incubi.

In a couple of places today, I see a shepherd with a small flock of sheep. This is a great change historically. Beginning in the Middle Ages, large flocks of sheep ranged over this part of Spain, making an agriculture of cultivated crops impossible. The wool was exported to Flanders. Some claimed that Spain was choking and dying on this wool, since the country needed the land to grow food for the people. Now, from the fields of grain, I see that the farmers have the upper hand over the sheepherders.

The two flocks that I saw were small, and the chief task of the shepherds seemed to be to keep the sheep out of the cultivated fields. They had to scrounge around in patches, ditches, and the fields where no crop was planted this year.

The shepherds were old men. What would it be like to accompany them for some weeks, to listen to their stories? Would solitude out here with their animals, perhaps many years' long, give them a special voice, a sensibility totally foreign to me? Would they reveal this to me? Would I be capable of hearing it? I think I did understand the shoemaker. Could I also understand a shepherd? But I don't believe that I can just walk up to him as I did in Belorado. It would take much more time to establish a certain familiarity between us. But what a revelation that might be!

In the seventeenth century, Laffi could have met a similar shepherd with his sheep. But he records a much more dramatic scene. As he came along here, just before reaching Burgo Ranero, Laffi and his companion found the body of a dead pilgrim, a man who had died right on the *camino*. Two wolves had begun to feast on the corpse. Laffi chased them away, covered the body with some rocks and, when he got to Burgo Ranero, sought a priest who could arrange a Christian burial.

It would seem that the people of this province did not do much to accommodate Laffi and other pilgrims of that time. But from various records I know that they were kept busy protecting their flocks from wolves; this was quite enough for their capabilities. Today, in a very different world, the people here want to do something for the pilgrims who pass through their region. And so they work—and spend much—to make the *camino* attractive and comfortable for walkers. But, it seems to me that all their good intentions and efforts have been decisively shaped by technological-machine-mathematical imperatives. The result is the very opposite of what was intended. I am overwhelmed by a heavy sadness. The *milieu technique* is so powerful, so all-pervasive, so deceptive, that it can ensnare these good people. The grotesqueness of "doing good" under the aegis of the technological imperative!

After about eight hours, I reach Mansilla de las Mulas, having walked maybe forty kilometers. I feel almost fresh, having stopped in one of the villages along the way for a short rest and a cup of coffee. A question or two easily brings me to the *refugio,* an older building in the center of town. It is under renovation, but much of the work has been completed and the finished rooms are attractively furnished.

I immediately run into David, the man who found my pen. He greets me with great enthusiasm and introduces me to the man in charge of the shelter and, with a highly imaginative account of my "reputation," demands that I be given the best bed in the dormitory. David and his friend are on their way out the door, planning to reach the next *refugio* yet today.

All the bunks and mattresses are new, and the man leads me to one next to the window—decorated with a lace curtain. This is something I have not seen before. Leaving my pack on the bed, I go in search of the kitchen. There I find three Spanish couples, perhaps a few years younger than myself, just finishing their lunch. They greet me heartily and invite me to sit down and share their meal; there are enough leftovers to make an excellent dinner for me. One of them had picked mushrooms along the *camino,* and the women cooked them. They also offered me a delicious fresh salad, bread, fruit, and wine. As I finished my coffee, one of the men took out a flask and asked me if I would like a drink of *aguardiente.* I was familiar with such a liquor from having lived in Latin America. The people of each region seem to make a strong brandylike drink from some common fruit of the area. Since I knew I would be given only a very small amount, I readily accepted. A tiny bit of powerful alcohol, slowly sipped among such friendly and generous people, seemed the ideal way to complete the convivial feast. The *aguardiente* was probably homemade and I could see that the men felt they were offering me a very special treat.

On my way out the building to get food for breakfast, I notice that there is a small parlor with a television set and, in a corner of the patio, an automatic clothes washer—more evidence of modern generosity. But since the building itself is old and somewhat haphazard in its arrangements, the place retains a certain genuine charm.

After my quick shopping trip—I find a market and bakery within a couple of blocks—I meet the two Canadians preparing their meal in the kitchen, and sit down to talk with them. While they are eating, a bicyclist —recognizable from his fancy clothing—comes in and orders them to wash up the pans they have used so that he can cook his food! Even without my command of Spanish, I could easily have picked up his arrogant tone and manner. Almost stunned by such a display of insolence, I manage to state quietly that they will be happy to do so the moment they finish eating but, if he is in such a great hurry, there are more clean pans in the cupboard.

Another example, this time even more graphic, more striking, of the great gap, the tremendous difference, between two kinds of Spanish people met on the *camino:* persons from what might be termed the "lower middle class"—open, friendly, generous and considerate; and others from the "upper" or "climbing toward upper"—haughty, impolite, selfish. I was deeply shocked by the attitude of this young man, and had difficulty maintaining some measure of restraint and composure. Are these young men representative of those who are coming to manage and govern

Spain? Do the older people belong to a generation that is passing, dying out? Are the older ones those who fail to be perfectly integrated into the *milieu technique?* Is it *this* artificial but all-encompassing rational network, made up of chimerical "gardens of delight," distracting but enervating pleasures, scientific wonders, and glamorous fads that has so effectively transformed these young men into boorish and repulsive cyclists? Perhaps I've been given a vision of the *milieu technique*'s power, of what it can produce: a young man devoid of elementary courtesy, deformed by the illusion of his own importance, ready to ride roughshod over all who inconvenience him. I shudder. Some have believed that World War II solved something. I seem to see that a new kind of being is coming out of the *milieu technique,* much more seriously lacking in the common decency one traditionally associates with a civilized creature than the aberrations fostered by National Socialism, Stalinism, and Pol Pot–ism. Underneath their high-tech equipment and fashionable "sportsman" outfits, is there still some spark of a *human* spirit in these men that could be kindled and grow into a virtuous person?

The *camino* now appears to me to be the ideal place where someone who is steeped in a tradition could empty himself or herself in such a way as to enjoy the freedom necessary for genuine reflection, a recollecting-thinking-feeling that involves the whole person and that is penetrating and powerful enough to break through the barriers and prejudices erected by the technological project. But I fear that these young men will never reach this *camino;* they will never know it; they are too tightly clothed in their uniforms and too intensely wrapped up in their machines; in terms of human possibility, it may not be too extreme to call them a lost generation. And the next?

20

Mansilla de las Mulas to León

May 23, 1993

A few kilometers from Mansilla, in 1142, Alfonso VII and his wife, Doña Berenguela, gave land to the Conde Don Ponce de Minerva and his wife, Doña Estefanía. Don Ponce was captured soon after in a battle with the Moors, and taken to Morocco. Knowing nothing about his fate, Doña Estefanía founded a monastery at Carrizo, on the Orbigo River, as a *hospital* for pilgrims going to and from Compostela, and worked there, attending to the needs of the travelers herself. Her husband was eventually set free, and went as a pilgrim to Compostela to fulfill a vow he had made while in captivity. One night, he stopped at Carrizo. It was sometimes the custom in the *hospitales* to wash the feet of the pilgrims—in imitation of the action of Christ Himself (John 13:1–17). That night as usual, Doña Estefanía washed the pilgrims' feet, but did not recognize her husband, now much changed after years of captivity. While she carried out this act of love, Don Ponce recognized her when he saw and felt her hands! The story goes on to say that they both then made vows of continence and the count, imitating his wife, founded the monastery of Sandoval nearby.

The truth of this story marvelously fit my thoughts on the *camino,* thoughts for which words do not seem adequate. The walking was somewhat difficult again today—enough to remind me of the reality of pain . . .

that, historically, has always been there, almost from the beginning, and that will always be there, almost to the end. There is no cure, no remedy, no effective painkiller. But all the agonizing questions—Why must this infant suffer so terribly? Why are the innocent persecuted?—all the actual suffering, received an "answer." Out of love, the Son was obedient, obedient to a horrible death. And such obedience was "exacted," was demanded, out of love. This love, although surpassing the love of these two twelfth-century *leoneses* for each other, is not contrary, not foreign, to the love they knew, the love and pain they experienced.

How foolish it all sounds—so much of what I have heard: If God is all-good and all-powerful—if this predication has any meaning at all—then why do the innocent suffer? True, such a question must occur to me, must torture me, if I have any sensibility at all, any capacity to love, any experience of being loved. And after today's *camino*, I don't see that any answer at all is possible, except to go deeply into the mystery of the Incarnation. The depth to which I go will determine how well I understand, how much pain I myself can accept, how passionately I shall love. All the words limp; they are poor, of extremely limited help. It is ultimately experience that leads to the truth. The simplicity of today's *camino*—around me, there is no spectacular scenery, inside me, there is the emptiness of self—the abandonment of rational abstraction, leave me open to the Mysteries of my prayer, the Mysteries of the Incarnation. I see more clearly than ever that one does not enter these Mysteries through academic reading and study, but by placing oneself in a place like this—of silence and solitude; and long reflection on the life stories of lovers long dead.

León—the last large city I shall walk through on the *camino*, well more than halfway to Compostela—is a city richly associated with pilgrims. At the end of the ninth century, when Alfonso III was king of León, it was the most important city in Christian Spain. Alfonso II (789–842), whose castle was in Oviedo, built the first basilica in Compostela to honor the tomb of Saint James the Apostle, whose body had been recently discovered there. He also worked to provide Oviedo with one of the greatest reliquaries in Europe. His successor, Alfonso III, built a second basilica at Compostela (877), assisting in its consecration in 899; the first one proved to be too small. In 910, Alfonso III moved the seat of the kingdom from Oviedo to León, where he died in that year. At the end of the tenth century (988), León suffered the distinction of being attacked by the great Muslim warrior Almanzor who, to the great relief of many in Christian cities, died in 1002.

In 1036, the relics of Saint Isidore (570–636), perhaps Spain's most illustrious saint, and a great encyclopedist, were brought from Seville—

then under Islamic control—to León. This was done through the initiative of Fernando I and his wife, Doña Sancha, following the pattern of collecting the relics of famous saints for the church of one's capital city. It is reported that numerous miracles then occurred through Isidore's intercession. This, in turn, attracted pilgrims, and is one of the few places in Spain that Aymeric Picaud notes as necessary to visit for their relics— the others being Santo Domingo de la Calzada, Sahagún—for the relics of the early saints, Facundo and Primitivo—and Compostela. The basilica honoring Isidore's relics is considered to be one of the great Romanesque treasures of the *camino*.

Aymeric Picaud, in his twelfth-century *Liber,* writes that the city is *llena de todas las felicidades*—full of all kinds of joys. Writing principally for French pilgrims, he refers most probably to the large number of good *hospitales* and to the fact that no Spanish city had more churches and monasteries during the High Middle Ages. In the minds of pilgrims, these would be important places to visit.

But I am tired, and interested in finding a new *refugio* whose opening I saw advertised on a bulletin board in Mansilla de las Mulas. Walking almost directly to it, I locate the place quite easily, right in the center of the city. It's in one of those monster buildings put up during the time of Franco, and it looks as if it was designed and built by the same people who disfigured the landscape of Burgos with that major seminary. This *refugio* was originally built as the Colegio de los Huérfanos Ferroviarios— for orphans of railroad employees—and looks as if it could hold more than a thousand children. There is a kind of park on two sides, so one does not enter directly into the building from the street. It appears that the place is now used for various different purposes, not as an orphanage, and the pilgrim shelter occupies only one wing of the third floor. It is open all day, except from nine in the morning to twelve noon, when two women come to clean. Altogether, there are ninety-one beds, four in the room to which I am assigned by the young man on duty at the desk. It's something like a hotel, with someone at this desk twenty-four hours a day, but there is no charge and no box for donations. The shelter is operated by the city, carrying on the tradition of being hospitable to pilgrims.

At the bottom of the stairs, I see something new: several machines that dispense soft drinks, coffee, and candy bars. Upstairs, there is a dining room, but no kitchen. Since it is Sunday, I hurry out to buy some food; I passed a small store that was still open on my way here. I can eat a cold lunch in the *refugio.* In some places, a food market will be open on Sundays—but not late in the afternoon.

On my way back to the shelter, I come to a pastry shop and my eyes are caught and held by all the fancy concoctions in the window. Why not get a treat to celebrate? I've covered well more than half the distance to Compostela, and it's Sunday. I can't resist the temptation, and go in, getting in line. When my turn comes, all my courage and excitement suddenly drain out of me; limp, I ask for some very plain, small donuts I see behind the glass, passing up all the more fantastic creations. What made me change so radically in the one instant? Is this the Spirit of the *camino,* keeping watch over my sense pleasures?

Back in the shelter, I do my laundry—the bathroom is huge—and shower. Then I eat lunch, ending with a cup of coffee from the machine and two donuts for dessert. There is a sign saying that one may stay here two days. In all other shelters, the rule has prescribed just one day. I feel certain, though, that one could get permission for another day, if needed to rest sore feet or muscles.

The young man at the desk tells me that a Frenchman came through last week, a retired army officer who was walking the *camino* for the eighth time! He averages forty kilometers every day. Another idea or wish: I would like to sit here in one of the *refugios* for some weeks or months and listen to the stories of the people who come through on the *camino.* I've learned that they come from the various countries of Europe, as well as North and South America, and I've even seen a guidebook—in Japanese—for Japanese pilgrims. Each traveler would have his or her personal history to tell, each with different dreams and hopes—as the Spanish say, with their *ilusiones,* an untranslatable word and sentiment. I have often wondered how people first hear about the *camino.* And the ancient question: What draws them to Compostela?

Today, I ask the question in León. The cathedral here is famous. And there are all those other monasteries and churches to see. But what does that mean? If I go out and pass by all these places this afternoon, will I *see* anything? I'm very uncertain. Seeing is not so simple. If I were to go out and take in all the "interesting" buildings, would that be an act of seeing or only an act of gross consumption? Instead of consuming some new gadget, some new cuisine, I would consume new "sights."

But, to begin with the basilica . . . I have no devotion at all to Saint Isidore; I know almost nothing about him. I have read only a few pages in his famous book, *Etimologías.* Would gawking at his tomb be anything more than morose curiosity?—according to medieval Scholastics, *not* a virtuous act!

This morning, as I walked, my eyes were opened—to see many snails on the path. I know that I saw them, because my seeing resulted in an action: I walked carefully so that I would not step on them; I recognized that it was more their soil than mine, and the good thing to do was to respect that truth.

There are many, many more remarkable buildings here in Spain to see—I've only come across a handful out of thousands. But I've looked at enough to recognize my confusion and ignorance . . . perhaps I've seen enough to begin to ask some good questions; perhaps if I see more, I shall only indulge an idle curiosity, only become a consumer of possibly memorable sights, only blunt and distort my capacity to frame the proper questions.

What lies behind the action of putting up these religious structures? What do they mean in the history of Spaniards? The direction from which to approach these questions seems clear: What is the connection between the Mysteries of the Rosary and the stones I see?

The Mysteries take me into the New Testament. There I see that Jesus was thoroughly respectful of Jewish custom. Out of their history, the Jews, too, had built in stone: the Temple in Jerusalem, of which they were proud, and synagogues in other cities, where they studied and prayed. Jesus never objected to these buildings. In fact, in the one recorded act of his life in which He displays some violence, He drives out all who are buying and selling in the Temple.

> He overturned the tables of the money changers and the benches of those selling doves. "It is written," he said to them, "My house will be called a house of prayer, but you are making it a den of robbers." (Matt. 21:12–13)

He is clearly zealous for the honor of this place. But, on another occasion, Jesus also said, "When you pray, go into your room, close the door and pray to your Father, who is unseen. Then your Father, who sees what is done in secret, will reward you" (Matt. 6:6). The worship of God does not require a building.

All the ecclesiastical monuments and churches are for us; God plainly has no need of them. They can do nothing for God. The only question then, is, What can they do for us? Their construction, maintenance, and use can give us the opportunity to honor God, can perhaps help us to move toward God, but can also promote our pride, serve our vanity. The matter requires some thought.

On the *camino,* I've learned that to enter the reality of pilgrim space, to join all who have preceded me, I must start with what I can touch, with what I feel. As is movingly illustrated in the story of Don Ponce and Doña Estefanía, perception occurs through the senses. Here in Spain, all construction that I have seen, all the buildings, belong to one of two classes. The first is precisely represented by what I saw as I entered León today. At the edge of the city, I saw a fence enclosing a large, grassy area with a very modern building set back at some distance from the street. Between the street and the Caja España office building—some kind of bank, I suppose—the professionally landscaped green area contained a fountain that shot water high into the air. The whole was put together by four groups of people: the financial decision-makers at the top, the office of architects and engineers who drew up the plans, the suppliers of materials, and the workmen who put the pieces together on the site. As one can see from the finished product, the workmen were only the adjuncts of the machines that prepared the materials. At no place in the finished work— unless there is some defect—can one see the sign of a workman's hand. An indication that this is a human creation can only be grasped in the overall design, in the abstract conception of the use of space, shapes, and materials. The fact that it doesn't fall down, that the grass has no weeds, shows that someone was behind the project, human intelligence was at work. But there is no evidence that anyone ever *touched* any part of the structure or its grounds.

Along the *camino,* I have also seen many examples of a very different kind of construction—small houses and buildings for farm animals, stone bridges and chapels, or very modest churches. In these structures, I can see that every stone was set individually in its place. It did not come from a stone factory, standardized, shaped, and ready to fit in any place. I saw that a man fitted each stone with his eye, hammer, and chisel. The result is a distinctively human work, the creation of a true artist. These ancient buildings required many skilled artisans on the spot; the modern ones require many machines at a great distance. The old way fostered maximum *use* value—joyful accomplishment in the act of building. The new one allows only *exchange* value—the worker puts in his time for his wages. Modern workers are engaged principally in assembling what someone else has designed and engineered. The difference is striking in the small bridges—the old ones, composed of individual stones, shaped in graceful arches; the new ones, with the gaunt steel, soon rusting, covered with dirty asphalt. Their frequent state of slight disrepair reflects a lack of interest in their careful maintenance. As with a TV set, would one want to pass it down to the grandchildren?

So, churchmen and religious inspiration at one time gave many men good work to do, fine human work, work that honored both God and man. I can thus marvel at the delicate stonework in the cathedral of Burgos, or in the cloister at Nájera, artistry that seems to defy the character of the material. I could see that individual men, working there, directly created beautiful things. These places are now eloquent testimonies to the gifts and disciplined workmanship of those unnamed and unknown artists. But so far on the *camino,* I have seen no evidence of this kind of work being done today. The best that modern society appears capable of doing is the repair and restoration of ancient achievements. I suspect that I don't see this astonishing quality of work today because all is constructed differently: the very conception of work and workman; the prima donna status assigned to a few and a lowly mass status given to the many. Modern technology reflects and abets the divisions. Here, the computer accurately stands for the new machines and their organization of society: Every technical advance means that fewer understand and control the centers of power, while more are relegated to stupefying tasks or to no place at all in the society. I conclude that such methods of construction cannot glorify God or honor men. Nobody needs it! The leap from one way of building to the other is like the jump from the oxcart to the tractor, from organic grace to blueprint coldness. The historical break is of great consequence, but I don't need to see more buildings to understand it better. Seeing more would mostly mean more consumption, more indigestion, more heartburn.

The ultimate purpose of religious building has not changed since men first set up a special pile of stones—*we,* not God, need them. Perhaps the time has come to examine more carefully the way we make the pile of stones. Why not get rid of all the old structures? Give them all to the government and let the ministries of culture and tourism do what they want with them. What is needed today, as the physical basis for prayer and worship, is good work. One of the essential aspects of the beauty that tourists admire in these ancient churches is the character of the work that produced them: good work makes beautiful things. If religiously minded people want beauty today—something humanly fitting as a setting for worship—they must foster the appropriate kind of work.

Why not found a new kind of religious order, one of men and women, married and single, to build new places of worship for today's believers? They could work in stone, or whatever materials are native or common to a place, using simple tools, making small buildings—of human dimensions—for the people of faith communities. The local people could house them, offering genuine hospitality while construction proceeded. Working austerely, lovingly, they would fulfill the vocation of true artists, working to express beauty rather than to get rich. Now, all this talent is lost to Spain, lost to history. But people must still possess the ability to conceptualize inspiring spaces, to carve and shape impressive forms. The machines are devastating the country, leaving behind a wasteland whose dreariness is relieved now and then only by one of these ancient handmade structures. But the Church has promoted beauty in the past. It must have some obligation to do the same today. The people require it, are thirsty for it. This would seem the historical moment to take up literally the command heard by Saint Francis in the early thirteenth century, "Repair my church." We know that once people erected buildings that respected both themselves and God. Today, the machines have made all such expressions of humanly made, *touched* beauty, impossible. The Church could move in, seize this great historical opportunity.

Every people on earth must constantly guard themselves from the temptation to let religiosity smother faith. The history of Spanish religious hubris is unique, very different from that of other nations and groups. Faith usually begins with religion. But then what? How avoid getting mired down in religion? How keep the community open to the transcendent? If one could learn to work with stone in a human way, on a human scale, which means that the individual artist would leave his or her imprint on both the design and the workmanship, one could then transcend religion, reach out to faith. One will ascend to the heavens only to the extent that one is rooted in the particularity of what one has grasped, touched, shaped.

The two Canadians arrive and are put in my room. They are so tired that they plan to take advantage of the rule allowing two days' stay in the *refugio*. Tomorrow, they'll rest and do some sightseeing in León. In other centuries, there were also rules for pilgrim use of the shelters. Laffi reports that when he arrived at a *hospital* here in León and requested the usual portion of food, they marked his pilgrim staff so that he could not return for more. Other historical accounts note that in certain periods beggars pretended to be pilgrims and attempted to live off the handouts and beds of the shelters. Even today, there is a general rule that a person should provide a letter from his or her parish priest, attesting to the fact that one is in good standing in a local parish and is genuinely a pilgrim attempting to walk to Compostela. So I should have presented such a letter in Roncesvalles before receiving my *credencial.* I had no letter, was not asked for one, and have not heard that anyone pays attention to the rule. In the eighteenth century, however, Albani carried documents from his local ecclesiastical authorities in Italy.

21

León to Villadangos del Páramo

May 24, 1993

I am out of the *refugio* and walking through the empty streets at my usual early hour. The only sound is the rhythmical tapping of my staff on the pavement, until I come to a bakery. Here, some workmen disturb the morning silence while loading a delivery truck with the day's fresh bread. Then, turning a corner, I surprise a woman coming out of a house—she looks as if she's going across the street to a neighbor because she has run out of coffee or milk. Startled by the sight of me, striding down the middle of the street with a large pack on my back and a long staff in hand, she stops, looks, then her face opens in a smile and she calls out, "¡Muy madrugador!"—"Well, you're an early bird!" Laughing, I return her greeting, without slowing my pace.

A few minutes later, it starts to rain heavily. Then, the street that the *camino* takes out of the city becomes a highway. Out here, people are up and speeding along in their vehicles. For the commuters and merchandise transporters, the day must begin early. The asphalt allows me to rush as well, and I soon come to a sign indicating the town, La Virgen del Camino.

According to an old tradition, the Virgin appeared nearby to a shepherd named Alvar Simón in the early sixteenth century. She asked Alvar to approach the bishop of León and tell him to build a church with her image in this place. Fearful that the bishop would never believe such a story, Alvar begged the Virgin to give him some sign that he could use to convince the bishop. She then requested Alvar's slingshot and, putting a small stone in it, shot the stone some six hundred paces from where they stood. She explained that when Alvar and his companions, including the bishop, returned, they would readily recognize the place for the church when they saw how much the stone, now invisible, had increased in size. And so it turned out.

Today, a newer church, built in 1961, marks the spot. It is dedicated to La Virgen del Camino, the patroness of León. This very modern structure, with its monumental sculptures of the Apostles and the Virgin on the facade, is thought to be representative of the vitality of contemporary religious architecture. It's true that the overall form seems to say that some imaginative architect (Fray Francisco Coello from Portugal) designed this. And the bronze statues, each six meters high, were obviously done by a sculptor (José María Subirachs). But the actual construction—the materials and the way they are used—is just as clearly the work of machines. All the surfaces shine with the smoothness of the artificial stone I saw in the benches before arriving in El Burgo Raneros.

The only persons who have left an imprint on this building, who are remembered and honored now by its physical presence, are the architect and the sculptor. No workman's handprint can be seen. The conception of the structure faithfully follows the bias of contemporary society: There is a radical division between artist and workman: one is allowed great freedom "to perform," to become a personality; the other is ignored or replaced by machines. The predictable result is that *no* honest, true work is done. Artists' work becomes more and more precious and false. Society is more and more flooded with monotonous and shoddy junk. Would that the rain could cleanse people's imaginations!

I have heard that there is also a good *refugio* here, but I've only completed about five kilometers. A hard rain is nothing to make me quit for the day. A few meters farther on the road, and I notice a sign for a bar and restaurant—just when the fury of the rain and wind has increased appreciably. In León, I had seen a notice on the bulletin board, advertising this business, and saying that they offered a special lunch to pilgrims. I decide to go in for a cup of coffee; perhaps the elements will calm somewhat in the meantime. I hang the poncho from the top of my staff, put the backpack against the wall, and sit down to enjoy a hot coffee with the last of the small donuts.

I look out the window, and at the clock. The rain has not relented, but it is much too early in the day to take advantage of the special lunch, so I resignedly shoulder the pack, put on and snap shut the poncho, grab my staff and step out the door. I have learned that rain and mud are nothing to complain about. Rain and asphalt—with cars and trucks speeding past—are unpleasant, even disturbing, but it would be truly foolish to call upon the intervention of the Virgin. If I think about it, the very discomfort should serve to provoke reflection on all this motor power continually rushing along, splashing me with dirty water.

For nearly three weeks, I have moved across the earth using only my feet. Occasionally, as today, I feel I am directly assaulted by cars; they mock me, they rebuke me, I imagine they would like to get rid of me—this stubborn pedestrian who insists that one's feet are the opening to a world of unimagined delights and wonders, a world closed to the occupants of cars. But I have to admit that my experience is not that of others. I own no car and hope that I never again live in a situation where I need one. In my present wealth, I am greatly privileged. But in every country where I have been, those who have cars are fanatically attached to them; those who do not have them, long for the day when their economic situation will permit the possession of this universal symbol. For the power of this mechanical object over people's imaginations and desires far surpasses the nature of any purely utilitarian good. As a friend in Mexico once told me when we discussed the possibility of reducing the number of cars in Mexico City that the people there might breathe, "That's a crazy idea; Mexicans will kill for their cars."

I suppose that for Spaniards, as for everyone else in the world—insofar as my experience extends—the car has become the perfect symbol of a modern, advanced, technical society, the society to which every nation apparently aspires. If one has a car, then freedom—perhaps the greatest of modern illusions—is physically in one's hands. The *feel* of a steering wheel, the immediate, surging response to a slight pressure on the accelerator, the kilometers rapidly dropping far behind—all create the delusion of personal power in a society where nearly everyone is trapped, and most are powerless, in the remorseless clutches of the economy. One can establish or raise his or her status with this magical symbol. I can hope to prove my worth by *its* style and value.

I have often wondered: Why do people get into their cars so often? Studies seem to show that usage has little to do with utility. Walking along here in the rain, feeling that I am truly *in* the rain—I am not going to get out of it; that is not the purpose of my movement—and seeing all these people whizzing by, I cannot but think that they are trying to escape. They're not going some place; they are attempting to leave some thing. Well, what can that be?

From the perspective of the *camino,* from the place of the *camino,* the great wonderworld of technological progress appears more and more artificial, more and more a vicious hoax. But it's a peculiar kind of artificiality. For example, all the people in the cars are enclosed in a perfect shell. If one of their new cars—and they all seem to be new—were to develop a leak, letting in rain, they would immediately return to the dealer with a righteous complaint. This kind of artificial covering—by general agreement—protects them from inclement weather, from nature. Not only does the car provide this wonderful control over nature but, in those places where a modern economy "works," it is universally accessible to all and, except for those times when one must be about earning the money to pay for it, is immediately available. Through my car, I can escape the reality of nature. I can be more than a mere creature.

In the Middle Ages, men who attempted to understand the human condition puzzled over a reference in Sacred Scripture to "the noonday devil." They came to name this *acedia,* a certain kind of weariness when one comes to feel that the effort to seek truth is just too much trouble; one becomes tired of moral and intellectual disciplines and seeks distractions, entertainments. Looking at people's faces, observing their interests and movements, I often have the impression that there is a modern *acedia,* more widespread among those who are higher in the world of technology; it is called boredom. As boredom rises among the affluent, so does the sophistication and glamour of their masquerades. Hoping to stimulate their dulled sensibilities, they continually seek novel amusements, among which the car occupies a unique place today.

Some who see the havoc and insanity of the car suggest the bicycle for those who want to move faster than their feet will carry them. I think of this when reflecting on my experiences with bicycle riders here on the *camino.* Further, in no large city or town where I've been in Spain do I see people riding their bicycles as a means of getting to some place. In fact, the roads and streets with their traffic are such as to make bicycles extremely dangerous, if not altogether impossible. I have only seen people *using* bicycles out in the villages—occasionally, I come across an older person on an old-fashioned bicycle. But from the omnipresent TV screen in the bars, I have noticed that there is a great interest in bicycle races—which today, I would guess, is a very high-tech and specialized sport for professionals. As farmers jumped from the oxcart to the tractor, so urban people jumped from walking to the car.

What a great distance separates me from all the people who flash past me! On what common ground could we ever meet? And what if they look closely as they hurry on, and notice the Rosary dangling from my hand? The students in 1928 prayed the Rosary as they made their way to Compostela from Madrid. They noted the surprise on the faces of people who passed them and saw this. In these times, today, what can automobile people think? Does my strange appearance invite them to reflect on where they are? Or do they experience only a fleeting, dismissive thought: That guy really is an anachronism!

Before noon, I complete the twenty kilometers from León and am at the edge of Villadangos del Páramo. I ask the first person I meet about the location of the *refugio,* not wishing to walk any farther than necessary in this rain. I learn that it's right here, just a few steps away, at this edge of town. I walk across the street and come upon a new building, seemingly just finished. It is surrounded by bare dirt, and several wheelbarrows are stood up at one side, resting in the mud. Some stones and planks make up a kind of bridge, and I can get up to the door. It is open! I can walk right in. The place is empty; I am apparently the first to arrive today.

The structure is designed specifically as a new *refugio,* and has some interesting features. Instead of one large dormitory, there are small rooms, without doors, containing two double bunks. In the center of the building, are a nicely constructed fireplace and a large table where people can meet and eat. Behind a wall is a modern kitchen with a coin-operated electric stove. There are lots of windows—which I like—and they give the place a cheery atmosphere even on this dark afternoon. In many of the older buildings, the scarcity of windows makes the *refugio* a rather gloomy place on cloudy and rainy days. It's very decidedly a machine-made product, but the workmanship of the stone fireplace contributes something unique, cries out with the claim that there *is* another way to build. This charming touch of a workman's artistry contrasts strongly with all the rest of the construction. I wonder if the architect, after viewing the finished shelter, saw the radical difference? Did she design it this way? Did she know what she was doing? Two very different modes of working gave two results, each having very little in common with the other. What a pity that there is no wood about to build a fire. A blazing fire after dark tonight would wondrously transform this place.

I wash out my socks and hang them up to dry, along with some things from yesterday's laundry, which didn't get completely dry in León. I see from the printed house rules that I can get my *credencial* stamped by the town's mayor, a woman, who is also the local pharmacist. She is available at the pharmacy during business hours—I can probably just reach her before she closes up for lunch. I put on my poncho and set out, looking for someone who can direct me to the pharmacy and places to buy food.

I come upon an older man who is busily loading boxes of empty soft drink bottles on the back of a truck, and ask for help. With great courtesy, he carefully explains where I have to go, and then asks me where I am from. He has obviously inferred where I am going, and then asks me—

candidly, simply—to give Santiago a kiss from him when I get to Compostela. I understand the request, for I've heard that on the main altar of the cathedral there is a large statue of Santiago. Behind the altar, there is a stairway leading up to this statue. At the top, one can reach the back of the statue's head, and it is the custom of pilgrims to kiss it. Yet another instance of the spontaneous friendliness I've encountered all along the *camino.*

In spite of the detailed directions, I experience some confusion in finding the pharmacy; another small town with twisting streets. There, the mayor/pharmacist stamps my *credencial,* and tells me that if I want to eat in a restaurant, there is a good one across the street from the *refugio.* I thank her, and go in search of a bakery and market. The bakery is easy to find, and I buy bread. When I arrive at the small market, I find it closed—but for no apparent reason. There is no one around to ask for further directions; the town does not seem large enough to support another store. Some rain continues to come down, so I decide to try the restaurant. I haven't had a hot meal since enjoying the fresh mushrooms in Mansilla de las Mulas.

The lunch nicely fulfills the mayor's promise, and the young woman who waits on me is singularly pleasant. Returning to the shelter, I notice one of those video machines in a corner of the foyer—the same machine I had seen in the Information Office—where was that?—Castrojeriz, I think. How daft! Why would anyone who is *on* the *camino* want to look at a video *about* the *camino?* Back at the Information Office, I was not curious enough about the machine to see what it actually contained, and I feel no desire to find out now.

Later, a young boy comes in and asks if he can help me in any way. His mother also has a stamp for the *credencial,* and she lives behind the *refugio.* She is available at all times, but one must walk around several streets to get to her house. I thank him for the information and the offer of help, explaining that I don't really need anything more. Again, people solicitous for the pilgrims, seeking to show them the town's spirit of hospitality. He plays a while with the video machine before going out.

The town's curious history has left a powerful image of "traditional" Spanish religiosity. In 1111, Villadangos del Páramo was the place of a bloody battle between the army of Queen Doña Urraca and that of her husband, Alfonso VI, El Batallador, king of Aragon. The town's parish church is dedicated to Santiago, and one of Europe's most famous statues of him is over the main altar. Here he is portrayed as the Matamoros on his white horse, sword in hand, a dying Moor beneath the horse's raised front hooves. Horse and rider are leaping out toward the congregation. What a queer place, this *camino!* Every person whom I've met in

Villadangos would seem to be the living heir of the Peregrino's, not the Matamoros's, spirit. What do they see when they enter their church and contemplate the bloodthirsty warrior?

Still alone, I happen later to glance out the window, and see one of the Spanish pilgrims who gave me the mushrooms. With his head bent down in the rain, he is walking right by, not seeing this building, set back some distance from the street, and unaware in any case that it is the *refugio*. I run to the door and shout. He turns, seems quite surprised to see me standing there, and then comes up on the makeshift walk. We happily exchange greetings, and then he watches the road for the rest of their group. When they all arrive, quite a festive atmosphere reigns in the somewhat sterile shelter. A fire in that fireplace would be the perfect accompaniment to the glowing cheer of these good people. They must have eaten earlier in the day, for they heat only some soup on the stove—which works with the money deposit!—and they insist that I take some. In the guest book, one pilgrim wrote, complaining, that she paid her one hundred pesetas, but got no heat.

One of the men tells me that he wants to found a group of people who would help in the maintenance of these *refugios*. One place might be lacking some furnishings that the group could then supply. Another might need some work and those skilled could volunteer their labor, and so on. I told him that I thought there were associations already formed for these various purposes. I had heard of several here in Spain, and of others in France, Belgium, and England. I had the impression that there were more—for example, in Germany. He might look into this and find that existing efforts needed only more interested people to collaborate. It was good to see someone who already had the idea of giving something back to the *camino,* even before he reached the end of his pilgrimage. The conversation made me want to find out more about these shelters—this one obviously represents a considerable investment. And I don't think the voluntary donations would ever cover such an expense.

Leafing through the guest book—usually called "El libro de peregrinos"—I see that someone else has written, "El camino es fe, sudor y esperanza"—"the *camino* is faith, sweat, and hope." Well, yes—if one had only a handful of words, it would be difficult to improve on that characterization.

The curious, spontaneous experience in the pastry shop yesterday has made me wonder. Without thinking about it, without any conscious plan of self-denial, I see that I never seek any extras, or sensual specialties except, when available, the daily *café con leche.* I have a vague feeling that that is the proper way to be on the *camino.* The one comfort about which I am unbending is to wear only clean, dry socks—two pairs with my shoes. To go back to my prayer of the very first day, it would seem that I need this to get to Compostela, as I need only a bearable amount of pain. But perhaps I have not gone deeply enough into this matter of physical comfort. I have good shoes, a fine sleeping bag, a well-designed backpack, a waterproof poncho. No pilgrim of former years traveled in such style and comfort—except possibly royalty and nobles. A couple of times Albani found that he had slept on a mattress that was full of bedbugs (I'm guessing that this is the insect he means). When he got out on the *camino* again, in the sunshine, he took off all his clothes and attempted to kill all the tiny creatures, one by one. He is quite expansive in his description of the annoyance caused by these bugs. Although I have often lain on filthy and greasy mattresses, I really slept soundly in my *clean* sleeping bag. I have experienced nothing of the discomfort of former pilgrims. Am I too comfortable to join them? to know the *camino?*

22

Villadangos del Páramo to Astorga

May 25, 1993

W hen I step out of the door, the overcast sky is so dark that it appears to be the middle of the night, but my clock says 7 A.M. Before I came to Spain, I would have said: Oh, what a miserable morning to begin a daylong walk! Can I put it off until tomorrow? But now, I just start out, feeling fresh each morning, eager to discover more new places, knowing that it will be a good day. For this has been the experience—every day, without exception.

After a couple of hours' threats, the rain begins, the heavens opening generously. And I'm still on a highway, being struck from all sides. First, gusts of wind and rain push in one direction, then a vehicle coming at me in another, a car or truck passing, coming at me from behind, in yet another, or I am buffeted several ways at once. About a meter away, the comfortable and protected drivers and passengers race along, listening to their stereos, to the kind of music that takes them to their preferred world. They look so dry and contented in their grownup's toys, being entertained all the way to their destinations.

But where are these places? Now they are securely enclosed in fashionable forms of glass, plastic, and metal. But this place is only the beginning. Beyond the body sculpted upholstery lie further successive layers of comfort and protection: employment, various kinds of welfare systems, insurance to cover property and life, webs of social obligations and favors, networks of information and entertainment and, always, corresponding bills and debts. If one scratches the surface, there is almost always fear. Behind all the supports and assurances, the economy seems never to cease being problematic. Each week or month, some new crisis in one sector or another, in one country or another. Just recently, the European Community again "forced" the current head of the Spanish government, Felipe González, to devalue the peseta. What if I can't keep up the payments on this marvelous machine? What if the economy really turns sour?

A Mercedes meets an old-fashioned pair of leather shoes—out here on the *camino* to Compostela. Are we in the same universe? What can these people think when they see me?—there's a fool, or a bum; an inexplicable anomaly; a public nuisance, cluttering up the highway. I suppose I appear very much out of place, a trespasser on *their* territory, in *their* world. Struggling to keep from being blown off the road, or from being sucked into the path of an oncoming car by the speeding trucks, I think it would be a great bit of luck if the *camino* were to head out through some nice, sticky mud.

As if in answer to my wish, I soon come upon an alternate route for the *camino*—down a dirt path. I know that the highway leads directly to Astorga, where I want to arrive today, but I jump at the opportunity to get out into the wet country soil, no matter how much farther or rougher it turns out to be. I should know by now, however, that good luck has nothing to do with a better or worse *camino*. Neither "luck" nor "better" make any sense. My attitude ought to be that of respectful and alert awareness, a limpid openness to what is. Here, Saint Paul can be taken quite literally, "In all things God works for the good of those who love him" (Rom. 8:28).

I approach a small town, Hospital de Orbigo, which must be as confusing as it is important in the history of the *camino*—while thinking of history as a possible way to enter the complexity of this place. Near here, in 1434, a gala monthlong tourney of knights provided footsore pilgrims with a spectacle of medieval valor and illusion, a strange medley of noble skills, courtly love, and religiosity. As an exercise intimately related to the *camino,* the festival can be approached by going back a hundred years earlier. In 1332, Alfonso XI made a pilgrimage from Burgos to Compostela. During the last few kilometers, from what is today called "El Monte de Gozo," he walked barefoot. When he got to the cathedral, he placed his medieval arms and armor on the high altar, and knelt in vigil throughout the night. He prayed. In the morning, the archbishop, Juan de Limia, celebrated Mass and blessed the weapons. He then returned them to Alfonso, thereby arming him as a Christian knight. Alfonso arose and went up to greet the statue of Santiago, kissing it, like any pilgrim. This action was partly in recognition of the fact that knights from all of Christian Europe looked on Santiago as their special saint, a patron of chivalry who, for them, incarnated the glorious deeds of a holy crusader in his miraculous appearances as a warrior against the Moors. These people had converted the disciple of Christ into the Matamoros, the invincible champion against Islam, the prototype of a Spanish knight fighting in the Reconquista, and of a European knight fulfilling the ideal of a crusader.

It was a custom then for the nobles of Alfonso's court in Burgos to invite passing knights on their way to Compostela to stop long enough for some knightly jousting before resuming their pilgrimage.

But one must go back yet farther. Some believe that history is written on the *caminos,* the great routes of warriors. Spain in the Middle Ages boasted of three routes: that of Charlemagne, that of Almanzor, and that of Mío Cid (Rodrigo Díaz de Vivar), the great historical and mythic hero celebrated in the *Poema del Cid* (1140). The paths of all three leaders led to Compostela. According to one legend, Charlemagne, inspired in dreams by Santiago, followed the Milky Way to Galicia, to free the Apostle's tomb from the control of the Moors, thereby opening the *camino* to French and other European pilgrims. Almanzor actually attacked the city in 997, destroying the basilica—but not touching the tomb of Santiago—and took the bells to Córdoba, where they were turned into lamps for the mosque. Christian captives were forced to carry them on their shoulders.

El Cid (Don Rodrigo) was *the* representative figure in Christian Spain at the end of the eleventh century, a fearless warrior in a warrior society. He made a pilgrimage to Compostela with his knights in 1064. On the way, they heard a terrible cry from a swamp along the road. Approaching, they saw a man, a leper, praying that someone, for the love of God and the Holy Virgin, would rescue him. El Cid pulled him out and put him in front of himself on his own horse. They arrived at an inn where they planned to spend the night. Sitting down to eat, El Cid let the leper eat from his plate. Such immoderate solicitude for this wretch greatly angered all the knights. But El Cid, the illustrious hero, simply ignored them, and went so far as to put the leper in his bed.

"Are you sleeping or awake, Rodrigo?" asked the leper.

"I cannot sleep," El Cid answered, "Please tell me—who are you? that such a light shines out from you?"

"I am San Lázaro, Rodrigo . . . I am the leper you cared for so well, for the love of God."

Three roads to Compostela, each filled with heroic deeds . . . and blood. This, indeed, is one history of the Peninsula. But around each of these roads, people also formed many *ilusiones*—wish-filled dreams, hoped-for goals, imagined ideals. When referring to this aspect of Spanish sensibilities, those from colder cultures speak disparagingly about "building castles in Spain." And now, with mid-twentieth century affluence, Europeans and others from farther away seek to inhabit an actual castle in Spain, permanently or during a holiday. To find the *camino,* one must clear away the vain dreams and search for the clear *ilusión,* the one some Spaniards have held steadfastly before themselves. This is the courage to believe in an impossible dream, tempered with humor. One is not embarrassed to tilt at windmills, or to believe in one's Guardian Angel.

There are records of many knights who went to Compostela to thank Santiago for saving them in some battle, or for redeeming them when they were captured by the Moors. Other accounts tell of knights who seemed to use the journey to Compostela as an opportunity to seek jousts and chivalric adventures along the way. One of the most famous of these pilgrims—if indeed he was a pilgrim—is Nicolás von Papplau from Breslau, who went to Compostela in 1480. He had a lance that was so heavy and large that a special cart carried it for him. It was said that he was the only man strong enough to lift it and use it in a tourney. The ancient chronicle adds that although he presented a fierce appearance, he behaved like any peaceful pilgrim when he approached the holy shrine.

The series of tourneys that began on July 10, 1434, near the Puente de Orbigo, was recorded by a witness (a notary, Pero Rodríguez de Lena), thus making the bridge and nearby town one of the most famous places in the history of chivalry. The games were organized as a "Passo Honroso" by a "great knight" from León, Suero de Quiñones. This kind of event took place next to a road on which people traveled. A knight or knights (here, Suero de Quiñones and eight friends) challenged all knights who came along and wanted to pass—in this instance, to continue their pilgrimage to Compostela. Sixty-eight knights from Germany, Valencia, France, Italy, Aragon, Brittany, England, Castille, Portugal, and "other places" accepted the challenge. During the month there were 727 jousts in which 166 lances were broken. They halted the festivities on only one day, the feast of Santiago, July 25th, which fell on a Sunday that year, making it a special Holy Year. Hence, more pilgrims than usual would be coming along the road and could stop for the entertainment. The chronicler adds that the knights had another motive, too, for taking a rest on this day: one of their fellows, an *aragonés* (someone from Aragon), was killed in the contests.

After all the games, Suero de Quiñones and many of the other knights went to Compostela. There, Suero prostrated himself before the statue of the saint, thanking him for the victories and the successful outcome of so many chivalric feats of skill and courage. One story relates that Suero de Quiñones claimed to be a prisoner of love, enslaved by his passion for a beautiful married woman. He proposed to free himself from these shackles by breaking a large number of lances, taking Santiago as his witness.

In the seventeenth century, Laffi stayed in this same place—Hospital de Orbigo—overnight. From his account, the reader soon sees that he always looks for a good place to sleep. For example, he seldom stays in the *hospitales* for pilgrims, seeking instead better accommodations for which, of course, he pays. In Hospital de Orbigo, the best he could find was a hut where he had to sleep on the bare ground. Commenting on the poverty of the place, he reports that the people were so miserable that he felt he should pay them for this radical minimum of hospitality. As one sees from Laffi's book—a "best-seller" in Europe when published—that he, too, no less than the knights of the fourteenth and fifteenth centuries, created his own Santiago, a magical-mythical figure with the power to fascinate and capture one's imagination.

In the twentieth century, Hospital de Orbigo appears, at first glance, as another fairly prosperous small town. But then a wonderful surprise, a vision out of folklore and the mysteries of creation: five stork nests—with storks in them! Four perched on top of a square church tower, and one more on the roof of an adjoining building—a regular colony. The town must possess some occult power of attraction to have been blessed by so many of these legendary creatures. Like silent nuns praying for the children of God, these still witnesses watch over the community.

I then come to a long and apparently ancient stone bridge, constructed of many graceful arcs, one after the other. This must be the historic Puente de Orbigo, near the site of Suero de Quiñones' medieval pageant. The bridge is truly a work of great art—the proportions are marvelous, the workmanship shines with the splendor of an artisan's skilled hand, the final construction is a beautiful and useful contribution to the community; a lovely human effort to complement the presence of nature seen in the storks, an inspiring work to place alongside the shoes I saw in Belorado.

I've heard that there is a very good *refugio* here, and the continuing rain tempts me to stop, but it's still quite early in the day. After being refreshed and strengthened by the sight of such wonders, I feel like pushing on. I'm eager to see what new thrill awaits me ahead. Shortly after, I come to an expensive-looking small hotel; it must be here for tourists. Well, why not stop for a coffee? At this early hour, on such a day, I'll probably not cause any problems for the employees—I would not want to embarrass them by my brashness, presenting them with a thoroughly unkempt and dirty customer. I haven't looked at myself, and have trouble imagining how awful I must appear: my old muddy shoes, the torn trousers, also caked with mud almost up to the knees, a much-used and rough pilgrim staff in my hand, the unwieldy backpack with rolled-up plastic mat tied on, the huge poncho covering me and pack, a greatly misshapen black felt hat and, underneath the poncho, an old gray sweatshirt. Curious. I don't have a single item of clothing in the backpack that would make me look more respectable, except for one decent short-sleeved shirt. But it's been much too cold to wear it. I lean the staff against the wall and enter. Taking off the poncho, pack, and hat, I find that I am alone—there is only the young man behind the bar. Good. Looking around, I see that the place is quite elegant, rather too polished for the likes of me today. But at this hour of the morning, we'll get along fine. He's probably happy to see someone come in out of the rain.

When I start out again, the rain slackens and then stops. A lovely, fresh spring day lights my path, and everything appears especially pleasant. I pass through fields, an occasional small village, climb into mountainous hill country, and walk through a stout and healthy-looking forest. Already an incredible variety of scenes and settings, yet the day is still young. Much of the time, my feet traverse a kind of cobblestone path. The farmers must find this useful to get to the fields on their tractors, or to lead their animals to pasture. The stones are just small enough to make themselves individually felt through the bottoms of my shoes. Thus, one might consider this a rough surface for walking, hard on the feet. But I think, rather, that the discomfort is an invitation to experience more fully the character of the day's *camino*—which is always particular, unique, sharp, never general, vague, or uniform.

After about six hours' walking, I see Astorga before me. It seems to be an especially confusing intermingling of hills with buildings rising from them on all sides and in all directions. I am reminded of El Greco's paintings of Toledo. The scene in front of me, however, is much more cheerful; there is no air of foreboding, no trace of hovering darkness. And I bring certain impressions with me, too. In the Middle Ages, no city on the *camino* except Burgos had more *hospitales* for pilgrims. The three students who came through here in 1928 were delightedly impressed by the loveliness of the young ladies they saw as they walked through the streets. And I've heard that some of the fantastic architecture of Gaudí is here. But I think I would need more time to enter the bizarre and daring world of his powerful imagination. From the pictures I've seen with my untrained eye, his wild creations appear to be profoundly distant from that glum seminary in Burgos.

A woman whom I meet at the edge of town tells me that there are two routes to the *refugio*. From her description, I decide to take the less complicated one, although it may be longer. This takes me downtown and near the episcopal palace, one of Gaudí's famous buildings. At a red light, I ask some people for further directions. This leads to a friendly conversation, and a small crowd gathers around me. They take a lively interest in me, as a pilgrim, asking the usual questions about where I come from. Someone asks my age, and the answer—sixty-five—evokes general astonishment. I have the impression that they are most concerned that I should dare to do this alone—at my advanced age! Laughing, I continue my way down the street and come to a complex of buildings that must be a large school, the place of the shelter. I have heard that this is operated by a group called the Hermanos Holandeses.

In the compound, I am directed to a small room at the end of a building that seems to be a residence—perhaps for the brothers. The room contains six or eight double bunks, one toilet with shower, and hot water. Outside the room, there is a broad porch with clothesline, and I hang my laundry there. Since there is no kitchen, I decide to hurry back and buy some food at a market I passed in town. There I find my usual supermarket cold lunch: a slice of ham, a can of mixed vegetables, bread, cheese, yogurt, fruit, and the cheap but good wine that comes in a paper carton.

Next to the shelter is a garden, about ten meters square, enclosed by a wall, containing a well cared for selection of flowers, shrubs, and a couple of small trees—the ideal place, with bright sun, to eat my lunch. It is rather cool in the shade, and I wonder whether I will ever experience any hot weather in Spain. But today has brought me everything I could possibly wish for. In the distance, coming over the mountains toward me, I see some angry-looking black clouds, creating a scene of moving, ever varying drama in the sky.

At times, I think that I should make a greater effort to know my fellow pilgrims better. Some days ago, I met three Frenchwomen in one of the *refugios*. Late last night, one of them arrived alone, in Villadangos. She said that her two companions were somewhere behind her. Now I see that she has arrived here, still alone, without any further knowledge of her friends. That means that she has been walking alone at least these last two days, knowing no Spanish. How wonderful to see another woman walking alone on the *camino,* just like the young American I met in Santo Domingo de la Calzada; then to meet the person herself, who is not afraid to do this. I admire her courage and independence. Several times she has arrived at a *refugio* some hours after me, but she has covered the same distance that day.

A young Frenchman also comes in—on his way *back* from Compostela.

He has also been to Fatima, the shrine of the Virgin in Portugal, and to Lourdes, the one in southern France. He shows me a large stack of stamped *credenciales*—he has stopped in a lot of places! On his hat he has a shell, the traditional sign of a Compostela pilgrim, together with a pin displaying the French flag. On a string around his neck, he wears a bigger shell. He also carries a rather large cardboard sign that identifies him as a pilgrim, lists the important places of pilgrimage he has visited, and states that he seeks a bed and voluntary offerings. Without these excellent *refugios* along the *camino,* one would need a good deal of money to pay for lodging each night. Not only have I found an extremely cheap—or costless—shelter each night, but I have passed up others when I wished to walk farther. There has been no problem at all in finding a bed when I wanted it.

Late in the afternoon, the other two Frenchwomen arrive and joyously greet their friend. How happy I am, too, to see them reunited. They seem to travel well together. The one walks faster, and goes at her preferred pace. The other two catch up with her now and then. They do not talk much with the young man, also from France, which seems strange to me. It's true that his appearance and behavior are a bit unusual, but my French is not good enough to form any clear opinion about him. From my experience so far, a knowledge of French, Spanish, and English would be sufficient to speak with nearly all pilgrims, since the other Europeans know English. I wish my French were more fluent. I can understand most of what is being said to me, but I cannot really maintain a decent conversation.

23

Astorga to Foncebadón

May 26, 1993

Yesterday, Wednesday, turned out to be the most unusual and thrilling day on the *camino* yet. I got an early start from Astorga and, after a few kilometers on a fairly quiet highway, came to a village. The yellow arrows indicated that the *camino* would continue to follow this road. But a street ran straight through the small village in the same direction, and a dirt road went on out past the few houses. Meeting some farmers, I asked them if I would get to Rabanal del Camino—a place that, according to my map, had a *refugio*—if I took the dirt road rather than the highway. They assured me that I would. Willing to risk a bit to avoid any highway, I decided to chance this trail into the country.

The path wound around trees and fields, alternately going up and down, but always in one general direction—toward the desired *refugio,* and gradually going higher and higher. After some climbing, I found myself in a forest that seemed to run along the top of the mountain. The path turned into a road, but it seemed to be some kind of service road, unused, and the scenery and feel suggested a national forest. After some hours, I decided that I had missed the turnoff to that town and *refugio,* but I seemed to be going always in the same direction. If this was true, then I was walking along a path parallel to that highway. And the map indicated another town, farther along the highway, Foncebadón.

It became more and more clear that this road was used by no one except forest service people, and that they had not been up here in a long time. If I broke a leg here, I would certainly not be found—I tended to watch where I was stepping! Whenever I came to a kind of higher or open place that allowed me to look out over the mountains, I saw nothing but more trees. No fields; therefore, there would be no people. And, of course, no villages.

Several times I came to a Y in the road. This I dreaded seeing, for I had to make a decision with no information or knowledge. The sky continued to be overcast, so I had no sun to help me on my directions. But I had the feeling that I was walking in a somewhat straight line. At each division of the road, I chose the side that seemed better for maintaining this line. But the forest showed no signs of ending in any direction I could look. I remembered having read somewhere that the forests of the world are diminishing. This one was thriving and apparently increasing. I was caught. On the one hand, I wanted somehow to get out of here; on the other, I rejoiced that the Spaniards were replenishing their forested mountains so bounteously. Being so lost, my pleasure was terribly mixed. A light rain began to fall, but I resolved not to go back. Surely I would come out of this before dark.

At another Y, the road to the left definitely went to the left—according to my estimation and guessing, toward that highway, maybe toward Foncebadón. I decided to take a chance and see if this led out. If not, I would wind around in some circle, no closer to getting out of the forest. But I had a feeling that this was a good turn, a time to change direction. After some hours more, the road became two water-filled ruts with the bushes on each side nearly covering it. Maybe it was just a dead end!

I think this is the first time I have been really lost. That, too, is another common experience of which I have been deprived . . . and perhaps a rich experience that can greatly benefit me. Thoreau wrote:

> Not till we are lost, in other words, not till we have lost the world, do we begin to find ourselves, and realize where we are and the infinite extent of our relations.

The meaning of what he says may extend to my situation today. Then, from what happened on the very first day, I learned who is out here with me, who wants me to make this *camino*. The more I am lost, then, the closer I may be to them. In the face of discouragement, the more I can relax, even rejoice.

But then I begin to wonder . . . Am I in some danger? Should I be afraid? But if there is danger and cause for fear, the journey today becomes more exciting, more heart-stirring. The absolute silence, the strongly sensed solitude, quickened all my senses and awakened my spirit. In this fantastic desolation, I required no stimulant except the damp air and the gray sky. I was definitely lost, somewhere on the heights approaching Monte Irago, one of the traditionally arduous and frightening mountains of the *camino*. An eighteenth-century document notes that the land around here is so rough, the rain, snow, and sleet so continual, that the pass is closed from about the beginning of September to the end of May . . . which means now! People who lived in this region would watch for pilgrims, then house and guide them. But I have seen no sign of any human presence since I left that village, except for the little-used road.

At every slight turn or opening in the trees, I looked up intently, taking in every detail, hoping to see some sign, some indication, of a direction. I had never before in my life looked so hard at what lay in front of me. I seemed to believe that everything depended on the intensity of my attention. But I never saw anything other than more forest. The trail, however, did not end. At one time, this was actually used by someone to go someplace. I felt sure it must be so. After innumerable disappointments, I thought I caught a glimpse, through the rain and mist, of a few roofs on a distant mountainside. Did I really see houses? Or was it a trick of light and shadow in the rain? And if there were houses, could I get from here to there? Before, in mountains, I had looked across gorges to another mountain or range, but there was no way to get from here to there. If I had to go "cross country," I would never make it—not on the slippery, wet ground with a heavy pack, and probably unable to maintain a sense of direction once plunged into the forest again. But the trail beneath my feet was still visible, and it led in the direction of what I thought I saw. The wet bushes were not yet so thickly entwined as to prevent my forward movement.

I then came to a kind of clearing, the trail becoming more open. Soon, a stone structure could be seen. When I got close, I saw that it was the ruin of a church. I had no reason why, but that seemed a good sign. The trail led on, clearly some kind of road now, and came out on a narrow one-lane asphalt road. This must surely lead to that village. And it did. I could really see houses! I was no longer lost! I have heard the expression, and always considered it trite; but now I felt genuinely confused: should I laugh or cry? All along the way, I must have chosen well at each Y, and the last one was exactly the one that brought me here. If I had chosen differently on any of the others, I would probably still be lost somewhere in that forest. Who was out there with me today? Other pilgrims who got lost and didn't find their way out? My Guardian Angel? I had no "sense" of help, but I always had the "feeling" I was going in the right direction—

without possessing any real evidence. But the feeling was there, and it never wavered; clearly, I do not live in a world of chance, I do not depend upon luck.

Strange. Albani, also walking alone, coming out of Astorga in the eighteenth century, writes that he got lost on a mountain. It must have been right here. He says that he met a hunter and this man pointed out the direction he should go. Continuing toward Compostela, he found shelter that night in a shed used to store straw. Since I'm arriving at an actual village, I should do even better than that.

Walking up the street, I see no one about. But all the houses are in fine condition and appear to be lived in. This is not the first time I have been in a village and seen no one on the streets. I stop at the town *fuente* for a drink, and hear some sounds nearby. Going toward them, I find two men working on an iron railing. Greeting them, I ask where I am. Then I ask if I can get to Foncebadón from here. Yes, that's possible. Can I arrive there before dark? Yes, that can be done. One interrupts his work, takes a paper and pencil, and draws me a rough map. I still have to cross several mountains, but they are not so high, the distance is not too great and, if I am careful, I will not lose the trail. He points out where I will meet crossing trails, and explains which to take. I warmly thank them, put some water in my bottle, and set off again—feeling like a new person, starting yet another new adventure—and it's still Wednesday! Providence is almost too clear, too pat.

After passing a few houses, I see a small sign, "BAR." That means coffee! Celebration! Surely I have time. Following the direction indicated by the sign, I come to what should be the bar. It looks like any other house, and there is no indication that it is indeed a bar. But, again, I *feel* that it must be the bar. I try the door. Locked. I knock—and wait. In a few moments, a woman comes to the door. Is this the bar? I ask. It is. And it's open. I don't bother to ask why the door was locked. Perhaps in such a small village, the few known customers come in later. I take off the poncho and pack, and joyfully relish the warmth and good taste of the coffee.

A man comes in and I ask him and the woman for directions to Foncebadón. They tell me essentially the same thing as the workman, adding a few small details that may turn out to be important when I get to those places where mountain paths cross. Neither these people nor the workmen seemed surprised to see me. I forgot to ask them if other lost hikers or pilgrims ever came to this village. It does seem to be a lost place up here in the mountains, with just that narrow road coming into it, and a footpath leading out the other side. This should be an excellent place to live.

In a minute, I am past some unfriendly dogs and out of the small village. The road or trail seems to be a kind of packed sand-dirt, a fine but unfamiliar surface on which to walk. It doesn't make the mud that sticks to your shoes, and I'm striding rapidly out across the mountains. The road climbs up and then drops down. I make my way around or over several small mountains. Sometimes one is separated from another by a deep gorge and the road winds down to one end and then switches back on the other side. From one side of the gorge, I can see the road on the other side, seemingly close, but I know that it will take a long time to get there. One cannot drop down into the gorge and come up over there; one must go around. Sometimes, I can see what looks like a road, high up on a neighboring mountain, and I think: That must be another road. I surely cannot get up *that* high from here. I always do! Up here, there are not many trees, only low bushes where anything at all is growing. I have a sense of great spaces or chunks of space, great heaps of mountains, the feeling that I'm covering enormous distances. I had forgotten to ask the people about actual distances and times. They had said that I can make it to Foncebadón, and I'm on the way they pointed out to me. This must be the fabled Monte Irago, so feared by pilgrims in the past.

The rain begins again with a whipping wind. I have no experiences at all of mountains, and am not prepared for the violence and erratic changes of the wind. But if I watch my footing and balance, I don't think it can blow me over.

It seems, then, that I've been out here for hours. I should have asked the villagers the time it would take to get from one landmark to another. Or maybe the directions were faulty . . . or I didn't understand them . . . or I took a wrong turn . . . A long discussion with myself . . . ending thusly: They know the country intimately; that was evident in the way they gave the directions. They are honest people who want to help me— that, too, was clear in the way they acted and talked. Every landmark that they described to me has turned out to be exactly as they said. And I made the turns they indicated—there was never a moment of confusion at the places where paths crossed. And it's not dark yet. So all is well! Or so I try to convince myself. I then come to a forested part of the mountain, and the path runs alongside, just as they said it would. I feel more confident. But then the terrible wind tears the strap off the bottom of my poncho, where the back is snapped to the front, thereby keeping me dry about down to my knees. The rest of the snaps hold; the poncho doesn't get blown over my head; I seem to be reasonably dry, at least from the waist up.

Now I begin to be tired. The walking has been good all day, but I've come a long way; I've been on the trail a long time, with just the one stop for coffee. This trail is supposed to come out on the highway. And then Foncebadón should appear. The place of the *refugio,* Rabanal del Camino, should be some distance back on the highway. If I get to Foncebadón, I've gone far beyond my planned destination, and I can surely find some shelter in the village.

At just about the time when I feel that I can go no farther, I see the highway! The directions were perfect. And then, just as the people said, I soon find the road, on the other side of the highway, leading up to Foncebadón. I turn off, suddenly feeling fresh and still strong. The road up to the village looks more like a thick grass and mud path, with rocks strewn in it here and there. It certainly doesn't look like a *used* road. In a short time, I come to a stone house. Its thatched roof has collapsed; it's obviously abandoned. The street now becomes mostly mud, flowing rainwater runoff and rocks. Another house—also abandoned. Every place I come to is utterly uninhabitable, or has been used as a makeshift stable for animals. I see one house that looks as if it could be used, but there is a padlock on the door, and no sign of anyone around. In a short time, I find myself in open country, or so it seems. It's getting darker, but I've definitely been through the entire village. In the distance, I think I can see the highway winding its way on up the mountain. This is *not* the town where I expected to buy food and find a room in some simple hostel! It is a very small *deserted* village . . . the first time I've seen this in Spain. I saw no signs of life at all—except for fresh cowshit on the ground.

In 1988, a pilgrim who walked along the same path through the village wrote, "A tightening noose closed around my throat, an invisible but cold hand grabbed my heart." Seeing all the fallen stones, hearing the mountain wind blowing through the eerie silence, he concluded: "Total desolation, the dominion of the Evil One, whom you expect to meet at every corner."

I did not see any church, but I remember that my map indicated one. I can't go on in this wind and rain, and I have no idea how far it is to the next village. It's too late to go back down the highway, looking for Rabanal del Camino. I turn around. Surely one of those houses that looked like an animal stable has a roof. And that's all I need. I start back through the village and come upon the church. I had missed it in the increasing darkness. It faces a cross street, sitting on what was a corner. The side is on this street, and is partly missing. I go in and find some roof still in place, but the ground or floor is all covered with cowshit. It too, is used only by the animals. As I turn to go out, I notice a room attached to the church, just beyond where the wall has a gaping hole. The room has walls on three sides and about three or four meters of roof. I look into this space and find fairly clean dry straw on the floor. The wind is coming from the side of the wall, so the back of the room is out of a draft and gets no rain. Perfect.

I put my poncho on the staff to dry out, take off the pack, throw down the plastic mat, roll out the sleeping bag, take off my wet clothes and lay them on the straw to dry, and ease myself into the sleeping bag to get warm. Although I've had nothing to eat since my usual breakfast, I feel no great hunger. I have three small peaches and a tiny piece of cheese that I'll save for the morning. The wind howls through some openings in the church, the rain beats fiercely on the roof, but I'm soon dry and warm.

Suddenly, I hear a noise. It sounds like a car door being slammed. What can that be? I decide to stay where I am and be quiet. I can't get dressed again and go out into that rain. Straining to look out the opening of my "room," which is perpendicular to the street, I see a man walk by. He seems intent on going someplace, so I decide to wait until he finds me before I start explaining myself.

Slowly relaxing, I am startled to see a large dog in the open wall. Every dog I have seen in Spain so far has been aggressively unfriendly—they always growled and threatened me like those three back there in that small village a few days ago. But they have always been chained, or I was able to protect myself with my staff. Now the staff is under the poncho, and I'm flat on my back in the sleeping bag. I'm not ready for this! Frantically trying to concentrate, think out some plan of defense, I notice that the mutt continues to look at me, but he makes no sound. We stare at each other . . . finally, he turns and goes out. How explain that? Is this another mystery of the *camino?* Like finding my way out of that forest? or coming on this dry place in a terrible storm? I don't think I've ever in my life been helped like this. But I've never been in such odd circumstances and places either.

Trying to make some sense of my good fortune, I notice a movement in the open space leading to the street. Raising my head, I see another dog—one of those very thin, very mean-looking mongrels. They are always the most vicious, their appearance faithfully expressing their violent character. They seem set on working a kind of revenge on people for having allowed such a genetic mismatch to take place. And I'm at his mercy. My only possible defense is the backpack—can I reach it? lift it? in some way thrust it between him and me? I'll never manage it, but every muscle in me tenses to try. All this time, we are staring at one another—in silence. He, too, makes no sound. After some minutes, he turns and goes out.

I'm shaking from the relaxed tautness of my nerves. I've read that people in the past had to face wolves, and I never imagined how one could actually meet a wolf. But I guess it could happen as it did here with these dogs. Why didn't they attack me? Why didn't they at least growl and bark? They are the first silent dogs I've encountered in Spain. And one looked really suspicious and threatening. What did they see or not see in me? They obviously saw me, and could smell me. They "knew" I was not a familiar fixture here. They looked right into my eyes. Are the barking, jumping, and growling of all the other dogs I've met nothing but a show, an empty threat?

I'm no longer trembling; my body starts to feel calm, slack; I think now I will sleep. How grateful I am for the day, the anxiety and thrills. I had never before thought of the *camino* as this kind of adventurous danger: walking into the category of missing person, or chewed up by mongrels as a trespasser. Maybe I share more than I realized with medieval pilgrims.

At some hour during the night, I am awakened by a cowbell. I have noticed that cows and sheep, here in the mountains, often have bells around their necks, that is, on at least one animal of the group. And I have assumed that this is to help the farmer find his stock in places where fences are not much used. The bell comes closer . . . and closer. A cow slowly walks across my open wall and into the church. Another follows, and then a bull. They seem to walk around inside the church for some minutes, and then one comes out, glances in my direction, and continues on into the rain and wind. I breathe easily and brace myself for the next. What will I do if one starts to explore my space? There is not enough room here for the cow and me. If she comes in, she will have to turn to get out again. But to do that, she will have to walk on me, or knock the backpack over, or trample on and tear the poncho—or all three.

The bull comes out of the church; moving slowly, he wanders out into the storm. One to go! In a few minutes, the other cow slowly puts her head out the destroyed wall of the church. She takes a step or two, the way cows do when they are in no hurry. Her head turns in my direction, and she looks—at me? at the straw? I don't know much about cows, what they can see or smell in the darkness. But she moves the way I have seen cows move when they are not being pushed or herded . . . a step or two in my direction. What does she "intend?" I decide it's time to start acting. This is a very different situation than with the dogs. I feel no fear, no real anxiety. Cows, I believe, are always "friendly." But I feel a kind of frustration—go away! leave me alone! I have to get this message to her. What can cows get? I sit up, wave my arms, yell at her. I have a flashlight, but am uncertain of what effect it would have. I watch, to see the next move. She stands there. Is she looking at me? Is she just curious? She takes a step. Is it toward me, or toward the street? How slowly these huge creatures move. But that's something in my favor. I wave my arms again, I shout. That should be enough. What can she possibly find attractive in this corner? I'm giving her every sign to make her feel unwelcome. But she's so slow—and I need my sleep.

After what seems a very long time of a kind of standoff, she slowly ambles out, out into the storm, out into the raging wind and rain, out into these glorious mountains, out into the village of Foncebadón.

Dare I relax completely? . . . I need the sleep . . . one had a bell . . . perhaps that was part of their nightly routine—to check out the church . . . I'm too tired to care . . . all has gone well . . . I have no need to fear . . . I can sleep . . .

24

Foncebadón to Ponferrada

May 27, 1993

The dry straw, the wind and rain, the wonderfully dark, fresh air, the warm sleeping bag, all contribute to a restful and refreshing sleep. I awaken early, feeling hungry now, and eat the meager bits of food left in the pack. In the dark silence of the morning I dress, put my gear in order, shoulder the pack, grab the staff and set out, attempting to avoid the rivulets of water and the numerous piles of cowshit. It's cold, but I can offset that by striding rapidly . . . the rain has ended. The village presents strange, conflicting images: The buildings are in various stages of ruin but, when seen closely, present impressive examples of well-conceived form, nicely hewn stone, and careful construction. High on the front wall of what was the church, two large bells bear silent witness to a forgotten community of faith. Everywhere, the grass is richly green, thick, gloriously vigorous. There seems to be enough to support a large herd of cows. People lived here, tilled this land, constructed all these once substantial dwellings. Why would they forsake such a lovely, silent place?

According to a document of the twelfth century (1103), Alfonso VI granted certain rights to a *hospital* and the church of San Salvador de Irago, on petition of the hermit, Gaucelmo. Some believe that Gaucelmo himself built the first shelter for pilgrims in Foncebadón. In addition, the place seems to have shared in the fame of the *refugios* at the other two high mountain places along the *camino,* Roncesvalles and Cebreiro—which I should reach in a couple of days. Monte Irago, the peak here, reaches about 1,500 meters. No wonder it's cool this morning. The winter snow probably disappeared only recently. In September 946, Ramiro II convoked a local church council here. It seems there was a monastery in the area, where the council fathers met. Now there are only ruins, an occasional whistling wind and, this morning, a cold, gray sky.

Leaving the scattered stones of the village, I reach the narrow highway, and soon come to one of the most famous monuments of the *camino,* the Cruz de Ferro, a plain iron cross mounted on the top of a tall wooden pole that is implanted in a cone-shaped pile of stones. This strange, lonely presence may be the most photographed object along the *camino.* Each passing pilgrim participates in the ancient practice of picking up a stone and throwing it on the heap. Before passing pilgrims took up this millennial practice, farmworkers from Galicia, on their way to seek jobs in Castille, threw their stones down at this spot. In Roman times, these piles of stones, located at boundary points, were called "Mounts to Mercury," the god of travelers, and each person passing them participated in the ritual. But the action reaches far back beyond the Romans. After the act of walking, throwing a rock on this mount must be the oldest continual ritual of the *camino.* Here I meet and touch people who lived long before anyone in Galicia ever heard of Santiago. My arm reaches far back beyond history. One account says that Gaucelmo, who died in 1123, and who also helped pilgrims find their way across these mountains, put up the first cross on the pile of stones, thereby marking a transition from paganism to Christianity. But how could a thrown stone be related to the crucified Christ? Here, to his empty cross? It appears to me more like a haphazard mixture of Christianity and paganism.

I soon come to another abandoned village, Manjarín. A few cows, enjoying the lush grass, turn their heads toward me when I walk over to the *fuente,* which is still in excellent shape. A fresh spring that probably supplies pure water the year round, an apparently rich soil, a goodly number of repairable stone houses, an uncluttered panorama extending out over valleys and distant mountains, everything needed to inspire and nourish a graceful life on earth is here—and yet no one seems interested. To what have the people turned? Where can they find a place in Spain more attractive than this?

Looking up, I see, on the other side of the road, a new, hand-lettered sign, "REFUGIO." A short distance up the side of the mountain there is a complete building, with roof! It appears to be a quite simple, elementary shelter, but that's all I needed last night. I suspect that no food is there, so I continue walking up the road. Getting near the top of the mountain, I see a small army installation higher up, on the right. I've heard that it's some kind of weather station, and the men have rescued pilgrims caught in snowstorms while walking along here in the winter. Immediately, my imagination takes control: Some soldier, looking out the window, sees me down here on the road, cold, hungry, and walking in wet shoes. Hearing the wind wailing through some cracks in his warm building, he comes out and yells at me, inviting me up to share his warm fire and hot breakfast. Oh, what a great fantasy! What a pleasant early morning dream.

But my eyes are drawn to the left. There, far away, I see a range of snow-covered mountains. It appears that I'm looking straight across at them, that we are exactly at the same altitude. But my mountain has no snow at all, only cold, clear air and rich, silent solitude in which the wind plays its evocative whistling in rhythms older than history, older too than the flora that covers the mountain. How lucky I am that no one sees me, that I'm not disturbed out here in the midst of this glorious experience, alone in a stark place too rugged, too awesome, too resplendent to be colonized and exploited.

The road then leads down on the other side of the mountain. The *camino* takes off across a field and I suddenly find myself at the top of a very steep path; I almost tumble and fall into the village of El Acebo. At this early hour, I see no one in the street. Even the dogs seem to be still asleep. I pass two bars, but they are closed—it's too early to open. At the farther end of the village, after I've given up hope of finding something to eat, I see a new small sign, "BAR," with pointing arrow. Hunger drives me to investigate, in spite of the quiet reigning in the village. Climbing up a side street, I come to a kind of porch piled high with boxes of empty bottles. There is no sign or formal entrance, but there is a door, and it's open. Going in, I find that I've entered the back door of the bar. Inside, I meet a young man and woman, working and cleaning. The place is newly constructed, not quite finished. Smiling, they greet me; friendly, they answer yes, they're open; yes, there is food. Amazingly, there is also an open fire in some kind of grill at waist height. I set down the pack, sit close to the fire, take off my wet shoes and place them on a shelf near the flames.

Shortly, the young woman brings me a delicious potato and green vegetable soup, along with some hunks of substantial, chewy bread. She sets the tureen on the table, and I help myself. Before she returns, I have emptied two large soup dishes. Just then she arrives with eggs and thick slices of bacon. She pours me a large glass of wine—have I ever eaten better in my life? I can't remember tasting anything so good. I ask for a large *café con leche* to end this sumptuous repast and prepare for the day's surprises.

I tell the young woman of my night in Foncebadón. She laughs, enjoying the story, and explains that the village is empty with the exception of
one old lady who lives there alone. The old woman's son, who has a farm
nearby, keeps some cows around the village. He must have been the person I saw from my sleeping bag; he and the dogs were checking on the
cows. The other village where I saw the *refugio,* is completely forsaken.
But the stone houses would not need much work to make them attractively habitable again. And there is enough level ground to plant some
crops. The land once supported people who built all the houses, including a pretty good-sized church. Why have they deserted such beauty? The
place could certainly support a fruitful subsistence agriculture. I thought
of the life of the shoemaker in Belorado, of the incredibly deep green
grass growing between the fallen stones, of the sparkling, clear water in
the springs, of the broad sky opened up to infinity. How blessed is this
spot of Spain! But so much wealth and loveliness ignored, abandoned.
Will no one come back and *see* what is here? Will no one reclaim the
country's national treasures? Will no one work this luxuriant earth?

When I decided that a well-paid and tenured university position, further
enriched with various perquisites and lifelong benefits, was actually a
kind of impoverishing imprisonment, I looked all over America for just
such a place as this. I'm surprised that I see no former bureaucrats or
professionals out here, working to build a domestic or household economy, the only one that exploits neither land nor people. From what I can
see, it would be difficult to find a more suitable and attractive place to
live a modest and graceful life, one far removed from the vanity and ugliness of a vicious consumption-disposal spiral.

Historians write about the Industrial Revolution; some social scientists
use the label "modernization"; Karl Polanyi terms the change "The Great
Transformation"; Marxists speak about the transition from feudalism to
capitalism. Many scholars have been fascinated with the emergence in
the late eighteenth century of the industrial or capitalist market econ-
omies of the Western world. Today, politicians and progress enthusiasts
still extol the possibilities of economic and technological development.
Ivan Illich wrote that one might better understand what has happened—
now categorized, sometimes propagandized, with these various concepts
and slogans—by looking at the change from a reign of gender to a regime
of sex, that is, the movement from a gendered society to an *economic*
society. Marx believed that the destruction of an agrarian peasantry and
the emergence of a labor force—conceptualized by him and others as
"free"—were necessary for the transition from feudalism to capitalism.
Many thinkers believe that the essential element in this process is agri-
cultural productivity. Living in a world that accepts the conventional nar-

row notion of productivity, one would certainly be tempted to leave Foncebadón and Manjarín. But can no one see what this kind of productivity does to people and places? Can no one see what is lost in this move? Can no one imagine the way of life that is discarded?

The woman says I can make it to Ponferrada, the next town with a *refugio.* I put on my shoes, now warm and dry, adjust the pack, and tell her how much I've enjoyed their attractive bar. She and her husband have built and furnished a welcome setting for a cold and hungry pilgrim coming down off the mountain. But most important, for me, they took the unusual step of opening early for business today.

I still have to make my way over many small mountains. Geographers might call this country "hilly," but the experience of my feet says "mountainous." The atmosphere continually changes—at times, a heavy mist or fog envelops me; some rain attempts to drench me; but the sun shines out, too. In one place, the path dips down into heavy and thick vegetation. I can almost imagine that I make my way through a cool tropical rain forest. I am then surprised by a mountainside completely covered with what look like rhododendron bushes. The air is heavy with their pleasant, strong scent. I cannot remember ever smelling anything that was at once so sweet and so real. The character of the air seems very different from what one gets in artificial, manufactured odors; it is *solid,* there to stay as long as the bushes bloom. I have arrived at just the right time of the year.

At one place, I can look out many kilometers across a rolling valley that seems to stretch the horizon out in front of me, just for my eyes' pleasure. Here and there, clusters of tiny buildings mark villages and small towns. Later, approaching one of these places, I cross a magnificent old medieval stone bridge. From a great distance, the village looks like a page out of fairyland; the closer I come, the more captivating the artistry of the stonework. Why are these ancient structures so attractive? And many modern ones so nondescript, so dull? Or even ugly, repulsive?

Molinaseca . . . A friendly storekeeper of the village appears to fit naturally in the graceful settings with their sturdy and well-maintained buildings. From him I buy two oranges to sustain me until I arrive at Ponferrada. I have about five more kilometers to go, and it looks like rain all the way. In the distance, the ominous shape of two atomic energy cooling towers destroys all my joy in the shape and strength of the old stone architecture. Have such simple, clear lines ever suggested so much destruction and terror, and pushed one so powerfully to ask what used to be more personal questions, What is a good life? and, How do I live it? Now, I must ask questions such as, How deeply am I plugged into the network? How much do I participate in the despoliation of creation?

What is the precise nature of my action when I participate in the rape of nature, in the attempt to control and direct nature? From all I have felt during these weeks, from all I have sensed, I have come to believe more certainly in creation. No other concept is anywhere near adequate to name the elementary ground of all my experience, of all my thinking and feeling. It is also clear to me that creation is contingent—I am, and everything through which I move is—only through participation. Nothing is its own author, nothing exists of itself. Therefore, all my understanding of and respect for both myself and all I see must be based on this ground. If this is true, then any destruction of creation must be blasphemy. I know this because of where I have come to be: The *camino* has carried me to an insightful space. I arrive at a new understanding of blasphemy; I feel a new horror of the sin; I question anew my place in the web of modern monstrosities.

Strange that today I am confronted with the two extremes: A graceful life of subsistence in a place of sublime beauty, and a "clean," "safe" fix for a life of frenetic activity. Subsistence is supposed to entail degrading labor, and economic society is supposed to offer an exciting life of leisure. The former was tried and found wanting, the latter is delivering on its promises. But it seems to me that many do not *see* either extreme. The beauty of one and the ugliness of the other are hidden. How can one come to see *what is there?* For me, the discipline of the *camino* has marvelously opened my eyes. I can *see* the possibility of a good life in Foncebadón or in Manjarín. And if the experience of my feet is true (and I feel that it is), I do not need all the electricity those towers provide. Happiness, indeed, is to be found in consuming less rather than more. One need not invoke all the powerful arguments about radioactive waste poisoning large areas of creation for thousands of years. But I am horrified to think that the places selected for hiding the awful waste will probably be those places, like Monte Irago, which modern people have abandoned, the places ideally suited for a gentle, comely way to live on the earth. When people do choose to live plainly, decently, will they be able to find uncontaminated places to settle?

In Ponferrada I find the *refugio* at one side of a small plaza, connected with the office or rectory of a church. Opposite is the church building itself, hugely monstrous, with a large billboard out front, detailing the sums the government is spending on renovations. A sign at the office door says that the *refugio* opens at 5 P.M. As I ponder this information, two laughing young people come out the door, heading for lunch. I ask them about the shelter, which appears to be in the basement under the office. As if the sign does not exist, they invite me to go right in and make myself at home. I descend the stairs and find a corridor with small rooms off one side. Each has a little window, high on one wall, through which I can see the feet of people walking by on the sidewalk. Each also has an old mattress on the floor. At the end of the corridor, I find the bathroom—where the shower has only cold water. After the adventures in the forest and Foncebadón, I feel a great need for a shower, no matter how cold. It is indeed chilling, but it wonderfully revives my tired body so that, when dry, I feel I could easily set out again on the *camino* . . . immediately. Two long days of clambering over mountains, most of the time beaten down by rain and buffeted by wind, lost for hours, and I feel eager to start out anew. Will I ever be given two such days again? Amazing the way my body recovers!

Crossing those mountains formerly involved much more than a tired body. As I noted yesterday, Albani, too, got lost when he left Astorga, but not because he chose to avoid the road. There was no clear indication of where the *camino* went. There is one tradition that the people of El Acebo did not have to pay taxes to the king, on condition that they put out and maintain 800 stakes on the mountain, marking the *camino.* But that was long before Albani came along. On his second day out of Astorga, Albani got lost again in the mountains. This time, he finally came across an old man gathering chestnuts. This man led him to Ponferrada and gave him shelter in his own house, an extremely modest dwelling. Albani was strongly touched by the generosity and kindness of these obviously very poor people. Before he left the next morning, he gave the children a few small coins. They regarded him as some kind of god descended from the heavens. He notes that among those people many never see any money at all—it's as far removed from their lives as sacred relics.

There is no kitchen in the *refugio,* so I decide to eat the customary cold dinner—a slice of ham, frozen vegetables, cheese, fruit, and yogurt. After finding these things in a market, I come upon a rather fancy bakery—it seems a fairly large town—and find something called high-fiber bread. So, "health food" fashions have reached the provincial towns of Spain. That enables me to enjoy a change from the daily white bread.

After the lunch hour, the tourism office on the other side of the plaza opens again. There, an attractive and friendly young woman stamps my *credencial,* and explains that I can go to a new *refugio,* just a few blocks away. It features hot water. Before approaching her desk, I noticed that she had directed some bikers to the same place. No longer needing the hot water or the night noise of cyclists, I ask if I may stay where I am—in the rather dark and cold basement. She looks at me as if I am a bit queer—I get the impression that the new place is also a lightsome and pleasant building—and says that I can certainly remain there across the plaza. Her smile and expression subtly change to suggest that she is ready to accept all idiosyncrasies, no matter how odd, without judgment. As has happened so often—recently with the woman in the bar this morning and the man in the market this afternoon—I again meet a person whose genuine spirit of friendliness shines out, giving off an unmistakable aura, brightening the world around them. I ask about a display of a dozen or more different wines that are in the room. She proudly explains that they are all from this region, Bierzo, a place especially blessed in the variety and quality of its wines.

The rain has finally stopped. A bench in the plaza invites me to enjoy the last lengthening rays of today's sun. I've heard that there is a famous castle in the town, but I think I prefer to sit quietly and look back over the day. Off and on, an idea has moved in and out of my thoughts and prayers: I should be doing this, walking the *camino,* for some clear purpose, perhaps to seek some end or goal. At first, I thought this might be to perform an act of penance. Everyone needs to seek his or her specific penitential form and measure. From the very first day, the pain and fatigue I experienced suggested that this might be the "reason" I was out here. I could work toward a certain equilibrium in my life, some degree of justice. But later it seemed that I was out here to seek faith, that I might find the pearl of great price in the *camino*'s mud or among the mountains' wildflowers. In some way I would come to participate in the faith of all those who preceded me. They would carry me along, showing me the way through the darkness of this world.

But today, a new, clear thought occurred to me: Perhaps I should go to Compostela to seek a certain favor, not for myself but for someone else. Perhaps all the pain and exhaustion are to be embraced for those I know or someone I love. Perhaps I'm supposed to ask *for them.* I'm not out there, lost on some mountain for myself, but for someone else; *they* receive some grace. It makes no sense at all to think about being on the *camino* in terms of myself. I'm already here; now I must seek to bring others, that they too might enjoy the company of Santiago and his pilgrims. My looking, my attention, must more and more go out away from myself. I've lived long enough attending to myself; I need to seek the Other, those I know, those I would love. In some way, this walk is really for them. And that's what I need to learn: How? And for whom? Well, something to think about tomorrow. Now it's time for bed. I return to the basement, spread the sleeping bag out on the mattress and crawl in. I'll sleep well tonight. No one else has arrived; they're all over in the new more up-to-date *refugio.* My good luck continues.

25

Ponferrada to Villafranca del Bierzo

May 28, 1993

As I get closer to Compostela, each day seems more lovely, more filled with charm, more resplendent with wonders. And the felt pleasure comes from different dimensions simultaneously. Today, making my way over several mountains, I rejoice in the warm sun; the heat penetrates deep into my body. As I saw from the mountain, the *camino* wanders through a few villages, each one more inviting than the last. Church towers are blessed with their nests of storks. The profuse colors of spring are especially evident in the narrow streets. The balconies and windows of almost all the houses are filled with pots and flower boxes, and the first blooms brighten the open spaces with their colors and scents. Those houses that have a small yard in front generously display their short gnarled rosebushes, which have already flowered. How fortunate the people who live in such surroundings!

In the open country, two pleasant surprises: large fields of vegetables and quiet dogs. I have never before walked through vegetable-growing country. Except for the two mongrels in Foncebadón, almost all the dogs I have met were chained. And all have acted viciously with their threatening bark. Suddenly, now all the dogs are loose, and all quietly lie in front of the rural houses, watching me pass. Another minor puzzle of Spain.

I reach Cacabelos, which was rebuilt in 1108 after an earthquake by Diego Gelmírez, the famous bishop of Compostela. Here, I am in no danger of getting lost. Like several other towns that grew up around the *camino,* the main street that goes straight through *is* the *camino.* The houses and other buildings are arranged along each side of the street. In a few minutes, I come to a winery with an adjoining restaurant, which from the street appears to be an elaborate complex with several large buildings. There is a sign near the high entrance gate inviting pilgrims in for a glass of wine. As I read the sign, a bus pulls up, and all the people get out and walk through the gate. They appear to be on an excursion or tour. Is this just a tourist trap that I would do better to avoid? There is a restaurant inside the outer wall, however, and that means coffee. Since I've had nothing this morning except my usual bread, cheese, fruit, and water, I decide that it's time to enjoy a hot drink; I can ignore the fact that the place is oriented to outsiders, such as tourists.

As I go in the yard, I notice a quaint gift shop, another building where wine-making equipment and procedures are set up, and a stairway that leads up to the restaurant. There, I find myself in a large room filled with heavy tables and chairs, the walls decorated with photos of winemakers and their prizes, and displays of wine bottles with many different labels. I am the only customer. A young woman comes over and I ask for a large *café con leche.* It seems now a long time ago that I first learned that coffee comes in two sizes. People often order a large one early in the morning, then small ones the remainder of the day. I have decided to celebrate all the vigorous and striking signs of spring. A few moments later, I am given the largest coffee cup I have yet seen in Spain. Shortly after setting this down, the young woman returns with a big piece of cake, which I didn't order. I have the impression that this is some kind of gift, thank her, and ask no questions.

Both the coffee and the cake are excellent. As soon as I finish, I go in search of the young woman, for she has disappeared. When I find her, I ask for my bill. "Oh no," she says, "there's no charge." She had recognized me as a pilgrim, of course, and served this favor from the winery! So the sign outside, inviting pilgrims in for a glass of wine, was just that, an invitation, not an advertisement to sell wine. What an invigorating feeling—to walk through a country so full of such munificent people, such gracious experiences.

In the fifteenth century, after walking along here through El Bierzo, the German monk Hermann Künig von Vach notes, in his guidebook for other European pilgrims, that one should be very careful of the wine. Sometimes it can burn up the soul, he said, as if one had swallowed a burning candle. Each writer fills his *relato* with advice, some trivial, some more

weighty. I've often wondered about the best mix of knowledge and ignorance that one should bring to the *camino*.

In the early afternoon, shortly before lunch, I arrive at the edge of Villafranca del Bierzo, another town that began and grew to be important in
the Middle Ages because the *camino* passed through it. French colonists
constituted an identifiable neighborhood here, and French monks from
Cluny established a large monastery. It looks like a town of several inter-
secting hills with a confusing labyrinth of streets and alleys between and
over them. The first building I come to is the famous Romanesque church
of Santiago. Walking down alongside the small church, I meet three or
four men dressed in coats and ties, who appear to be solid citizens of the
community. I ask them for directions to the *refugio*. As one answers me, I
think I see an enigmatic smile exchanged between the others. I learn that
the *refugio* is just down the hill, immediately in front of the church.

In a few moments, I come to a small, one-room building with various
"pious" signs related to the *camino*—for example, the slogan, "Ultreya"
(roughly, "Upward and Onward") and souvenirs such as imprinted T-
shirts. A huge dog—loose—lies there sleeping. Just beyond, I see some
workmen building a stone retaining wall. In front of them are two large
Quonset-type structures, covered with semitransparent plastic that is
torn and patched in places. At first, I wonder if this is some kind of joke,
and I am reminded of the smile I noticed a few moments ago.

I look inside the door of the first "building." Out of a general picture of
confusion, I see a bar on the left, rough tables with plank benches on the
right, boxes of rotten apples at the back, and various items of clothing
and junk scattered around or hanging from the ceiling/roof. In the adjacent Quonset, I find double bunks, some divisions into rooms, the floor
paved with stone in places, covered with a damp carpet in other places. I
look for a bunk with a dry mattress toward the back of the room, and
drop my pack there. In the "bar," I learn that the *menú del día* will be
ready soon. The price is quite reasonable—600 pesetas—so I decide to
take a chance on a hot meal.

There is an outdoor sink, a semi-enclosed shower with water that seems
to be heated by the sun, and some trees out back from which I can string
my clothesline. With all this sun and a good breeze, I'll get everything
washed and dry today. Later, hanging up the wet clothes, I have to work
my way around the piles of tin cans, crates of empty bottles, and trash.
I've never yet seen anything like this on the *camino!*

When it's time to eat, the woman who seems to be both cook and
waitress invites me to sit down at one of the tables. I am the only pilgrim,
and am immediately joined by the three workmen who were constructing
the stone wall. The courses are served "family style," and each of us is

free to eat as much as he wants. The food is excellent, the wine good, and the conversation exciting. Shortly after we sit down, a Spanish pilgrim whom I had not seen before comes into the room, greets the workmen, and plunges immediately into an animated and polemical discussion of Spanish political economy with the man at my left, who seems to be the leader of the workmen. I have heard such conversations before, and always marveled at their combination of strong, committed opinion and curiously unconcerned detachment. People would argue fiercely as if the fate of the nation hung on the victory of the best—the most passionate?—presentation. But today, as on other occasions, the confrontation suddenly ends with a general condemnation of all politicians, parties, and policies—proposed or already in place.

Before we get up from the table, the French woman pilgrim, whom I had met before, walks into the room, alone. The man at my left, when he notices her standing there, and that she is uncertain where to go, gruffly orders her not to move. Since she does not understand Spanish, I translate. Without any greeting or introduction, he arises, walks up to her, and tells her to close her eyes, and to keep them closed until he gives the word to open them again. Although he appears a rough and seasoned workman, his presence and manner of speaking permit no argument or doubt—he speaks with authority.

He slowly moves his hands over her entire body, keeping them about ten centimeters away, never actually touching her. Occasionally, he draws away and snaps his arm and fingers, as if shaking water or mud off his fingertips. When he finishes, he tells her to open her eyes, and asks her how she feels. With a perplexed and dazed look on her face, "Different," she says. She then turns and walks slowly out of the room, as if she were wandering through a dream. Everyone was silent throughout the ritual. Curious about what has happened, I am the first to speak—except for my earlier translations. I turn to the man and ask him directly, "Usted es curandero?" He looks at me for a moment; we both smile, but he does not answer. He did not have to. I think we clearly understand one another.

Curandero can mean very different things, depending on the people and their relationship, the circumstances, and the local traditions. I intended my question to be candid and simple: Do you have healing powers? And I'm pretty certain he got that. I look at him again, standing there in his workman's slightly soiled clothes, needing a shave, absolutely calm, no trace of arrogance or of false humility. I smile, we part, he to his wall and I in search of the Frenchwoman. I have never come so close to one who seemed to be a genuine *curandero,* and I want to look into this further.

I find her seated on a bunk in the "dormitory." She is taking off her shoes and socks, and tells me that she has a broken blister that seems to be infected. I look at it; indeed, it looks ugly. So, the *curandero* somehow knew that there was something wrong with her when he looked at her, although he did not see her walk into the room—she might have walked with a limp. What did he remove from her? the infection? a fever? She tells me she might rest the next day; the foot would no doubt be better and her companions would probably catch up with her by then.

I wonder—should I talk to the *curandero* about my left heel? Once every two or three days the pain becomes so severe that I cannot continue walking. But I found a remedy. I carry some wide adhesive tape with me, my principal medical supply. Whenever the pain became unbearable, I stopped, took off my shoe and two socks, and carefully covered the heel with a smooth layer of tape. After that I am able to walk on the heel with almost no pain at all. Since I've treated myself successfully, I decide not to bother the *curandero*.

I get up and go into town to buy food for supper and breakfast, thinking that the shelter serves only a lunch/dinner. As I go out, I pass the workmen, placing stones in their new wall. Walking a few meters farther, I see that other workers, hired by the government, are grading the approach to the church, having finished paving the area in front with flat stones. Looking up, I see the north door, called the Puerta del Perdón—the Door of Pardon. One tradition records that a Spanish pope, Calixtus III (1455–58), granted to this church the privilege of substituting for the cathedral in Compostela under certain conditions. Those pilgrims who reach Compostela in a Jubilee Year—that year when the feast of Santiago falls on a Sunday, as this year—can obtain all the spiritual benefits ordinarily obtainable only by making a pilgrimage to Rome or to the Holy Land. But if a pilgrim in such a year is prevented from reaching Compostela through some obstacle such as serious sickness on the journey, he or she can still obtain the graces by going through the door of this small church dedicated to Santiago. Another tradition informs us that a large *refugio* stood on the place now occupied by the Quonset huts.

The Romanesque church is small and attractive and, contrary to my usual practice, I step in to look around. Some believe that Romanesque *is* the architectural style of Christianity. I see that much work has been done to restore the interior to its former clean, simple form. At one side, there is a tiny chapel with a sanctuary candle burning next to an altar with tabernacle. The Blessed Sacrament is reserved there. Stopping to reflect on what this might mean, I am jolted out of my thoughts by the brash appearance of a young woman, a guide, leading a handful of tourists around the church. She walks right by the Blessed Sacrament chapel with no acknowledgment or sign whatever of the Real Presence. How can she be a guide in this place? Into what nonsense does she lead these people? What can she possibly explain to them? I am so confused and disturbed by her evident lack of any awareness of where she is—as indicated by her behavior—that I cannot move to speak to her. For her, the place seems to be just another museum, another example of the country's store of Romanesque architecture. If the tourists are not there to gawk, it's just another artfully crafted arrangement of stones, special only because of its empty elegance. Perhaps yet another entrepreneur will come along and photograph the building for his coffee-table book. Was the artistic expression of Christianity frozen in this graceful architecture? Is there a living breath warm enough to bring it back to life? Should the modern pilgrim disavow these stones? Leave them to the tourists?

Governments often use or make up the history of their countries in order to create the myths that legitimize their own policies and authority, a sometimes ruthless and generally ignoble exploitation of the past. But here I see a new, added dimension. All along the *camino,* I come upon these restoration projects. They appear to transform the spirit and imagination of earlier faith communities into artistically attractive but definitively dead museum space. Each project of this official governmental cultural revitalization that I have examined seems to bury the past, making the truth of these very different historical people more and more beyond contemporary reach. I suspect that guides such as the young woman I saw in the church cannot provide any link. The past can only become grossly utilitarian, an idle distraction for the jaded tourist and a fairly good investment risk for the government. Each renovation project flaunts a large sign indicating the millions of pesetas invested in the work. That translates into jobs, a healthy profit for contractors, a noncontroversial achievement for politicians and a general upgrading of local property values. Perhaps the well-dressed men I met when I approached the town were real estate speculators. This church fits the pattern—the creation of a picturesque and historically interesting monument that attracts yen, Deutschmarks, and dollars. From being expressions of a living faith, the buildings have become desiccated cultural artifacts—but valuable economic assets.

Walking down into town to buy some food supplies, I see that the community boasts a huge, ancient castle and an unusually large number of substantial monasteries and churches. If the *camino* contributed greatly to the growth of Villafranca del Bierzo, I wonder if one could work out some kind of relationship between the vitality of the physical evidence and the power of the *camino*'s spirit? Or would one find that the stones *never* had any life in them? How would one approach the *camino* as a social phenomenon? I suspect that some of the claims—for example, graceful Romanesque churches and crowded monasteries translate into a flowering of faith—are too vague to have any meaning. True, a faith lived in humility seems to have been at the origins of much that I see, but a founder's simple virtue can easily be transformed into a follower's vain ambition.

As I walk back to the Quonset huts, several pieces of information and recent experience fall into a pattern of recognition. Somehow, I suddenly realize that the rough workman is the owner of the *refugio,* and his name is Jesús Arias Jato! The woman who served us dinner, his wife! The two huts are operated as a unit by a family, somewhat like the *refugio* in Cizur Menor. Although appearances are radically different, each place reveals the distinctive stamp of a personality dedicated to the spirit of the *camino,* to the possibility of contemporary people entering the luminous space of the pilgrimage to Compostela.

When I return, I see the Señora de Arias behind the bar, and ask her if she can make me a *café con leche.* Certainly, she answers. Up until now, I have always seen this prepared in a special machine that, I think, is imported from Italy. There is no such machine here. La Señora simply heats a pan of milk on her gas burner and sets it on the table with the morning's coffeepot. The taste is different, but good enough that I drink two cups. Then I have to go search for La Señora. When I find her, I tell her that I've drunk two cups. She seems a bit awkward about taking the money.

The pilgrim who was talking politics earlier comes into the room. A thick cord over his shoulder has a wineskin tied to it. As we talk, Arias the workman walks up and asks for the wineskin. He unscrews its cap, holds it above his head about twenty-five centimeters away, tips it, and squeezes. A thin stream of wine is neatly caught by his mouth with not a drop spilled. So this is the way people drink from these things. One drinks without touching the "bottle."

A Spanish couple come in to have their *credencial* stamped. When the man learns that I am an American, he makes several emphatic statements about the United States being the only great country left in the world. Arias quietly replies that maybe *that* country alone is great that is noble in its spirit. As in his earlier action as *curandero,* so now in his opinion as world observer, Arias speaks with unmistakable authority. He is a man I would like to get to know better. When he stamps my *credencial,* he writes over the stamp's logo, "Qúe tu camino sea luz interior"—not very easy to translate: "May your pilgrimage be filled with interior light."

The next morning I am ready to start before dawn. I come out of the dormitory, and am surprised to see a light in the "bar." Inside, a couple of other early risers are waiting for Arias to finish making coffee. Bread, sausage, and cheese are already on the table. Commenting on the cool morning air, Arias builds a quick-starting fire in an old potbellied stove. With our coffee, we gather round. I look up and see that the metal flue runs over to the end of the hut and then out the plastic wall, apparently in defiance of physical laws.

I ask Arias about his dreams for the place, since I had seen architectural blueprints and sketches of a new *refugio* on the bulletin board. He expresses some criticism of the new government *refugios* that I have passed, and says that the architect of the new *refugio* in Burgo de Raneros has designed one for him. He likes the simplicity of this man's work. I had walked by this place in Burgo, but had not stopped. Arias says that he wants something more modest than the one, for example, in Villadangos del Páramo, where I *had* stayed. But his big problem is money. I immediately recognize that this is a complicated matter that would take a long time to unravel. For example, he is obviously a very independent character—any government rules or requirements would not sit well with him. So he probably must depend on private funding. On the wall, I had seen a list of associations in various countries, pledged to support specific aspects of the new construction. Apparently, he must depend on the rate at which money comes in from them. I make a resolution to look into this when I return to Germany. But now I feel that I must get back out there on the next mountain.

I ask him the price of the breakfast, and he waves me away. "You can drop something in the box, if you wish"—there is a donation box near the door. He gives me a firm, warm *abrazo*—hug—and I set out, eager for yet new wonders, having slept well in what must surely be the most unusual and *simpático refugio* on the entire *camino*. I've heard that some people believe that strong telluric forces operate at certain places along the *camino*. Without knowing of any such reference to Villafranca del Bierzo I feel, from my experiences of the place and the Arias Jato family, that some unique and special quality marks this spot.

26

Villafranca del Bierzo to El Cebreiro

May 29, 1993

I start out on a highway that winds this way and that, cutting right through the mountains. The road follows the Valcárcel river, so all the climbs and downgrades are gradual. I feel uneasy; it's all so unreal; these mountains shooting up all around me, continually changing form, with their resulting lights and shadows, but I'm not climbing them. The river provides a way through them. It's a magnificent, swift-flowing stream, now and then cascading down in an abrupt waterfall of a meter or two, or rushing in rapids through rocks, then moving quietly in a broad and calm channel. Dropping or striking the rocks, its sound reaches me through the trees and brush, revealing its elementary power, its living presence. The passing cars and trucks, with their machine noise, continually violate the space and sounds of this lovely valley. But then I notice an ugly residue, a more permanent desecration: Between the highway and the river, the ground is littered with rubbish—soft drink cans and plastic water bottles predominating. Gazing up at the mountains, or resting my eyes on the lush vegetation, enjoying the water's varied rhythms, breathing in the warmth of the sun, I feel sick with the sight of the trash. How can people wreak such destruction?

Persons enclosed in a fast-moving vehicle, comfortable in a sealed-up capsule, cannot hear the river, and the vegetation hides it from their eyes.

They have no time to stop and feast on the mountains. The astonishing order and the awful havoc are accessible only to someone actually in it, moving slowly through it, to someone with their feet on the ground and all their senses open to the experience. Here I plainly and forcefully see that it is not just pedestrians who suffer from smog and noise, who pay for automotive convenience; it is not just the rich earth sucked empty of its minerals. The resplendent glory of creation, the wild flourishing of nature, is wantonly besmirched by these invasive monsters. The beliefs and actions associated with the acquisition, ownership, and use of automobiles encourage the tossing of one's garbage out the window while speeding ahead—to a place far removed from one's thoughtless, personal acts that despoil this pleasant valley. I suspect that people's sensibilities and dreams are caught by the car so firmly, and the resulting clouding of their perceptions is so complete, that the only places safe from such trashing are remote mountaintops like those I crossed yesterday. There is no economic advantage in driving up there, and developers have not yet added the amenities necessary to exploit the region for the distraction and amusement of bored urban parasites searching for an unspoiled spot of nature.

I pass more of the new roadside signs, "Camino de Santiago." At the bottom, they read, "Consejo Cultural de Europa." Perhaps this entity, whatever it is, pays for the signs, and the present Spanish government, eager to appear enlightened—in favor of culture, and anxious to be considered a part of Europe—rejecting the isolation sought by Franco, puts them up. But anyone reflecting on the history of the *camino* would have to resist this easy and superficial association. Individuals, each coming out of an unique story, walked along here from all over Christendom. There was no European culture, no rapid transport, and no modern maps. When the path was most filled with pilgrims—probably in the twelfth and thirteenth centuries—each person set out in a certain darkness, ignorant of what lay at *finis terrae,* at what was believed to be "the end of the earth." I see no way to relate today's pretentious signs to those wandering walkers of old.

I arrive at Vega de Valcarce around noon. It seems a good time and place to stop for a short rest and coffee. While relaxing, I look out and see that the rain has started again. The woman tending the shop tells me that I still have about thirteen kilometers to walk before reaching El Cebreiro, which sits on top of a mountain! Emphasizing the mountain, she gives a certain warning character to her voice. I think about what she says . . . but I've climbed in the rain before. Why be apprehensive? What is there to fear?

As I make my way up the street, another woman stops me and asks if I am looking for the *refugio*. No, I answer, I hope to reach El Cebreiro today. She thinks that's a very bad idea. It's raining, it's not going to stop, and I still have to get up that mountain. It would be much more prudent to take advantage of the *refugio*, get a good night's rest and start the ascent tomorrow morning. Smiling, I thank her for her friendly solicitude, and repeat that I want to walk farther today. I don't mind the rain, and I feel certain that I can make it long before dark. She shakes her head, and I am intrigued by the expression on her face, as if to say, "Well, there goes another crazy American . . . you can't tell them anything!" On my part, I feel the warmth of being blessed again, of meeting another good person looking out for my welfare. This is the story of the *camino:* Day after day of friendliness and thoughtfulness, of gifts and graces. I am jolted out of such reveries by my memory of the subway station in Paris, when I had to change train stations on my way to the French-Spanish border. There, attempting to figure out how the electronic ticket-vending machine worked, I looked up and simultaneously saw a sign and a person: The large, clear letters warned people to accept *no* help from anyone met in the station; and a young man, who spoke like a hustler, asked for a hundred-Deutschmark bill that he might buy my ticket for me!

Warmed by the coffee and the spontaneous outpouring of generosity, I smile, thank the woman, and resume my journey.

The trail increases in steepness; the rain in relentlessness. I appear to be the only person out in such rugged weather. Working my way up the mountainside, I lose all sense of how far I've come or how long I've climbed. I have a sense, however, that I should be reaching the village soon. Now and then, I look up from the ground and search for signs of houses. And then, far ahead, I discern what looks like a village. But when I get closer, I see that it's on a mountainside across a wide and deep canyon; worse, it's on my left and the trail turns to the right.

The path has a wonderful and wild character. No vehicles, no people, nothing out here except the elements, ever changing, ever challenging. As long as I can continue to find the yellow painted arrows, I feel I can make it. No matter how steep and tortuous the trail, no matter how violent and erratic the wind and rain, I can certainly cover thirteen kilometers this afternoon. I feel quite relieved of all concern, of any worry, free to enjoy the fresh and raw beauty of the darkening, windswept mountainside. But in my struggle to keep my footing, I am careful. I don't want to fall on a slippery rock or smooth patch of grass. With the heavy pack, I might have difficulty getting up again. I'm grateful for my third leg, the strong staff. It helps make each step possible. I recall a comment made by Albani. He wrote that this part of the climb is so difficult that a horse or donkey would be exhausted by the required effort.

I strain to see some sign of the village. As at other times of tiredness, I am again attacked by an agony of doubt: I made a wrong turn, and I'm lost on this mountain. I'll never get to El Cebreiro today; I'm doomed to wander around up here all night, for I've seen no place to stop and come in out of the rain. Then, when I feel that I am approaching the absolute limits of my strength, I think I see some buildings almost directly ahead. El Cebreiro! Finally! Again, at the last moment, rescued! I am ashamed of my doubt.

I reach a farmyard, right alongside the path, and walk up to the barn. In the open doorway there is a farmer, keeping dry, quietly observing the rain . . . and now, me. I greet him and ask the name of this place. I don't quite catch his pronunciation, but I'm certain that he does not say, "Cebreiro." "Where is El Cebreiro?" I ask. "Oh, that's about two more kilometers up the mountain." He must have noticed the disheartened look on my face and the desperate weariness of my stance, for he adds, "Your climbing is just about over; it's pretty level going from here." I thank him and try to stand up straight as I turn and go out of the yard.

Surprisingly, I feel a surge of strength. When I stopped in front of him, I believed I could not take another step. But that break, even though I did not sit down, seems to have renewed me. Strange, the way my body works—always so well. The path continues to go uphill, but the grade is definitely not so steep. After about two kilometers, I reach the top—I've made it to El Cebreiro. I feel as if I've been climbing and struggling with the mountain and mud for at least twelve hours. But when I later check, it turns out to have been only seven or eight. Well, that's quite enough for this terrain. Perhaps I can even allow myself to take a bit of pride in my endurance.

I cannot but step into this hallowed space with a certain trepidation and awe: El Cebreiro, maybe the highest mountain one climbs along the *camino*, well more than a thousand meters, the place of a miracle whose telling eventually reached all of Europe. Today, one can find slight variations of detail in the different accounts preserved, and there is no certainty of the event's date, but opinion inclines toward the beginning of the fourteenth century. There was a monastery and a *hospital* for pilgrims here, on the top of the mountain. The story begins on a winter day, either during or just after a heavy snowfall, when a monk was saying Mass in the chapel. All the accounts record that he was a man *de poca fe*—of weak or little faith. Shortly after beginning the Mass, he noticed that one of the farmers or peasants from a village farther down the mountain had entered and was kneeling in the back of the chapel. A thought ran through his head. . . . What a foolish man to venture out and climb up here through all the snow . . . just to look at some bread and wine. . . . Then, after speaking the words of the Consecration: This is my body . . . This is the chalice of my blood . . . he trembled with terror. The bread and wine had all the appearances of flesh and blood!

The monk and the peasant were both buried in the chapel of the monastery. In 1486, *Los Reyes Católicos,* Ferdinand and Isabella, donated a finely wrought reliquary to hold the remains of the miracle. Emperor Charles V (d. 1558) was once passing nearby. A story relates that someone asked him if he did not want to stop at the monastery and see the miracle—the flesh and blood. Without hesitation, he answered no. He then went on to explain that he did not doubt the mystery of the Sacrament; the miracle was to confound heretics, those who deny the Real Presence. Laffi writes that a pope, Paschal II (1099–1118), wanted very much to see the miracle, put on the traditional habit (clothing) of a pilgrim, and journeyed there for this purpose. But there must be some confusion in the story, since the most probable date for the miracle is the early fourteenth century. Before being elected pope, Paschal served as a papal legate in Spain under Pope Urban II, whom he later succeeded.

In the sixteenth century, before Laffi visited the place, there were only four monks left in the monastery and the church was reported to be in very bad shape. Now, many buildings in the village are being restored, and Don Elías Valiña Sampedro, for many years the parish priest and an enthusiastic worker in recovering the tradition of the *camino* in this century, is also buried in the church.

As I walk up through the frequently photographed stone gateway to the most prominent building—what I take to be the restored monastery—I am confused by what I see inside the enclosure: a goodly number of new and very expensive parked automobiles. Wet and cold, I think of the comfortable ride they offered their occupants. But why did they drive up here? Out of respect for the miracle? Will I find some new kind of faith in El Cebreiro today? Seeing no one around in the rain, I hesitantly open the door a crack and look inside; I see a small bar. More confident, I walk in and am met by a young woman. I ask her about the *refugio,* and she cheerily replies that it opens at 6 P.M., in a couple of hours, and she has the key. Somewhat discouraged, achingly exhausted, and feeling my feet soaked and cold, I ask where I might sit down and rest. Still smiling, she unhesitatingly answers, "Right here, make yourself comfortable," gesturing toward another room beyond an open door.

I take off my poncho, pack, wet shoes, and socks, and put them in a corner of the tiny bar. After putting on dry socks, I step just inside the other room, seemingly a dining room and, attempting to be as inconspicuous as possible, sit down at a table in the nearest corner. Entering, I had noticed a large number of well-dressed people clustered in the center and at the far end of the room, finishing their lunch. It appears that the monastery has been converted into an expensive and stylish restaurant. How far have these people driven to eat lunch? This is, indeed, incredible.

Because my clothes are damp and I am still shivering from the cold, I order an *aguardiente*—perhaps the alcohol will warm me. The young lady asks if I want to eat. I apologetically explain that all this elegance is far beyond the settings of where I am accustomed to eat lunch, meaning that I feel the place beyond my means. Ignoring my perhaps foolish remark, she promises to bring me a substantial meal at a quite reasonable price. I am too wet and tired to inquire further, so I weakly acquiesce.

In a few moments, she returns with a tureen of white bean soup and a basket of compact, crusty bread. Before she can come back, I have hungrily consumed three bowls of hot and hearty soup. Almost immediately, she appears and sets a plate filled with boiled potatoes, pork, and a piece of sausage. The pork is mostly fat and rind, but I learn that one is supposed to cut it in such a way that each bite contains fat, a bit of lean, and a large piece of potato. It's definitely a poor man's cut of meat. For dessert, there is a dish of custard—all for 700 pesetas, an eminently fair price. The *aguardiente* was fifty more, and I decide on another to celebrate my ascent to El Cebreiro.

Curiously, as the fashionable patrons leave, someone starts a fire in the fireplace at the far end of the room, and the young woman invites me to go over. It has stopped raining, but I decide to warm myself at the fire before going out in the sun—the air will be chilly out there at this altitude. When I get near the fireplace, I stop in shock, seeing the unbelievable before my eyes: Some cyclists, who have come up on the highway and entered while I was eating, have surrounded the fire with their bicycle packs! I can't get anywhere close. Although I have never met the same cyclist twice—they travel much faster than I—they all behave in exactly the same way. I am tempted to believe that they have some secret conspiracy of brutishness worked out among themselves. Resignedly, I get up, leave the room, gather up my wet gear and seek the sun. Since we are so high on a mountaintop, the rays still reach the monastery-restaurant patio. I find a quiet spot, sit down, and look out over the village. I can see a couple of the ancient *pallozas*, prehistoric circular dwellings with cone-shaped thatched roofs. This is supposed to be the best place in Spain to see these preserved and restored structures.

In the middle of the eighteenth century, Albani arrived here at night, and found only one monk left at the monastery. He counted thirty-four *pallozas*, and noted that each had a large pile of firewood stacked outside for the winter. The *hospital* for pilgrims was one of the *pallozas*, and there were four sacks of straw on the ground inside, to be used as mattresses. There he met a Spanish pilgrim lying on one of the sacks, where he had been for three days, quite sick. He writes that a lovely thing (*un bonito hecho*) happened to him then. Seeing that the Spaniard appeared to be failing, that he hardly breathed at all, he hurried to the monastery to get the priest. He didn't want to see the poor man die without the Last Sacraments. He learned, however, that the priest had gone off to another village to say Mass.

Returning to the shelter, he held up his pilgrim's crucifix before the eyes of the dying man to encourage him as best he could, and silently commended his soul to God. Within two hours, "he passed to the other life nicely contrite." After the death, the old woman who watched over the pilgrim shelter prepared a turnip soup, and they ate their supper together, "like a mother and her son." Albani then arranged one of the straw sacks and tried to sleep. But there in the darkness, on top of that mountain, with the dead body right beside him, he could not relax enough to drift off. Sleepily arising at dawn, he said good-bye to the old woman and continued his pilgrimage to Compostela. In the account of this incident, as throughout his *relato,* Albani shines out as an attractive and generous pilgrim, one you would enjoy meeting at night in a shelter along the *camino.*

Promptly at six, the young woman comes out of the restaurant and leads the way to the *refugio,* a large new building at the other end of the village. I had suspected, and now see, that the collection of buildings is another European "living" Disneyland. About thirty people actually live here, most apparently employed to serve tourists and wait on dinner guests who drive to the top of the mountain to eat. A government sign calls the place a "Conjunto histórico-artístico." All the buildings are restored or in the process of being rebuilt. Two of the *pallozas* contain an ethnographic museum. Perhaps when the building program is complete, the authorities will install authentic artists and "folk" to entertain visitors. I see three cows leisurely enjoying the abundant green grass. But everything is cleanly antiseptic—sharply contrasting with the shit-littered, rich-smelling yard of the farmer I met two kilometers down the mountain.

The new *refugio,* a large, multistoried building, seems equipped with everything. However, the kitchen and washing machines, new and shiny, are not yet ready for use. A lounge is filled with large plastic-covered easy chairs and finely made wooden tables. The windows admit a generous amount of light. The bathrooms, separate for men and women, have the latest style of chrome fixtures. But everything fits so tightly that the hot shower fills the room with steam. The cold efficiency is not quite perfect.

After a shower, I step outside to bathe in the beauty beneath my feet. With the sky cleared and the sun still lighting the distant, low valleys, I sense my own insignificance in this huge, pure space. Far out on the horizon, many kilometers away, mountains etch a smoothly rising and falling line separating dark land masses from the delicately colored sky. To me, with almost no experience of mountain terrain, the patchwork of fields and villages, seemingly at my feet but more than a thousand meters below me, is magically evocative of a fairy wonderland. What must it be like, to live up here and to stop in one's work, look out, contemplating this rich pattern—nature so carefully and lovingly cultivated? Creation is indeed beautiful, beyond all imagining. And I am especially blessed at this moment, able to see all the way to the horizon, for the mountaintop could have been shrouded in the rain clouds of this afternoon, or by a heavy mist and fog. Since it is spring, the tiny, neatly divided fields shine out in various shades of clean, washed green, beginning another season of re-newed growth, a silent but powerful witness to the earth's goodness. When I reached this magnificent summit, I felt almost no pain, only ex-treme exhaustion. Now, refreshed and in dry clothes, privileged to fix my eyes on the work of God and the Spanish people, I'm ready to begin an-other day. The complex pattern of distant fields, the fresh colors, the fine clarity of the air, the very height itself give me new vigor. This day is undoubtedly unparalleled, incomparably unique. Reflecting on that judg-ment, I have to smile to myself, for I've repeated a similar thought each evening.

The silence and solitude of the *camino* were particularly suggestive, resonant today. I had come to think that I should be making a pilgrimage for the gift of faith, for those whom I know and love, for those tied most closely to me. Today, that idea appeared too narrow, indeed, quite wrongheaded. If I were to believe that my intention and the gift of faith are confined or limited in this way, then I would be equating these goods with the goods of economics, with the world of scarcity. But that is mani-festly, monumentally false. Neither intention nor faith are diminished by the number of persons affected or touched.

But because I am a mere creature, there must be some criterion of limit; limit is necessarily a defining characteristic of myself as creature. Only the intention and gift of the Lord are infinite, reaching out to touch all persons. I cannot presume to act in this way. I must search for the mode proper to me. With the rain beating me down, unable to see more than a few meters ahead, I seemed to arrive at the certainty of a possible position: My intention can affect all those whom I have touched since my birth. These are the people whose lives I have entered, the people who are a part of *my* life. If intention is possible, if it can reach another, then these are precisely all those whom I can hope to affect.

This is what is real: what I can touch . . . my own flesh, the ground under my feet, the aura of this place, the young woman who befriended me today, my family, and all those whom I have known or who have known me. For me, this is the limit of the real. I cannot reach out to some hungry child in the confusion of Africa, to some drugged young man in the hell of New York, to a yuppie in the golden ghetto of Scottsdale. For me, all these are abstract chimeras; they are not real.

In the purity of this wonderfully crystalline air, my firm presence on this sacred ground, my contact with El Milagro del Cebreiro (The miracle of Cebreiro), the deliberate, slow movement toward Compostela—all move me to see my action more intelligibly. I have walked into the luminous realm of the *camino,* seeking what lies at the end of the peninsula, beyond the legendary *finis terrae.* I have already experienced an overwhelming plethora of graces, which increase each day. Now all my attention must be focused on the other, all the others, of my life. My intention must be directed to them, away from my self.

27

El Cebreiro to Samos

May 30, 1993

I wake up at the usual hour, shortly before 6 A.M., warm, uncomfortably warm. This has never happened before. As I become more alert, I realize that the room is filled with radiators, and they have come on during the night. Later, downstairs, looking out the glass and chrome door, I see that it is still quite dark . . . and raining furiously . . . I must step out into a storm on a mountaintop! I hesitate to open the door . . . but after a few moments of enduring the antiseptic warmth of the new building, I shoulder my pack and hesitantly venture out. The wind and rain strike and confuse me. I'm uncertain which way to go in the darkness. And a mistake now, at the beginning of the day, can only place me in a progressively worsening situation.

The trail seems to lead down a gently graded road, and I soon spot an arrow indicating that I've started well. My only challenge now is the wind and rain, which if not friends, are certainly old companions. Later, the *camino* takes off for some solid cross-country hiking up and down a winding mountain path. After some hours, I arrive at Alto do Poio, a high mountain village, and stop for a small coffee. The rain has ceased, but a cold wind gusts now and then, chilling me through to my bones.

Some kilometers later, I approach a small town, Triacastela. On the outskirts, along the path, I come to a long, low stone wall. About seventy-five meters back from the wall, in a nicely landscaped yard, is a new *refugio.* It's smaller than the one up at El Cebreiro, and looks much more attractive . . . its design appears to express some imagination and spirit. The building and the entire setting would present an especially welcome sight to a tired pilgrim at the end of a day's walk. But it's much too early for me to stop, so I only look without changing the rhythm of my stride.

In a few moments, I am surprised by coming upon a man sitting in the open doorway of his shop, carving wooden shoes. I've often seen people out in the country wearing these shoes, and I would guess that they are cheap and practical for keeping one's feet dry. I also know that animal manure is hard on both leather and rubber. We talk a bit about his work, and I continue on the path, my spirit considerably lightened and enriched by the meeting. What good fortune to meet yet another craftsman who possesses a complete and consummate skill and who, as an upright member of his community, creates something good and useful for his neighbors. Again, I am happy for Spain—still able to count such persons among its citizens.

In the center of town, I try to buy bread, but the bakery is closed. I hope I can find something open in Samos, my destination today. As I make my way up the street, I spot an open, welcoming bar, and decide on a second cup of coffee. I also need to take off my wet shoes and socks and put on dry socks. My feet continue to perform admirably, but I attribute that largely to the fact that I keep them dry. I notice that on the bar there are some plates of small pieces of bread with thin slices of *chorizo* (sausage) on top—*bocadillos* or *pinchos.* They are free, so I help myself to two . . . perhaps out of proportion to my minor purchase. As I enjoy my snack, a young German couple also come in for coffee. I have met them earlier on the *camino,* and they had explained to me that they are making the *camino* in two years, half last year—to Sahagún—and the other half this year. Their vacation is not long enough to do the entire *camino* in the same year. How fortunate I am to have this time, and the money to buy food each day. They remind me that today is Pfingsten, Pentecost Sunday. I had not realized the day. How strange my accounting of time and dates. I only think in terms of entering the space of the *camino* each day, and attempting to plunge myself as deeply as possible in it. I have lost my sense of other kinds of measure.

Here, the *camino* divides into two routes, which join again in Sarria, about twelve kilometers farther. The one to the right is reputed to be more picturesque, but the one to the left goes through Samos. I will take this latter one, since I want to stay at the famous Benedictine monastery tonight. The Germans are taking the other one. After putting on my shoes and saying good-bye to them and the town, I find that the path takes on a distinctively new character: huge, ancient trees on each side completely shade the *camino*. This would be a welcome, cooling relief on a hot day, but only an interesting variation today. I meet a farmer and his cows, as he accompanies them out to their pasture. As in many places, the *camino* also serves as a path to fields and pastures for local farmers.

Passing through a number of small farm villages, the narrow path brings me right up to the old houses and other buildings. I am greatly impressed by the stonework, and immediately jump to the comparative judgment I've been pushed to make before: These structures are substantially different from what one sees in more recent and new construction. In the new buildings, everything is rigidly uniform; it looks, and is, factory-made. The old buildings appear, and are, handmade. I am confronted with the radical differences between industrial and vernacular construction and work, symbolizing the expressions of two very separate modes of living, of two very different worlds, far distant from each other. It is clear that workmen must follow the demands of manufactured building materials today, whereas formerly the artistry and imagination of individual craftsmen were continually required to fit each stone into the whole.

In this part of the country, the difference is also obvious in the roofs. Many of these are made of slate that was mined, I would guess, nearby. Some of the old roofs are an amazing and variegated patchwork of various odd pieces of different size and shape, artfully fitted together to make a weatherproof covering. The new ones are made of uniform machine-cut squares or rectangles, all the same size, requiring only the most elementary carpentry skills: snap a chalk line and follow it. From the numbers and relative ages of the two kinds of roofs, I can easily infer that the new is replacing the old. Why? Jacques Ellul believes that if a new technique is known, it will inevitably be applied. But I wonder about the precise character of that inevitability. I suspect that at least two separate factors enter: a curious sense of order, and laziness. Because of the ubiquity, apparent efficiency, and up-to-date sheen of machine-made objects, together with an increasing lack of direct, sensible experience of natural and handmade objects, people are inclined to choose the new and to reject the old as dowdy, old-fashioned. This inclination is given a decisive push by one's inherent laziness. Ultimately, this is why technological inventions tend to be bad in themselves, and to be used badly. One must see how the impulse to technological novelty interacts with human nature. I conclude, and this is amply confirmed by the historical record, that this nature is somehow wounded, and believe that the ancient schema expressing an aspect of this—the seven capital sins—is true. So men are powerfully moved to abandon an art requiring, not textbook manuals— they would be largely useless—but long apprenticeship under a master workman. It appears easier to buy factory-cut slate or factory-made tiles, and the result looks more citified and modern.

I have never before seen such roofs; I would never have dreamed that hand-crafted work can extend so far, creating such art. Looking at them closely, I see that, as with everything—people, natural scenes, man-made objects, paintings—one cannot truthfully imagine their beauty: one simply cannot rely on the inevitably falsifying picture; one must look at them directly with the eye, *and* in the actual place where they grew out of a people's way of living. Here, as I walk through the villages, able to touch the very walls that support such intricate roofs, able to inhale some slight whiff of these people's lives, I can sense something of the depth of this human work. I know that these roofs, when first conceived and constructed, formed an integral and vital part of a people's life, resulted from the way a people lived. But I don't know the details and skills of the work or the character of the people. Since I am a stranger, I do not know if such people still exist in these villages. I have had the good fortune to meet two different shoemakers, two men who come from a world where such roofs were also made. But I know them only from a few fleeting moments of conversation. I infer something of the lives of the people here only from a few roofs, lives that probably exist today only in these vestiges of a community once characterized by a certain wholeness and an inventive autonomy.

After Triacastela, the arrows indicate a little-used highway. Following this route, I am surprised and confused to come upon two massive mud-slides and one rockslide, each of which covers half the road. There are no warning signs or flags for approaching cars. Perhaps this is because the slides are so recent—they look quite fresh, as if they have come thundering down, just before I reached these places. Now and then I look up, with some apprehension, at huge rock and earth formations that seem to jut out over the road, threatening to come crashing down at any moment. Will the recent rains loosen yet another huge slice, just as I am passing, and bury me under tons of mud and debris? Or will I have time to jump out of the way? In the Middle Ages, pilgrims had to worry about wolves and thieves at certain places along the route. I have not been warned of any danger, except for sunburn. But those landslides were large enough to bury two dozen pilgrims, if they were caught under them.

Coming down from El Cebreiro in a fog that must have been even thicker than the one I walked through, Albani got lost again. He notes that he would sometimes walk all day without meeting a single person. Some-times the exception would turn out to be a fellow pilgrim. But on that day, after walking what turned out to be twice the actual distance to Triacastela, he finally met a muleteer who showed him the way. Before

Albani got there, he passed several crosses stuck in the ground, each indicating the place where a pilgrim had been killed or robbed and left for dead. Whenever he passed one of these, he shuddered and thought, "Who knows but that they will have to erect one of these crosses for me? But by the grace of God, I met no robbers, and arrived safely." He also records that the region was so poor, and bread from wheat flour so rare, that it was sold as if its value equaled that of a holy relic.

After about eight hours of continual walking, interrupted briefly for the two small cups of coffee, I arrive at what must be Samos. In the middle of the village, I am confronted by the towering walls of the monastery, the Real Monasterio de San Julián de Samos that, together with its church, has been declared a national monument. I see that much restoration work has already been finished, even extending to the streets and approaches to the buildings. The physical plant, covering about two acres, is reputed to contain a shelter for pilgrims, and I have come here to learn something about the history of hospitality. Saint Benedict (d. 547), one of the truly important figures in the direction and shape of Western civilization, and the founder of Western monasticism, wrote in chapter 53 of his Rule (which inspires and governs Benedictine monasteries to this day):

> All guests to the monastery should be welcomed as Christ, be-cause He will say, "I was a stranger, and you took me in" (Matt. 25:35). Show them every courtesy, especially servants of God and pilgrims. When a guest is announced the superior or brothers should greet him with charity; and they should pray together in order to be at peace . . . all shall honor in the guests the person of Christ. For it is Christ who is really being received.

There is no sign or indication of where the *refugio* is located—only lofty, solid-looking walls, and some small doors tightly closed. The sun is shin-ing now, and I had hoped to do some laundry. But how to get inside? Starting around the building, I come to a small gas station on the street, and a young man there points to one of the closed doors. That is the entrance to the shelter, but it only opens at 6 P.M. That means no laundry today; no time for it to dry.

I ask about a place to buy food. The gas-station attendant says that the bar across the street might offer something to eat, and there is a small *tienda* (store) farther in the town that, he believes, might still be open. Following his directions, I go around the monastery and soon come to the *tienda*. It's open. I buy their last loaf of bread and the usual items for a cold dinner and breakfast, suspecting that I shall not be offered anything at the monastery. The young man had said that a monk sometimes comes out before six and opens the door, so I return and sit down in the street, letting the sun dry my shoes, while I wait. The Rule, again:

> Guests, after reception, are to be led in prayer. The superior or his delegate shall sit with them.

> Let the Divine Law be read to the guest for his spiritual uplifting, and let every courtesy be shown him. . . . The abbot will wash the guest's hands and, together with the brothers, his feet. . . . Special care should be taken of the poor and pilgrims for Christ is truly made welcome in them.

At about four o'clock, a door opens, a monk comes out. Seeing me sitting there on the ground, he comes over to talk. He is friendly, and he, too, mentions that the monk-guestmaster might come out before six to open the *refugio* door. Not too much later, three young monks come out and greet me. Curious, I suppose; they ask me about myself. In our conversation, I learn that they are novices—young men preparing to be monks—from Puerto Rico, and one was born in New York City! At this very moment, an older monk appears and leads them away, giving me the impression that I might be a questionable influence on his young charges.

Becoming resigned to the position of an outsider, I again sit down in the street. The sun still reaches me; I can relax in its warmth. Soon, the monk-guestmaster appears, opens the door to the *refugio,* and immediately disappears. I go in and see that the shelter is a long, cold and damp, dark room with several small nonopening windows, and a row of double bunks along each wall. The mattresses are quite dirty, but they are all I need to support my sleeping bag. At the end of the dormitory, there is a large, tiled, and well-lighted bathroom with wonderfully hot water. Feeling grateful for this blessing, I hope for a place to do laundry tomorrow.

The first monk I met had invited me to Vespers, and I said that I would like to attend. Then, just before the scheduled hour, the guestmaster comes for me and leads me up to a small chapel where about fifteen monks are gathered. I wonder . . . is this the entire community? in a place that could house hundreds? Vespers is sung solemnly, with exposition of the Blessed Sacrament, which had begun before I arrived. After the blessing with the Monstrance, I understand that I am to return to the dormitory. Since I am the only pilgrim here tonight, the dungeonlike hall will be a quiet place to rest . . . and to ponder the enigma of today's Benedictine hospitality.

No one has told me, and there is nothing in the dormitory except the

bunks, and one small bare table with chair, but I know that Benito Jerónimo Feijoo (1676–1774), the eldest of ten children from a distinguished
Galician family, received the monk's habit here when he was just fourteen
years old. Although I have not been shown it, there is a cloister garden
inside a quadrangle of monastery buildings with a statue of Padre Feijoo
in the center—I have seen a photograph. After finishing his studies, Feijoo was assigned to the monastery of San Vicente in Oviedo, and remained there—except for two short trips to Madrid—until his death. In
volume 3 of his study, *Historia crítica del pensamiento español,* José Luis
Abellán entitles the chapter on this monk, "El espíritu del siglo: Feijoo"
(The spirit of the century: Feijoo). Some authors, such as Gregorio Marañón, believe that the eighteenth-century Enlightenment began in Spain
only with the publication of the first volume of Feijoo's *Teatro crítico,* in
1726. Up until that moment, Spain was "a desert submerged in the most
profound darknesses."

Marañón's mixed metaphor suggests the confusion surrounding the figure of Feijoo. In Feijoo's writings, one often comes upon the phrase, "me
duele España" (the tragedy of Spain pains me greatly) . . . an idea familiar
to twentieth-century readers in the more recent formulation by Miguel de
Unamuno. A polymath, Feijoo did not begin to write and publish until
after he was fifty. From then until his death, he carefully crafted a body of
essays and letters, directed both at intellectuals and the general public,
attempting to speak about what seemed to him to be the cultural back-
wardness of Spain. He attacked both superstition among the general pop-
ulation and academic sterility among scholars.

Feijoo was not, however, a child of the Enlightenment à la Voltaire. In
his essay, "On the Moral Senescence of the Human Race," after covering
ancient history, Feijoo writes,

> With the coming of the Redeemer, the world takes on a different
> color, one part of it being transformed into heaven. Those who
> then embraced the truth wedded themselves to virtue. A small but
> lovely flock, feeding on the pasture of sound doctrine, lived as
> innocents. The harmony, candor and faith of the primitive Church
> produced, not at the beginning of history—as poets have imag-
> ined—but in the very middle of time, a golden age.
>
> But this happiness did not last long. As soon as the persecutions
> ended, one finds Christianity in the same state we see today. It
> appears that the blood of the martyrs fertilized the field of the
> Church, but when this sustenance ended, the harvest of virtues
> turned out to be a poor crop indeed. The similarity of those times
> to these is established by witnesses beyond all suspicion.

Contemplating the whole Church from the height of the pontifical throne, Saint Gregory the Great, who flourished in the sixth century, compared the Church to Noah's ark, where there were few humans and many brutes. In the Church also, the huge number who live brutishly, following the impulses of the flesh, is out of all proportion to those who live rationally, following the Spirit. Was there any change for the better in the times that followed? None at all.

One sees that the pain Feijoo suffered came not only from the intellectual, but also from the moral, poverty of his native land.

When I first learned that Feijoo was closely associated with Samos, I immediately wondered: Will I walk from one Spain to another? Will I find some great contrasting clash between the Milagro del Cebreiro and the sophisticated thinker? And then I found this in a letter by Feijoo, "The Examination of Miracles":

[Here] is the way I proceed in this matter [of whether or not a miracle has occurred]: to believe those miracles which are well authenticated, to doubt those which do not possess strong evidence, and to judge those false which after careful examination I have judged to be such.

And, later in the same letter: "Am I convinced by the number of witnesses? No, by the quality."

Feijoo dedicated the third volume of *Teatro crítico* to the abbot and monks of Samos.

My love for that holy monastery is measured by my obligation; and the obligation is so great that it can only be satisfied with love.

As the greatest benefit which I have received from that monastery is the healthy instruction which I got there in my youth, so the greatest of its glories, although they are many and sublime, is the continual record of the most austere monastic observance for so many centuries.

The Benedictines have been important in the historical origins of offering hospitality to impecunious travelers and pilgrims in what is today called Europe. In this history, one can note a certain tension between the spontaneous action of personal gift and the institutionalized ritual of organized service. Over the centuries various individuals and groups have offered hospitality—food, shelter, and other kinds of assistance—to pilgrims on the *camino*. As someone following these pilgrims' footsteps, I have now stayed in places maintained by private laypersons, religious orders and congregations, individual parishes, and governmental jurisdictions. Without any hesitation, I would state that my favorite is the miserable hovel of Arias Jato in Villafranca del Bierzo. In spite of the rudimentary facilities and the accumulated trash, all the physical necessities were present: first of all, access to the place when one arrived; the door appears always to be open. Actually, I don't remember seeing a door that could be securely closed; then, a quiet place to sleep, warm water for bathing and washing clothes—and a good place to hang them—inexpensive, simple, and good food. There was also something else: a man and his family, who seemed to live in the spirit of the *camino,* who seemed to have penetrated something of its mystique, and who generously shared the little he possessed of physical resources and the much he possessed of spiritual gifts. People in the government have erected impressive and sometimes attractive new buildings. And I have found all the public employees friendly and helpful. But Maribel Roncal—with her lovely garden and house for pilgrims in Cizur Menor—and Jesús Arias Jato—with his markedly unusual accommodations—offered a kind of spirited welcome that seemed true to the *camino,* to the glories of its history. All the other shelters, some of them fine places to spend the night, nevertheless fall into a category different from these two unique expressions of contemporary hospitality. From all the good persons I've met, two stand out especially as memorable hosts.

28

Samos to Portomarín

May 31, 1993

Today's events seemed more interesting; they seemed to reveal more facets of my presence in Spain; the earlier days appeared less rich, less meaningful. The new experience began in the early morning, shortly after I left the monastery—without having met any of the monks. I was again greeted by the call of the cuckoo, the friendly sound coming down the valley from a great distance away. As on other days, I did not see this Spanish "morning's minion" (Gerard Manley Hopkins).

Continuing through country fields, twice I met small flocks of sheep, watched over by women shepherds . . . the first time I had seen women doing this work. Once I met a man whose two oxen pulled a cart filled with firewood . . . someone getting in his supply for next winter—if it's already dead and seasoned; if it's green, it will need a year to dry out. A rough beam was fastened to the animals' horns, with the tongue of the two-wheeled cart attached to this. The arrangement seemed too simple or rigid—thinking of the animals' comfort. I wish I knew more about ways of harnessing these beasts' strength. Later, I met a man guiding a donkey, who pulled a wagonload of hay. This was the most direct evidence I have seen that not all Spanish farmers are totally mechanized. But I was puzzled: How should I think about the two women and the two men? What does their presence mean in that other world, the one that buffeted me as I walked along those busy highways a few days ago?

Today, the actual path was more appealing, more attractive, than ever. Often, an ancient stone wall, built as a fence, ran along each side, marking the narrow *camino*. Here and there, trees grew within the wall, or just beside it. The intricacy with which the stones fitted together complemented the sinuous vigor of the old trees. The interlacing of art and nature shone out as an exemplary combination of a craftsman's work and nature's powers of graceful growth. In some places, I had to watch my step carefully, for the path cut deeply between the trees and walls, and was filled with puddles or an actual running stream. Along one stretch, the rushing water covered the entire path, and all stepping stones—if there were any—had been submerged. I searched for a place to climb up out of what had become a deep ditch so that I could continue on higher ground. Getting out and over the wall, I found myself in a meadow of thick grass, shining in the sunlight. But when I tried walking on the grass in a direction parallel with the wall, I found that the meadow shone because it was a sheet of moving water! There was no "high ground," no way to keep my shoes dry. But after about half a kilometer, I could again descend to the path and find rocks or dry places to avoid the water.

During all this time, I felt as if I were being treated to some rich feast, as if I were stepping into a new dimension of aesthetic possibility. The most famous account of someone's experience of the *camino* is found in the *Liber Sancti Jacobi,* where Aymeric Picaud, after noting distances, gives most of his attention to the people and some of the physical conditions he encountered in the twelfth century. Extensive and detailed accounts of a pilgrim, found in the books of Laffi and Albani, note the characteristics of all the impressive buildings they saw, civil and religious, together with much information on their contents: ornamentation and relics. In none of these reports is there an awareness or appreciation of the natural world enveloping the wayfarer; this enthralled me today. I find that I am as delighted with what I see out-of-doors as they were with church interiors.

I would guess that interest in landscape, in the world from which I come, finds its origins in the English Romantics of the eighteenth and nineteenth centuries. For example, Thomas Gray, looking out over Cumberland meadows and wooded slopes in 1769, wrote of the "sweetest scene I can yet discover in point of pastoral beauty." For these men, a landscape entered the mind, was an experience, a state of perception. Gazing on the English countryside was like a dream, tranquil or intoxicating, seemingly of the creative imagination itself. What they saw appeared profoundly meaningful to them: Nature offered a "countenance or intellectual tone [which] must surpass every imagination and defy every re-membrance" (Keats).

After today, I feel that this Romantic sensibility and vision are incom-plete in a sense that induces a certain passive sterility in the person con-templating nature in this way. The construction of the stone fences, with their trees, the farmers I met today, the shoemakers, the ancient stone houses with their slate roofs, exemplify an insertion *in* nature, a way of living *with* nature that does not dominate or destroy it. These and similar actions, works of art, are also expressions of specific communities, works flowing integrally from these communities *as* communities. Their makers might not share the aesthetic sensibilities of the Romantic poets, they may not have stopped to admire a landscape. On the other hand, maybe they *did*. My conversations with American farmers have given me clear and striking evidence of their appreciation for the beauty that surrounds them. For me, after experiencing these magnificent examples of a *common* art, one manifesting the response of gifted individuals to the needs of their communities, I see that the Romantic perception is deficient. A truer appreciation of nature results from seeing the interweaving gracefulness of a sensitive human touch—today, most clearly evident in the trees growing out of the stone fences.

But how come to such a seeing? Some Romantics believed that one's eyes could be opened by walking. Wordsworth celebrated walking as a life-journey toward renewal and knowledge. Going out into the country, he sought a pastoral tradition that, he believed, would be a path to per-sonal enrichment. These writers thought that intentionality was sufficient to give them a particular configuration of walking that leads to some kind of redemption and renewal. For them, "cultivation" rather than "civiliza-tion" became the appropriate metaphorical description of the walker's accomplishment.

I find that Thoreau has a more complete understanding of walking, and suggests how one may come to a much more real and vital experience of the world, of both oneself and nature.

> He may travel [by walking] who can subsist on the wild fruits and game of the most cultivated country. A man may travel fast enough and earn his living on the road. I have frequently been applied to do work when on a journey. . . . The cheapest way to travel, and the way to travel the furthest in the shortest distance, is to go afoot, carrying a dipper, a spoon, and a fish-line, some Indian meal, some salt, and some sugar. When you come to a brook or a pond, you can catch fish and cook them; or you can boil a hasty-pudding; or you can buy a loaf of bread at a farmer's house for

four-pence, moisten it in the next brook that crosses the road, and dip it into your sugar—this alone will last you a whole day. . . . I have traveled thus some hundreds of miles without taking any meal in a house, sleeping on the ground when convenient, and found it cheaper, and in many respects more profitable, than staying at home.

Thoreau did not restrict himself to taking an afternoon stroll, contemplating landscapes along the way. He knew that one had to seek to insert himself *in* nature. Walking is not done to position oneself for the enjoyment or edification of inspiring views. Some sweat of human purpose must infuse one's hiking.

Aymeric Picaud, writing on the nature of pilgrimage, provides another dimension of the difficulties encountered when walking. All walking/pilgrimage begins with Adam who, having disobeyed God, was expelled from Paradise and condemned to walk through the "wilderness of this world." This journeying was "continued in Abraham, Jacob and all the children of Israel up to Christ, to be complete in him and his apostles."

As the Jews entered the Promised Land only through much suffering, so pilgrims, that they might enter the celestial fatherland promised to the faithful, must put up with cheating innkeepers, climbing mountains and clambering down into valleys, endure the terror of being robbed and the worries of finding one's way.

There is another witness, the uniqueness of whose journey points to yet a further dimension in this primordial activity: The Wandering Jew. According to the legend, as Jesus carried his cross through Jerusalem, he stumbled outside a shoemaker's shop. The shoemaker was asked to help the weakened "criminal," and he refused, saying (in the Spanish version of the story), "¡Anda! ¡Camina!" —get on with you. In Spanish, these words would forever echo throughout the heavens with their ominous association, for the shoemaker, in punishment, was condemned to walk the earth until the end of time. An Italian astrologer claimed that the forlorn fellow was in Compostela as a pilgrim in 1267. One sees, then, that the act of walking goes much further than the well-intentioned meanderings of the Romantics.

Today, I made another step into this world of walking—through nature. I saw something new: nature, with an immediate sensory vividness, with a direct clarity never before experienced. But this only happened because I also saw how people have learned to live gracefully in nature, in creation. My senses were prepared for this, were purified by the very difficulties of each day—the pain, the exhaustion, the confusion . . . and the prayer. I needed the daily ascetic exercise to rid my sensibility of all the artificial, pseudo-experiences of sense to which one is exposed in contemporary mainstream living. But I also needed to go far beyond what now appears as the superficial experience of the Romantics.

Looking back at the Romantics from the privileged place of the *camino,* I can see the strange paradox of their moment in history. They looked, and believed that they were seeing the natural world. Their action was, indeed, a step toward this seeing. But their experience of nature occurred precisely at the time when factories in England were beginning to replace unique handmade objects with standardized machine-made products. From the moment of its inception, the Romantics' new historical sensing—their singular immersion in nature as sensed—would face increasing imperilment and, in fact, practical extinction for many or most people. This was recognized early and expressed by the powerful voice of William Blake. Gerard Manley Hopkins's incisive and imaginative poetic voice, witnessing to the possibilities of this experience in the late nineteenth century, still stands unequaled. His sight was purified, and he achieved what he called "inscape," partly through a rigorous pilgrimage, both interior and geographic. He, too, expanded and enriched our notion of walking.

A few hours after leaving Samos, I come to Sarria, another town whose rich history is closely associated with the *camino.* But I cannot find the yellow arrows, and the streets confuse me. I want to go directly through the town and continue farther today. Since it is quite early in the morning, I meet a lot of children and young people on their way to school. Several times I ask different students, but no one knows the street to take. This is the first time I have met people on the *camino* who do not know the actual route. What are these young people learning in their schools? or in their community? Will no one tell them of the ancient path that winds through their town? of the fascinating history trod out by thousands walking right through their midst? Fortunately for me, I come upon a police station and go inside. The officers are, as usual, friendly and eager to demonstrate their knowledge; they also offer to stamp my *credencial.* I then explain that I get a stamp only in the places where I spend the night. That way I will have a clear record of where I was each day.

Cheered by the warmth of the officers, I find the streets to get out of town, and then wind my way through a number of small farm villages, each comprising a few households, obviously the homes and barns of working farmers. I feel a slight tinge of regret—I should have searched for a bar in Sarria. I will not find any coffee today in these small places. Then, some kilometers from Portomarín, I see a small Romanesque church and another new *refugio.* The government has certainly carried out an extensive building program this year; all the new places have just been built. From the plaques I see on their walls, they seem to be financed by the local communities or regions.

After about eight hours, covering as much as forty kilometers, I see Portomarín on a hill overlooking a large lake. In 1956, government engineers started damming the river Miño, which flooded the site of the old town. All was moved to the top of a nearby hill to create a new city. It looks somewhat artificial, but undoubtedly attractive. As I walk down the clean, broad streets, I remember that today marks four weeks on the *camino.* In Germany, I had made a rough guess that I would need a month to reach Compostela. Since I am getting close, I did not make such a bad estimate. A few kilometers back, my spirits were given a boost. I was happy to see a graffito on the side of a building: "¡Animo!"—take courage, you don't have far to go.

Visually, the glory of the town is the fortress-church of San Nicolás, a high boxlike structure, impressive and imposing, moved and rebuilt here, stone by stone. Its clean lines and severe design conceal a history that I find obscure and confusing. French monks from Cluny, with the support and encouragement of Spanish rulers, established or reformed many monasteries in Spain, beginning at the end of the tenth century. After 1141, Cistercian monasteries were introduced in Spain, and then multiplied. They were part of another reform movement within the Benedictine tradition, following, yet different from Cluny. The Cistercians imposed on themselves absolute separation from the world, rigorous practice of poverty, and refusal to accept ecclesiastical benefices and rents. They attempted to support themselves with their own manual labor, believing that this is an integral part of the Benedictine Rule. Cistercians sought to employ no servants or tenants to work their land. They observed perpetual silence, and extended their practice of poverty to the liturgy, ecclesiastical ornamentation, and architecture.

Urban II called for a crusade against the Muslims in 1095. In 1119, Hugh de Payens founded the Templars (*la orden de los Templarios*) in Jerusalem, to protect pilgrims traveling to the Holy Land. At his request, Saint Bernard, the leader of the reform Cistercian movement, wrote a short book, *Liber de laude novae militiae* (In praise of the new militia [1136]). Bernard takes the traditional idea of a *miles Christi*—a soldier of Christ—and, in view of the persistent aggression of Islam, combined the principles of monasticism and chivalry to create a rationale for a permanent *Christian* army, a legion of knight-monks who were prepared to fight in a continual crusade against those defined as infidels. Orders modeled on the Templars and influenced by the preaching and writing of Bernard were then founded in Spain. Los Caballeros de Calatrava (1158) was the first, and was directly affiliated with the monastery of Cîteaux, the source of the monastic reform movement. A half dozen or so more followed, such as the Caballeros de Alcántara and the Caballeros de Santiago. All the major Spanish foundations, with the exception of the Caballeros of Santiago, which followed the Rule of Saint Augustine, were associated with the Cistercians, following their rule of life. Members of these orders took the traditional monastic vows, and in some the knight-monk could add another vow: *consagrarse a la guerra santa contra los infieles*—to consecrate oneself to the holy war against the infidels.

Other military orders, such as the Teutonic Knights, came to Spain to join the Spanish orders in the Reconquista, the war against the Moors. Some of the military order fortresses also helped to protect and shelter pilgrims on their way to Compostela. Américo Castro believes that these orders were a response to and an imitation of policies initiated by the Almorávides (1086–1115) and the Almohades (1121–1269), warlike sects of Muslims who came to Spain from Africa and that held power in al-Andalus during those years. Other authors strongly contest this opinion. Saint Bernard, in the *Liber de laude novae militiae,* wrote that "to die fighting for the defense of the faith is to be a martyr for Christ." He makes no allusion to the spirit of Islamic warriors.

Three of these orders had fortresses around Portomarín, but the magnificent church of San Nicolás is the only substantial physical reminder of their presence. Records indicate that San Nicolás belonged to the Caballeros de San Juan de Jerusalén. It was established by the Templarios, the original military order. These knight-monks came to Spain in the twelfth century, and participated significantly in the Reconquista. After a particularly devious and gruesome intrigue, they were suppressed by Rome in 1312. Much of their extensive property holdings, such as San Nicolás, passed to the Caballeros de San Juan. The two orders had been in conflict with each other, and sometimes this deteriorated into open warfare. The distance from this situation to the idea of Bernard—to be a martyr for Christ—appears to be filled with impenetrable clouds of obscurity and human inclinations toward wickedness.

Climbing up the final steep hill into the town, I come directly to the *refugio*. It is another new government construction—and open. I set the pack down next to a new, clean corner bunk and get out all my dirty clothes. In a utility room, I find two new washers and a dryer. To use them, one gives his clothes to a woman who then operates the machines. There is a small charge, enabling her to earn a few pesetas. I ask the shelter attendant if I may do my own laundry, since I find it hard to change this habit. This is quite agreeable to him, but he is surprised and ready with advice when he sees what I plan to do. I have learned that the laundry sinks are not usually supplied with hot water. So, when I come to a place like this, I take a bucket to the shower, fill it with hot water, and pour this in the laundry sink. From the expression on his face, and his muttering, I suspect that I have inspired another Spaniard to think, "These crazy Americans!" In the large backyard, there is a clothesline and enough sun to dry my wet shoes. What a joy to find a shelter with the basics!

In addition, there is a fully equipped kitchen, but the new refrigerator is not yet connected. Well, I don't have any need for that. In the corner, there is a beautiful old wood-burning cookstove, with a box full of wood. I wonder . . . does anyone know how to work it? Although I cooked on just such a stove for about fifteen years, while living on our subsistence farm, I decide not to experiment tonight. One must know well the idiosyncrasies of each stove. And the usual gas range is against the other wall. Someone has left instant coffee behind, so I can make my own *café con leche*. At the market, I buy the same supplies: a slice of ham, frozen vegetables, fruit, cheese, yogurt, and add a liter of milk. I can heat a large cup tonight and another tomorrow morning. The night air will be cool enough to keep the yogurt and milk if I set them outside the window.

As I enjoy my hot dinner in the large kitchen, an article in the local newspaper catches my attention. There is a full-page list of instructions on how to prepare for the *camino*. I can read it, but don't get every word since it is written in Gallego (Galician), the local language, different from Spanish. Fortunately for me, all the people I've met here in Galicia also speak Spanish, since I can't catch their language when spoken. Almost every item of the advice offered by the newspaper provokes a smile from me. For example, one should walk long distances fifteen to thirty days before setting out, to get in condition—I had walked all of seven days. One must take two pairs of hiking shoes, not new ones, and alternate them frequently—I have one pair. From my experience of four weeks, I find the information and counsel rather overly protective.

I feel good . . . it's been a fascinating, revelatory day. I had never thought of *using* the Rosary, of saying these prayers to pass the time or relieve the pain. But today, the slow, deliberate recitation seemed to open my spirit, seemed to discipline my sensibility, so that I *saw* creation anew, as if bathed in a sparkling light. The direct power of my senses was increased, my awareness was enlarged and sharpened. I think I was taken far beyond the Romantics. The *camino* carried me deeper into that mysterious place, creation. How superficially I have lived; how little I have known the creation. But tonight my thoughts go in another direction; I stumble over a dark, brooding image: Santiago, Matamoros—the Moorkiller, the special patron of the Caballeros de Santiago.

29

Portomarín to Palas de Rei

June 1, 1993

R egularly striking the pavement, my staff makes a strangely loud sound . . . no one is yet in the streets, the sound echoes off the silent stone buildings. I would enjoy meeting someone and wishing them a hearty "¡Buenos días!" . . . but the solitude and silence seem particularly appropriate. There are no distractions . . . I am refreshingly free to walk out into the *camino,* to learn where it leads me today. I come down the hill, leaving this picturesque town, and reach a crossroads. Which way do I go? I must think clearly, practically, try to remember what I was told last night about the route. Straining to bring back that too casual conversation, I see an approaching car . . . a Guardia Civil jeep. For the pilgrim, there were times and places in the past when the sight of the policing authority immediately translated into fear and alarm. Local warriors sometimes lived off extortions and spurious duties that they forcefully demanded from pilgrims. But I joyfully greet these men, relieved to know that I shall not lose my way at the very beginning of the day. They know precisely in which direction I should go, and display their customary courtesy and friendliness.

A local person told me that I would have to do some climbing at the beginning today, but that the path would then level off. There is, indeed, a lot of climbing, but my informant failed to tell me that I would encounter a *series* of high hills or low mountains. That means much descending, always more or less painful. And it takes a long, long time before anything like level ground begins to appear. People who live here develop perceptions very different from mine. Plodding on, I meet a farmer who looks up at the sky and then tells me that it's going to rain. I want to thank him, but feel rather awkward about it. I know that he offered his knowledge of the weather to help me. Smiling to myself, I wonder how I can thank him for telling me that I will soon get soaked with rain.

When the climbing ends, I feel that I'm in a new place, as if I'm walking *on top* of the world, as if I'm in a place altogether above the normal world, the everyday world. I've experienced this before, but each time the sensations are new, fresh, as if it is a first time. I skirt level fields, while everything takes on a special, quite different character. The wind and rain are not the same up here; they are not the elements I grew up with in central Illinois. I move through air that, I suppose, is "thinner"—some science-influenced book no doubt has suggested that term. What I know is that my body or, more correctly, I feel the space, I breathe and walk differently up here. Only the rain is familiar. Because I've simply walked into it whenever it strikes, I think I've come to know it better; I've not tried to avoid or curse it. Perhaps the elements, too, have worked to cleanse my sight.

After some hours, I reach Ligonde, where only a couple of houses are visible from the *camino.* Then I come upon yet another new *refugio,* with a farmhouse nearby. In front, a farmer stands, maybe thinking about what indoor work he can do in this rain. I greet him and we talk. Eagerly and openly, with a touch of pride, he speaks of the new shelter, offering to unlock it and show me around. I assume that he has volunteered to keep the key and watch over the building. I thank him, declining the invitation, saying that I want to keep going farther, and I am anxious to keep moving. Noticing his own modest house, aware of the few needs that anyone walking the *camino* has, knowing that these new places are rather richly appointed, and thinking of the real hardships and dangers thousands have endured in the past, I suggest the possibility that these new *refugios* are overly built, too well equipped. From his eyes and the hesitation in his voice, I can see that such thoughts have occurred to him. But he has mastered these temptations; he is reluctant to make any explicit criticism. Over many generations, people in his position have learned to guard themselves in what they say to strangers who arrive suggesting heterodox opinions. I am quite content to say no more, not wanting to embarrass him; I wish him a good day, and continue my journey.

The texture of the atmosphere and the fresh spring look of the fields enthrall me with their special beauty, specific to this time and place. But I see machines and then smell strong odors that raise, for me at least, disturbing questions. Next to the barns on many farms are stainless steel electrically powered cooling units for the milk. I remember that, on my grandfather's farm, the milk cans were set in the large water tank where the stock drank to keep them cool until the milk truck arrived. Obviously, perhaps, a much less efficient way to handle milk. But is this the proper question to ask? At what cost did these farmers insert themselves deeply enough into an industrial agriculture to be able to imagine and then carry out *this* mode of life? to live in the industrial economy? Would they still be able to recognize the shoemakers?

From America, I know the strong smell of liquid manure that comes out of swine confinement operations, out of these scientifically efficient ways to produce pork. From seeing the kinds of meat sold in the markets, I know that, economically, Spain is heavily into hogs. For the last two days, I have been strongly assaulted by a noxious stench when I pass some farms. During all my days on the *camino*, I have yet to see a living pig. So I arrive at certain conclusions: Swine production is carried out only in farm factories utilizing a confinement system; all the animals are tightly enclosed in an efficiently engineered space. This production is concentrated in certain areas, such as those I walked through these last two days. The peculiar manure smell, although recognizable, is more foul, more offensive, than any I have ever before experienced around such operations. Do Spanish farmers have a higher tolerance than their American counterparts for disagreeable odors? Or have they not yet learned to fine-tune the system so as to bring the smell down to a more acceptable level? In any event, this horrible befouling of the pure mountain air is a terrible blight. I wonder . . . do the farmers ever reflect on all the costs of their conversion to an industrial mode of production?

In Portomarín, I heard that a new *refugio* was being constructed in Palas de Rei, but no one knew if it was ready for use. My map showed some kind of sports complex on the near side of the town. From this I inferred that the place would be large enough to support at least one small inn or hotel. Therefore, I would be able to find a place to stay and something to eat. Cold and wet, my fingers are so stiff now that I can't get them to undo a button or snap on the poncho.

I come to the football field and town. I'm exhausted . . . unable to walk any farther, and the pain has returned . . . it's found new places in that left leg to torment me! That piece of information about pain lasting only through the first few days must apply only to young people, or to those whose constitution is very different from mine.

Following the arrows, I easily reach the new *refugio,* located in the center of town, across the street from the Ayuntamiento (City Hall) and its plaza. I read the sign on the door and learn that it is finished and open to receive pilgrims, but only after 5 P.M. I turn and walk up the street, meeting a young man within the block, and ask him if there is a place nearby where I can get a good *menú del día,* the daily special. Without hesitation, he confidently says yes, and directs me to a restaurant. I find that it's only about two blocks away—at this point, a highly important fact, for I am thoroughly sore, tired, and wet.

Outside a plain door, like that of any ordinary residence on the street, I see a very small sign, "Casa Curro," but no suggestion of what that means, or any indication that this is a place open for business. Cautiously, I open the door and look in—a large, unadorned room, crates and boxes stacked here and there, some bare tables and chairs and, in the far corner, a small bar. The place is deserted but dry, and the bar probably has *aguardiente*—just what I need to move my fingers again. I manage to get the dripping poncho off and draped from my staff, lean the pack against the wall and drop into the nearest chair.

After a short time, a door at the end of the room opens, revealing what seems to be a kitchen, and a woman comes out to greet me. I ask her if there will be a meal later, for I know it is still too early to eat in Spain. She says yes . . . and believes that she can work me in. Her remark strikes me as strange, but I am too tired to question her about its meaning. Trusting that food will appear at the appropriate hour, I order an *aguardiente.*

There is a small window looking out on the street, and I notice that the rain has stopped . . . the sun has appeared . . . just after I reach a dry place. There is also a bar across the street, and a crowd of young people milling about in front, going in and coming out. Observing them more carefully, I see that they have backpacks; they must be walking on the *camino,* as a group. This is the first time I have come across a large group of young people walking together, and have heard that they can reach into the hundreds. I feel rather confused about the meeting. It's so quiet and peaceful, being alone in this room, cut off from the distraction of their noise. But it might be interesting to see such a group close up, to know something about them . . .

While musing on the experiences of the day, I am startled by the woman who brings me a large plate of soup and bread—but not the tureen, unfortunately. So, there is food for me. Moments later, the door suddenly swings open and all the young people come crowding in, laughing and talking. They noisily push tables together, pull up chairs and sit down. Without a word being spoken, the woman brings them dishes and utensils, and they set the table. Then comes the soup. Watching these movements, I conclude that they had made some previous arrangement to eat here today; and I am a special, added guest.

I have the feeling, from the turning of heads now and then, that the young people wonder who I am. Since they can see the poncho and pack, they know I am on the *camino*. After finishing their dinner, a young woman, more courageous (or curious) than the others, comes over to my table, says hello, and gradually asks me about myself: Where do I come from? How old am I? then, somewhat wonderingly, Do I walk alone? How far did I come today? At what time did I start? Have I had any trouble with my feet? and so on. As we talk, I notice that the entire group becomes silent, turns toward us and listens intently. The young woman first, then the others, too, express frank amazement. They find it difficult to believe that someone my age has the strength or stamina to survive the *camino!* They are surprised to learn that I have come so far today. They think it simply incredible that my feet are not covered with blisters. Several of them are tenderly treating such problems on the bottom of their feet. I recall what an older man said one night in a *refugio* during just such a conversation with a couple of young people: "¡Los viejos somos los fuertes!"—"we old folks are the strong ones!" I have to smile inwardly at the reactions of the friendly young woman and her companions.

The one aspect of my action that they find most unimaginable, most incomprehensible, is that I walk alone. Apparently the idea has never occurred to them . . . or to most others. The people whom I have met, and who have expressed some question about my presence on the *camino,* are always most intrigued, not by my age, but by this practice of walking in solitude. The deliberate stepping out into the space of the *camino* alone seems to have been done by very few. The most extensive and interesting account of a solitary pilgrim is that by Albani. I have met only three other persons who set out in this way: the French physician, the young man from the Canary Islands, and the young woman from California. One of the three Frenchwomen occasionally walks alone for a day or two before rejoining her companions. I wish I could meet her again to ask her about the different experiences of the two situations.

Are people afraid to be out there by themselves? What would be the nature of this fear, since I have heard of no dangers? Are people afraid of themselves, of facing themselves in the silence of the fields and mountains? Have they no intimation of the delights, the wonders, to be experienced in the historically vast space of the *camino?* How could the *camino* speak to you if you are listening to your companion? How could you ever hope to enter the mystery of this place beyond places unless you are silent, alone, open to the secret voices? After the experience of walking the *camino* by myself, I cannot imagine setting out with others. How could I meet all the old pilgrims, who speak so strangely and softly, if I am engrossed with my friends?

It's true that solitude can be terrifying. Fearful ghosts and demons can move into the space of one's quiet. In my tradition, I know this has happened many times, the most famous early instance being that of Saint Antony, when he lived as a hermit in the Egyptian desert. Before he died in 356, he was tormented by the Devil in shapes and manners beyond all description or imagining. This very challenge inspired many European artists to attempt portrayals of his temptations. Within Western monasticism, any attempt to live as a hermit has been subjected to rigorous rules and cautions. Spiritual directors know that solitude is not to be sought lightly. So is it not dangerous to be alone out here? I cannot speak for others, but I feel that I am not alone; I walk with many—all who came here before me. As they assisted me on the first day when I thought I could not get across the Pyrenees, so they have often taken my hand to lead me through the dark and fearsome regions of solitude.

The young people eating with me today will probably meet no *pícaro* anywhere along the *camino*. But this was the experience of pilgrims over all the centuries: to meet people along the way who attempted to cheat, trick, or even kill them. The *pícaros* have come in many forms, and almost all the records mention them. Picaud writes at great length about evil *mesoneros*—innkeepers.

> They let [the pilgrim] taste a good wine, and then actually sell him a bad one. Others sell cider for wine, others adulterated for good wine. Others, fish or meat cooked two or three days ago, which makes people sick. . . . Others promise soft and clean beds, and give guests filthy ones. . . . The evil innkeeper gives strong wine to his guests to make them drunk. Then, when they are sound asleep, he robs them. . . .

> Servant girls in the inns along the Camino de Santiago who, for shameful motives and to obtain money, through the instigation of the Devil, approach the beds of pilgrims, manifestly deserve condemnation. The prostitutes who, for the same motives, between Portomarín and Palas de Rei, in mountainous regions, come out to tempt pilgrims, should not only be excommunicated, but also be stripped, tied up and embarrassed, cutting off their noses, exposing them to public shame. . . . There are so many ways, my

brothers, that the Devil throws out his cursed nets and opens the door to perdition for pilgrims, that it disgusts me to describe it all.

Picaud's prescriptions for punishment were in accord with a belief in the power of salutary and graphic example. Such practices were still current in the eighteenth century. Several times, Albani mentions seeing the bodies of hanged or beheaded men prominently displayed alongside the road. This was a common chastisement for men convicted of robbing pilgrims. It was hoped that their putrefying corpses would serve as a vivid deterrent to further depredations on travelers.

In his guidebook, Picaud also counsels pilgrims to be careful not to allow any quarrels to arise among themselves. He relates that in the church of San Gil, a popular stopping place on the *camino,* north of the Pyrenees,

> I saw once on a certain night [pilgrims in the church] fighting over the chair of the saint. The French were sitting there next to the saint's tomb and the Basques, wanting to sit in the same place, attacked them. And it happened, naturally, such was the struggle with fists and stones, that one person received a serious wound, fell to the floor, and died. Another one, with a head wound, fled to Castelneu, on the road to Périgueux, and died there. Therefore, you must strive to root out all fights and drunkenness among yourselves as pilgrims.

Picaud has several more pages of such detailed description. From him and others who have written of their experiences, it appears that one must struggle to reach and stay on the *camino.* Another way of saying this is to acknowledge that there is also a way of truth here, proper to this place, to the space of the *camino.* And truth is never grasped easily; it does not fall like a ripe apple. In former times, the hardships and dangers were a given. One had to arrive at a peculiar trust in God to set out at all, to practice a certain kind of fidelity to avoid temptations. Today, all this is changed. The obstacles may be our companions and friends who would accompany us on the *camino,* distracting us from its illuminations. In each age, there was a distinctly proper way to reach Compostela, to taste the mystery of Santiago Peregrino. That has not changed today. The task is to identify the contemporary way. All my experience inclines me to believe that this is the way of silence and solitude, not distracting oneself with books or companions. One needs a certain discipline, an appropriate *askesis,* to find the *camino.*

Well, it's time to step outside and let the sun dry my shoes. This is an amazing establishment. No one else came in to eat—only the group of youths and myself. Once, two men came in and had a drink at the bar. They appeared to be old familiars. The woman who served us a fine meal is the only person working here. Another local idiosyncrasy to add to my list.

The young people had only walked a short distance before lunch, and continued farther after eating. I walk back to the *refugio* and sit on the sidewalk, letting the sun warm me. At exactly five o'clock, a woman comes and opens the shelter. Each pilgrim must show his or her *credencial*—which is then stamped—to be admitted . . . a friendly but "by the book" reception. The building is not just a dormitory, but a complex and pleasing arrangement of rooms, surprisingly spacious overall. There is a fine kitchen, though not yet functioning, a large dining room and dormitories divided into men's and women's sections. Many windows admit a cheerful light to the interior, but I notice that, after I have opened them, a Spanish pilgrim comes along and closes them. I'm beginning to believe that many of the Spanish I meet are allergic to fresh air. I then decide to take a chance. There are balconies outside some of the windows where I can string a clothesline in the late afternoon sun. So I quickly wash all my dirty socks and hang them out to dry.

The showers introduce me to a novel technological gimmick. There are no faucets, only one button. I push it and shower water comes down at a comfortably hot temperature. After about two or three minutes, the water automatically stops flowing. If one is not finished, he must press the button again. There is hot water in the sinks, and radiators to heat the rooms. The authorities have tried to be attentive to all possible physical and aesthetic requirements of pilgrims. Although I am tempted to find fault, I must admit that such generous attention is genuinely impressive.

The dining room also serves as a kind of lounge. The attractive fireplace will be a welcome center for gathering when it is working. But now there is nothing in the room except furniture and a lot of promotional material designed to attract tourists to Galicia. One pamphlet, in French, effusively praises all the natural, culinary, and historical attractions. There is a passing mention of Santiago, too. The author states that the *camino* of Santiago constitutes one of the stages in the history of Galicia. The Council of Europe has now declared it to be the first cultural European journey (*itinéraire*). Again, "cultural" appears to mean anything and nothing. It is claimed that the religious pilgrimage route brought to this corner of the world various intellectual and cultural movements during the Middle Ages. It "covered" the *camino* with Romanesque churches, monasteries, hospitals, and pilgrim shelters. Then, lauding the cuisine of the region, the author asks, "What better time to visit Galicia?" I feel certain that one can never find the *camino* as a tourist. I have heard that some see the origins of modern tourism in the pilgrimage to Compostela. If there is any truth in that, is the secularization of such a journey, in fact, a perversion? The prostitution of foreign and exotic places and people in order to entertain the affluent is surely a despicable use of the other. I fall asleep, troubled. Am I, too, a tourist?

30

Palas de Rei to Arzúa

June 2, 1993

S everal small villages today. Passing through one, I meet a woman who comes out to the *camino* from her house, holding something up on a clean towel. I stop, uncertain what she has or intends. Then I see that she carries a round cheese, and offers to sell it. I hesitate, trying to imagine what I will do with it: It's more weight to carry, and I can't eat so much cheese myself. I smile, mumble some excuse, refusing her offer. But as I walk on, I slowly come to feel deeply chagrined. This was the first time on the *camino* that I had the opportunity to get something directly from the hands of the person who made it. And I failed miserably to act! How could I have been so obtuse? I don't have any food in my pack, and I could have shared the cheese with others when I reach the next *refugio*. I missed the chance to share in the honest life and work of someone who lives beside the *camino*. How could my thinking have been so clouded? so narrowly calculating? Does the consideration of my own comfort and convenience take such a repulsive form? Why couldn't I *see* what was being offered me?

In other places, I do not miss what is immediately under my feet. I come to an ancient stone bridge . . . the usual grace and proportion. Later, there is another. Oh, that I could sit here for hours and look at these marvels. Perhaps I need more time, time to contemplate such workmanship, in order to recognize living examples of good work. Perhaps modern images have corrupted my vision more thoroughly, more deeply, than I had ever imagined. The meeting with the cheese lady was an important test, and I failed it shamefully. I had thought that the discipline of the *camino* had worked to purify my vision. What vanity! How low I have fallen. How far I have yet to climb.

Then I come upon another small bridge, this one constructed of that cast concrete, the kind made in imitation of stone. I have no trouble recognizing what it is—a bridge—but its provenance is patent, its ugliness blatant. Why would people construct a bridge with such an ersatz material and method of work? Within a few kilometers, they have outstanding examples of genuinely *human* work, remarkable analogs of an ideal bridge, of a Platonic form. Could the exemplary idea of "bridgeness" be more perfectly realized? Have people lost the capacity to recognize such ideal types?

I pass by Leboreiro, an ancient town whose name comes from the word for rabbit, *liebre.* This place has been famous for hundreds of years because of the number of rabbits here. In the country, I often come upon signs indicating that hunting is not open to the public in that area. But I have yet to see any evidence of a wild animal. Of wild creatures, I have seen only birds and a great number of snails. I suppose everything else has been hunted out years ago. There are places, however, where small game should flourish. And I have seen signs permitting fishing along certain streams.

As I walk on a rather wide road through a village, I see a woman on the other side, coming toward me, shouting and waving furiously. My suspicions are aroused when she gets closer; she's dressed rather strangely and her demeanor suggests nothing so much as a wild witch. It appears that she wants to stay on that side of the street, so I walk over to find out why she is so excited by my presence in the village. Gesticulating crazily, she loudly proclaims that I'm going the wrong way, that I'm lost, that I've gotten off the *camino.* From my appearance, she must have judged that I am a pilgrim. But that's pretty easy to do. And it's possible that I have missed a turn here in the village. But how can I trust her? The closer I get to her, the more outrageous, if not insane, she appears. I suddenly recall several strong, moving drawings by Goya of just such women. Some art historians call them drawings of foolish or evil hags.

I ask her where I should go. "Follow me!" she says. She goes on up the street in the direction from which I had come. After a hundred meters or so, she turns into a narrow lane with a row of attached houses or farm buildings on each side. When we come out of the village, she points down a kind of path or modest road. I don't see any yellow arrows, but I also don't want to embarrass her by raising this question as a challenge. Perhaps she has really saved me from getting lost and walking some kilometers off the *camino*. I thank her and head off in the direction she pointed, but I hope that I meet someone else whom I can question. After less than a kilometer, I do meet another woman, this one solidly respectable in appearance. I ask her if I am on the *camino*. "Yes, you're right on it," she answers. "But I don't see any yellow arrows," I protest. "You will . . . don't worry . . . just keep going straight ahead." I thank her and continue. And she was right. The arrows again appear. Really, quite amazing . . . within minutes of having lost the *camino*, a fantastically disheveled creature appears to warn me and set me straight. This walk is indeed an experience without chance encounters. But that's what the world is; I need only recognize the fact. I feel I'm on the edge of grasping something about the true character of my life as creature . . . .

Albani reached a village along here just as it was getting dark. It was raining, and he went from house to house, asking for shelter. But no one had a place for him. He says that he was then forced to become a *predicador* (preacher), wandering through the streets. This must mean that he walked along, shouting out his predicament, something like house-to-house salesmen and craftsmen who call out what they have to offer as they walk through the streets. Sometimes they have a special bell, whistle, or horn that identifies their service or product. Finally,

> a poor man with a small lantern in his hand came out and led me to his hut, for the houses of this village were huts with thatched roofs, and he treated me most kindly, although he was the poorest devil in that village. He had six children and they lived in great misery. I gave them all the bread which I had begged that day, along with a *peseta* of twenty-four grams. They kissed my hands and feet a thousand times, and I passed the night comfortably.

Over the centuries, the adventures of pilgrims with people who live alongside the *camino* have been preserved in many such stories. One recounts how a poor pilgrim, on reaching a village like the ones Albani and I walked through, went from door to door, asking that the householders, for the love of God and Santiago, give him shelter.

> All closed their doors in his face, with the exception of the last one, who received him generously. That same night a terrible fire raged through the village, reducing all the houses to ashes, with the exception of the one where the pilgrim slept.

Another tells how a pilgrim comes upon a woman, just as she is putting her bread in the oven to bake. He asks her for a small piece. She replies that she doesn't have a crumb in the house. "May God grant that your bread [in the oven] not turn into a stone," he says, going his way. The woman turns to her oven, opens it, and finds only a large round stone inside. Frightened out of her wits, she runs after the pilgrim, but he has disappeared.

Such stories were told all over Europe. People knew and understood them. But did they believe them? Did I believe the "witch"? Perhaps my action is some kind of link to the world of these people, to the world of their faith. This is a distant, foreign place. It is definitely not the world of the automobiles that passed me some days ago: They operate in the universe of money, insurance systems, and safety measures. Albani and the unknown pilgrim left their homes trusting that someone along the way would open a door for them. The other one felt that he, out of charity, should pray that God not turn a stingy woman's bread to stone. I half believed that the "witch" was sent to guide me. Was our trust and faith foolish or misplaced? Does one see nature and the other through the beliefs of conventional wisdom, or through the truths of ancient tales?

Later, I come upon three Spanish pilgrims who have sat down beside the path to eat their lunch. I know them, since we have met one night in a *refugio.* They wave, laughing and calling out, insisting that I stop and join them. The pain in my left leg has returned and is so intense that I decide to accept their generous invitation and rest for a few minutes. Apparently, they had noticed something irregular in my step as I approached, for one offers me a box of individually sealed tablets. "Here, take one of these," he orders. "Well, but how do I know what it will do to me?" I ask, smiling. "No le hace nada"—"It won't hurt you at all." He explains that it's a special glucose pill for energy and to relieve muscle pain. I had heard about them from another pilgrim in one of the *refugios,* but had never seen them. He adds that they are popular with athletes, and I have the impression that other pilgrims use them as well. Not to refuse his kindness, I take one and let it melt in my mouth, following the procedure he explains to me. He offers me more, suggesting I take them along for future relief. I thank him, saying that one is enough.

After eating a bit of bread and cheese, I shoulder my pack and wave good-bye. Within a few minutes, the pain returns, as excruciating as ever! I suspect that one would have to go far on the road of drugs in order to walk the *camino* "comfortably." But would one then still be on the *camino?* I no longer doubt that pain and the *camino* are intimately related. But I wonder whether I have sought too many comforts, too much security, avoided too many opportunities to enter into the experience of Albani and so many others who struggled over this path before me . . .

More than eight hours of walking . . . a long day . . . I reach Arzúa with the leg pain penetrating more deeply than on any previous day! I thought I would become much stronger as I approached the end; now that I approach that goal, I feel that's certainly true. After several days of relative comfort, however, I'm completely taken aback by the intensity of today's pain. But looking back at the whole of what has happened since leaving Palas de Rei this morning, I can only conclude that this has been another glorious and moving day on the journey. Reflecting on my good fortune as I search the town for the shelter, I again meet the Spaniards. They have learned that the *refugio,* at the other side of town, does not open until five o'clock, and that a woman in a small shop on a side street near the church in the center of town stamps the *credencial* for pilgrims. Making our way through a somewhat complicated maze of streets, we find this woman's shop. While she stamps our documents, I reflect on the time and additional walking I would have needed to ferret out this information and find this place. Another timely and "lucky" meeting.

They then invite me to a bar for a cup of coffee. After that refreshment and some pleasant conversation about our aches and exhaustion, we set out for the edge of town, where we find the *refugio.* The sun shines brightly; we sit on the steps or lie on the grass, waiting for the place to open. A smooth grass lawn surrounds the building, and a wooded hill rises behind it. Then, at five o'clock, a friendly woman arrives with the key and opens the door. It's an older building, formerly a school of music, with one large room containing new double bunks. There is a small bathroom, boasting of two hot showers, a toilet, and a sink.

While sitting on the front steps, I saw that there is a large *lavadero* only about fifty meters from the shelter. This is a special structure I have noticed in some of the villages and towns. Traditionally, women gathered there to do their family laundry by hand. This one is rather spacious, maybe eight by fifteen meters, completely roofed but open on three sides, with a spring continually supplying water at the closed end. The center of the building is a large shallow pool contained by a slanting and ribbed concrete edge, making a continuous washboard all around the pool. Outside this, just inside the roof line, people doing their laundry can stand on a stone ledge or floor. Luckily, I find a bucket in the bathroom, fill it with hot water, and immediately head for the *lavadero* with my soap and dirty, sweaty clothes. There may be enough sun left to dry them this afternoon.

Only one other person is doing laundry so late in the day, an older woman who greets me pleasantly when I arrive. Out of the corner of my eye, I watch to see if there are any special tricks one should know to use this facility. Basically, we go through exactly the same motions. For centuries, people—in most societies, I would guess, women—have washed their clothing in pretty much the same fashion. One repeatedly strikes the wet, dirty clothes against a rough surface, and then wrings out the water. I notice that the woman, although using soap, depends more on physical pounding, while I am more generous with my soap and hot water. We both rinse out our clothes in the pool, and the drain, at the opposite end from the spring, carries off the soapy water slowly down the hill.

This is the first time I have been able to use the traditional *lavadero.* At other times, I was limited to a sink in the *refugio.* I am delighted, and grateful for the opportunity to do my laundry in this way at least once before leaving Spain. This experience, too, is a link to another world. And in that place, they took care to make a structure that is nicely designed and engineered. What a striking contrast: The distance between the charm of the *lavadero* and the steely whiteness of a modern laundromat.

Two or three dozen persons could comfortably wash their clothes at the same time, all facing one another around the pool. Perhaps this is— or was—one of the important meeting places for the women of the town. Doing one's laundry here, in this open, sylvan setting with one's friends, neighbors, and relatives would be quite a different experience from working alone with a washing machine in one's apartment or house. I wonder . . . does anyone other than this old woman use the *lavadero?* Perhaps no one comes any longer. Such a change would be an important and significant break . . . like others I have observed along the *camino.* I look around . . . at the hill with its graceful trees, at the colors of the year's first wildflowers, at the gentle slope's bright grass, and feel the restful silence. What must it be like when many women are here, laughing, chatting, pounding their clothes? If I intruded in their space, I'm certain I would provoke glances, smiles, whispering. Perhaps this space no longer exists; perhaps the world has shrunk. How thankful I am for having found this mark of the past, for having stood on these worn stones, for having actually moved in these traces. I found a *lavadero* at the last possible hour with just the right amount of sun.

After hanging up my laundry and taking a hot shower, I sit on the lawn in front of the shelter, happy to let the sun warm me, for the air is still cool, and allow my tired legs to replenish their vigor. Two women from the town stop and ask if they might look inside the building. They are delighted to see all the new bunks, and explain that the old *refugio,* located in the center of town, had no beds in it. After talking with them, I walk back into town to buy food for my cold dinner. The *refugio* lacks only a kitchen.

Today, the *camino* took me to unusual places in my prayer. The idea of
God as Father filled out all of my awareness . . . nothing else *was.* But
then, from I know not where, my own father came before me, and I came
before myself as father. At first, I tried to rid my mind of these earthly
notions, thinking they were distractions. But they stayed. Then I thought
that I should be careful to distinguish . . . I had before me two images and
one unimaginable presence; I should be careful not to confuse them: the
idea, if one can use that term, of God the Father, the images of my own
father, and myself as father. But in the movements of my awareness, the
three somehow stuck together, then separated, then came together in
different configurations. I felt strongly that I should not fear the associations; there was indeed some real connection between them. One relation
of father and child threw light on another, reflected back, then illumined
the third, and so on. If I simply let myself see what was there, what revealed itself to me, I would understand all three relations better. I should
not attempt to differentiate to achieve some greater conscious clarity.
Rather, I should quietly rest in what I was seeing, not attempting to guide
reflection, not seeking any special knowledge. I should not fear to let
myself learn . . . to look at what I saw . . .

My father grew before my eyes . . . I saw him more clearly than when he
was alive . . . he spoke to me more simply. It seemed that, for the first
time in my life, I could hear him . . . I now knew him better than ever
before . . . it now seemed possible to become his son, to live the life
toward which he had pointed me by the integrity, generosity, and openness of his own life. But then the scene changed. As I have set out on the
path of earlier pilgrims, so I must set out on the path of my father. He
lived a virtuous life, not for himself, but for his family, for me. Now I must
take up the task. As I begin each day anew on the *camino,* so I must begin
each day resolved, not to be a self, *my*self, but to be my children's father.
The truth may be that I have no other vocation, no other being. And all
this is learned from the Father. His being, if one can make such a stumbling predication, is His love for the Son, and their mutual love, the Spirit.

Slowly, my awareness took on a very different form . . . I could not
imagine or think of anything except the pain. Everything else was shut
out, definitively excluded. The pain gradually became a darkness, a terrible night. But in the midst of what seemed a bottomless pit, I saw something: I realized that, in a very real sense, the pain is not mine, it does not
belong to me at all, it is not something for which I am responsible.
Rather, it is a gift that settles down on me, that takes up a kind of abode
in me. And it is precisely this gift that allows me to love, that gives me the
capacity to love. Yesterday, I had prayed that I might come to love as I
should. But any child who has begun to study the catechism knows what

this is: To love as I have been loved. In a sensible, fleshly way, one sees what this is in the Lord; it is He who fully reveals the way of love to us. If I wish to share in this love, I must participate in his pain. Paul is quite clear on this point: "I want to know Christ . . . the fellowship of sharing in his sufferings . . . (Phil. 3:10). Further, he explains the necessity of this pain for the community: "I fill up in my flesh what is still lacking in regard to Christ's afflictions, for the sake of his body, which is the church" (Col. 1:24).

I can know the love of the Father, that is, love in this way, to the extent that I share in his Son's love, the one sent as the way (in Spanish, the *camino*). This way was crowned with suffering. This must then be my way/*camino*, too. And this is necessary, not only for me, for my well-being, but for those I love. As I need *His* pain, so they need my pain, that they, too, might know love, be able to love. To love, they wait for me to make up what is lacking in the pain of the community. So the terrible pain I have endured today is not an evil, is not something I should attempt to avoid or alleviate. It is a special kind of good, a pure gift, a grace given for those whom I would love. To accept this pain today is the greatest, most sublime thing I can do for my children, my parents, and all those I seek to love. I possess no greater gift to give them. And the marvelous, extraordinary character of this gift is that it is hidden. No one can ever know it, except the Lord, for no one can look into my muscles and bones, into my groaning spirit, to know what I feel. It is good, then, that pain is so private, so secret; this is eminently fitting; it is more difficult for me to boast . . . it is easier to guard against vanity . . .

How would I ever have come to this pain . . . to this knowledge . . . if I were not on the *camino?* This is indeed a place of grace, of the workings of grace.

31

Arzúa to Monte del Gozo

June 3, 1993

I'm nearing the end of the adventure; I could probably get to Compostela by this evening. But already,
early in the morning, the pain in my lower legs has begun again. It might
be better to stretch the journey into two days, arriving in Compostela
tomorrow, more alert to the complexity and wonder of that place, with no
"distraction" from pain. On the other hand, the pain might be the most
fitting condition to accompany me to the legendary city. Mulling over
these conflicting thoughts, I come to a large village. There, something
takes shape inside me: an all-consuming thirst for a coffee . . . *that* presents itself as the immediate and proper companion to the pain.

I meet a young man on the street and tell him I'm looking for a bar
where I can get a cup of coffee. Is there one open in the village at this
early hour? "Yes, in just one minute," he answers, "Come with me." After
half a block, I see a camping trailer parked next to a small plaza, where
several streets meet. The side of the trailer opens to reveal a kitchen and
bar, at which people could stand. There are chairs and tables near a tree
in the plaza. In a few moments, a pleasant outdoor café is created. I sit
down and am soon enjoying the invigorating refreshment of a *café con
leche.* The meeting with the young man places the pain in a different
region of my awareness; for the moment, the day is transformed. But I

cannot wait for the local people to come out of their houses and begin their daily tasks. I have met the only one of them I needed to know this day, and it's time to push on.

Later, the realization reaches me: I haven't seen any yellow arrows for some time. Have I been dwelling in my pain and neglecting to watch for the path? Have I become lost again, so late in the journey? I continue plodding in the direction that I think is forward, toward Compostela, hoping that I will meet someone whom I can ask. Soon, in fact, I do: a man painting shutters on a large house near the road. I ask him if I'm on the *camino,* and he puts down his brush, telling me to wait a moment. He comes over to talk . . . I'm not lost . . . indeed, I'm right on the *camino.* He himself is just putting the finishing touches on a new *refugio.* This is his land and house, and he has converted the house into a shelter for pilgrims. Smiling, he invites me to come in and be the first guest. I thank him, but explain that I've only been walking a few hours, and want to get much farther today.

He says that he knows Jesús Arias Jato in Villafranca del Bierzo, and Maribel Roncal in Cizur Menor. Now that his *refugio* is ready, there are three shelters owned and maintained by private persons along the *camino.* He talks about the *fuerzas magnéticas* (literally, "magnetic forces," taken to mean something like "cosmic vibrations") found in certain places on the earth, and says that the *camino* is especially rich in such significant and powerful phenomena. He believes that his house lies in a center of these mysterious powers. Evidence of these possibly epiphanic places in Galicia can be traced to pre-Roman times. Some would argue that the celestial signs indicating the presence of James the Apostle's body in what is now Compostela were part of a longer and more varied history of such preternatural manifestations in the area of the *finis terrae.* There is much literature, and books on the subject continue to be published. Some of the more recent ones have a distinctly New Age flavor, but the older studies and speculations reach back into ancient hermetic traditions. I had hardly thought about it, but now believe that Arias Jato must possess some such connection or authority. Well, it would be interesting for me to pursue the matter with this man, but I am eager to be out on the *camino,* moving toward my destination. Getting so close to the end of this long journey, I am anxious to reach its conclusion, to find what awaits me at the *finis terrae.* I congratulate the new innkeeper, wish him well, and start up the next hill.

Some hours and kilometers later, I feel that I can endure the pain and continue walking today, if only I can stop long enough to eat. I believe that the combination of rest and food will work some magic in my body. Unable to think of anything else, I come to a bar where the *camino* crosses a road. A rather run-down, modest building . . . I enter the door . . . Adjusting my eyes to the darkness, I find myself to be the only person in a small, disorderly room. At the left, through an open door, I see an older woman talking with two farmers. Her appearance fits the unkempt and dirty rooms well. I ask her if she serves any food here. "No hay comida"—"There is no food," she answers bluntly, her face expressing no interest whatsoever in me as a potential customer. I then inquire how far I have yet to go before finding something to eat. "Cinco kilómetros"— "Five kilometers," again in her deadpan voice. Rapidly running through what I imagine to be the bar's resources, my needs, and a possible match, I order a *copita de aguardiente*. With my drink in hand, I return outside to the welcoming sun, sit down on a rock, and sip slowly, savoring the sharp sensation of the powerful alcohol.

Looking out, letting my eyes rest on the distant hills, I see a farmer come out on the road, leading a team of oxen that pulls a cart filled with hay. This is probably the first cutting of the new growing season. I wonder . . . How does he cut it? . . . How long does he let it lie in the field? . . . How does he throw it on the cart? . . . How does he store it? . . . To what animals does he feed it? I have done all these actions myself, and I wonder how he carries them out. I keep touching, all too lightly, so many lives along the *camino*. But I can only question myself about them . . . I cannot know them . . .

Then my eyes are drawn to the ditch that runs along the road. It's actually filled with blooming calla lilies. American dictionaries define this flower as a "house or greenhouse plant." And here they are, as large and beautiful as any I've ever seen, bursting out like wild weeds along the public road. The incongruity of the three scenes: a gruff and somewhat surly old woman in her haunt, a poor farmer with his slow-moving beasts, and the pure, clean lines of the profuse calla lilies—in this odd juxtaposition drive out all awareness of pain. I restfully contemplate the strangeness, not knowing how to make any sense of what my eyes take in. Although I will never know the stories of the woman or the farmer, or carry away some lilies to adorn my home, I feel that I've entered their space, I've walked into their world; they are not just scenes which pass before my eyes. To attempt to photograph them would be to violate them, to betray their presence, to grossly *use* them.

In a short time, I am again struggling with real mud, the kind that clings to and builds up on your shoes so that your feet, seeming to weigh several kilos each, have to be pulled up out of the sticky glue for each step. But I am surrounded, enclosed, by huge eucalyptus trees. I've lost all sense of a landscape, something pictured "out there," separate from me, which I observe or contemplate. Neither am I in an environment, some kind of natural setting, a reality apart from my presence. The pain, mud, and a month's walking have brought me to a new place; that is, one I had not hitherto visited. Just as there is no mind-body dualism in my experience of this place, so there is no human-nature dualism in the reality of my presence here. But I am not in some network of connections, relationships, and continuities. I am brought to ask: What gives shape and content to my life here and now? It seems that precisely because of the pain and effort, still demanded after a month's exercise, I have entered the space of the old lady, the farmer, and the lilies. Here I have found a place unknown to the people in the automobiles who threw their trash out the window as they sped past a real world from which they had removed themselves.

Is this some new experience of nature? I'm certainly not in the position of those who would follow Locke and make nature a reality apart, an object that one can contemplate, work on, attempt to control and conquer. Nor am I with those who, inspired by the ideas of Spinoza, the animism of Native American Indians, English nineteenth-century Romantics or New England Transcendentalists, call for some sort of assimilation with a larger natural setting. I feel that the exercise and pain have allowed me to enter this place through a full, sensory involvement; my senses have made me into a being of fine and delicate awareness; I am—for me—a new kind of rational sensorium. Seeing the old woman, the farmer, and the lilies, I realize that nature groans in them, just as Saint Paul first instructed us: "The whole creation has been groaning as in the pains of childbirth" (Rom. 8:22). I am distinct from the woman and the farmer, as I am distinct from these trees, from this sweet air that bathes all of us in its life-giving power. Our basic unity is to be found in the fact that we are all creatures, we are one in the creation; we are not the reason for our own existence; ultimately, our being is one of participation. But to live in this unity, one must share in its fallen condition, that of struggling to come to be. The world is not Eden. Because of the pain and work of walking, I have become a part of creation. In *that* place, I can hope to join the Romans addressed by Paul, and to

> groan inwardly as we wait eagerly for our redemption as sons . . .
> We do not know what we ought to pray for, but the Spirit himself
> intercedes for us with groans that words cannot express. (Rom.
> 8:23–26)

Finally, about two in the afternoon, I find a restaurant in Lavacolla. I am so exhausted that I almost stumble on the threshold, and just barely manage not to fall on the table of some people eating their dinner. The three Spaniards have also stopped here, and get up to leave as I enter. They have finished eating and want to continue walking all the way to Compostela this afternoon. We say good-bye, for I shall probably not see them again in this life, since they do not intend to remain in Compostela, but will return to their homes after they reach the holy city. I feel that if I can just sit down, take off my shoes, and eat something, I can make it to Monte del Gozo today.

Without asking what is being offered on the *menú del día,* or the price, I simply tell the young woman that I wish to eat. I am too tired to think or form any words beyond making the elementary request. As my body rejoices in the comfort of the chair, unburdened by the pack, the woman brings me my dinner: two substantial plates of well-prepared food, tasty tough bread, and about half a liter of wine—all for 650 pesetas. It turns out to be one of the very best meals I have enjoyed on the *camino.* Curious . . . the rhythms of the *camino.* After hours of painful personal struggle in which I participate in the universal groans of a fallen creation, I suddenly fall into an idyllic, lightsome room, am served by an attractive and friendly young woman, and discover new powers of renewal in myself.

Starting out on the final steps for today, I soon come to the Lavacolla river. There is an ancient custom, mentioned by Aymeric Picaud, of pilgrims washing their private parts and all their bodies in this river before proceeding to Compostela. From the way the custom is described, one sees that the washing had both a practical and a ritual significance. But I feel too far away from it to know how to join them, and mechanically walk past the river.

After eight or nine hours, dragging my feet, I reach Monte del Gozo (Mount of Joy), only about six kilometers from Compostela. The place gets its name from the fact that it is a small mountain from which one can first see the city of Compostela. Laffi, arriving here with a friend in the seventeenth century, records that

> we could see the longed-for and often-mentioned Santiago, about half a league away, appearing so suddenly that we fell on our knees, the excess of joy bringing tears to our eyes. We began to sing the *Te Deum.* But after only two or three verses, we could sing no more because of the abundance of tears pouring out of our eyes.

A century later, Albani writes that when he first saw the city,

> I threw myself on my knees, kissed the ground a thousand times, took off my shoes and, singing the Holy Litany, rapidly headed for the holy city on my bare feet.

A custom of the French, the origin of which is unknown, determined that, out of any group of pilgrims, the first to see the two towers of the cathedral would receive the name "Roi." Some believe that the name—Roi, Leroy, Roy—became popular in France because of this custom. Those who had received it would pass the name on to their children.

I look out and, in the distance, see buildings in the haze. But I cannot distinguish the cathedral towers. Perhaps the smog is too thick. Below my feet, stretched down the hill toward Compostela, an eerie vision of straight lines and square corners strikes my eyes, rows and rows of identical one-story buildings. I count thirty rows, one below the other. This is the new hotel for "pilgrims" built by the government this year. I learn that the reception office, where I must register, is in the last building at the bottom of the hill. Working my way down the many steps, I pass shops among the terraces of hotel rooms—tourist shops?—a large restaurant and cafeteria, a post office and a medical building. In the special reception building, I find people seated at computers and telephones, and many items of promotional literature. One desk handles pilgrims who arrive on foot. The smiling young woman records my name, stamps my *credencial,* and gives me a card with my building and room number. I shoulder my pack and start back up the long flight of stone stairs. Four of the buildings, at the very top of the hill, are reserved for those who are walking to Compostela, and there is no charge for staying in them. All the others are for people who arrive in vehicles, and one pays for a room there.

In my building, a young man shows me to the room. It contains four double bunks. He tells me that the other buildings, for paying guests, have one or two beds per room. Each building seems to have about twenty-five rooms. At the end of the corridor, there are showers and toilets, separate for men and women. Since there is still a bright sun, I immediately wash out some clothes, and tie a clothesline from my window to a nearby newly planted tree.

Later, the young man, a hired attendant, tells me that after building this complex the government leased all the operations—rooms, shops, food facilities—to a private firm. I ask him about any possible conflict with hotel and restaurant owners in the city. He acknowledges that there is a lot of controversy about the project, and complaints from the service people in Compostela. He also adds that one can get a room more cheaply there. The new rooms on the Monte cost 2000 pesetas. So, the complex was not built to solve the historical problem of gouging and dishonest innkeepers. I wonder . . . Does it promote pilgrimage? or tourism?

Refreshed by a shower, I walk to the shopping area, about halfway down the hill. Not everything is finished and open for business. I find no food markets, only a cafeteria. All the architecture is strictly functional, not what one could call "plastic," but definitely machine-made, absolutely uniform in design, all situated in a regular and rigid gridwork. In such a place, I decide to limit myself to one small coffee. I have a bit of bread and cheese in my pack, and that will suffice for tonight and tomorrow morning. Perhaps after a few years, when the carefully planned landscaping results in some shrub and tree growth, the place will appear slightly less monotonous and programmed. But I suspect that the critics are right: This huge facility is designed for the tourists, those who arrive by plane, train, bus, and car. It is a blight on the hill, seriously damaging a terrain blessed by the tears of thousands like Laffi. This monster building project effectively separates and distances the pilgrims of yesterday from those of today. On the sterile cleanliness of the white stone steps, in the glass and stainless steel cafeteria, using the most up-to-date plumbing, I find it difficult to form any link with the past . . . with one possible exception.

Diego Gelmírez, bishop and then archbishop of Compostela for forty years (1100–1140), is the most famous historical figure associated with Santiago de Compostela as an important place of pilgrimage in Europe. In 1105, he ordered the construction of a church here on the Monte del Gozo, the Ermita de la Santa Cruz. After the church was consecrated, Gelmírez led a solemn procession to it from the cathedral in Compostela. The great crowd of clergy and people inspired witnesses to claim that the ceremonies were strictly on a par with those of the Roman Curia. Later, this church was torn down to make way for another. And so, perhaps, the constructions have continued until today . . .

Some believe that Gelmírez was one of the most ambitious and intriguing men of his time and, because of his connections with powerful people—popes and abbots, kings and queens—made Compostela one of the three most important places of pilgrimage in the Middle Ages, along with Rome and the Holy Land. Although it seems impossible to determine, the number of people going to Compostela may have been greater than those going to Rome, and was certainly more than those traveling to the Holy Land. But a historical work that he commissioned leads one to question his singular importance.

Gelmírez ordered a history of Compostela to be written, known today by the title *Historia Compostelana.* In it, one finds the first documentary evidence of large numbers of pilgrims, not because records were kept of numbers, but because an interesting event that occurred. The emir, Alí ben Yúsuf (1106–42) sent ambassadors to Galicia on a delicate diplomatic mission to Queen Doña Urraca in 1121. On the public highway, these ambassadors, surprised to see so many Christian pilgrims going to and coming from Compostela, asked their Christian guide, Pedro, "Who is it who inspires such a huge multitude of Christians to travel so devotedly? . . . There are so many coming and going, that we can barely make our way westward on the road." Pedro replied that it was Santiago, "whose body is buried at the remote end of Galicia, and is venerated [by people] in France, England, Italy, Germany and all Christian territories, especially Spain, whose patron and protector he is."

The diplomatic mission occurred before the *Liber Sancti Jacobi* (c. 1140), also commissioned by Gelmírez, appeared. Organized propaganda promoting pilgrimages to Compostela is believed to have been most effective after this date. If this is true, people were coming to Compostela independently of Gelmírez's efforts to get his see raised to the rank of an archbishopric (1104), and to obtain a form of cardinal-priest rank for seven of his clerics (1109). The climax of his influence resulted in Calixtus II's raising Compostela to the rank of a metropolitan see in the province, in place of Mérida, then governed by Muslims (1120). Gelmírez's goal, apparently, was to obtain for Compostela the ecclesiastical primacy over all of Spain, replacing what he considered the great rival, Toledo. Calixtus II died in 1124, however, and his successor, Honorius II, did not look with favor on the ambitious dreams of Gelmírez.

Perhaps this new building project, together with all the various events promoted, not by any archbishop but by a decidedly lay Spanish government, will result in more people appearing here, visiting the cathedral and other local places associated with historical pilgrims. But what will these persons be? Why will they come? What will they find? Attempting to unravel my thoughts, I see a list of current events in the city: art exhibits, lectures, plays, and concerts. Tomorrow night the Chicago Symphony is playing. As I walked along in the *camino,* and came across evidence of these cultural celebrations planned for this Holy Year, I always felt a lack of interest or, if I thought about the matter, a certain repugnance. But maybe I should allow myself this one diversion before returning to Germany. Maybe beneath the appeal to tourists, such events hide some secret of the *camino.* Tickets for "retired persons and students" are half-price (1,500 pesetas), so I can afford to go. But I'm still left with the problem of dress. Although I have that one decent short-sleeved shirt in my pack, the evenings are quite cool and I'll have to wear my old gray sweatshirt. Well, the blue jeans are freshly washed, so I will not look too bad.

Although a few other persons have been assigned to this building, I recognize none of them, and they have been put in other rooms. The young woman at the reception desk, in effect, has given me a private room . . . yet another gesture of the kindness and thoughtfulness I have received from everyone along the *camino*. I can recall no time or occasion this past month when I was not so blessed.

The pain of the *camino* revealed something further to me today. All my life I have heard that one should pray for others. People sometimes ask me to pray for them. And I make the same request. Saint Paul is especially and repeatedly clear about this. But today it seemed to me that I have never really believed any of this—in the necessity and efficacy of prayer for another . . . until the pain entered deeply enough into me to enlighten me. Pain is there . . . always; that's simply a fact of life. Everyone, at some time, receives his or her share in this universal human experience. Finally, there is no way, short of death, to avoid it. What, then, to do with it? Yesterday, it seemed clear to me that one experiences pain for someone else, for another, for those whom I would love.

To pray for another is to wish that person well, that he or she reach happiness and, finally, the ultimate Good. But if the pain is for the other, then this specific wish must accompany it. What further good could I wish for the person I love? Since I am human, able to think and voice such wishes, I must direct them to those others for whom I care. I *must* pray for them. This is not a formal and empty exercise. It is as real as the pain. The very intensity of the physical sensation argues to the reality of the spiritual wish, the word directed toward the other's good.

As I already understood, pain is necessarily, inevitably, efficacious to the extent that it participates, and goes to make up what is lacking in the Lord's pain. Thus, my prayer for another must be similarly efficacious. If such were not true about the pain, then one would have to say that the pain of the Lord is not efficacious—assuming that one accepts and welcomes the pain as a gift making up what is lacking in the suffering of the Lord. The effectiveness of my pain, and prayer, is limited by the impurity of my intention and the coolness of my love. If I simply love, simply pray, accepting the pain given me as it comes, then my intention and action do really reach out to touch all those to whom I direct my attention, all those to whom the *camino* has brought me.

To learn these truths about pain and prayer may be, for me, the principal grace of the *camino*. As I have come to realize so often, each day seems more blessed than the one before. Now, so close to the end of my journey, the same pattern holds. Today, unequivocally a day of great, unimaginable discomfort, maybe the "worst" of the *camino,* is no exception. I have traveled yet further into the world of the ancient pilgrims.

32

Monte del Gozo
to Compostela

June 4, 1993

L ong before dawn, I'm awake and alert. Excited, I
quickly eat the piece of bread and cheese, take up
my pack and staff, and step out into the darkness. In spite of a few lights, I
can see the stars, the vision revealed to Charlemagne in a dream. In the
dream, Santiago urged Charlemagne to clear a path for pilgrims to follow
the *iter stellarum, el camino de estrellas, la Vía Láctea* (The Milky Way),
to his tomb in faraway Galicia, so that they would be safe from the preda-
tions of Muslim *razzias*. Charlemagne was told that "all peoples, from sea
to sea, will journey there . . . to the end of time," forming a sacramental
procession of innumerable people in permanent pilgrimage. The idea of
the holy thus received another powerful push in the direction of identify-
ing it with the action of pilgrimage, thus historically completing the journey that originated with Moses and Abraham, and was sanctified in a
unique way by Jesus. Another link between the sensible and the supernal
was established.

Once people imagined a new epiphany in distant Galicia, the direction
of earlier Christian pilgrimages was radically changed. All roads no longer
led to Rome. The ancient Roman roads now made a new direction for
people possible. Instead of walking to Rome, and through Rome, to the
Holy Land, pilgrims in greater and greater numbers traveled westward.

Instead of seeking the known center of Western civilization, people coura-
geously set out on uncertain and dangerous roads for the limiting boundary of the known earth, *finis terrae*. And their numbers far exceeded any
earlier peaceful movement of peoples across the Western world. From
archaeological evidence, we know that places as distant as Sweden were
significant starting places for pilgrims going to Compostela.

But Compostela did not become the new Rome. For example, Diego
Gelmírez, credited by some authors as being the one person most responsible for making Compostela famous among pilgrims, was studiously sub-
missive to Rome in all his grand plans and actions. For forty years (1100–
1140), he governed Compostela as bishop and, later, as archbishop, working ambitiously and imaginatively among the powerful of his time to make
the shrine the greatest place of pilgrimage in Christendom.

I look up at the stars, the same stars that shone over the hermit Pelayo,
early in the ninth century; but they reveal nothing of his mystery to me.
According to the legend, Pelayo saw "supernatural lights" among the
stars. The region was not populated, so he had to travel some distance to
reach a city, Iria Flavia, where he reported the strange celestial fireworks
to the bishop, Teodomiro. The bishop accompanied Pelayo to the place
of his hermitage, kept vigil, and was vouchsafed the same heavenly vision. Awestruck, he proclaimed three days of fasting for the people who
had come with him to that remote wilderness retreat. At the end of that
period, the witnesses scraped the ground over which the angelic messen-
gers, the new stars, seemed to hover, and discovered the tomb of Saint
James the Greater—Santiago. Almost immediately, Alfonso II, from his
court in Oviedo, ordered a church constructed on the site (814?). About
sixty years later, Alfonso III had this small structure destroyed and a
much larger one, *de gran hermosura* (of great beauty) built in its place.
As people came there from all over the West, the idea of Europe, of a
people with shared beliefs and customs, with a common *telos,* began to
be experienced by more and more from farther and farther away.

Two of the twenty-two miracles worked by Santiago and recorded in
the *Liber Sancti Jacobi* (Book II), relate how the saint rescued two pilgrims from drowning. Each man, in a separate incident and story, was
returning from the Holy Land. Of all possible miracles dreamt or remembered, why were these two recorded?

Among all the accounts of pilgrims walking to Compostela that I have
read, the richest and most colorful, the most revelatory of the character
of the pilgrim himself, the most detailed *relatos,* were written by two
Italians, Domenico Laffi, who walked from Bologna in the seventeenth
century, and Nicola Albani, who started from Naples in the eighteenth
century. As I look at the stars over my head, I wonder . . . What kind of

Fig. 3. Jost Amman, "The Jakobsbrüder," 1568. Bayerische Staatsbibliothek, Munich.

evidence is this? That Italians—and there were many—would go all the way to Compostela, and not to Jerusalem? How did Santiago move people's religious orientation from the Holy Land and Rome to this wild outpost of the Western world? Rome and Jerusalem were ancient and important centers where people had met and crossed back and forth for centuries. The place that came to be called Compostela—it had no name when Pelayo looked up at the new configurations in the night sky—lacked any history at all. There are only archaeological conjectures about Celtic settlements and ceremonies. But now my shoes fit directly into the footsteps of thousands, maybe millions, who came here before me and who walked exactly to the place where I now go. But I know, from the *relatos* and reflection on my own awareness, that each of us is very different; each seeks his or her own grace, an intimate, incommunicable secret in each soul.

Along here somewhere—but in the darkness I cannot see it—is the *ermita* de San Lorenzo. Centuries ago, pilgrims stopped here to venerate the *Santo Cuerpo* (the holy body) of another pilgrim, their last stop at such a shrine before reaching the cathedral. Picaud tells the story—so it happened earlier than the twelfth century—of how thirty pilgrims from Lorraine, before starting out for Compostela, swore an oath to help one another so that all could arrive at their goal. One, however, refused to bind himself by the oath. Before reaching the Pyrenees, one of the pilgrims fell seriously ill and had to be carried along—at times by a horse, other times by his companions. This slowed them down so much that, on reaching the mountain range, they left their sick friend there. The one who had not taken the oath decided to stay with the sick man. These two spent the night at a place called San Miguel. In the morning, the sick man insisted on attempting to cross the mountains into Spain. They reached the summit, but the invalid died there the next night. Perplexed, his companion implored the help of Santiago. A horseman appeared, and asked him what he was trying to do. He answered that he wanted to bury his dead friend, but had no way to dig in the rocky terrain. "Put the body across the saddle, and ride on the horse behind it, until you get to a place where you can bury your friend," said the man, and they started out that very night, the stranger having disappeared.

When the sun rose, the pilgrim saw that they had arrived at a stone cross, just at the edge of Compostela, a distance of about one thousand kilometers from where they had started the evening before. He buried his friend, who became the *Santo Cuerpo,* there. Immediately, the unknown apparition appeared again and spoke:

> When you return to your own country, you will meet your other companions in León. Tell them that because they showed such a lack of loyalty to their comrade, the Apostle Santiago will not hear

their prayers or accept their pilgrimage until they have performed the necessary penance.

The pilgrim finally recognized who was speaking to him, but when he tried to prostrate himself before the saint, Santiago disappeared. Along with many other moments on the *camino,* this event, too, was captured by European artists.

From the streetlights, I can now wend my way to the cathedral, and in a short time I find myself alone in the immense Plaza del Obradoiro, looking up at the towers of the church. Everyone still sleeps . . . all is silent . . . no one disturbs the cool morning air except a few pigeons who continually fly up, alight, walk around me, and rise again into the early dawn light. This, too, must be a singular experience. I have never heard of a pilgrim who arrived here and found no one except for a few pigeons. Writers describe the crowds, the babble of many different tongues, the colorful costumes from their respective regions, the music and, always, the merchants. Already in the twelfth century, they offered shells (the traditional symbol of a Santiago de Compostela pilgrim), wine, shoes, leather bags (like modern backpacks), purses, straps, belts, every kind of medicinal herb, and food. But now, not even a scrap of paper blows across the enormous stone sweep of the plaza, a vast space designed for thousands. Selfishly, gluttonously, I try to breathe in all the atmosphere of twenty centuries of prayer and hope, try to hear the sighs of a million pilgrims, try to offer the dreams of so many who started but died on the *camino* before reaching this sacred spot.

Perplexed by the solitude, the silence, too stunned to fall on my knees or kiss the ground, awed by the enormity of the towers before me, I slowly turn around and see a magnificent architectural facade, the twenty-five arches across the front of the Palacio de Rajoy, named for an eighteenth-century prelate Archbishop Rajoy. Turning farther, I face the restored splendor of the Hostal de los Reyes Católicos, originally built for pilgrims by Ferdinand and Isabella when they finally conquered al-Andalus. After 750 years of the Reconquista, the last Islamic kingdom on the Peninsula fell.

The construction and administration of the *hospital* encountered many difficulties, mirroring the general situation in Compostela for pilgrims. In the twelfth century, Picaud warns of the many dishonest innkeepers. Jerome Münzer, a physician from Nuremberg, arriving in Compostela in the fifteenth century, notes in his *relato* that many in the city live off the exploitation of pilgrims. When Laffi was in Compostela, he chose to pay for his lodging and food at what we would call commercial establishments. Albani, a century later, stayed at the *hospital* for the three nights allowed each pilgrim, and mentions that the beds were filthy. No food was served there. He ate well, however, at the monasteries in the city, especially with the Franciscans.

I walk over, noting that the Hostal is the only building open at this early hour. At the magnificent glass doors, I hesitate, then push one open. A quick glance inside at what is now a five-star world-class hotel tells me that I will not be welcome here. I am so intimidated, in fact, that I cannot satisfy my curiosity to find out what a room costs in a place like this. As unobtrusively as possible, I let the door swing shut and turn again toward the empty plaza.

Slowly, as in a dream, I walk across the enormous expanse of stone, hearing no sound except the regular tap . . . tap . . . tap of my staff on the pavement. How should I imagine the people who arrived here before me? Many English, who often sailed to La Coruña, and walked from there; Polish knights, since a pilgrimage to Compostela was considered part of the ritual preparation for knighthood; royalty, like Louis VII of France and Countess Sofía of Holland; saints, like Brigid of Sweden and Francis of Assisi; and the thousands known only to God . . . Do I walk in their footsteps? Do I know anything of the Interior Castle of their spirit? Am I truly one of them? Am I moving in the sacred time where they dwell? I look up at the sky . . . the stars are no longer there . . . the ether is suffused with a pale light . . . Did I miss the stars of Pelayo? Or does that question take me across a threshold into vanity and presumption?

Just beyond the Obradoiro, I find a small, charming plaza with "dwarf" trees to match it, and sit on a park bench to rest. It's true that I'm here, in Compostela, after thirty-one days of tough, painful hiking across all kinds of terrain, through sharp, biting variations in weather. In some sense, I've joined those who came here before me. And I have a clear, undeniable feeling that they brought me here. If they had not come, there would be no *camino*. If they had not sanctified the path with their faith, their courage, and their very lives—the records show that many died and were buried along the way—I would never have heard of this fantastic journey into a sacred space. If they had not accompanied me, I would never have been able to endure the pain and exhaustion, as I learned on the very first day.

I hear a few sounds. The city is beginning to awaken to another day. Several people walk by, hurrying to their jobs. I smell coffee brewing. The sky is clear . . . it will be a glorious day of sun! But I'm troubled . . . some shadow begins to form inside me . . . a vague disquiet creeps over me. I feel a slight tinge of fear. I begin to perceive internal motions that I don't recognize . . . I try to breathe more deeply, to relax, but the unease grows greater. I can't figure out what's happening . . . it seems that a weighty sadness descends and muffles my spirit . . . a bleak discouragement blocks any hope of relief. I force my mind to search. If only I could find the proper word to name this empty darkness . . . I cannot move . . . it's as if I have been poisoned by some malignant nerve gas.

Finally, I stumble onto an idea. This must be what people mean today when they talk about suffering from depression! Or what the ancients would call being afflicted with melancholy. If I remember those old texts well, one of the remedies is to soak in a hot bath. Well, the closest I can get to that here is a hot cup of coffee. I look across the street at a rather elegant bar . . . it's not yet open.

Perhaps, since I've never before in my life been attacked in this way, I can determine what strange demons have invaded my private space. Slowly, I begin to get through the sticky cobwebs and murky darkness. This is a *new* day, radically different from all the other thirty-one. I got up this morning and walked only about six kilometers . . . and then sat down. I've never done that before. Today, I will go no farther . . . I will not climb any more mountains . . . I will never again step out in the darkness and be hit in the face with a gust of rain—my early morning welcome. I will not feel the sun on my back, warming me as it rises in the sky . . . I will never again struggle to lift my feet out of the mud, hour after hour . . . the cuckoo bird will not greet me as I set my pace for the day. I will not gaze at a horizon, knowing that just on the other side, an ever new vision of creation awaits me. I will not see different varieties of wildflowers . . . *every day!* The pain is past, the thrills are over, the magic is finished.

Now there is traffic in the street, people on the sidewalks. Two pretty young women walk by, laughing and talking. They look like students, going to an early morning class. I think the building on the Obradoiro opposite the Hostal de los Reyes Católicos belongs to the university. And it's time for me to think of my next move. I must get up from this bench. I have to walk out in some direction. And then I remember—the post office . . . mail, maybe, from family and friends. I get up, ask, learn that the building is only a block away. There, another friendly person takes my name, looks in the pigeonholes, and returns with some letters. A big smile now, "They haven't forgotten you!" Returning her smile, I thank her and head for that bar, now open. The waiters wear white shirts, ties, and neatly creased black pants. I'm back in the city, for sure.

It's only two weeks since I received word from family and friends— when I found mail in Carrión de los Condes—but it seems like a time measured differently, the time of a distant dream, far away in different senses simultaneously. And so the pleasure is correspondingly greater. Such letters and the coffee, taken together, do much to restore some balance to my sensibilities. The lingering sadness is not quite so bleakly hopeless, not so heavily oppressive.

I walk out into the sun, but don't feel its warmth. Going around the side of the cathedral, I search for the Oficina de Peregrinos. Near the door, waiting for the office to open, about ten or fifteen pilgrims mill about, laughing and exchanging stories. I don't recognize any of them, and feel disinclined to greet anyone. But someone comes up from behind, touches my shoulder and extends his hand, obviously happy to see me. It's the French physician I met on the first day, just before reaching Valcarlos on the road to Roncesvalles! I don't have to force a smile. I have not seen him for some days, and did not expect ever to meet him again. I'm as surprised as I would be if I met the young American woman, another person who walks alone. I should sit down and ask him about his experience. But I can't manage speech . . . the weight is too great, the cloud too dense. I will never know his story.

The office opens, I file in. A young woman puts the final stamp in my *credencial.* It's quite a colorful record now, since each place has designed its own logo or seal. My name is entered in a register, so it will be here and back there at the beginning in Roncesvalles. Another person fills in my name and the date on the "Compostela," a document (written in Latin) that looks like a diploma and that originated in this form in the fourteenth century, attesting to the fact that I am officially a pilgrim who arrived at Santiago de Compostela. Reading the historical record, one sees that people formerly placed great importance on this document; in some accounts it takes on a certain mystical significance. But today, one can receive it if he or she claims to have walked at least 150 kilometers of the *camino.* Is this a concession to contemporary flabbiness? A novel version of cheap grace? A recognition of dried-up faith?

In my bilious state, I narrowly examine the images and words. At the top, there is a drawing of Santiago as a pilgrim. But from many such drawings I have seen in the catalogs of European exhibitions, I know that this one did not come from the fourteenth century. It looks more like those sentimental, washed-out, anemic figures apologizing for their existence that so-called artists first started producing, I think, in the eighteenth century. At the bottom of the page, the official seal of the dean and chapter of the cathedral is printed. It portrays a much more vigorous figure— Santiago Matamoros on his white horse, raised sword in one hand and a flag in the other. The flag is one that was carried by the Caballeros de Santiago, the military order—a red sword or cross on a white background. Matamoros's horse, reared up, is preparing to come down on two unfortunate and prostrate Moors, one raising his arm in supplication. The Latin says that I have visited *hoc sacratissimum Templum pietatis causa devote*—this most holy temple with a devoutly pious intention. "Pious" here refers to the virtue of piety that, according to medieval thought, belonged to the cardinal virtue of justice, through which one attempted to honor God, as is His *just* due. But the young woman only asks me how to spell my name . . . The sharply conflicting images of Santiago clash before me again. How can these good people sit there, complacently filling out forms?

I step out of the office and start walking. But where am I going? What do I intend to do? Confused, I stop to consider. The next logical step would be to find a *refugio* and drop off my heavy pack and staff. But where is it? I return to the office, wait my turn again, and then ask if there is a *refugio* in the city. The first young woman is uncertain, and asks another. This one says, yes, there is one, in the Minor Seminary; and returns to some other task. I apologetically explain that I am a foreigner and quite unfamiliar with the city. Where is this Minor Seminary? She gives me a street . . . I thank her and start out again.

Near the pretty plaza where I had sat earlier in the morning, I stop a gentleman and ask him about directions to the Minor Seminary. He graciously draws me a simple map and points me in the right direction. I am surrounded by the old city, with its narrow and irregular stone streets, ancient and attractive stone buildings, churches, monasteries, and schools. There is a legend that *gallegos* (people from this region) are especially skilled in working stone since they learned the craft from those surviving the catastrophic end of Atlantis. Everything is beautifully restored, immaculately clean, glowing with history and local color . . . the kind of place tourists love . . . the miasma still hangs over me, shaping my sentiments.

Climbing a hill, I reach what appears to be the Minor Seminary at the top, a huge nondescript building. The door opens to a large foyer, and I see a kind of reception window on the left wall. On the other side of the wall, through the window, an unsmiling middle-aged man, heavy-set, watches me approach. I try to smile, greet him, and ask if this is the *refugio*. He answers sharply that it is *not* a *refugio* and, once it appears that I have accepted this truth, condescendingly explains that the administration graciously allows pilgrims to stay on the top floor of this seminary. There is a charge of 300 pesetas per day, payable in advance. Since this is eminently reasonable, I see no point in objecting, and hand him a 500-peseta note. He has no change, and tells me that I can pick it up when I go out again. He warns me to leave no money or valuables upstairs with my belongings, for he has no control over the kind of people—pilgrims, presumably—who go up there. I thank him and head for the stairs.

On the top floor, I pick out a bunk in the dormitory—they seem quite clean—set my pack on it, and walk to the train station. There I learn that the next train for the border where I want to cross, Irún, leaves at 9:15 tomorrow morning. I'll be in the holy city only one day. I walk to the cathedral and arrive just in time for the noon Mass—the Misa de Peregrinos.

The cathedral is considered a great Romanesque monument, one of the most perfect examples of this genre. The Pórtico de la Gloria, one of the entrances, done by Maestro Mateo in the second half of the twelfth century, is judged to be the most beautiful and finely executed Romanesque portico in the world. Beginning with Aymeric Picaud, most of those who arrive here and write an account provide detailed and enthusiastic reports on what they see and their reactions to it. But I cannot look . . . or, I do not see anything . . . I climb the stairs and go into the cavernous church.

Laffi says that he entered the building and, "kneeling before the [main] altar, with a joy and heartfelt contrition never before experienced [said my prayers]." Albani records that

> I entered rapidly, my heart and mind were immediately illumined; it seemed that I had walked into heaven! My legs and entire body trembled, my head was reeling, my eyes shot here and there, searching for the mysterious chapel of the glorious saint. Going up before the altar, I genuflected and, with my face pressed to the floor, gave thanks.

Below the main altar, the saint's body rests in a large silver reliquary in the shape of a box or coffin. Picaud notes that some doubted that this was true, claiming that the body was really in France. He says the doubters were Frenchmen, and dismisses their opinion. Arnold von Harff, a German knight who traveled to Compostela at the end of the fifteenth century, wrote that some maintained that the body was really in Toulouse:

> I tried, by making large offers, to get them to show me the holy body. They answered that custom forbade this, that the holy body of Santiago is in the main altar, and that if anyone were to doubt this he would, in that very instant, go crazy, just like a rabid dog. That satisfied me.

This knight of many desires recorded another in his diary one day, "Oh lovely maiden, come share my bed with me."

It is noon . . . time for the Misa de Peregrinos to begin. The large cathedral is filled with people. I notice two or three who, from their dress, may have walked here on the *camino*. The only sounds come from the floor—people shuffling their feet, moving around for a better position in the church. After the clergy file in, the Mass begins. One cleric climbs into a pulpit and leads the people in singing. His voice, resounding throughout the enormous space from loudspeakers, cancels out the weak and listless participation of the people. In the twelfth century, during the night,

> barbarian peoples, and those who live in all the regions of the world, come to this place . . . [people] of every language, tribe and nation, in caravans and phalanxes, fulfilling their vows in actions thanking the Lord. . . . To contemplate the choirs of pilgrims at the foot of the venerable altar of Santiago in perpetual vigil inspires joy and admiration. The Germans on one side, the French on another, the Italians on yet another. They stand in groups, holding lighted candles in their hands. Therefore, the whole church is illuminated like a sunny clear day. . . . Some play zithers, others lyres, and others small drums or flutes, flageolets, trumpets, harps, violins, British or Gallic psalters, some singing with zithers, others accompanied by various instruments, all passing the night in watch. Some weep for their sins, others read the Psalms, and some give alms to the blind. Here, one hears different tongues, different voices in barbaric languages—conversations and songs in German, English, Greek, and in other languages of other tribes and diverse peoples from all over the world. There exist no words or languages which are not heard here. . . . A continuous solemnity is celebrated, the festivities are carefully prepared, the distinguished celebration offers up worship day and night, praises and outpourings of joy. . . . There is uninterrupted solemnity. . . . The doors of this basilica never close.

The Mass continues. I notice that a man, standing near me, leaning against a pillar with his back to the altar, reads his newspaper. His wife follows the distant movements of the clergy . . . From all the accounts I have read, people in earlier centuries were seized by a powerful *libido videndi*—a passion to see—the holy relics. As soon as possible, Albani rushes to the Capilla del Tesoro, the special chapel containing the treasure (*tesoro*) of relics. There he was thrilled to look at

> many bodies of saints, not to speak of all the heads, legs, feet, hands, fingers, arms, the bellies, vials filled with the blood of martyrs . . . and two other vials, one filled with the milk from her [the Virgin Mary's] breasts, the other with the tears shed from the eyes

of the Virgin at the tomb of her most holy Son; one also sees the hair and clothing of the Virgin, along with so many other relics.

Some of these relics were obtained by Diego Gelmírez in a trip to Portugal in 1102. After he gathered up a large collection—the action was then called a "pious theft"—he instructed his archdeacon and another canon from the cathedral to return to Compostela by way of hidden and unused paths so that people would not meet them and find out what they were carrying away. The numerous men and women in the congregation moving about around me seem to be innocent of such strong beliefs and passions . . .

A custom developed quite early: one should spend the first night in vigil before the tomb, as close as possible to the holy relics. When many pilgrims arrived on the same day, and all wished to get a good place for the night, savage fights sometimes erupted, blood was shed, a pilgrim killed. According to canon law, the church then had to be purified of this crime. The process of reconciliation required a trip to Rome to obtain the necessary documents. On June 12, 1207, Innocent III authorized the archbishop of Santiago to purify the church with a special blessing using holy water, wine, and ashes, and with no need to visit Rome.

The Mass ends, and when the crowd disperses, I see no one shoving another. I climb up behind the altar to give the traditional kiss to the back of the statue, and then step down under the altar to view the silver reliquary with the holy relics of Santiago inside. In the Middle Ages, the cities, with their churches, nurtured pilgrimages of devotion. The people were drawn to these places because they contained relics, the physical remains of saints. One could touch the holy there, one could reach out to the salvific love of these great heroes and heroines, one might even be blessed with a display of thaumaturgic power. All was symbolized and concretized in the relics. The life of faith was viewed *sub specie peregrinationis*—in the light of pilgrimage—to the sacred places. But my religious sensibility must be very different; I have no desire to see or touch any relic. Then a perhaps impious question occurs to me: Are any left here?

I have learned something in these thirty-one days of solitude and silence: that I'm not alone, that I don't even exist as some kind of self-conscious individual, that I am not an autonomous self with some potential to realize. Rather, I exist only to the extent that I participate in the innumerable practices that collectively establish the living tradition that is my heritage, which my parents and the pilgrims have given me. All the "inner" experiences of these four weeks only occurred insofar as they had real links with the experiences of the dead who accompanied me. I have learned how to speak a truthful "we," a radically different act than the spurious and aggrandizing "we" one so often hears today. The relics I touch are they, their real presence. I have met, embraced, and kissed them . . . and their lips were not cold. Looking around me, I don't recognize any of them here today; perhaps there are a few hidden among the great throng of tourists. But most of them are out there . . . on the *camino,* waiting to welcome today's pilgrim. All my thought, all my intense longing, is to walk back out there, and to join them in their journey.

Notes

How It All Began

Page xi ". . . *el ser español.*" Américo Castro, *La realidad histórica de España* (México: Ediciones Porrúa, 1962), 22, 80–81, 393.

Page xi ". . . on the subject." Jaime Cobreros, *Camino de Santiago* (Barcelona: Ediciones Obelesco, 1991). There is an enormous literature on the *camino,* in several languages. The latest bibliography is by Maryjane Dunn and Linda K. Davidson, *The Pilgrimage to Compostela: A Comprehensive Annotated Bibliography* (New York: Garland Publishing, 1994), vol. 18 in the Medieval Bibliographies Series.

Page xii "'. . . even criminal rebellion.'" Castro, 389. I have done all translations from foreign languages in the book.

Chapter 1: St. Jean Pied de Port to Roncesvalles

Page 3 "'. . . exploited their pilgrims.'" "Veneranda dies," *Liber Sancti Jacobi. "Codex Calixtinus"* (Pontevedra: Xunta de Galicia, 1993), Book I, p. 223. Translation (Latin to Spanish) by A. Moralejo, C. Torres, J. Feo.

Page 4 ". . . Santiago de Compostela pilgrim." Serafín Moralejo and Fernando López Alsina, eds., *Santiago, camino de Europa* (Santiago: Xunta de Galicia, 1993), p. 23.

Page 4 ". . . vagrants or criminals." Pierre Barret and Noël Gurgand, *La aventura del Camino de Santiago* (Madrid: Ediciones Xerais de Galicia, 1982), p. 42.

Page 5 "'. . . carries in himself.'" Javier Martín Artajo, *Caminando a Compostela* (n.p.: Editorial Católica, 1976), p. 36.

Page 5 ". . . whom were infants." José María Tome López, *Andando en solitario por la ruta jacobea a Santiago de Compostela* (Zaragoza: Caja de Ahorros y Monte de Piedad de Zaragoza, Aragón y Rioja, n.d.), p. 24. The author walked in 1987. Marta González Vázquez, *Las mujeres de la Edad Media y el Camino de Santiago* (Santiago de Compostela: Xunta de Galicia, 1989). Luis Vázquez de Parga, José María Lacarra, Juan Uría Ríu, *Las peregrinaciones a Santiago de Compostela* (Pamplona: Gobierno de Navarra, 1993), vol. 3, pp. 91–108.

Page 5 ". . . Compostela—from Germany!" Klaus Herbers, "Las peregrinaciones alemanas a Santiago de Compostela y los vestigios del culto jacobeo en Alemania," in Paolo Caucci von Saucken et al., *Santiago, la Europa del Peregrinaje* (Barcelona: Lunwerg Editores, 1993), p. 324.

Page 6 ". . . merchants, and robbers." Elías Valiña Sampedro, *El camino de Santiago: estudio histórico-jurídico* (Madrid: CSIC, 1971), pp. 43–49, 72–80.

Page 6 ". . . to be English." Teodoro Martínez, *El camino jacobeo: una ruta milenaria* (Bilbao: Publicaciones de la Excma. Diputación de Vizcaya, 1976), p. 176.

Page 6 ". . . of two of them!" Artajo, pp. 61, 72.

Page 6 ". . . be quite indispensable." Artajo, p. 31.

Page 8 ". . . Palestine, to Galicia." *Liber Sancti Jacobi,* Book III.

Page 8 ". . . wounded, to die." *Liber,* Book IV. Juan G. Atienza, *En busca de Gaia* (Barcelona: Robin Book, 1993), p. 274.

Page 9 ". . . Charlemagne left Spain." *The Cambridge Medieval History* (Cambridge: Cambridge University Press, 1964), vol. 2, pp. 604–5, 778.

Page 9 ". . . Roland never existed." Martínez, p. 209.

Page 9 ". . . a sharp knife." Domenico Laffi, *Viaje a poniente* (Santiago de Compostela: Biblioteca mágica del peregrino, 1991), pp. 80–90.

Page 9 ". . . shelter to pilgrims." Vázquez de Parga, vol. 1, p. 292.

Page 11 "All: Amen." After returning to Germany, I wrote a letter to the priest in Roncesvalles, asking him for a copy of the Blessing.

Chapter 2: Roncesvalles to Zubiri

Page 18 ". . . in God's service." Nicola Albani, *Viaje de Nápoles a Santiago de Galicia* (Madrid: Consorcio de Santiago, 1993), pp. 225–26.

Page 19 ". . . lands to Compostela." Christian Krötzl, "Del mar báltico a Santiago de Compostela. Peregrinajes e influencias culturales," in Caucci, p. 388.

Page 19 ". . . some free horsehide." Vázquez de Parga, vol. 2, p. 130.

Chapter 3: Zubiri to Pamplona

Page 22 "'. . . his rainy days.'" "A Week on the Concord and Merrimack Rivers," in Henry David Thoreau, *Walden and Other Writings* (New York: Bantam Books, 1989), p. 83.

Page 25 ". . . were highly organized." Vázquez de Parga, vol. 1, pp. 281–399.

Page 26 ". . . relics in Spain." *Liber Sancti Jacobi,* pp. 508–72.

Page 26 ". . . medieval religious imagination." Valiña Sampedro, p. 5.

Page 26 ". . . or to forgive." Juan Blázquez Miguel, "Pueblos y brujos malditos del Camino de Santiago," in Gonzalo Torrente Ballester et al., *Heterodoxos en el Camino de Santiago* (Pamplona: Ayuntamiento de Pamplona, 1990). John S. Strong, "Relics," in Mircea Eliade, ed., *The Encyclopedia of Religion* (New York: Macmillan, 1987), vol. 12, pp. 275–82.

Page 26 ". . . against the Moors." *The Cambridge Medieval History,* vol. 2, pp. 371–409.

Page 26 ". . . or from Compostela." Juan Ignacio Ruiz de la Peña Solar, "La peregrinación a San Salvador de Oviedo y los itinerarios asturianos del camino de Santiago," in Caucci, p. 234.

Page 26 ". . . in the Middle Ages." José María Lacarra, "Espiritualidad del culto y de la peregrinación a Santiago antes de la primera cruzada," in *Pellegrinaggi e culto dei santi in Europa fino alla 1a crociata* (Todi: Presso l'accademia Tudertina, 1963), p. 116.

Page 27 ". . . it was written." In a long (forty-nine pages) and learned article, Christopher Hohler attempts to prove that the *Liber Sancti Jacobi* was written to teach schoolboys Latin and music. "A Note on *Jacobus,*" *Journal of the Warburg and Courtauld Institutes,* vol. 35 (London: The Warburg Institute, 1972), pp. 31–80.

Page 27 ". . . like a cassock." Silvino Pérez Alonso, *Por Dios, por la Patria y por el Rey* (Vileña, 1937). This is an unpaginated, mimeographed manuscript written by Pérez Alonso, the parish priest of Vileña. He was accompanied on this pilgrimage, in the midst of the Civil War, by the young *requeté navarro,* Fidel Pinellos. A *requeté* was a member of a Falangist youth militia.

Chapter 4: Pamplona to Cizur Menor

Page 30 ". . . been done badly." Carlo Melchers, *Das grosse Buch der Heiligen* (Münich: Südwest Verlag, 1980), pp. 471–74. A recent biography is Philip Caraman, *Ignatius Loyola* (San Francisco: Harper and Row, 1990).

Page 31 "'. . . all eternity. Amen.'" *The Spiritual Exercises of St. Ignatius,* George E. Ganss, S.J., trans. (Chicago: Loyola University Press, 1992), p. 20. One form of the prayer is found as early as 1370. It was widely used in the sixteenth century, but the author is unknown. Ignatius presupposes that the prayer is known. It was popularized by Ignatius's use of the prayer and it is associated with him. In the chapel at Heathrow airport (London), my eye was caught by two books among the religious literature offered to modern travelers, the *Spiritual Exercises* and another collection of Ignatius's writings. Both volumes contained the prayer I quote, and in each, the same line is missing:

> *Sangre de Cristo, embriágame*
> Blood of Christ, inebriate me.

I wonder how far such embarrassment goes. It seems a strange omission in an age when the instances of people drunk on the blood of others are legion.

Page 31 ". . . of the place." Barret and Gurgand, p. 281. "Compostela is essentially a sanctuary, and its splendor depends on the degree of something more important, the splendor of its faith. If [its] faith were dead, the city would be dead." Gonzalo Torrente Ballester, *Compostela* (Madrid: Afrodisio Aguado, 1948), p. 260.

Chapter 5: Cizur Menor to Puente la Reina

Page 39 ". . . the experience of prayer." While reciting the prayers of each decade—one Our Father, ten Hail Marys, and the doxology—the person meditates on the Mystery of that decade; for example, the Angel Gabriel appearing to the Virgin Mary, telling her that she will be the Mother of God. This is the first of the Joyful Mysteries, The Annunciation. See Luke 1:26–38.

The prayers:

> Our Father, Who art in heaven, hallowed be thy name. Thy kingdom come, thy will be done, on earth as it is in heaven. Give us, this day, our daily bread, and forgive

us our trespasses as we forgive those who trespass against us. And lead us not into temptation, but deliver us from evil.

In the last few years, before the "Amen," the following has been added: "For thine is the kingdom and the power and the glory, for ever and ever. Amen."

Hail Mary, full of grace, the Lord is with thee. Blessed art thou among women, and blessed is the fruit of thy womb, Jesus. Holy Mary, Mother of God, pray for us sinners, now and at the hour of our death. Amen.

Glory be to the Father and to the Son and to the Holy Spirit, as it was in the beginning, is now, and ever shall be, world without end. Amen.

Before beginning the five decades, one generally recites the Creed:

I believe in God, the Father Almighty, Creator of Heaven and earth, and in Jesus Christ, his only Son, Our Lord, conceived by the Holy Spirit, born of the Virgin Mary, suffered under Pontius Pilate, was crucified, died, and was buried. He descended into hell. On the third day He rose from the dead, ascended into heaven, and sits at the right hand of God the Father Almighty. From thence He will come to judge the living and the dead. I believe in the Holy Spirit, the Holy Catholic Church, the communion of saints, the forgiveness of sins, the resurrection of the dead, and life everlasting. Amen.

Page 42 ". . . in the eleventh century." Yves Bottineau, *Les chemins de Saint-Jacques* (Paris: Arthaud, 1966), p. 112.

Page 42 ". . . several *hospitales* here." Vázquez de Parga, vol. 2, p. 124.

Chapter 6: Puente la Reina to Estella

Page 45 ". . . Saint James the Apostle." Vázquez de Parga, vol. 1, pp. 31–32.

Page 46 ". . . throughout the Peninsula." Lacarra, p. 128.

Page 46 ". . . part of Christendom." Lacarra, pp. 138–41.

Page 46 ". . . 'to one another.'" Moralejo and López Alsina, p. 432.

Voto y súplico para lograr descubrir un ARS con que se demuestren a los infieles las verdades cristianas, para que broten los hombres piadosos que la asimilen y expongan, para que Papa, Emperador, reyes y príncipes fomenten el estudio del árabe y el hebreo, faciliten las expediciones misioneras y promuevan una cruzada de alcance universal. Todo ello, orientado a alcanzar la concordia entre cristianos y saracenos, incluido su respectivo clero; porque en el fondo se encuentran muy próximos.

Page 47 ". . . hurry on nervously." Artajo, pp. 59–60.

Page 48 ". . . thoughts of pilgrimage." Geoffrey Chaucer, The Prologue, *The Canterbury Tales*.

Page 49 ". . . by a *cofradía*." Vázquez de Parga, vol. 2, pp. 133–49.

Page 49 ". . . in the country." Carta Pastoral de los obispos del "Camino de Santiago" en España, *El Camino de Santiago. Un camino para la peregrinación cristiana* (no place or publisher, 1988), p. 44.

Page 49 ". . . were called in." Váquez de Parga, vol. 1, pp. 247–54.

Page 50 ". . . patron saint of Estella." Vázquez de Parga, vol. 2, pp. 138–39.

Page 50 "'. . . the worldly, too.'" Vázquez de Parga, vol. 3, p. 67.
Page 51 "'. . . having reached Santiago.'" Artajo, p. 28.
Page 51 ". . . just outside Estella." Vázquez de Parga, vol. 2, p. 143.

Chapter 7: Estella to Los Arcos

Page 57 ". . . only very narrowly." An introduction to some aspects of the relationship between Romanesque art and the *camino* can be found in Serafín Moralejo, "Artistas, patronos y público en el arte del Camino de Santiago," *Compostellanum*, vol. 30, nos. 3–4 (Santiago de Compostela, 1985), pp. 395–430.
Page 59 "'. . . a mental activity!'" Fergus Kerr, *Theology after Wittgenstein* (Basil Blackwell: New York, 1986), p. 42.

Chapter 8: Los Arcos to Logroño

Page 64 ". . . his only existence." Serafín Moralejo, "Santiago y los caminos de su imaginaría," in Caucci, p. 86; Paolo Caucci von Saucken, "Vida y significado del peregrinaje a Santiago," in Caucci, p. 97.
Page 64 ". . . honor with Santiago." Américo Castro, *Santiago de España* (Buenos Aires: Emecé Editores, 1958), p. 134.
Page 64 ". . . kind of peace." Martínez, p. 103.
Page 64 ". . . in their lives." Castro, *La realidad,* p. 344.
Page 65 ". . . and Santiago Matamoros." Claudio Guillén, "En torno a *Santiago de España* de Américo Castro," *Revista Hispánica Moderna* (New York, 1959), vol. 25, pp. 207–17.
Page 65 ". . . promotor of the *camino*." Vázquez de Parga, vol. 2, pp. 149–51.
Page 65 "'. . . fear of trouble.'" Martínez, p. 98.
Page 66 ". . . established in Córdoba." Anwar G. Chejne, *Historia de España musulmana* (Madrid: Ediciones Cátedra, 1980), pp. 10, 149, 368.
Page 66 ". . . or the tomb." Robert Plötz, "Peregrinatio ad límina Beati Jacobi," in Caucci, pp. 27–28.
Page 66 ". . . to dictate loyalties." Chejne, pp. 54–55.
Page 66 ". . . from the Moors." *The Cambridge Medieval History,* vol. 6, pp. 394–99.
Page 67 ". . . of San Francisco." Vázquez de Parga, vol. 2, p. 152.

Chapter 9: Logroño to Nájera

Page 72 "'. . . paradoxical about that!'" Ludwig Wittgenstein, *Culture and Value* (Oxford: Basil Blackwell, 1980), p. 32.
Page 73 ". . . Don García, in 1052." Vázquez de Parga, vol. 2, pp. 155–61.
Page 74 ". . . at her feet." Millán Bravo Lozano, *Guía práctica del peregrino* (León: Editorial Everest, 1993), p. 97.

Chapter 10: Nájera to Santo Domingo de la Calzada

Page 79 ". . . de la Calzada." Vázquez de Parga, vol. 2, pp. 162–63.

Page 83 ". . . daughter were punished." Laffi, pp. 102–9.

Page 84 "'. . . made a Nun.'" Robert Southey, *The Poetical Works of Robert Southey* (London: Longman, Orme, Brown, Green, and Longmans, 1838), vol. 7, p. 263.

Page 84 ". . . *La Farce du pendu dépendu.*" The play was also staged in Paris the same year, 1920. For a discussion of it, see Henry Ghéon and André Gide, *Correspondences* (Paris: Gallimard, 1976), vo. 2, pp. 970–71.

Page 84 ". . . buried in Galicia." Miguel de Unamuno, *Andanzas y visiones españolas* (Madrid: Espasa-Calpe, S.A., 1975), p. 58. The chapter from which the quotation comes, on Santiago de Compostela, is dated August 1912.

Page 84 ". . . still alive today." Guillén, p. 209.

Page 84 ". . . take a shit." *Liber Sancti Jacobi,* Book II, chap. 10, p. 357.

Page 85 "'. . . only understand wrongly.'" Wittgenstein, p. 32.

Chapter 11: Santo Domingo de la Calzada to Belorado

Page 88 ". . . everyday collective action." Kerr, pp. 64–65.

Page 90 ". . . in the field." *The New Cambridge Modern History* (Cambridge: Cambridge University Press, 1968), vol. 2, p. 581.

Page 93 ". . . it was born." *The New Cambridge Modern History,* vol. 2, p. 312.

Page 93 ". . . clergyman and lawyer." Pierre Vilar, *Historia de España* (Barcelona: Editorial Crítica, 1980), pp. 26–27.

Chapter 12: Belorado to San Juan de Ortega

Page 98 ". . . work of Cervantes." Castro, *Santiago de España,* p. 43.

Page 99 ". . . killed, and expelled." Isidore wrote *De fide católica contra judeos* at the request of his sister, Florentina. *Diccionario de historia eclesiástica de España* (Madrid: Consejo Superior de Investigaciones Científicas, 1975), vol. 2, p. 1213. Isidore's full text is in J. P. Migne, PL (*Patres Latini*) (Paris, 1850), vol. 83, cols. 449–538.

Page 99 ". . . the Visigothic king, Recaredo (586–601)." The complete text of these ancient laws, called the *Fuero Juzgo,* can be found in Marcelo Martínez Alcubilla, *Códigos antiguos de España* (Madrid: J. López Camacho, 1885), vol. 1, pp. 63–72. Some modern authors judge this legislation to be anti-Jewish; for example, Harold Livermore, *A History of Spain* (New York: Grove Press, 1960), p. 62; Yitzhak Baer, *A History of the Jews in Christian Spain* (Philadelphia: Jewish Publication Society of America, 1961), vol. 1, pp. 19–20. From reading the actual text of the laws, I do not think one's judgment can be so simple.

Page 99 ". . . antiquity is Rome." *The Cambridge Medieval History,* vol. 7, pp. 633–35.

Page 100 ". . . a Christian church." Vicente Cantarino, *Entre monjes y musulmanes. El conflicto que fue España* (Madrid: Alhambra Editorial, 1978), pp. 197–98.

Page 100 ". . . rather than die." *The Cambridge Medieval History,* vol. 7, pp. 641–61, 594.

Page 100 ". . . Christians against them." Abraham A. Neuman, *The Jews in Spain* (New York: Octagon Books, 1969), vol. 2, pp. 262–64.
Page 100 ". . . bloody war followed." Livermore, p. 194.
Page 100 ". . . Battle of Covadonga." Cantarino, p. 34.
Page 100 ". . . capture of Granada." Cantarino, p. 96.
Page 100 ". . . uninterrupted until today." Carta pastoral de los obispos, p. 14.
Page 100 ". . . in this century." Klaus Herbers, *Der Jacobsweg* (Tübingen: Gunter Narr Verlag, 1986), p. 7. Angel Rodríguez González, "Privilegio de los votos," in Moralejo and López Alsina, p. 416.
Page 100 ". . . the Battle of Clavijo." Martínez, pp. 28–29, 49; *Diccionario de historia eclesiástica de España,* vol. 4, p. 2189.
Page 100 ". . . earlier Christian defeat." Fernando López Alsina, "Santiago, una ciudad para el apóstol," in Caucci, p. 61.
Page 101 ". . . defeated the Moors." Martínez, p. 50.
Page 101 ". . . symbol of the Reconquista." Cantarino, pp. 183–84.
Page 101 ". . . Moor-killer is known." Martínez, pp. 244–47.
Page 101 "'. . . for the Spaniards!'" Martínez, p. 72.
Page 101 ". . . meant to symbolize." Martínez, p. 29.
Page 101 ". . . ideology of the state." Plötz, in Caucci, p. 36.
Page 101 ". . . the Christians there." *The Cambridge Medieval History,* vol. 5, pp. 265–77; vol. 6, p. 791.
Page 101 ". . . powerful and Christian." Artajo, p. 106.
Page 101 "'. . . purified and cleansed.'" Pérez Alonso, 26th day.
Page 102 ". . . could not lose." Robert Plötz, "El apóstol Santiago el Mayor en la tradición oral y escrita," in Moralejo y López Alsina, p. 205.
Page 102 ". . . conquest and booty." Castro, *La realidad,* p. 387.
Page 102 "'. . . St. James!'" Castro, *La realidad,* pp. 346–50.
Page 103 ". . . to honor him." Arturo Sorio y Puig, "El camino y los caminos de Santiago en España," in Caucci, pp. 196–211. Vázquez de Parga, vol. 2, pp. 173–77.
Page 103 ". . . monastery and church." Laffi, p. 110.

Chapter 13: San Juan de Ortega to Burgos

Page 107 ". . . and artistic patrimony." José María Ballester, "Introducción," in Caucci, p. 12.
Page 109 ". . . and deserted gymnasium." Vázquez de Parga, vol. 2, pp. 181–99.
Page 109 ". . . blood every Friday." Vázquez de Parga, vol. 2, pp. 194–96; vol. 3, p. 139.
Page 109 "'. . . of such feeling.'" Laffi, p. 112.
Page 110 ". . . crucifix in Galicia." Pablo Arribas, "En el camino de Santiago," *Peregrino* (December 1993), p. 13.

Chapter 14: Burgos to Granja de Sambol

Page 116 ". . . a considerable annoyance." Laffi, p. 114.
Page 120 ". . . *that* exact experience!" M. K. Gandhi, *Key to Health* (Ahmedabad: Navajivan Publishing House, 1992), pp. 40–43.

Chapter 15: Granja de Sambol to Castrojeriz

Page 122 ". . . have affected them." Tome López, p. 36.

Page 123 "'. . . feast on him.'" Laffi, p. 114.

Page 123 ". . . form emphasizing eremitism." Saint Athanasius, *The Life of St. Antony* (Mahwah, N.J.: Paulist Press, 1950).

Page 123 ". . . especially disfiguring diseases." Melchers, pp. 46–48; Vázquez de Parga, vol. 2, p. 203.

Page 123 ". . . the castle's defenses." Vázquez de Parga, vol. 2, p. 204. There is no agreement among historians on the reasons for the Moorish invasion. For example, one opinion is that a Visigothic leader invited them, to help him in his struggles with a rival. There are other opinions, too.

Page 124 ". . . up the Peninsula." *The Cambridge Medieval History,* vol. 2, pp. 371–409.

Page 124 ". . . advanced in Europe." Chejne, pp. 18–22.

Page 124 ". . . kingdom to another." Vázquez de Parga, vol. 2, p. 204.

Page 126 ". . . in the *parador*." Marco Finetti, "Pilgern ganz pauschal," *Die Zeit,* 2 April 1993.

Chapter 16: Castrojeriz to Frómista

Page 132 ". . . owner's best friend." Tome López, pp. 124–25.

Page 133 ". . . Sancho III el Mayor." Vázquez de Parga, vol. 2, pp. 207–8.

Page 135 ". . . faith from religion." Lens and Ruth Kriss-Rettenbeck, Ivan Illich, *"Homo viator*—Ideen und Wirklichkeiten," in Lenz Kriss-Rettenbeck and Gerda Möhler, *Wallfahrt kennt keine Grenzen* (Münich: Verlag Schnell & Steiner, 1984).

Chapter 17: Frómista to Carrión de los Condes

Page 138 "'. . . European culture then.'" Unamuno, pp. 58–59.

Page 138 ". . . Pyrenees into Spain." Gonzalo Torrente Ballester, "Introducción al camino de Santiago," in Torrente Ballester, pp. 1–9.

Page 138 ". . . make a pilgrimage)." Vázquez de Parga, vol. 1, pp. 122–24.

Page 139 ". . . restored to health." Alfonso X, El Sabio, *Cántigas de Santa María,* Walter Mettman, ed., 3 vols. (Madrid: Editorial Castalia, 1986–89), vol. 1, pp. 123–26; pp. 249–51; vol. 2, pp. 279–81. Vázquez de Parga, vol. 2, pp. 208–12.

Page 140 ". . . returned to life." *Liber Sancti Jacobi,* Book II, chap. 17, pp. 367–71. Another version of the young man who castrates himself is found in the book of Guibert de Nogent (d. 1124), *De vita sua.* This is discussed by J. E. Ruiz Domenec, "La prodigiosa historia de un peregrino a Santiago de Compostela en el siglo XII," *Anuario de estudios medievales* (Barcelona, 1987), no. 17, pp. 43–47. See also Paul J. Archambault, *A Monk's Confession: The Memoirs of Guibert of Nogent* (University Park: Pennsylvania State University Press, 1996).

Page 141 "'. . . much to the poor.'" Vázquez de Parga, vol. 2, pp. 213–16; Lacarra, p. 117.

Page 141 ". . . as a museum." The building was a convent of the Poor Clares, a congregation of nuns founded by Saint Clare (d. 1253), the friend of Saint Francis of Assisi.

Chapter 18: Carrión de los Condes to Sahagún

Page 146 ". . . on divine truth." *Summa theologiae,* I-II, q. 83, art. 4, corp.
Page 147 ". . . of the pyramids!" Richard F. Burton, *Personal Narrative of A Pilgrimage to Al-Madinah and Meccah,* 2 vols. (London: Tylston and Edwards, 1893), vol. 1, pp. 29–30.
Page 148 ". . . relates a detailed story." Vázquez de Parga, vol. 2, pp. 222–34.
Page 149 "'. . . Spain [what it is].'" Cantarino, p. 117.
Page 149 ". . . a *religious* war." Castro, *La realidad,* p. 29.
Page 149 ". . . certain Spanish character." Cantarino, pp. 302–3.
Page 149 ". . . under its jurisdiction." Vázquez de Parga, vol. 2, pp. 223–24. Martínez, pp. 27–30, 105–9. Plötz, in Caucci, p. 28. Isidro G. Bango Torviso, *El camino de Santiago* (Madrid: Espasa-Calpe, 1993), p. 34. Valiña Sampedro, p. 9.
Page 150 ". . . a Cluniac *camino.*" Cantarino, pp. 150–51.
Page 150 ". . . claim is ridiculous." Raymond Oursel, "Cluny y el camino," in Caucci, p. 142.
Page 150 "'. . . put on it.'" Wittgenstein, p. 28.
Page 150 ". . . in the town." Vázquez de Parga, vol. 2, pp. 224–25. Hermann Künig von Vach, a monk and pilgrim, wrote his book, *La peregrinación y camino de Santiago,* about 1450. Torrente Ballester, *Compostela,* p. 132.
Page 151 ". . . of the Aztecs." Bernardino de Sahagún, *Historia general de las cosas de Nueva España,* Angel María Garibay K., ed., 4 vols. (Mexico City: Editorial Porrúa, S.A., 1977).

Chapter 19: Sahagún to Mansilla de las Mulas

Page 154 ". . . technical criteria alone." Jacques Ellul, *The Technological Bluff* (Grand Rapids: Wm. B. Eerdmans, 1990).
Page 155 ". . . image and reality." Ellul, p. 145.
Page 155 "'. . . of compacted earth.'" Bravo Lozano, p. 150.
Page 156 ". . . they cannot reflect." Ellul, p. 145.
Page 156 ". . . the twelfth century." Ivan Illich, *In the Vineyard of the Text* (Chicago: University of Chicago Press, 1993), p. 21.
Page 156 ". . . for the people." *The New Cambridge Modern History,* vol. 2, p. 322.
Page 157 ". . . a Christian burial." Laffi, p. 117.

Chapter 20: Mansilla de las Mulas to León

Page 161 ". . . of Sandoval nearby." Vázquez de Parga, vol. 2, pp. 237–38.
Page 162 ". . . died in 1002." Sorio y Puig, pp. 218–22. Vázquez de Parga, vol. 2, pp. 243–59, 357–58. Victor M. Rodríguez Villar, "San Salvador de Oviedo en la peregrinación jacobea," *Peregrino* (November 1993), pp. 12–13. Martínez, p. 2.
Page 163 ". . . through Isidore's intercession." Lacarra, p. 117.
Page 163 ". . . kinds of joys." *Liber Sancti Jacobi,* Book V, chap. 3, p. 504.
Page 164 ". . . and churches to see." Later, I learned that there are two principal churches in the city: the Real Basílica de San Isidoro, a Romanesque treasure consecrated December 21, 1063; and the Catedral de Santa María de la Regla, a later Gothic church.

Chapter 21: León to Villadangos del Páramo

Page 170 ". . . it turned out." Vázquez de Parga, vol. 2, p. 260.
Page 172 ". . . 'the noonday devil.'" The expression comes from the Latin Vulgate (Psalm 90), the translation most widely used among western readers in the Middle Ages. A representative discussion can be found in Evagrius Ponticus, *The Praktikos and Chapters on Prayer* (Kalamazoo, Mich.: Cistercian Publications, 1981), pp. 18, 20, 26. Evagrius was an eastern monk but his work greatly influenced western monasticism.
Page 174 ". . . King of Aragon." Vázquez de Parga, vol. 2, p. 262.

Chapter 22: Villadangos del Páramo to Astorga

Page 179 ". . . resuming their pilgrimage." Bango Torviso, pp. 43–45.
Page 179 ". . . on their shoulders." Plötz, in Caucci, p. 28. Martínez, p. 51.
Page 179 ". . . a warrior society." *The Cambridge Medieval History,* vol. 6, pp. 399–403.
Page 179 ". . . the love of God." José Filgueira Valverde, *El libro de Santiago* (Coruña: Diputación Provincial de la Coruña, 1989), pp. 111–12.
Page 181 ". . . as his witness." Bango Torviso, pp. 43–45.
Page 181 ". . . minimum of hospitality." Laffi, p. 119.
Page 182 ". . . through the streets." Artajo, p. 73.

Chapter 23: Astorga to Foncebadón

Page 186 "'. . . of our relations.'" Thoreau, *Walden,* p. 232.
Page 187 ". . . and guide them." Vázquez de Parga, vol. 1, p. 317. Because of the number of last testaments preserved, it is argued that many did not expect to return. Bango Torviso, p. 33.
Page 188 ". . . to store straw." Albani, p. 216.
Page 190 "'. . . at every corner.'" Vicente Malabia Martínez, "Camino de Santiago. Notas de un peregrino conquense," *Boletín Oficial del Obispado de Cuenca* (enero-marzo 1989), p. 42.

Chapter 24: Foncebadón to Ponferrada

Page 196 ". . . council fathers met." Vázquez de Parga, vol. 2, pp. 280–82.
Page 196 ". . . paganism to Christianity." Vázquez de Parga, vol. 2, pp. 282–83.
Page 201 ". . . marking the *camino.*" Vázquez de Parga, vol. 2, p. 283.
Page 201 ". . . as sacred relics." Albani, p. 216.

Chapter 25: Ponferrada to Villafranca del Bierzo

Page 204 ". . . a burning candle." Bravo Lozano, p. 198.
Page 205 ". . . imprinted T-shirts." "Ultreya" is derived from the medieval French words

outrée (forward) and *susée* (upward); both, in turn, from the Latin, *ultra* and *sursum,* respectively. See Martínez, p. 142.

Page 207 ". . . the Quonset huts." Vázquez de Parga, vol. 2, pp. 301–2. Valiña Sampedro, p. 11.

Page 207 ". . . style of Christianity." Martínez, p. 27. Malabia Martínez, p. 39.

Page 210 ". . . return to Germany." I learned that progress on the new building occurred, thanks to help from La Asociación Jacobea de Aquisgrán (Deutsche St. Jacobus Gesellschaft e.V. Aachen). See Liliana Simon, "Con los mismos ideales," *Peregrino* (December 1993), p. 4.

Chapter 26: Villafranca del Bierzo to El Cebreiro

Page 213 ". . . the required effort." Albani, p. 217.

Page 215 ". . . flesh and blood!" Tome López, p. 91.

Page 215 ". . . the Real Presence." Vázquez de Parga, vol. 2, pp. 314–15.

Page 215 ". . . for this purpose." Vázquez de Parga, vol. 2, p. 317.

Page 217 ". . . pilgrimage to Compostela." Albani, p. 217.

Chapter 27: El Cebreiro to Samos

Page 223 ". . . inevitably be applied." Ellul, pp. 153–54.

Page 225 ". . . a holy relic." Albani, p. 217.

Page 225 "'. . . really being received.'" *The Rule of St. Benedict,* Timothy Fry, O.S.B., ed. (Collegeville, Minn.: Liturgical Press, 1981), pp. 254–56. This is from chap. 53, "The Reception of Guests."

Page 226 "'. . . welcome in them.'" *The Rule,* pp. 256–58.

Page 227 "'. . . most profound darknesses.'" José Luis Abellán, *Historia crítica del pensamiento español* (Madrid: Espasa-Calpe, S.A., 1981), vol. 3, pp. 491–92.

Page 228 ". . . None at all." Benito Gerónimo Feijoo y Montenegro, *Obras escogidas,* Biblioteca de Autores Españoles (Madrid: Imprenta de Perlado, Páez y Compañía, 1903), vol. 56, pp. 76–77. (This is vol. 2 of the *Teatro crítico.*)

Page 228 "'. . . by the quality.'" Feijoo, *Obras escogidas,* vol. 56, p. 524. (This is from *Cartas eruditas.*)

Page 228 "'. . . so many centuries.'" Feijoo, *Obras escogidas,* Biblioteca de Autores Españoles (Madrid: Ediciones Atlas, 1961), vol. 141, p. 259.

Chapter 28: Samos to Portomarín

Page 231 ". . . Gerard Manley Hopkins." Gerard Manley Hopkins, "The Windhover."

Page 232 "'. . . of pastoral beauty.'" Gray wrote this in a journal entry, sent as a letter to Thomas Wharton. *The Selected Letters of Thomas Gray,* Joseph Wood Krutch, ed. (New York: Farrar, Straus, & Young, 1952), pp. 152–53.

Page 233 "'. . . every remembrance.'" Cited by Grevel Lindop, *Times Literary Supplement,* 17 September 1993. See also T. J. Diffey, "Natural beauty without metaphysics," in Salim Kemal and Ivan Gaskell, eds., *Landscape, Natural Beauty and the Arts* (Cambridge: Cambridge University Press, 1993), pp. 43–64.

Page 233 ". . . to personal enrichment." *The Prose Works of William Wordsworth,* W.J.B. Owen and Jane Worthington Smyser, eds., 3 vols. (Oxford: Oxford University Press, 1974), especially volume 2.

Page 234 "'. . . staying at home.'" Thoreau, *A Week on the Concord and Merrimack Rivers,* p. 83.

Page 234 "'. . . finding one's way.'" *Liber Sancti Jacobi,* Book I, "Veneranda dies," p. 208.

Page 234 ". . . pilgrim in 1267." F. Bouza-Brey, "El judío errante peregrino a Compostela," *Cuadernos de estudios gallegos,* Santiago de Compostela, 21 (1952), pp. 167–68.

Page 237 ". . . inclinations toward wickedness." "Ordenes Militares," in *Diccionario de historia eclesiástica de España,* vol. 3, pp. 1811–30. Cantarino, pp. 209–17. Martínez, pp. 116–20, 157–58, 251–56. *The Cambridge Medieval History,* vol. 5, pp. 265–77.

Chapter 29: Portomarín to Palas de Rei

Page 244 ". . . with my friends?" Gerhart B. Ladner, *"Homo Viator:* Medieval Ideas On Alienation and Order," in Ladner, *Images and Ideas in the Middle Ages* (Rome: Edizioni di Storia e Letteratura, 1983), pp. 937–74.

Page 244 "'. . . he robs them.'" *Liber Sancti Jacobi,* Book I, "Veneranda dies," pp. 214–15.

Page 245 "'. . . describe it all.'" *Liber Sancti Jacobi,* ibid., pp. 215–16.

Page 245 ". . . alongside the road." Albani, p. 188.

Page 245 "'. . . yourselves as pilgrims.'" *Liber Sancti Jacobi,* Book I, p. 211.

Chapter 30: Palas de Rei to Arzúa

Page 250 ". . . or evil hags." Pierre Gassier, *Francisco Goya: Drawings* (New York: Praeger Publications, 1973).

Page 251 "'. . . the night comfortably.'" Albani, p. 218.

Page 252 ". . . he has disappeared." *Liber Sancti Jacobi,* Book V, chap. 11, pp. 575–76. This is the last chapter of the book, entitled, "How Pilgrims of Santiago Should be Received."

Chapter 31: Arzúa to Monte del Gozo

Page 258 ". . . to be published." Manuel Mandianes, *Peregrino a Santiago. Viaje al fin del mundo* (Barcelona: Ronsel, 1993). Claudio Sánchez Albornoz, "El culto de Santiago no deriva del mito dioscórido," *Cuaderna histórica de España* 28 (1958), pp. 5–42. Gonzalo Torrente Ballester et al., *Heterodoxos en el Camino de Santiago* (Pamplona: Ayuntamiento de Pamplona, 1990). Juan G. Atienza, *En busca de Gaia* (Barcelona: Robin Book, 1993). Cobreros, *Camino.*

Page 261 ". . . a ritual significance." *Liber Sancti Jacobi,* Book V, chap. 6, pp. 512–13.

Page 261 "'. . . of our eyes.'" Laffi, p. 127. This may be the most important prayer of thanksgiving recited during the Middle Ages. Monastic choirs chanted it in common once a week, and it was said or sung for all special occasions when an individual or corporate body wished to solemnly thank God. It is attributed to Saint Ambrose (4th century):

Te Deum laudamus: te Dominum confitemur.
Te aeternum Patrem omnis terra veneratur.
Tibi omnes Angeli, tibi Caeli et universae Potestates,

Tibi Cherubim et Seraphim incessabili voce proclamant:
Sanctus,
Sanctus,
Sanctus Dominus Sabaoth.
Pleni sunt caeli et terra majestatis gloriae tuae.
Te gloriosus Apostolorum chorus,
Te Prophetarum laudabilis numerus,
Te Martyrum candidatus laudat exercitus.
Te per orbem terrarum sancta confitetur Ecclesia:
Patrem immensae majestatis;
Venerandum tuum verum et unicum Filium;
Sanctum quoque Paraclitum Spiritum.
Tu Rex gloriae, Christe.
Tu Patris sempiternus es Filius.
Tu, ad liberandum suscepturus hominem, non horruisti Virginis uterum.
Tu devicto mortis aculeo, aperuisti credentibus regna caelorum.
Tu ad dexteram Dei sedes, in gloria Patris.
Judex crederis esse venturus.
Te ergo quaesumus, tuis famulis subveni, quos pretioso sanguine redemisti.
Aeterna fac cum sanctis tuis in gloria numerari.
Salvum fac populum tuum, Domine, et benedic heriditati tuae.
Et rege eos, et extolle illos usque in aeternum.
Per singulos dies benedicimus te.
Et laudamus nomen tuum in saeculum, et in saeculum saeculi.
Dignare, Domine, die isto sine peccato nos custodire.
Miserere nostri, Domine, miserere nostri.
Fiat misericordia tua, Domine, super nos, quemadmodum speravimus in te.
In te, Domine, speravi: non confundar in aeternum.

We praise you, Oh God: we profess you Lord.
All the earth venerates you, eternal Father.
All the angels, the heavens, the universal powers,
The Cherubim and Seraphim with unceasing voice proclaim:
Holy,
Holy,
Holy Lord God of Hosts.
The heavens and the earth are filled with the majesty of your glory.
The awesome choir of Apostles,
The great number of Prophets,
The white-robed army of Martyrs, all praise you.
The holy Church proclaims you throughout the earth:
Oh Father, of immense majesty;
Your venerable, true and only Son;
And the Paraclete, the Holy Spirit.
You, Oh Christ, are the King of Glory.
You are the eternal Son of the Father.
You, to accomplish men's liberation, were not horrified by the Virgin's womb.
Overcome by the sting of death, you opened the kingdom of heaven to believers.
You are seated at the right of God, in the glory of the Father.
You are believed to be the judge who will come.

Therefore, we ask that you help your servants, whom you redeemed with your precious blood.
Grant that they be numbered with your saints in eternal glory.
Save your people, Lord, and bless your inheritance.
Rule them and hold them up forever.
We will bless you each day.
And we will praise your name forever and ever.
Oh Lord, deign to keep us from sin this day.
Have mercy on us, Oh Lord, have mercy on us.
Let your mercy descend on us, since we have hoped in you.
In you, Lord, I have hoped: let me never be confounded.

Page 261 "'. . . my bare feet.'" Albani, p. 218.
Page 262 ". . . to their children." Vázquez de Parga, vol. 2, pp. 354–55. Moralejo and López Alsina, p. 21.
Page 263 ". . . way for another." Vázquez de Parga, vol. 2, p. 350.
Page 263 ". . . the Holy Land." Cantarino, pp. 170–71.
Page 264 "'. . . protector he is.'" *Historia Compostellana,* ed. Emma Falque Rey (Turnhout: Brepols, 1988), pp. 307–8. This is the first critical edition of the text. Alí ben Yúsuf, a leader of the Almoravide sect of Muslims, had invaded the Peninsula from Africa. See R. A. Fletcher, *Saint James's Catapult: The Life and Times of Diego Gelmírez of Saniago de Compostela* (Oxford: Clarendon Press, 1984), p. 131.
Page 264 ". . . dreams of Gelmírez." Castro, *Realidad,* p. 330.

Chapter 32: Monte del Gozo to Compostela

Page 267 ". . . in permanent pilgrimage." *Liber Sancti Jacobi,* Book IV, chap. 1, pp. 407–8.
Page 267 ". . . supernal was established." Martínez, pp. 81–82.
Page 268 ". . . going to Compostela." Christian Krötzl, "Del mar báltico a Santiago de Compostela," in Caucci, pp. 385–88.
Page 268 ". . . in its place." Bango Torviso, pp. 14–15.
Page 271 ". . . saint, Santiago disappeared." *Liber Sancti Jacobi,* Book II, chap. 4.
Page 271 ". . . Compostela for pilgrims." Vázquez de Parga, vol. 2, pp. 391–92.
Page 271 ". . . exploitation of pilgrims." Vázquez de Parga, vol. 2, p. 379.
Page 271 ". . . call commercial establishments." Laffi, p. 131.
Page 272 ". . . with the Franciscans." Albani, p. 219.
Page 272 ". . . walked from there." Brian Tate, "Las peregrinaciones marítimas medievales desde las islas británicas a Compostela," in Moralejo, pp. 161–75.
Page 272 ". . . preparation for knighthood." Martínez, p. 146.
Page 272 ". . . Louis VII of France." Martínez, p. 87.
Page 272 ". . . Sofía of Holland." Vázquez de Parga, vol. 1, p. 66.
Page 272 ". . . Brigid of Sweden." Vázquez de Parga, vol. 1, p. 77.
Page 275 ". . . end of Atlantis." Torrente Ballester, p. 8.
Page 276 ". . . in the world." Vázquez de Parga, vol. 2, p. 361.
Page 276 "'. . . [said my prayers].'" Laffi, p. 128.
Page 276 "'. . . floor, gave thanks.'" Albani, p. 218.
Page 276 ". . . dismisses their opinion." Vázquez de Parga, vol. 2, p. 398.
Page 276 "'. . . That satisfied me.'" Vázquez de Parga, vol. 1, pp. 229–30.

Page 276 "'. . . bed with me.'" Plötz, in Caucci, p. 31.

Page 277 "'. . . basilica never close.'" *Liber Sancti Jacobi,* Book I, "Veneranda dies," pp. 198–99.

Page 278 "'. . . many other relics.'" Albani, p. 221.

Page 278 ". . . were carrying away." Vázquez de Parga, vol. 2, p. 372.

Page 278 ". . . to visit Rome." Valiña Sampedro, pp. 7–8. Martínez, p. 143.

Index

acedia, 172
Albani, Nicola, 16, 17, 18, 168, 176, 188, 201, 213, 216–17, 224–25, 232, 243, 245, 251, 252, 261, 268, 271, 276, 277
Albelda, 102
Alexander II, 101
Alfonso II, 162, 268
Alfonso III, 162, 268
Alfonso VI, 65, 66, 73, 79, 100, 149, 150, 174, 195
Alfonso VII, 124, 161
Alfonso VIII, 108
Alfonso X, 100, 139
Alfonso XI, 178
Alí ben Yúsuf, 263
Almanzor, 66, 148, 162, 179
Alvar Simón, 169–70
Andrew the Apostle, Saint, 49–50
angel, 8, 145, 148, 180, 187
Antony, Saint, 123, 244
architecture, 13, 54, 57, 74, 75, 81, 106, 133–34, 138, 165–68, 170, 173, 207–8, 223–24, 263
Arias Jato, Jesús, 209–10, 229, 258
Aristotle, 104
Athanasius, 123
Atlantis, 275
Averroes, 65
Avicenna, 65

Benedict, Rule of Saint, 225, 226
Bernard, Saint, 236
Blake, William, 235
Bohn, Peter, ix
Brigid of Sweden, Saint, 272
Buñuel, Luis, xi, 95, 98
Burton, Richard, 147

Calixtus II, 8, 27, 264
Calixtus III, 207
Cantarino, Vicente, 149
Cántigas de Santa María, 139, 140
Castro, Américo, xi, xii, 98, 102, 149, 150, 237
Cervantes, Miguel de, 98
Chanson de Roland, 8
Charlemagne, 8, 9, 104, 148, 179, 267
Charles V, 215
Chaucer, Geoffrey, 48
Christian, William A., Jr., ix
Cistercian, 236–37
Civil War, Spanish, 27, 97, 98, 101
Cluny, 149–50, 205, 236
Coello, Fray Francisco, 170
Constantine, 99
Cortés, Hernando, 124
creation, 14, 15, 38, 39, 94, 199–200, 238
credencial, 9, 16, 25, 28, 42, 48, 56–57, 67, 89, 104, 107, 111, 127, 132, 168, 173–74, 184, 209, 246, 253, 262, 274
crusade, 46, 101, 104, 149, 179, 236
curandero, 206–7, 209
cyclists, 68, 69, 104, 129–30, 145, 158, 201, 216

d'Aulnoy, Mme., 109
dead, the (pilgrims), 8, 15, 20, 40–41, 51, 59–60, 147, 271–72, 278–79
Descartes, René, 59, 154, 156
Díaz, José Ignacio, ix
Domingo de la Calzada, Santo, 78–79, 103
Don García, 73, 74
Doña Estefanía, 161, 165
Duden, Barbara, ix

Eco, Umberto, 35
El Cid, 66, 179–80
El Greco, 182
Ellul, Jacques, 154–56, 223
Estefania (daughter of Sancho III), 42
Evil One, the, 190
exhaustion, 7, 15, 20, 23, 41, 48, 56, 193, 214, 235, 241, 260
expulsion of Jews, xii, 93

faith, 41, 51, 65, 78, 84, 87–88, 110, 127, 134, 135, 138, 141, 146, 149, 151, 202, 209, 218
Feijoo, Benito Jerónimo, 227–28
Ferdinand and Isabella, 25, 66, 93, 126, 215, 271
Fernando I, 163
Fernández de Córdoba, Gonzalo, 110
Fernán Martínez, 100
Folbert, 5
Francis of Assisi, Saint, 66, 168, 272
Franco, Francisco, 101, 163

Gandhi, Mahatma, 120
García Ramírez, 51
García Villoslada, 149
Garrigós, Alfons, ix
Gastón de Bearn, Count, 51
Gastón de Dauphiné, 123
Gaucelmo, 195–96
Gaudí, 182–83
Gelmírez, Diego, 204, 263, 264, 268, 278
Ghéon, Henri, 84
Gómez Díaz, 140
González, Felipe, 178
Goya y Lucientes, Francisco, 41, 47, 54, 95, 98, 250
grace, 10, 23, 156, 202, 219, 256, 265
Gray, Thomas, 232
Guardia Civil, 6, 239

Harff, Arnold von, 276
Hernando de Talavera, 100
Historia Compostelana, 263
Holy Year, 27–28, 38, 105, 126, 180, 264
Honorius II, 264
Hopkins, Gerard Manley, 231, 235
hospital, 13, 25, 33, 42, 46, 49, 73, 75, 79, 108, 109, 126, 150, 161, 168, 182, 214, 271
Hugh de Payens, 236

Ignatius of Loyola, Saint, 29–31, 108
Illich, Ivan, ix, 198
Innocent III, 278
Isabella, 100, 110
Isidore, Saint, 98, 162–63, 164

James the Apostle, Saint, xi, 8, 26, 45, 66, 84, 134, 162, 258, 268
Jews, xii, 50, 93, 99–100, 135, 149, 165, 234
John of the Cross, Saint, 155
Juan de Limia, 178
Juan de Ortega, San, 103

Keats, John, 232–33
Künig von Vach, Hermann, 109, 124, 150, 204

Laffi, Domenico, 9, 82, 87, 103, 116, 123, 157, 181, 215, 232, 261, 263, 268, 271, 276
lavadero, 253–54
Leonardo da Vinci, 38
Liber Sancti Jacobi (Codex Calixtinus), 2, 8, 15, 17, 19, 25, 26, 49, 104, 139, 148, 163, 232, 264, 268, 277
Locke, John, 260
Louis VII of France, 272
Lull, Raymond, 46–47

Maestro Mateo, 276
Manier, Guillermo, 109–10
Marcio, Pedro, 100
Marx, Karl, 198
Mayor, La (Doña Mayor), 42, 133
Merton, Thomas, 63
Military Orders, 236, 237
miracle, 49–50, 51, 82–85, 109–10, 139–40, 214–15, 219, 228, 251–52, 268, 270–71
Mitcham, Carl, ix
Moreno, Maite, ix
Münzer, Jerome, 271
Musa, 124

New Age, 258

Ortega y Gasset, José, 98
Oursel, Raymond, 150

pain, 6–7, 9, 10, 13, 15, 20, 21, 23, 28, 41, 54, 56, 141, 146, 151, 161–62, 235, 241, 252, 253, 255–56, 257, 260, 265, 273

Papplau, Nicolás von, 180
Pascal II, 215
Pelayo the hermit, 45–46, 148–49, 268, 270, 272
penance, 7, 202
Peregrino (*revista*), 33, 79
Pero Rodríguez de Lena, 180
Philip II, 29
pícaros, 6, 17, 36, 138, 244, 271
Picasso, Pablo, 95
Picaud, Aymeric, 2, 15, 17, 18, 19, 27, 31, 42, 43, 47, 69, 148, 163, 232, 234, 244, 245, 261, 270, 271, 276
Poema del Cid, 102, 179
Polanyi, Karl, 128, 198
Ponce de Minerva, Don, 161, 165
prayer, 7, 28, 30, 39–41, 45, 48, 65, 78, 101, 111, 144, 218, 235, 265
Pyrenees mountains, 1, 4, 8, 19, 25, 26, 46, 66, 138, 244, 245, 270

Rajoy, archbishop, 271
Ramiro I, 100
Ramiro II, 100, 196
Recaredo, 99
Reconquista, 46, 100, 101, 102, 148, 149, 179
relics, 26–27, 49, 277–78, 279
Roland, 8, 9
Roncal, Doña Maribel, 32, 36, 49, 229, 258
Rosary, 28, 39, 44, 48, 59, 62–63, 71, 78, 82, 88, 108, 127, 144, 151, 165, 172, 238

Sahagún, Fray Bernardino de, 151
Saint Antony's Fire, 123
Sancha, Doña, 163
Sancha (Leofás), 51
Sánchez Albornoz, 150
Sancho III, 42
Sancho Panza, 5
Sancho Ramírez, 48
Santiago Matamoros, 46, 63–65, 100, 101, 102, 104, 174–75, 179, 238, 274
Santiago Peregrino, 46, 54, 63–65, 104, 245, 274
shell, 4, 18–19, 82, 271

Sofia of Holland, countess, 272
Southey, Robert, 83–84
space (and place), 14, 20, 23, 35, 37, 44, 60, 69–70, 77, 82, 87, 88, 95, 113–16, 137, 165, 211–12, 240
Spinoza, Benedict, 260
Spiritual Exercises (Ignatius Loyola), 30
staff, 6, 53, 82, 130, 137, 169, 213, 239, 272
stork, 95, 135–36, 181
Subirachs, José María, 170
Suero de Quiñones, 180–81

Tarif, 124
technology, 2–3, 4, 22, 33–35, 38, 69–70, 90–94, 121–22, 129–30, 153–57, 159, 171–72, 177–78, 199, 211–12, 223–24, 240–41, 246
Teresa, Countess, 140–41
Teodomiro, bishop, 45, 46, 268
Thoreau, Henry David, 22, 98, 186, 233–34
Torrente Ballester, Gonzalo, 38, 140
Transcendentalists, 260
Trapp, Sebastian, ix
Turpin, archbishop, 8, 148

Unamuno, Miguel de, 84, 98, 137–38, 140, 227
UNESCO, 107
Urban II, 101, 215, 236
Urraca, Queen Doña, 174, 263

Valiña Sampedro, Don Elías, 215
"Veneranda dies," 2, 3, 27
Velázquez, 95
Vincent Ferrer, Saint, 100
Voto de Santiago, 100–101

Wandering Jew, the, 234
Wittgenstein, Ludwig, 59, 60, 72, 85, 150
Wordsworth, William, 233

Xenophon, 156
Ximénez de Cisneros, 100

Die Zeit, 126